D1273169

LECTURES ON THE ESSENCE OF RELIGION

LECTURES ON THE ESSENCE OF RELIGION

by

LUDWIG FEUERBACH

Translated by Ralph Manheim

HARPER & ROW, PUBLISHERS
NEW YORK, EVANSTON, AND LONDON

FIRST EDITION

LIBRARY OF CONGRESS CATALOG CARD NUMBER: 67-21548

H-R

Contents

cracy and sympathy.—Examples: dog, lotus flower, rivers, stars, stones.—Immature and culturally conditioned behavior in religion.—Wonder and insight into the essence of nature. —Human nature as constant determinant of animal worship.—Animal worship the theoretical and practical expression of degree of intellectual development.

49 SEVENTH LECTURE

Animal worship typifies the fundamental character of religion.—Egoism, its rational justification.—Self-preservation the basis of religious veneration.—The Supreme Being a concentrate of all instincts, needs, and doubts.—Rejection of life.—Life as the supreme good, and religion as directed at its preservation and enhancement.—The nature of the gods conditioned by the cultural level.—Worship, advantage, and benefit.—Examples from the classics.

58 EIGHTH LECTURE

Advantage and benefit in pagan and Christian worship.—Views of classical antiquity, the Church Fathers, the Bible, and Luther.—Mosheim.—The efficacy of God dependent on mankind, serving its "egoism."—Common objections: religion as self-denial and self-sacrifice.—Examples of seeming denial of egoism.—Examples of religious self-sacrifice.—Its meaning and purpose: indirect self-affirmation.

68 NINTH LECTURE

The meaning of sacrifice: atonement and conciliation.—Customs among early Germans and neighboring peoples.—Human sacrifice among Greeks and Hebrews.—Human sacrifice in the eighteenth and nineteenth centuries.—Psychological human sacrifice.—Meaning and purpose of religious self-sacrifice.—Future bliss, religious ecstasy.—Sacrificial offerings, niggardly and lavish.—Common and refined egoism in sacrifice.—Patriotic sacrifice.

attitude.—The identity of reverence for divine and secular authority.

227 TWENTY-FIFTH LECTURE

Idol worship and divine worship.—Religion a public declaration of love.—Divine jealousy.—A special "religious sense" would make the distinction between true and false gods unnecessary; source of the distinction in the imagination prompted by desire for happiness.—Polytheism and monotheism the fruit of religious imagination.—The difference between wishes and gods.—Supernatural and superterrestrial Christian desires.—God and world.—Emptiness of the world a condition of heavenly bliss.

235 TWENTY-SIXTH LECTURE

The miracle.—True miracles always benefit man. Wishing and miracle.—Faith in miracles necessary for faith in God. —Miracle as confirmation of the truth of faith.—Luther's view of Biblical miracles.—Miracles as "example" of the Word: miracle working presupposed in the God of faith.—Inconsistency of intellectual faith.—Necessity of nature and divine perfection.—Rationalism "dehumanizes" the divine by subjecting it to laws of nature.—The essence of will and of miracles.

245 TWENTY-SEVENTH LECTURE

The irrational element in the belief in miracles.—Religious desire allegedly fulfilled in faith.—Impossible to grasp Gospel fiction historically.—On the alleged inexplicability of miracles: the question of their possibility is meaningless.—Miracles as wish fulfillment; miracles always worked by and for man.—The necessity of a limitation of desires.—Duty and happiness; cultural tendency of religion.—The essence of desire: pagan and Christian desires.—Prayer, desire, magic:

faith in imortality.—The negative attitude of theology, its rejection of reality.—Atheism alone a positive view, resting on true understanding of nature and human nature; theism a parasitical formation.—Practical consequences of the abandonment of religious conceptions.

287 ADDITIONS AND NOTES—Pages 287–356

357 *Bibliography*

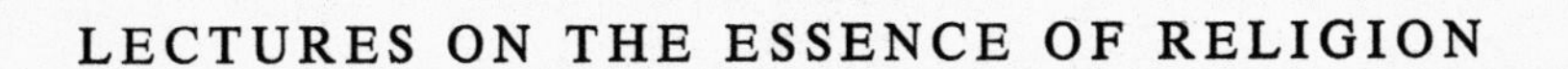

LECTURES ON THE ESSENCE OF RELIGION

First Lecture

IN OPENING MY SERIES of lectures on the essence of religion, I wish first of all to state that what prevailed over my prolonged reluctance to take such a step was the appeal, the express desire of the students at this university.

Today it is not necessary, as it was in ancient Athens, to promulgate a law requiring every man to support one party or the other in a civil war; today every man, even if he supposes himself to be supremely nonpartisan, is at least theoretically a partisan, though he may not know it or want to be; today political interest engulfs all other interests and political events keep us in a state of constant turmoil; today it is actually the duty—especially of us nonpolitical Germans—to forget everything for the sake of politics; for just as an individual can accomplish nothing unless he has the strength to devote himself exclusively for a time to the branch of endeavor in which he wishes to succeed, so likewise mankind must at certain times forget all other tasks and activities for the sake of one particular task and activity if it wishes to achieve something complete and worthwhile. Religion, the subject of these lectures, is to be sure closely connected with politics; however, our consuming interest today is not theoretical but practical politics. We wish to participate directly and actively in politics; we lack the peace of mind, the inclination, the desire to read and write, to teach and learn. We have busied ourselves and contented ourselves long enough with speaking and writing; now at last we demand that the word become flesh, the spirit matter; we are as sick of political as we are of philosophical idealism; we are determined to become political materialists.

But apart from this reason, implicit in the character of the times, for my reluctance to lecture there are other personal reasons. With my theoretical bent, I have less aptitude for teaching than for thought and inquiry. A teacher does not, and may not, hesitate to say the same thing a thousand times; I am content to have said something once, provided that I am confident of having formulated it correctly. A subject interests me and holds my attention only so long as it presents me with difficulties, only so long as I am at odds with it and have, as it were, to struggle with it; but once I have mastered it I hurry on to something else, to a new subject; for my interest is not confined to any particular field or subject; it extends to everything human. This does not mean that I am an intellectual miser or egoist, who amasses knowledge for himself alone; by no means! What I do and think for myself, I must also think and do for others. But I feel the need of instructing others in a subject only so long as, while instructing others, I am also instructing myself.

Now I long ago settled my accounts with the subject matter of these lectures, namely, with religion; in my works I have exhausted all its most essential, or at least its most difficult, aspects. Moreover, I do not write or speak easily. To tell the truth, I can speak and write only when the subject matter grips me emotionally, when it commands my enthusiasm. But emotion and enthusiasm are not products of the will; they do not take their cue from the clock, arising on appointed days or at set hours. I can speak and write only about things that strike me as worth speaking and writing about. And to me only what is not self-evident or has not already been fully dealt with by others is worth speaking and writing about. Accordingly, even in writing I deal only with that part of a subject which has not been dealt with in other books, or at least not in a way that fully satisfies me; the rest I leave aside. Consequently my thinking is aphoristic, as my critics say, but aphoristic in a very different sense and for very different reasons than they suppose. It is aphoristic because it is critical, that is, because it distinguishes essence from appearance, the necessary from the superfluous. I have spent many years, twelve whole years, in rustic seclusion, solely occupied with study and literary activity, and as a result have lost, or at least neglected to develop, the gift of oratory, of oral delivery, for it never occurred to me that I should ever again address an audience—I say *again* because I did, long ago, deliver lectures at a Bavarian university —and least of all in a university town.

The period in which I said goodby forever to the academic career, or so I thought, and went to live in the country, was so abominably dismal that such an idea could never have come to my mind. That was the period in which all public life was so poisoned and befouled that the only way of preserving one's freedom of spirit and one's health was to abandon all government service, every public function, even that of a university instructor; when no public position, even as a teacher, was obtainable except at the price of political servility and religious obscurantism, and only the written word devoted to learned matters was free—though only to a very limited degree and not because learning was respected, but rather because it was disparaged for its real or supposed ineffectualness or lack of influence on public affairs. What was one to do at such a time, especially if one was conscious of holding ideas opposed to the prevailing system of government, but withdraw and resort to writing as the only means of escaping the impertinence of a despotic state power—though that, too, demanded resignation and self-restraint.

But it was not only political disgust that drove me into retirement and condemned me to the use of the written word. Not only was I living in an incessant inner conflict with the political system of the day; I was also at odds with the ruling intellectual systems, that is, the dominant philosophical and religious doctrines. But in order to gain clarity as to the substance and causes of this conflict, I needed protracted and uninterrupted leisure. And where are they better to be found than in the country, where freed from all the conscious and unconscious servitudes, compromises, vanities, distractions, intrigues, and gossip of city life, one must rely wholly upon oneself? A man who believes what others believe, who teaches and thinks what others think and teach, in short, who lives in intellectual or religious unison with others, has no need to withdraw from them physically, no need of solitude; but it is a very different matter when a man goes his own way, breaks with the whole world of those who believe in God, and then wants to clarify and justify the breach. For that he needs free time and freedom of movement. It is ignorance of human nature to suppose that a man can think and study freely in any place, any environment, under any conditions, if only he has the determination to do so. No! Truly free, uncompromising, unconventional thinking, thinking that aspires to be fruitful, not to say decisive, requires an unconventional, free, and uncompromising life. And anyone who wishes in his thinking to get to the bottom of human affairs must have his two feet physically, bodily on their foundation. That foundation is nature. Only in direct communion with nature can man become whole again, can he cast aside all extravagant, supernatural, and unnatural ideas and fantasies.

But a man who spends years in seclusion—not, to be sure, in the abstract seclusion of a Christian hermit or monk, but in humane seclusion; whose only communication with the world is by way of the written word; loses the desire and ability to express himself by word of mouth. For there is an enormous difference between the spoken and the written word. The spoken word is addressed to a specific audience which is physically present; the written word to an absent, indeterminate audience which exists only in the writer's mind; speech is addressed to persons, writing to minds, because the people I write for are beings who, as far as I know, exist only in my mind, in my idea. Consequently writing lacks all the charms, the amenities, the social virtues as it were, which attach to the spoken word; the writer grows accustomed to rigorous thinking, to saying nothing that cannot be defended against criticism, and by that very fact becomes terse, rigorous, deliberate in his choice of words, incapable of speaking easily. Gentlemen, I call your attention to that fact; remember, if you please, that I have spent the better part of my life not on a speaker's platform, but in the country, not in the lecture hall but in the temple of nature, not in drawing rooms and reception chambers, but in the solitude of my study. I should not like you to attend my lectures with unwarranted hopes, expecting to find an eloquent and brilliant speaker.

Since thus far I have communicated with the public exclusively through my written works; since I have devoted my happiest hours, my best energies, and my whole mind to my writings and owe my name and reputation to them alone, it seems only natural that I should take my books as the foundation and guideline of these lectures. Accordingly, they will serve as my text, my role in speaking will be that of a commentator. My purpose, then, in delivering these lectures is to explain, to elucidate, to demonstrate what I have said in my books. What makes this seem all the more fitting is that I tend to write with the utmost brevity and succinctness, confining myself to the most necessary and essential, omitting all tedious transitions, leaving all self-evident parentheses and consecutive clauses to the reader's intelligence—thereby exposing myself to extreme misunderstandings, as the critics of my works amply demonstrate. But before I name the works I have chosen as the text of these lectures, it seems advisable to give a brief survey of my literary work as a whole.

My works can be divided into two groups, those dealing with philosophy as such, and those concerned more specifically with religion or the philosophy of religion. To the first group belong my *History of Modern Philosophy from Bacon to Spinoza,* my *Leibniz,* my *Pierre Bayle: A Contribution to the History of Philosophy and of Mankind*, my *Philosophical Critiques and Principles.* To the second belong: my *Thoughts on Death and Immortality, The Essence of Christianity,* and finally, the *Explanations and Additions to the Essence of Christianity*. But regardless of this classification of my writings, all have strictly speaking only one purpose, one intention and idea, one theme. This theme, of course, is religion or theology and everything connected with it. I am one of those who very much prefer a fertile one-sidedness to a sterile, futile versatility and prolixity; who throughout their lives have only *one* purpose in mind, upon which they concentrate all their powers; who study widely and intensively and never cease to learn, but who teach only one thing and write about only one thing—in the conviction that such singlemindedness is the only means of exhausting a subject and accomplishing something in the world. Accordingly, I have disregarded religion and theology in none of my works, though of course I have treated this central concern of my thinking and my life in different ways according to the time of writing and the viewpoint of each particular work. Still, I am obliged to admit that before publishing the first edition of my

History of Philosophy I deleted all direct references to theology, not for political reasons but out of youthful caprice and antipathy. In the second edition, however, which was reprinted in my *Collected Works,* I filled in these gaps, though from my present rather than my original point of view.

The first name that this work mentions in connection with religion and theology is that of Francis Bacon of Verulam, the father of modern philosophy and natural science, as he has often, and not without justification, been called. Because he solemnly professed that he had no intention of applying to religion and theology the profane critique which he developed in the field of science, that he was an unbeliever only in human matters, but in divine matters an absolute and utterly submissive believer, many regard him as the model of a scientist who is a pious Christian. It was he who wrote the famous words: "A little philosophy inclineth men's minds to atheism, but depth in philosophy bringeth men's minds about to religion" (*Essays,* 16), a statement which, like so many statements of past thinkers, was once a truth but is so no longer, although it is still upheld by our historians, who draw no distinction between past and present. But in my account of Bacon, I showed that in dealing with physics he negated the principles he professed in matters of faith, in theology; I showed that the old manner of considering nature, teleology—the doctrine of intentions or purposes in nature—was a necessary consequence of the Christian idealism which derives nature from a being who acts with purpose and consciousness, and that Bacon deprived the Christian religion of the all-encompassing character it had held for the true believers of the Middle Ages; I showed that he applied his religious principles only as a private individual, but not as a physicist or philosopher, not in that aspect of his thinking which was to exert an historical influence, and that it is therefore quite mistaken to regard Bacon as a religious Christian scientist.

The second thinker to present an interest from the standpoint of the philosophy of religion is Bacon's younger contemporary and friend Hobbes, known chiefly for his political views. He was the first modern philosopher to be stigmatized as an atheist. The learned gentlemen, it is true, have long argued the point: was he really an atheist? I have settled the argument by pointing out that he is just as much a theist as an atheist: like modern thinkers in general he posits a God, but this Hobbesian God is to all intents and purposes no God at all; for Hobbes identifies reality with corporeity, so that according to his own philosophical principle his God, to whom he is unable to impute any corporeal predicates whatever, is a mere word and no being at all. The third significant thinker, though from the standpoint of religion he does not essentially differ from the first two, is Descartes. However, I did not deal with his attitude toward religion and theology until later, in my *Leibniz* and *Bayle,* because it was only after the appearance of my first volume that Descartes came to be proclaimed the model of the religious, and specifically Catholic, philosopher. But I showed that Descartes the philosopher and Descartes the believer were two diametrically conflicting individuals.

The most original, and as regards the philosophy of religion the most significant, figures I treated in the same volume are Jakob Böhme and Spinoza, both distinguished from the other philosophers mentioned by the fact that they not only describe the conflict between faith and reason, but that each sets forth independent doctrines concerning the philosophy of religion. The first, Jakob Böhme, is the idol of the philosophizing theologians or theists, the other the idol of the theological philosophers or pantheists. Böhme's admirers have recently advertised him as the best antidote to the poison of my ideas—the ideas underlying the present lectures. In connection with the second edition of my book, however, I reexamined Böhme in detail. And my renewed study merely corroborated my first conclusion, namely, that the secret of his theosophy is on the one hand a *mystical* philosophy of nature and on the other hand a *mystical* psychology; and accordingly that his work does not refute but rather substantiates my view that all theology consists in two things: a doctrine of nature and a doctrine of man. The same volume concludes with Spinoza. He is the only modern philosopher to have provided the first elements of a critique and explanation of religion and theology; the first to have offered a positive opposition to theology; the first to have stated, in terms that have become classical, that the world cannot be regarded as the work or product of a personal being acting in accordance with aims and purposes; the first to have brought out the all-importance of nature for the philosophy of religion. I was glad to express my unstinting admiration and respect for him; I found fault with him only for continuing, under the influence of the old theological ideas, to define this being who does not act with purpose, will, or consciousness as the most perfect being, in short, as the Godhead, and so barring himself from a development which would have led him to look upon conscious man as a mere part or—to employ Spinoza's term—a mode of the unconscious totality, and not as its summit and fulfillment.

The opposite pole to Spinoza is Leibniz, to whom I have devoted a special volume. If Spinoza is to be honored for having made theology the handmaiden of philosophy, the first modern German philosopher earned the honor, or dishonor, of having once again tied philosophy to the apron strings of theology. In this respect Leibniz, in his celebrated *Theodicy,* outdid all others. It is generally known that Leibniz wrote this book out of gallantry toward a Queen of Prussia whose faith had been troubled by Bayle's doubts. But the lady for whom Leibniz really wrote and whom he really courted was theology. Even so, the book did not suit the theologians. Leibniz sat on the fence between the two parties, and for this very reason satisfied neither. He wished to offend no one, to hurt no one's feelings; his philosophy is a philosophy of diplomatic gallantry. Even the monads, the entities of which in his view all sensible beings consist, exert no physical influence on one another, lest any of them suffer injury.

But a man who is determined to offend no one—even unintentionally—can have no energy, no force; for it is impossible to take a step without trampling on some creature or other, or to drink a sip of water without swallowing a quantity of small organisms. Leibniz is an intermediary between the Middle Ages and modern times; he is, as I have called him, the philosophical Tycho Brahe, but precisely because of his indecision he remains to this day the idol of all those who lack the energy to make up their minds. Already in my first edition of 1837, I not only criticized Leibniz's theological attitude, but took the occasion to criticize theology in general. The standpoint from which I criticized it was Spinozan, or abstractly philosophical; I drew a sharp distinction between man's theoretical and practical attitudes, identifying the former with philosophy, the latter with theology and religion. In his practical attitude, I said, man relates things only to himself, to his own profit and advantage; in his theoretical attitude he considers things only in relation to each other. Consequently, I went on, there is a necessary and essential difference between theology and philosophy; to mix the two is to mix essentially different attitudes, and the result can only be a monstrosity. Reviewers of my book were greatly disturbed by this distinction; but they overlooked the fact that Spinoza in his *Theologico-Political Treatise* already considered and criticized theology and religion from the same standpoint, and that if even Aristotle himself had criticized theology, he could not have criticized it differently. As a matter of fact the standpoint from which I criticized theology at that time is not that of my later works; it was not my ultimate and absolute standpoint, but only relative and historically conditioned. Accordingly, in the new edition of my *Exposition and Critique of Leibniz's Philosophy,* I criticized Leibniz's theodicy and theology, as well as his related pneumatology, or doctrine of the spirit, in a different way.

Second Lecture

Just as Leibniz is the opposite pole to Spinoza, so Leibniz's opposite pole from a theological point of view is the French scholar and sceptic Pierre Bayle. The maxim *audiatur et altera pars* applies not only in jurisprudence, but in all science. In accordance with that maxim, I thought it appropriate that the German philosopher, a believer at least in a philosophical sense, should be followed in the series of my works by the unbelieving or at least sceptical French philosopher. Actually my reason for writing this book was not only philosophical, but practical as well. All my works have been written in opposition to a period when every effort was made to force mankind back into the darkness of bygone centuries. This is also true of my *Bayle*. It appeared at a time when, particularly in Bavaria and Rhenish Prussia, the old conflict between Catholicism and Protestantism had flared up anew with the most repugnant violence. Bayle was one of the first and most outstanding champions of enlightenment, humanity, and tolerance unfettered by either Catholic or Protestant faith. The purpose of my *Bayle* was to teach and to shame a present immersed in folly and malice by arousing such a voice from the past.

In the first chapter I show that Catholicism, with its monasteries, its saints, its celibate clergy, etc., differs from Protestantism in that its essence lies in the antithesis between flesh and spirit. In the second, dealing with Protestantism, I show that it differs from Catholicism in that its essence lies in the antithesis between faith and reason. The third deals with the contradiction between theology and philosophy or the scientific spirit in general; for to theology, I say, only what it holds sacred is true, whereas to philosophy, only what it holds true is sacred. Theology is grounded on a particular principle, a particular book, which, it believes, contains all truths, or at least those that are necessary and salutary to man; consequently it is of necessity narrow-minded, exclusive, intolerant, bigoted. Philosophy and science, on the other hand, are not based on any particular book, but find the truth only in nature and history as a whole; they are grounded on reason, which is in essence universal—not on faith, which is in essence particular.

The fourth chapter treats of the conflict or contradiction between religion and ethics, or of Bayle's ideas on atheism. Bayle held that man can be just as moral without religion, since most men are immoral and live immorally with and in spite of all their religion; that atheism does not necessarily imply immorality, and that a state can therefore perfectly well be made up of atheists. Bayle uttered these thoughts as early as 1680; yet only a year ago* a baron and deputy was not ashamed to declare before the assembled Prussian Diet that he favored state recognition and political rights for all denominations, but not for atheists. The fifth chapter treats expressly of the autonomy of ethics, its independence of religious dogmas and opinions; what in the fourth chapter is proved by examples from history and daily life, is here demonstrated by the very nature of ethics. The sixth chapter treats of the contradictions between the Christian dogmas and reason, the seventh of the significance of the contradiction between faith and reason in Bayle. For Bayle lived at a time when faith still possessed such authority that men believed, or forced themselves to believe, what their reason recognized to be false and absurd. The eighth chapter treats of Bayle's importance as an opponent of the religious prejudices of his day. The ninth and last chapter deals with Bayle's character and his place in the history of philosophy.

The book on Bayle is the last of my historical studies. My approach to more recent philosophers has been exclusively that of a critic, not that of a historian. The more recent philosophers differ in one striking respect from their predecessors. For the

* I.e., in 1847.—TRANS.

earlier philosophers separated philosophy and religion and even set them in opposition, arguing that religion is grounded on divine wisdom and authority, while philosophy is grounded solely on human wisdom—or, as Spinoza put it, that religion aims solely at the advantage and welfare of man, while philosophy aims at the truth; while the most recent philosophers stand for the *identity* of philosophy and religion, at least as far as content and substance are concerned. It was this identity that I set out to attack. As early as 1830, when my *Thoughts on Death and Immortality* appeared, I found myself involved in an argument with a dogmatist of the Hegelian school, who maintained that there is only a formal difference between religion and philosophy, that philosophy merely raised to the level of the concept what religion possessed in the form of images. I replied in the following verse:

> Essence itself is form. You therefore destroy the content of
> Faith by destroying the image, its own appropriate form

I criticized the Hegelian philosophy for regarding the essential as nonessential and the nonessential as essential in religion. The essence of religion, I declared, is precisely what philosophy regards as mere form.

A work deserving of special mention in this connection is a short pamphlet which appeared in 1839 under the title: *On Philosophy and Christianity*. Despite all attempts at compromise, I wrote, the difference between religion and philosophy is ineradicable, for philosophy is a matter of thought, of reason, while religion is a matter of emotion and imagination. But religion does not, as Hegel maintains, merely translate speculative ideas into emotionally charged images, but also contains an element that is distinct from thought, and this element is not merely its form but its very essence. This element can in one word be termed sensuousness, for emotion and imagination are also rooted in sensibility. Those who take umbrage at the word because it connotes carnal appetite are asked to consider that not only the belly, but the head as well, is a part of the human body. In my work sensuousness is nothing other than the true unity, a unity that is not cogitated or constructed but really exists, between matter and spirit; thus it is in my work tantamount to reality.

To clarify this distinction between religion and philosophy, let me cite—but only as one example out of many—a doctrine which throws special light on it. The early philosophers, or some of them at least, postulated immortality, but only the immortality of the thinking part of us, of man's spirit as opposed to his body. Some went so far as to teach explicitly that even memory died away and that only pure thought, an abstraction which of course has no existence in reality, remained after death. But this is an abstract, derived immortality, not what is meant by immortality in religion. Rejecting this philosophical immortality, Christianity professed the survival of the whole, real man body and soul, for this is the only kind of survival that means anything to feeling and imagination, and precisely because it is a bodily survival. What is true of this particular doctrine is true of religion in general. God himself is a sensuous being, an object of vision; not of physical vision to be sure, but of spiritual, that is, imaginative vision. Thus we can reduce the difference between philosophy and religion to the simple statement that religion is sensuous and aesthetic, while philosophy is nonsensuous and abstract.

Now, although even in my earlier works I recognized sensuousness to be the essence of religion as opposed to philosophy, I was unable to accept this religious sensuousness, first of all because it is merely imaginary and affective, in conflict with reality. The body—to stay with our example—the body, which is stressed in religious as opposed to philosophical immortality, is a mere product of the imagination and of emotion, a "spiritual" body, that is, to all intents and purposes no body at all. Accordingly religion is a recognition, an affirmation of sensuousness against sensuousness. A second reason why I was unable to accept the sensuousness of religion was that in this connection I myself still took the position of an abstract thinker, and had not yet grasped the full importance of the senses. At least I had not yet achieved full clarity in the matter. I arrived at a full appreciation of the world of sense on the one hand through further and more penetrating study of religion, on the other hand through the direct study of nature, for which my life in the country gave me excellent opportunity. Thus it was only in my later work on philosophy and the philosophy of religion that I resolutely attacked both the abstract inhumanity of philosophy and the fictitious, illusory humanity of religion. It was only then that, fully aware of what I was doing, I replaced the abstract, merely cogitated cosmic being known as God by the reality of the world, or nature; that I replaced the rational being deprived of his senses, which philosophy has extracted out of man, by the real, sensuous man endowed with reason.

Among my works on the philosophy of religion, those which provide the best over-all view of my intellectual development and its result are my *Thoughts on Death and Immortality* and my subsequent works on the same theme. I have dealt with the subject on three occasions: in 1830 in the book so titled, my first published work; in 1834 in *The Author and the Man,* and in 1846 in *The Question of Immortality from the Standpoint of Anthropology*. I first dealt with the matter as an abstract thinker; on the second occasion I emphasized the contradiction between thought and sensibility; on the third I took the standpoint of a thinker reconciled with the world of senses. Or, to put it differently: I wrote the first book as a philosopher, the second as a humorist, the third as a human being. Nevertheless, the *Thoughts on Death and Immortality* of 1830 already contain in the abstract what was fully developed in the later books.

In my more recent works I have given nature precedence over man, but already in that first book I took up cudgels against the idea of a natureless, absolute, and consequently eternal personality, in short, against the idea of a personality infinitely extended and free from the limitations of reality, as conceived in the usual doctrine of God and immortality. An excerpt from this book is published in my collected works. The first section is entitled "The Metaphysical and Speculative Ground of Death." It deals with the relation of the personality to being, or nature. The limit of the personality, I say in substance, is nature; everything that exists outside of me is a sign of my finiteness, a proof that I am not an absolute being, that I have my limit in the existence of other beings, that I am consequently not an immortal person. This truth, first expressed in general or metaphysical terms, is developed in the other sections. The next is titled: "The Physical Ground of Death." In it I write that the essence of human personality, of personality in general, implies spatial or temporal determinateness. Indeed, man is not only a spatial being, he is also essentially an earthly being, inseparable from the earth. How absurd it is, then, to impute eternal, supraterrestrial existence to such a being! I framed this idea in the following verses:

> Where you awoke to the light, there one day you will slumber;
> Never will Earth release any man from its precinct.

The third and last section is titled: "The Intellectual or Psychological Ground of Death." The simple underlying idea is: the personality is determined not only in a bodily or sensuous, but also in an intellectual sense; a man has a limited vocation, position, task in the great community of mankind, in history; and with this limitation eternal life is not compatible. He endures only in his works, in the influence which he has exerted within his sphere, his historical task. Moral, ethical immortality means nothing else. This idea, contained in the third and last section, is also that of my "humoristico-philosophical aphorisms." Intellectual, ethical, or moral immortality is solely the immortality a man gains through his works. A man's soul is what he passionately loves, what he does with passion. Men's souls are as diverse, as particular as men themselves. Accordingly, immortality in the old sense of eternal boundless being is consonant only with a vague, indeterminate soul that does not exist in reality but is merely a human abstraction and fantasy. However, I demonstrated these ideas, the fundamental ideas of the book, only for a special case, the example of the writer whose immortal spirit is nothing other than the spirit of his works.

For the third and last time I dealt with immortality in my treatise *The Question of Immortality from the Standpoint of Anthropology*. The first section treats of the common faith in immortality, found among most if not all peoples in their state of childhood or ignorance. Here I show that those who believe in immortality impute their own ideas to primitive peoples: that these peoples actually do not believe in another life, but only in this life, that for them the life of the dead is merely a life in the realm of memory, and that the living dead are merely personified images of the dead in the minds of the living. I show further that if you insist on a personal or individual immortality, you can only take the view prevailing among primitive peoples, for whom a man after death is in every respect the same as before death, endowed with the same passions, occupations, and needs, because a man is inseparable from these. The second section deals with the subjective necessity of the belief in immortality, that is, with the inner, psychological motives which give rise to man's belief in immortality. The concluding proposition of this section is that immortality is really needed only by dreamy, idle people, whose imagination carries them away from their real lives, and not by energetic people concerned with the things of real life. The third chapter deals with the "critical belief in immortality," that is, the view of those who no longer hold that the whole man with his flesh and bones continues to exist after death, but draw a critical distinction between the mortal and immortal essence of man. But this view, I say, is itself subject to doubt and criticism; for it is contrary to man's immediate sense and consciousness of unity, which leads him to reject with incredulity any such a critical division and cleavage in man's nature. The last chapter deals with the belief in immortality that still prevails among us, the "rationalistic belief in immortality," which, torn as it is between belief and unbelief, seemingly affirms but actually negates immortality by confounding unbelief with belief, this world with the next, time with eternity, nature with God, and the profane heaven of astronomy with the heaven of religion.

Here I have given a brief and superficial survey of my ideas on immortality and death. I have done so because ordinarily, and quite justly, the problem of immortality forms a main chapter in any discussion of religion or the philosophy of religion, whereas I shall disregard the belief in immortality, or rather treat it only insofar as it is connected with, or rather is one with, the belief in God.

Third Lecture

I NOW COME to those of my writings which embody my doctrine, religion, philosophy, or whatever you may choose to call it, and provide the subject matter of these lectures. This doctrine of mine is briefly as follows. *Theology is anthropology*: in other words, the object of religion, which in Greek we call *theos* and in our language God, expresses nothing other than the essence of man; man's God is nothing other than the deified essence of man, so that the history of religion or, what amounts to the same thing, of God—for the gods are as varied as the religions, and the religions are as varied as mankind—is nothing other than the history of man.

Let me illustrate and clarify this assertion by an example, which however is more than an example: the Greek, the Roman, or any other pagan god, as even our theologians and philosophers admit, is merely an object of pagan religion, a being who exists only in the faith and imagination of a pagan, but not in those of a Christian people or individual; consequently, he is only an expression, an image, of the pagan spirit and disposition. Similarly, the Christian God is merely an object of the Christian religion and consequently only a characteristic expression of the spirit and disposition of Christian man. The difference between the pagan god and the Christian God is solely a difference between pagan and Christian man, taken both collectively and individually. The pagan is a patriot, the Christian a cosmopolitan; consequently the pagan's god is a patriotic god, while that of the Christian is a cosmopolitan; the pagan, in other words, has a national, limited god, because the pagan did not rise above the limitations of his nationality but placed the nation above man; the Christian has a universal, world-encompassing God because he rises above the limitations of nationality and does not restrict the dignity and essence of man to any particular nation.

The difference between polytheism and monotheism is merely the difference between the species and the genus. There are many species, but only one genus, since it is in the genus that the different species come together. There are different species of man, different races and peoples or whatever else we may choose to call them, but they all belong to the one genus, the genus *homo*. Polytheism is at home where man does not rise above the concept of the species, where he recognizes only men of his own species as his equals in rights and endowment. But the concept of species implies multiplicity; consequently there are many gods wherever man regards the essence of the species as the absolute essence. Man rises to monotheism where he rises to the concept of the genus, in which all men come together and their differences of species, race, nationality disappear. The difference between the One or its equivalent, namely, the universal God of monotheism, and the many or their equivalent, namely, the particular national gods of the pagans or polytheists, is merely the difference between the many different varieties of men and the genus *homo* in which all are one. The visibility, palpability, in short, the sensuous character of the polytheistic gods is nothing other than the sensuous character of the human distinctions of species and nationality—the Greeks, for example, differed visibly, palpably from other peoples; the invisibility, the nonsensuous character of the monotheistic God is nothing other than the nonsensuous character, the invisibility, of the genus, in which all men come together, but which does not exist visibly and palpably as such; for only the species exist.

In short, the difference between polytheism and monotheism reduces itself to the difference between species and genus. Genus is indeed different from species, for in considering the genus we disregard specific differences. But this does not make the genus a distinct independent reality, since it is merely the common head under which we subsume the many species. The generic concept stone cannot be said to transcend the mineral realm, though it is equally far removed from the concept of flint, limestone, or fluorite, and indeed designates no particular stone to the exclusion of others. Similarly God as such, the one universal God, from whom the bodily, sensuous attributes of the many gods have been removed, does not transcend the genus *homo;* he is only the most objectified and personified generic concept of mankind. Or put more clearly: as the polytheistic gods are human beings, so likewise is the monotheistic God a human being, just as man, though he transcends the many particular varieties of human being—Jew, Greek, or Indian—is not for that reason superhuman. Accordingly, nothing can be more absurd than to say that the Christian God descended from heaven to earth, or to trace the origin of the Christian religion back to the revelation of a being distinct from man. Just like the pagan gods, the Christian God originated in man. If He differs from the pagan gods, it is only because Christian man is different from pagan man.

I first developed this view or doctrine of mine—to the effect that the secret of theology is anthropology and that, objectively as well as subjectively, the essence of religion reveals and expresses nothing other than the essence of man—in my book *The Essence of Christianity,** and subsequently in certain shorter books and articles relating to that book, for example, *The Essence of Faith According to Luther,* 1844,† *The Difference Between the Pagan and the Christian Deification of Man,* and finally, in the second edition of my *History of Philosophy,* where it is dealt with in various contexts, and in my *Principles of Philosophy.*

The view, or doctrine stated in *The Essence of Christianity,* or more exactly that part of my doctrine which it was possible to set forth in a book on Christianity, shows an important gap. For that reason the book gave rise to the most preposterous misunderstandings. Because, confining myself to my subject, I disregarded nature in treating of Christianity; because Christianity itself ignores nature; because Christianity is idealism, an edifice crowned by a natureless God or spirit who makes the world by merely thinking and willing, and apart from whose thinking and willing the world has no existence; because *The Essence of Christianity* therefore starts from, and deals exclusively with, the essence of man; pre-

* George Eliot, trans. (New York: Harper Torchbook, 1957).
† Melvin Cherno, trans. (New York: Harper & Row, 1967 .

cisely because Christianity does not worship the sun, moon, and stars, fire, earth, or air, but only the human essence as distinguished from the forces underlying nature; because it worships will, intelligence, consciousness as divine powers and beings—for these reasons it was thought that I looked upon man as a *creatio ex nihilo,* a being without premises or antecedents, and this supposed deification of man on my part was held to conflict with our immediate feeling of dependency, with our natural insight that man did not make himself, that he is a dependent being who originated in something, in other words, that the ground of his existence lies outside himself, that he points outside and above himself to another being.

You are perfectly right, gentlemen, I said inwardly to those who attacked and ridiculed me; I know as well as you, perhaps even better, that a human being conceived absolutely, exclusively, in terms of himself is an absurdity, an idealistic chimera. But the being which man presupposes, to which he necessarily relates, without which neither his existence nor his essence is conceivable, this being, gentlemen, is none other than nature, and not your God. I first filled in this gap in *The Essence of Christianity* with a short but significant book, *The Essence of Religion,* a book which, as the title page itself indicates, differs from its predecessor in dealing with the essence not only of Christianity but of religion in general, and accordingly takes in the pre-Christian, pagan religions of nature. Its far wider range gave me an opportunity to counteract the stigma of idealistic one-sidedness which in *The Essence of Christianity* I had brought upon myself in the eyes of my uncritical critics; my enlarged field enabled me to make good the deficiencies of *The Essence of Christianity*.

Yet here again, needless to say, I did not proceed along the lines of theology and theistic or theological philosophy. The purpose of these two books and their relation to one another can best be stated as follows: Theologians, or theists in general, distinguish between the physical and the moral attributes of God—but God, as we have already said, is the name by which the object of religion is generally designated. God, says Leibniz, must be considered in two ways: *physically* as the author of the world, *morally* as the monarch, the legislator of mankind. According to His physical attributes, chief of which is *power,* God is therefore the cause of physical beings, of nature; according to His moral attributes, chief of which is goodness, He is the cause of moral beings, of men. In *The Essence of Christianity,* my sole subject was God as a moral being; thus it was impossible for me to give a complete exposition of my view and doctrine. Inevitably I disregarded God's other half, His physical attributes, with which I was obliged to deal in another work. But a suitable and objective treatment of them was possible only in a book comprising also nature religion, the religion which has the physical God as its primary object. However, as I showed in *The Essence of Christianity,* God, considered in his moral or spiritual attributes, God as a moral being, is nothing other than the deified and objectified mind or spirit of man, and in the last analysis theology is therefore nothing other than anthropology. Accordingly, in *The Essence of Religion* I showed that the physical God, or God regarded solely as the cause of nature, of the stars, trees, stones, animals, and of man, insofar as they too are natural, physical beings, expresses nothing other than the deified, personified essence of nature, that the secret of physicotheology is therefore nothing other than physics or physiology—physiology not in its present restricted sense, but in its old universal sense of natural science in general. A moment ago I summed up my doctrine by saying that *theology is anthropology*. I should now like to complete that statement by saying: anthropology *and physiology*.

My doctrine or view can therefore be summed up in two words: *nature* and *man*. The being which in my thinking man presupposes, the being which is the *cause* or *ground* of man, to which he owes his origin and existence, is *not God*—a mystical, indeterminate, ambiguous word—but *nature,* a clear sensuous, unambiguous word and thing. And the being in whom nature becomes personal, conscious, and rational is man. To my mind, unconscious nature is the eternal, uncreated being, the first being—first, that is, in time but not in rank, *physically* but not *morally;* man with his consciousness is for me second in time, but in rank the first. This doctrine of mine, insofar as it takes nature as its starting point, invokes the truth of nature and opposes this truth to theology and philosophy, forms the substance of the last-mentioned book. But it is dealt with on the basis of concrete historical material, namely, nature religion;

for I never develop my ideas in the thin air of abstraction, but always ground them in real historical facts and phenomena, independent of my thinking. Accordingly I have developed my view or doctrine of nature on the basis of nature religion.

In that book, by the way, I not only set forth the essence of nature religion, but also in a brief survey described the entire development of religion from its first elements to its conclusion in the idealistic religion of Christianity. It thus comprises a succinct intellectual or philosophical history of human religion. I stress the adjective "intellectual," for it was not my purpose to write a formal history of religion, one of those histories in which the various religions are reeled off one after the other, and as a rule classified according to highly arbitrary hierarchical distinctions. Apart from the major distinction between nature religion and the spiritual religion of man, I was more concerned with the common (i. e., similar or identical) factor in religions than with the arbitrary and usually so trifling differences between them. In general I concentrated in this book on the essence of religion, and went into history only insofar as religion cannot be understood without it. In this book, as in all my writings, my reasons for dealing with the essence of religion were not only of a theoretical or speculative character, but essentially practical. The principal reason for my interest in religion has always been that, if only in the imagination, it is the foundation of human life, the foundation of ethics and politics.

My primary concern is and always has been to illumine the obscure essence of religion with the torch of reason, in order that man may at least cease to be the victim, the plaything, of all those hostile powers which from time immemorial have employed and are still employing the darkness of religion for the oppression of mankind. It was my purpose to demonstrate that the powers which man worships and fears in his religious life, which he seeks to propitiate even with bloody human sacrifices, are merely creatures of his own unfree, fearful mind and of his ignorant unformed intelligence; to demonstrate that the being which man, in religion and theology, sets up as a distinct being over against himself, is his own essence. It was my purpose to demonstrate this so that man, who is always unconsciously governed and determined by his own essence alone, may in future consciously take his own, human essence as the law and determining ground, the aim and measure, of his ethical and political life. And this will inevitably come to pass. Whereas hitherto misunderstood religion, religious obscurantism, has been the supreme principle of politics and ethics, from now on, or at some future date, religion properly understood, religion seen in terms of man, will determine the destinies of mankind.

It was this aim, an insight into religion that would promote human freedom, independence, love, and happiness, that determined the scope of my historical treatment of religion. Everything that was irrelevant to this purpose I set aside. Historical expositions of the various religions and mythologies of the peoples of the earth *without a true insight into religion* are to be found in innumerable books. And I shall lecture as I wrote. The purpose of my lectures as of my books is to transform theologians into anthropologists, lovers of God into lovers of man, candidates for the next world into students of this world, religious and political flunkeys of heavenly and earthly monarchs and lords into free, self-reliant citizens of the earth. Thus my purpose is far from negative. It is positive; I negate only in order to affirm; I negate the fantastic hypocrisy of theology and religion only in order to affirm the true nature of man. No word has been so much abused in our day as the word negative. When I negate something in the field of knowledge, of science, I have to give reasons. And reasons instruct, cast light, create knowledge within me; every negation in the realm of science is a positive act of the mind. True, it follows from my doctrine that there is no God, no abstract, disembodied being distinct from nature and man who decides the fate of the world and of mankind as He pleases; but this negation is merely a consequence of an insight into the essence of God, of the knowledge that it denotes nothing other than on the one hand the essence of nature and, on the other, the essence of man.

Of course it is possible, since there must be a nickname for everything, to call this doctrine atheism, but it should not be forgotten that like its counterpart "theism" this name means nothing. *Theos,* God, is a mere name, which covers everything under the sun, whose content is as varied as are times and men; the crux of the matter is what we mean by God. As late as the eighteenth century, for example, Christian orthodoxy put so pedantically narrow a definition on the word that even Plato was looked upon as an atheist because he did not teach the *creatio ex nihilo* and hence failed to distinguish properly between Creator and creature. Similarly in the seventeenth and eighteenth centuries, Spinoza was almost universally regarded as an atheist; in fact, if my memory does not deceive me, a Latin dictionary of the eighteenth century goes so far as to translate "atheist" by "*assecla Spinozae*" (follower of Spinoza); but the nineteenth century has struck Spinoza off the list of atheists. Times change, and men's gods with them. It is equally meaningless to say "There is a God" or "I believe in a God," and "There is no God" or "I do not believe in a God." Whether we speak of theism or of atheism, what matters is the content, ground, and spirit.

And now I shall proceed to the subject itself, namely, my book *The Essence of Religion,* which I have chosen as the basis of these lectures.

Fourth Lecture

I SHALL briefly summarize the first paragraph of *The Essence of Religion*: the foundation of religion is a feeling of dependency; the first object of that feeling is nature; thus nature is the first object of religion.

The paragraph breaks down into two parts. The first explains the subjective origin or ground of religion; the second designates the first or original object of religion. To begin with the first part: the so-called speculative philosophers have ridiculed me for putting down the feeling of dependency as the source of religion. They have held the words "feeling of dependency" in low esteem ever since Hegel, in response to Schleiermacher—who, as we know, found the essence of religion in man's feeling of dependency—remarked that then a dog must also have religion because he feels dependent on his master. The so-called speculative philosophers, be it noted, are those who, instead of fitting their concepts to the facts, fit the facts to their concepts. Thus it matters not at all whether my explanation appeals to the speculative philosophers; what matters is whether it is in keeping with the facts. And that it is.

When we consider the religions of so-called savages, as reported by travelers, and of the civilized peoples as well, when we look into our own inner life, which may be observed directly and without fear of error, we find no other appropriate and all-embracing psychological explanation of religion than the feeling or consciousness of dependency. The ancient atheists, and even a great many theists both ancient and modern, have called fear the ground of religion; but fear is merely the most widespread and obvious expression of the feeling of dependency. As the Roman poet said: *Primus in orbe Deos fecit Timor*—Fear first made the gods in the world. Among the Romans the word fear, *metus,* actually carries the meaning of religion, and conversely the word *religio* sometimes signifies fear or awe; thus a *dies religiosus,* a religious day, was taken to mean an unlucky day, a day that was feared. Even our German word *Ehrfurcht* (awe, piety)—expression of the highest religious veneration—is composed of *Ehre* (honor) and *Furcht* (fear).

The explanation of religion by fear is eminently confirmed by the fact that most primitive peoples take the frightening aspects of nature as the principal if not exclusive objects of their religion. According to Meiners,* the more primitive peoples of Africa, northern Asia, and America are afraid "of rivers, especially in places where they form dangerous whirlpools or rapids. When they navigate such places, they implore mercy or forgiveness, or beat their breasts and throw propitiatory sacrifices to the angry gods. Certain Negro kings who have chosen the ocean as their fetish are so much afraid of it that they do not dare look upon it, much less travel it, because they believe that the sight of this terrible god would kill them on the spot." And W. Marsden tells us that when the Rejang of inland Sumatra first see the ocean, they sacrifice cakes to it and implore it to do them no harm.† According to the reports of theistic travelers biased by their own religious ideas, the Hottentots believe in a supreme being but do not worship him; instead they worship the "evil spirit," whom they regard as the author of all the evils that befall them in the world.

I note, however, that these travelers' reports, especially the earlier ones about the religious conceptions of the Hottentots and of savages in general, are full of internal contradictions. In India too there are regions "where the greater part of the inhabitants observe no other religious cult than that of the *evil spirits.* . . . Each of the evil powers has a name of his own and the more forbidding and powerful he is thought to be, the more conscientiously he is worshiped." Similarly, even those American tribes which according to theistic observers recognize "a supreme being," worship only "evil

* See Bibliography, p. 357.
† See Bibliography, p. 357.

spirits" or beings, to whom they attribute all the evil and trouble, all the aches and ailments that come their way; this they do in the hope of mollifying them, in other words, out of fear. The Romans made objects of religion even out of *diseases* and *plagues, fever; grain blight*, to which they devoted an annual festival; *infant mortality*, to which they gave the name of Orbona; and *calamity*. Obviously such worship, as the ancients themselves, Pliny the Elder for example, pointed out, had no other ground than fear, no other purpose than to disarm the unfriendly gods; this was also noted by the ancients, Aulus Gellius for example, who writes that men worshiped or celebrated some gods in the hope that they might be helpful, and conciliated or appeased others in the hope that they might refrain from doing harm. Indeed, Fear itself had a temple in Rome and also one in Sparta, where, however—at least according to Plutarch—it had an ethical significance, namely, fear of evil, shameful actions.

The explanation of religion by fear is further confirmed by the fact that even among culturally more advanced peoples the supreme Godhead is a personification of those natural phenomena which arouse *the highest degree* of fear in man; he is the god of storms, of thunder and lightning. Certain peoples, indeed, have no other word for God than thunder, so that their religion expresses nothing other than the shattering impression which nature's thunder makes upon man through the ear, the organ of terror. Even among the so highly endowed Greeks, the supreme God was named simply the Thunderer. Similarly the god Thor or Donar—i. e., the thunder-god of the ancient Germanic peoples, or at least of the Norsemen and of the Finns and Letts as well—was their oldest, first, and most universally worshiped god. The English philosopher Hobbes derived the intelligence from the ears, because he identified intelligence with the audible word. Considering that it was thunder which pounded religion into man, we may with greater justice term the eardrum the sounding board of the religious sense and the ear the womb of the gods.

Indeed, if man had only eyes, hands, and the senses of taste and smell, he would have no religion, for all these senses are organs of critique and scepticism. The only sense which, losing itself in the labyrinth of the ear, strays into the spirit or spook realm of the past and future, the only fearful, mystical, and pious sense is that of hearing. Of this the ancients were well aware when they said: "An eyewitness is worth more than a thousand auditory witnesses"; "the eyes are more reliable than the ears"; or "what we see is more certain than what we hear." That is why the last and most spiritual of religions, Christianity, deliberately bases itself solely on the word, the word of God, as they call it, and consequently on the sense of hearing. "Faith," says Luther, "comes from listening to the Lord's preaching." And elsewhere: "In the Church of God nothing is demanded but hearing." This, by the way, shows how superficial it is, in speaking of religion and particularly of its first grounds, to serve up hollow phrases about the absolute, the supersensory and infinite, as though man were without senses; as though the senses had no bearing on religion. It is senseless to speak in any context whatever of a man without senses.

But I have digressed long enough. Our explanation is further confirmed by the fact that although Christians in theory at least attribute a purely supersensory, divine origin and character to religion, it is chiefly in moments and situations which arouse fear that a religious mood comes over them. When, for example, His Majesty the reigning King of Prussia,* venerated by the pious Christians of our day as the "Christian king" par excellence, convened the unified Diet, he decreed that prayers for divine assistance should be offered up in all the churches of the land. But what was the reason for His Majesty's religious impulse and for this decree? Simply the fear that the evil appetites of the modern age might disrupt the plans and projects conceived in connection with the unified Diet, that masterpiece of Christian-Germanic statecraft. Or, to give another example: a few years ago when the harvest was poor, God was fervently besought in all our churches to send His blessings and special days of prayer and penance were even set aside. What was the reason? Fear of famine. And that is why Christians wish "godless" unbelievers every known calamity, and why, purely out of Christian love and solicitude, it goes without saying, they experience the utmost pleasure when a misfortune befalls the godless, for they are convinced that trouble will bring them back to God and turn them into good believers. Of course Christian theologians and

* Friedrich Wilhelm IV (1840-60).

thinkers deplore, at least from the pulpit or in their writings, the fact that such phenomena as those I have just mentioned should be set down as characteristic of the religious principle; but the truth of the matter is that religion—at least in the usual or rather in the historical, dominant sense of the word—is characterized not by what is written in books, but by what happens in real life.

The only difference between Christians and uncivilized peoples or so-called heathen, is that Christians do not transform the phenomena that arouse their religious fear into special gods, but rather into *special attributes* of their God. They do not pray to evil gods; but they pray to their God when they think He is angry, or when they fear that He may become angry with them and strike them with harm and disaster. Just as evil spirits are virtually the sole objects of the worship of primitive peoples, so the angry God is the chief object of worship among Christian peoples; here too, in other words, the chief ground of religion is fear. In final confirmation of my contention, I cite the fact that in their attacks on Spinoza, on the Stoics, and on pantheists in general (whose God, viewed candidly, is nothing other than the naked essence of nature), Christian and other theologians or religious philosophers contend that their God is no God at all, that is to say, no true religious God, because he is not an object of love and fear, but only of cold reason, free from emotion. Thus, though rejecting the view of the ancient atheists that religion originates in fear, they implicitly admit that fear is at least an essential component of religion.[1]

Nevertheless fear is not the complete and sufficient ground and explanation of religion, and not only for the reason stated a little while ago, namely, that fear is a passing emotion; for the object of fear is enduring, at least in our imaginations, indeed it is a specific characteristic of fear that it reaches out beyond the present to tremble at possible future evil. No, the true reason why fear does not offer a complete explanation of religion is that, once the danger is past, fear gives way to an opposite emotion, and that, as a minimum of reflection suffices to show, this opposite feeling attaches to the same object as the fear. This is the feeling of release from danger, from fear and anxiety, a feeling of delight, joy, love, and gratitude. Indeed, the phenomena of nature that arouse fear and

[1] For numbered notes, see Additions and Notes, pp. 287 ff.

dread are by and large those with the most beneficial consequences. The god who destroys trees, animals, and men with his thunderbolt is the selfsame god who fructifies the fields and meadows with his rain. The source of evil is also the source of the good; the source of fear is also the source of joy. Why, then, should human feeling not combine effects which even in nature spring from a single cause? Only peoples who live in the mere moment, who are too weak, too dull, or too frivolous to combine different impressions, experience nothing but fear of their divinities and devote their cults to none but evil, terrible gods. Among other peoples, the fear aroused by an object does not cause its good and beneficial qualities to be forgotten; the object of fear becomes an object of veneration, love, and gratitude. Thus among the ancient Germanic peoples, or at least among the Norsemen, the god Thor, the Thunderer, is "the beneficent, kindly champion of mankind," "the protector of agriculture, the mild philanthropic god,"* because the god of thunder is also the god of the fructifying rain and sunshine. Thus it would be quite one-sided, indeed, unjust to call fear the sole ground of religion.

At this point I differ *radically* from the earlier atheists and from the pantheists (I am thinking of Spinoza in particular) who in this connection held the same views as the atheists, for I cite not only negative, but also positive grounds of religion; not only ignorance and fear, but also the emotions opposed to fear, the positive emotions of joy, gratitude, love, and veneration as grounds of religion; and I maintain that not fear alone, but also love, joy, and veneration are makers of gods. "The feeling of those who have overcome affliction or danger," I say in my notes on *The Essence of Religion,* "is very different from that aroused by existing or feared affliction or danger. In the first case attention is focused on the object, in the second on myself, in the first case I sing hymns of praise, in the second songs of lamentation, in the first case I give thanks, in the second I implore. The feeling of affliction is practical, teleological; the feeling of gratitude is *poetic, aesthetic*. The feeling of affliction is transient, but the feeling of gratitude enduring; it forms a bond of love and friendship. The feeling of affliction is base, that of gratitude noble, the former worships only in adversity, the latter also in happiness." Here we have a psychological explanation of

* W. Müller, *Geschichte und System der altdeutschen Religion.*

religion not only in its common, but also in its noble aspect.

Thus I cannot find the ground of religion in fear or in joy and love alone. But what universal term embraces both aspects, if not the feeling of dependency? Fear relates to death, joy to life. Fear is a feeling of dependency on an object without which I am nothing, which has the power to destroy me. Joy, love, gratitude are feelings of dependency on an object thanks to which I am something, which gives me the feeling, the awareness that through it I live and am. Because I live and subsist through nature, or God, I love Him; because I suffer and perish through nature, I fear it and stand in awe of it. In short, man loves the being who gives him the means or reason to enjoy life and hates the being who deprives him of these or has the power to do so. But both are combined in the object of religion—the very same thing that is the source of life is also, negatively speaking—that is, if I am without it—the source of death. "Good things and evil," says Ecclesiasticus, "life and death, poverty and riches, are from God." "Knowing therefore by these things that they are not gods," we read in the Book of Baruch, "fear them not. . . . [For] whether it be evil that one doth to them or good, they are not able to recompense it; neither can they set up a king or put him down." Addressing idolaters, the Koran speaks in similar terms (Sura 26): "Do they [idols] hear you when you call on them? Can they help you or do you harm?"* In other words: only that being is an object of religious worship, only that being is a god, who can curse and bless, harm and help, kill and restore to life, bring joy and terrify.

Thus the feeling of dependency is the only truly universal name and concept by which to designate and explain the psychological or subjective ground of religion. Of course there is no such thing as a feeling of dependency as such, but only specific, particular feelings of dependency—e. g. (to draw examples from nature religion) the feelings of hunger or discomfort, the fear of death, gloom when the weather is bad, joy when it is good, grief over wasted pains, over hopes shattered by natural catastrophes; all these are particular feelings of dependency; but to subsume particular phenomena of reality under universal names and concepts is precisely the task implicit in the nature of thought and speech.

Now that I have corrected and amplified the explanation of re-

* N. J. Dawood, trans. (London: Penguin Books, 1956), p. 199.

ligion by fear, I must mention still another psychological explanation of religion. Certain Greek philosophers said that admiration of the regular course of the heavenly bodies gave rise to religion, i. e., to the worship either of the luminaries themselves or of a being who regulates their course. But it is immediately obvious that this explanation of religion applies only to the sky, not to the earth, only to the eye and not to the other senses, only to theory and not to human practice. The stars, it is true, were also causes and objects of religious worship, yet not as objects of theoretical, astronomical observation, but only insofar as they were regarded as powers governing the life of man, in other words as objects of human hopes and fears. Actually the example of the heavenly bodies shows that a being or thing becomes an object of religion only when it is an object, a cause, of the fear of death or the enjoyment of life, hence of the feeling of dependency. The author of a French work entitled *De l'Origine des principes religieux,* which appeared in 1768, was quite right in saying: "Thunder and storm, the sufferings of war, plagues and death have done more to convince man of the existence of God (i. e., incline him to religion, convince him of his dependency and finiteness) than the constant harmony of nature and all the demonstrations of the Clarkes and Leibnizes." A simple and constant order does not hold men's attention. Only happenings bordering on the miraculous can reawaken it. I have never heard the common people find proof that God punishes drunkards in the fact that they lose their health and reason. But how often I have heard the peasants of my village cite as proof of God's punishment the fact that a certain drunkard broke a leg on the way home.

Fifth Lecture

We have justified the reduction of religion to a feeling of dependency by historical examples. But to the unclouded eye this contention provides its own immediate justification; for it is evident that religion is only the hallmark or attribute of a being who necessarily considers himself in relation to another being—of a being who is not a god, that is, not an independent, infinite being without needs. But the most sensitive, most painful of man's feelings of finiteness is the feeling or awareness that he will one day end, that he will die. If man did not die, if he lived forever, if there were no such thing as death, there would be no religion. Nothing is mightier than man, says Sophocles in *Antigone*; he sails the sea, furrows the earth, tames wild beasts, protects himself against heat and rain, finds answers to every situation—from death alone he knows no escape. To the ancients man is synonymous with mortal, god with immortal. That is why I say in my notes on *The Essence of Religion* that man's tomb is the sole birthplace of the gods. In hoary antiquity —and here we have a visible indication of this connection between death and religion—tombs were also the temples of the gods; with most peoples the cult of the dead was an essential part of religion, with some it was the whole of religion. The thought of my dead ancestors is what most reminds me, the living, of my own death.

"Never," says the pagan philosopher Seneca in his letters, "is the mood of mortal man more divine (or in our language, more religious) than when he thinks of his mortality and knows that man is born to die some day." And in the Old Testament we read: "Lord, make me to know mine end, and the measure of my days, what it is." "So teach us to number our days that we may get a heart of wisdom." "Think of him, how he has died, so too must thou die." "Today a king, tomorrow dead." But quite independently of the idea of a God, the thought of death is a religious thought, because in it I confront my finiteness. But if it is clear that without death there can be no religion, it must be equally clear that the feeling of dependency is the most characteristic expression of the ground of religion; for what can impress on me more forcefully, more incisively than death the feeling that I do not depend on myself alone, that the length of my life does not depend on my will? Nevertheless I must state before going any further that for me the feeling of dependency is not the whole of religion, but only the source, the base, the foundation of religion. For in religion man looks for defenses against what he feels dependent on. Thus his defense against death is the belief in immortality. Indeed, the one religious plea of primitive man to his godhead is that stated in the prayer of the Cachinic Tatars to the sun: "Do not strike me dead."[2]

I now come to the second part of the paragraph, to the *first object* of religious worship. On this matter I waste few words, for today it is almost universally recognized that man's oldest or first religion is nature religion, that even the later spiritual and political gods of peoples such as the Greeks and the Germanic tribes were originally natural phenomena. Though Odin later became a primarily political being and especially a war-god, originally, like the Greek Zeus and the Roman Jupiter, he was nothing other than the sky—and that is why his eye was the sun. Among primitive peoples then and now nature is not a symbol or instrument of a god or being hidden behind it, but is itself, as such, as nature, the object of religious worship.

Stated briefly, the second paragraph says that religion is indeed essential to or innate in man, but that this is not the religion of theology or theism, not an actual belief in God, but solely the religion that expresses nothing other than man's feeling of finiteness and dependency on nature.

To this paragraph, I wish chiefly to remark that in it I distinguish religion from theism, the belief in a being distinct from nature and man, whereas in a previous lecture I said that the object of religion is generally termed God. It is true that today theism, theology, the belief in God have become so identified with religion that to have no God, no theological being, is considered synonymous with having no religion. But here we deal with the original elements of religion. It is theism, theology, that has wrenched man out of his relationship with the world, isolated him, made him into an arrogant self-centered being who exalts himself above nature. And it is only on this level that religion becomes identified with theology, with the belief in a being outside and above nature as the true God. Originally religion expressed nothing other than man's feeling that he is an inseparable part of nature or the world.

I said in my *Essence of Christianity* that the secrets of religion find their solution and clarification not only in anthropology, but even in pathology as well. Strangers to nature, the theologians and philosophers were horrified. But what does nature religion, with its feast days and rites relating to and expressing the most important natural phenomena, represent but an aesthetic pathology?* What are all these spring, summer, autumn, and winter festivals that we encounter in the ancient religions, but reenactments of the diverse impressions made upon man by diverse natural forces and events? Grief at someone's death or sorrow at the decline of light and warmth, joy at the birth of a child or the return of light and warmth after the cold of winter, or at an abundant harvest; fear and dread over phenomena which are frightening in themselves or at least to the human mind, such as eclipses of the sun or moon—all these simple, natural emotions are the subjective content of nature religion. Originally religion was not a thing apart distinct from the life of man. Only by and by, in the course of a later development, does it take on a separate existence and put forward special claims. And it is only against this arrogant, presumptuous ecclesiastical religion, which, being ecclesiastical, is now represented by a special official class, that I take up cudgels.

Though I myself am an atheist, I openly profess religion in the sense just mentioned, that is, nature religion. I hate the idealism that wrenches man out of nature; I am not ashamed of my dependency on nature; I openly confess that the workings of nature affect not only my surface, my skin, my body, but also my core,

* Or often very unaesthetic.

my innermost being, that the air I breathe in bright weather has a salutary effect not only on my lungs but also on my mind, that the light of the sun illumines not only my eyes but also my spirit and my heart. And I do not, like a Christian, believe that such dependency is contrary to my true being or hope to be delivered from it. I know further that I am a finite mortal being, that I shall one day cease to be. But I find this *very natural* and am therefore perfectly reconciled to the thought.

I have further maintained in my books and will prove in these lectures that in religion man projects his essence. Of this assertion nature religion itself provides a first confirmation. For what are the feast days of nature religion (and the religion especially of the simple, earthy peoples of antiquity expresses its essence most unmistakably in their feast days) if not expressions of the feelings and impressions which nature with its seasonal changes and other striking phenomena arouses in man? Certain French philosophers have seen nothing but physics and astronomy in the religions of antiquity. That is correct, provided we think of physics and astronomy not in a scientific sense as did the French philosophers, but in a purely *aesthetic* sense. The original elements of the ancient religions are merely projections of the sensations, the impressions which physical and astronomical phenomena arouse in man so long as he does not see them as objects of science. Later, of course, even among the ancient peoples, notably in the priestly caste who alone had access to science and learning, observations—the rudiments of science—took their place side by side with the religious view of nature; but such observations cannot be regarded as the original version of nature religion.

Besides, even though I identify my view with nature religion, I must ask you to remember that even nature religion contains an element which I reject. For although, as the name itself indicates, the object of nature religion is nature and nothing else, nevertheless, to man in his earliest stage, that of nature religion, nature is not an object as it is in reality, but is only what it seems to his uncultivated and inexperienced reason, to his imagination and feeling. Even here, accordingly, man has supernatural desires and consequently makes supernatural—or what amounts to the same thing, —unnatural demands on nature. Or to put it differently and more clearly: not even nature religion is free of superstition, for in their natural state, that is, without education and experience, all men, as Spinoza recognized, are subject to superstition. And when I speak in favor of nature religion, I do not wish to be suspected of also favoring religious superstition.

In nature religion I recognize neither more nor less that what I recognize in all religion, including the Christian, namely, *its simple fundamental truth.* And this truth is only that man is dependent on nature, that he should live in harmony with nature, that even in his highest intellectual development he should not forget that he is a part and child of nature, but at all times honor nature and hold it sacred, not only as the ground and source of his existence, but also as the ground and source of his mental and physical well-being, for it is only through nature than man can become free of all morbidly excessive demands and desires, such as the desire for immortality. "Learn to know nature, recognize it as your mother; then you will descend peacefully into the earth when the time comes." No more than I deify man—the absurd accusation leveled at me in connection with *The Essence of Christianity*—no more than I try to set him up as the God of theologico-religious faith (whom precisely I dissolve into His human, antitheological elements by defining Him as the goal of man)—no more do I wish to deify nature in the spirit of theology or pantheism when I define it as the ground of human existence, as the reality on which man should know himself to be dependent, from which he should know himself to be inseparable. Just as I can honor and love a human individual without deifying him, without even overlooking his faults and failings, I can also recognize that without nature I am nothing, and yet not for that reason forget its lack of heart, reason, and consciousness, which it first acquires in man; I can recognize nature for what it is without falling into the error of nature religion and of philosophical pantheism, namely, of making nature into a god.

Man's true culture and true task is to take things as they are, to make *no more,* but *also no less* of them than they are. Nature religion, pantheism, makes too much of nature, while conversely, idealism, theism, Christianity make too little of it, and indeed ignore it. Let us try to avoid the extremes, the superlatives or exaggerations of the religious emotion, to look upon nature, to speak of it and revere it as what it is—as our mother. But just as we show our earthly mother due respect without worshiping her, without forgetting the limitations of her person and of her sex, just as in our relationship with our human mother we do not remain forever a child, but confront her with the free mind of a grown man, so also we should look at nature not with the eyes of religious children, but with those of self-reliant adults. The ancient peoples with their exaggerated religious emotion and humility worshiped everything conceivable as a god and looked upon almost everything with exclusively religious eyes—as we read, for example, in a maxim of Menander, they also called their parents gods.

Our parents have not become indifferent to us just because we no longer look upon them as gods, because we no longer invest them with the power of life and death over their children as the ancient Romans or Persians did. By the same token nature, or any object whatsoever, need not lose its significance for us just because we divest it of its divine nimbus. On the contrary: an object first takes on its true intrinsic dignity when the sacred nimbus is stripped off; for as long as a thing or being is an object of religious worship, it is clad in borrowed plumes, namely, the peacock feathers of the human imagination.

In the third paragraph I say that, insofar as a man has specific, particular essence, he owes it to a particular nature, the nature of his country, and that consequently he is not only justified in making the nature of his country an object of his religion, but does so of necessity.

On this paragraph I have only this much to say: if it is not surprising that men should have worshiped nature in general, it is also no ground for surprise, regret, or ridicule that they should have made the nature in which they lived and breathed, to which alone they owe their individual character, in short, the nature of their country, an object of religious worship. If we wish to reprove or ridicule them for this, we shall have to ridicule and reject all religion; for if the feeling of dependency is the ground of religion, and if the object of this feeling is nature, the being on which man's life and existence depend, then it is only natural that he should worship not nature in general but the *nature of this country,* for it is to *this* country alone that I owe my life and what I am.

I myself am *not man as such* but this *particular, individual man.* I, for example, am a man who speaks and thinks in German—in reality there is no language as such, but only this and that language. The specific character of my being, of my life, is inseparably bound up with a specific soil, a specific climate, and this is especially true of the ancient peoples.

Thus it is not the least bit absurd or surprising that they should have worshiped their mountains, their rivers, their animals; especially when we recall that for lack of experience and education those early peoples looked upon their country as the whole world, or at least as its center. How, indeed, can we wonder at such worship of the homeland among early peoples living in isolation, when we stop to consider the religious role that patriotism still plays among civilized modern nations linked by the most thriving international commerce. Why, even the French say that "God is a good Frenchman"; and the Germans, who at least from a political standpoint have no reason at all to be proud of their country, speak even today unashamedly of the *German* God. And not without reason, I say in a note to *The Essence of Christianity,* because as long as there are many nations, there will also be many gods; for a nation's God, at least its true God, who must indeed be distinguished from the God of its dogmatists and philosophers of religion, is nothing other than its national feeling, its national *point d'honneur*. And among the early primitive peoples this *point d'honneur* was their country. The ancient Persians, for example, as Herodotus relates, esteemed other nations solely according to their distance from Persia: the closer they were, the higher they stood in the scale. And the Egyptians, according to Diodorus, looked on their Nile muck as the original and fundamental substance of animal and even of human life.

Sixth Lecture

AT THE END of the last lecture I opposed Christian supernaturalism and justified the position of nature religion, in which a particular and finite man worships a particular and finite nature, the mountains, rivers, trees, animals, and plants of his country. In the ensuing paragraph I take up the most paradoxical part of this religion, namely, the animal cult, and justify it on the ground that animals were indispensable to man, that his existence depended on them, that they enabled him to rise to a higher level of civilization, that man deifies what his existence depends on, and that consequently, in his object of worship—in this case the animals—he was merely objectifying the value he set on himself and his life.

There has been much argument on the questions of whether, in what sense, and for what reason animals have been objects of religious worship. The first question, as to the fact of animal worship, has been raised chiefly in connection with the religion of the ancient Egyptians, and answered sometimes in the affirmative, sometimes in the negative. But when we read the eyewitness reports of recent travelers, we see no reason to doubt that the ancient Egyptians, unless special arguments can be adduced to the contrary, worshiped or at least may have worshiped animals, since these reports confirm the existence of animal cults today or in the very recent past among many peoples of Asia, Africa, and America. Thus, as Martius relates, llamas are held sacred by many Peruvians, while others worship the corn plant.* The bull is an object of worship among the Hindus. "Once each year they show him

* *Rechtszustand der Ureinwohner Brasiliens.*

divine honors, deck him out with ribbons and flowers, and prostrate themselves before him. In many villages the people keep a bull as a living idol, and when he dies, bury him amid great pomp and ceremony." Similarly "all snakes are sacred to the Hindus. There are idolaters who are so blindly enslaved by their prejudices that they regard it as good fortune to be bitten by a snake. They see the hand of Providence and have no other thought than to end their life in rejoicing, because they believe that in the other world they will obtain an important post at the court of the snake king."*

Pious Buddhists and to a still greater degree the Jains, an Indian sect related to the Buddhists, look upon "the killing of even the lowest vermin as a deadly sin, equivalent to human murder."† The Jains set up "regular animal hospitals even for the lowest and most despised varieties, and pay poor people to spend the night in these places set aside for vermin, and let themselves be eaten alive. Many wear a piece of canvas in front of their mouths lest they swallow some flying insect and so deprive it of life. Others take a soft brush and, for fear of crushing some animal, sweep the place where they mean to sit down. Or they carry a little bag of flour or sugar or a jar of honey with which to feed the ants or other animals."‡

"The Tibetans too are as kind to bedbugs, lice and fleas as to tame and useful animals. In Ava, *the people treat domestic animals like their own children.* A woman whose parrot had died cried out with grief: my son is gone, my son is gone! And she had him buried with as much ceremony as a son."§ Curiously enough, as the same authority informs us, most of the animals worshiped in ancient Egypt and the ancient Orient are still considered *inviolable* by the Christian and Mohammedan inhabitants of those countries. The Christian Copts, for example, build *hospitals for cats* and make bequests in order that vultures and other animals may be fed at specified hours. According to W. Marsden, the Sumatrans hold alligators and tigers in such religious awe that instead of exterminating them they allow themselves to be exterminated by

* Ersch und Gruber, *Encyclopädie,* s.v. "Hindostan."
† Bohlen, *Das alte Indien,* Vol. 1.
‡ Ersch und Gruber, *Encyclopädie,* s.v. "Dschainas."
§ Meiners, *Allgemeine kritische Geschichte der Religionen.*

them.* They dare not even call tigers by their customary name, but refer to them as their ancestors or as the ancients, "either because they really regard them as such or in order to flatter them. When a European has traps set by less superstitious persons, these persons go to the place at night and perform ceremonies whose purpose it is to persuade the animal, when it is caught or smells the bait, that the trap was not set by them or with their consent."

Having with these few examples established the fact— the deification and worship of animals—I come to the cause and significance of the phenomenon. As to the cause, I reduce it to the feeling of dependency. Animals were necessary to man; without them he could not exist, certainly not on a human level. But the necessary is what I am dependent on; just as nature in general, as the fundamental principle of human existence, became an object of religion, so it was not only possible but also inevitable that animal nature should become an object of worship. Accordingly I consider the animal cult principally in relation to the period when it was historically justified, the period of nascent civilization, when animals were of the utmost importance to man. But consider the importance that animals still hold for us who laugh at animal cults. What is a hunter without a hunting dog, a shepherd without his sheep dog, a peasant without his bull? Is dung not the soul of our economy? Is not then the bull, with us as with the ancient peoples, still the supreme principle, the god, of agriculture?

Why should we ridicule the ancient peoples for according religious honor to what is still of the highest value for us rational beings? Do we not still in many cases prize animals above men? In the armies of the Christian Germanic nations is not greater value attached to the horse than to the rider, does not a peasant set more store by his ox than by his hired hand? And in the same paragraph I quoted a passage from the Zend Avesta as an historical example. The Zend Avesta (distorted, it is true, in its present late recension) is the religious book of the ancient Persians. In one of its parts, known as the "Vendidad," we read (unfortunately in Kleuker's old and unreliable translation): "*The world subsists thanks to the dog's intelligence. . . . If he did not guard* the roads, robbers or wolves would steal all property." Because of this important function, though also on grounds of reli-

* W. Marsden, *op. cit.*

gious superstition, the laws set forth in this same Zend Avesta, not only set the dog as guardian and protector against beasts of prey "on an equal footing with man, but even accord him privileges in accordance with his needs." For example: "Anyone who sees a hungry dog is under obligation to give him his fill of the best food." "If a bitch with puppies goes astray, the headman of the locality where she is found must take her in and feed her; *if he does not, he will be punished by maiming.*" A man, then, has less value than a dog. And in the religion of the Egyptians we find still more drastic ordinances setting man on a lower level than animals. "Any man," writes Diodorus, "who kills one of these (sanctified) animals, is liable to the death penalty. But if it is a cat or an ibis, he must die in any event, regardless of whether he has killed the animal on purpose or unintentionally; a crowd gathers and maltreats the offender in the most cruel way."

But the examples I myself have cited seem to argue against my derivation of animal worship from their indispensability. Are tigers, snakes, lice, and fleas necessary to man? Only useful animals are necessary.

> Though on the whole [writes Meiners] useful animals were worshiped more than harmful ones, we cannot conclude that their utility was the reason why they were worshiped. Useful animals were not worshiped in proportion to their utility, nor harmful animals in proportion to their harmfulness. The reasons why one animal was favored here and another there are unknown and unfathomable; and certain manifestations of the animal cult are inexplicable and contradictory. For example, the Negroes of Senegal and Gambia worship tigers, while in the kingdom of Ante and other nearby kingdoms those who kill a tiger are rewarded.

It is true that on first entering the domain of religion we encounter a chaos of the most baffling contradictions. On closer scrutiny, however, these reduce themselves to the motives of fear and love (though these, in accordance with the differences among men, are related to the most divergent objects), in other words to the feeling of dependency. Even though a given animal does no real, scientifically demonstrable good or harm, man's religious imagination, often for reasons that are quite accidental and unknown to us, associates magical influences with that animal.[3] But what miraculous medicinal powers have been attributed to jewels!

For what reason? Out of superstition. Thus the inner motives of worship are identical; such cults differ only insofar as the worship of certain objects is based on an imaginary utility or harmfulness, existing only in faith or superstition, while the worship of others is based on a real utility or harmfulness. In short, the alternative between fortune and misfortune, well-being and suffering, sickness and health, life and death depends in truth and reality on certain objects of worship, and on others only *in imagination, in faith,* in the mind.

I must also note in this context, where the diversity of religious objects seems to conflict with the explanation of religion I have offered, that I am far from reducing religion or anything else to any one-sided, abstract principle. When I contemplate an object, I always keep its totality in mind. My feeling of dependency is not a theological, Schleiermacherian, nebulous, indeterminate, abstract feeling. My feeling of dependency has eyes and ears, hands and feet; it is nothing other than the man who feels and sees himself to be dependent, in short, who knows himself to be dependent on all sides and in every respect. And what man is dependent on, what he feels and knows himself to be dependent on *is nature, an object of the senses.*

Thus it is not to be wondered at that all the impressions which nature makes on man through his senses, even if they are purely idiosyncratic, can and do become motives of religious worship, that even those objects which relate only to the theoretical senses and do not stand to man in the immediate practical relationship that provides the basic motives of fear and love, should become objects of religion. Even when man makes a natural being into an object of worship because of its frightfulness or harmfulness (to render it harmless) or because of its beneficence and utility (to thank it for its kindness), such an object presents *other* aspects which also strike the eye and consciousness of man and consequently become factors of religion. When the Persians worship the dog for its vigilance and fidelity, or, as it were, for its political and moral indispensability to man, they are not considering it only *in abstracto* as a guardian, but as a whole with all its other natural traits; and it is self-evident that all these traits should contribute to the formation of a religious object.

Other traits of the dog beside its utility and vigilance are expressly mentioned in the Zend Avesta. For example: "He has eight noteworthy traits; he is like an *athorne* (priest), like a warrior, like a tiller of the soil, he is the source of wealth; he is like a bird, like a robber, like a beast, like an angry woman, like a young man. As priest, he eats what he finds . . . as priest he goes to all who seek him . . . the dog sleeps a good deal, like a young man, and like a young man he is ardent in action. . . . [etc.]" Similarly the lotus, *Nymphaea lotus,* which was a principal object of worship among the ancient Egyptians and Indians, and is still worshiped almost throughout the Orient, is not only a useful plant—its roots are edible and were formerly an important source of food especially in Egypt—but also one of the most *beautiful* aquatic plants. Among the more rational, practical and civilized peoples, to be sure, the cult of an object is based exclusively on those of its properties that are significant for human existence and culture, but among those of opposite character an object may be worshiped solely for irrational features without bearing on human existence and culture, including some that are merely curious.

Indeed, things and beings may be worshiped for no other identifiable reason than a special *sympathy* or *idiosyncrasy*. If religion is nothing other than psychology and anthropology, idiosyncrasy and sympathy are bound to play a part in it. All the strange and conspicuous phenomena in nature, everything that strikes and captivates man's eye, surprises and enchants his ear, fires his imagination, induces wonderment, affects him in a special, unusual, to him inexplicable way, may contribute to the formation of religion and even provide an object of worship. "We look with awe," says Seneca in one of his letters, "upon the sources of the larger rivers. We set up altars to a brook that bursts with sudden power from concealment. We worship warm springs and certain lakes are sacred to us because of their darkness or unfathomable depth." "Rivers," says Maximus of Tyre in his eighth dissertation, "are worshiped either for their utility, as is the Nile by the Egyptians, or for their beauty, as the Peneus by the Thessalians, for their size, as the Ister by the Scythians," or for other random reasons that are of no concern to us here. "A child," writes Clauberg, a seventeenth-century philosopher, a German though he wrote in Latin, and a brilliant disciple of Descartes, "is moved and captivated chiefly by bright and glittering objects. That is why the barbarian peoples allowed themselves to be deluded into sun and star worship and similar idolatry."

All these impressions, emotions and moods, aroused by the shimmer of light on stones—for stones, too, are worshiped—by the dread of night, the darkness and stillness of the forest, the unfathomable depth and vastness of the sea, the strangeness, charm, or frightfulness of animal shapes, can be factors in religion; they are elements to be reckoned with in any attempt to explain and interpret religion. But in this stage, where man surrenders indiscriminately to such impressions and emotions and derives his gods exclusively from such impressions and emotions, he is still outside the realm of history, still in a state of childhood, the human individual is not yet an historical person (though he will later become one). Such gods are mere shooting stars, mere meteors of religion. Only when man turns to the attributes which remind him continually and enduringly of his dependence on nature, which make him feel keenly that he is and can be nothing without nature, only when he makes these attributes the object of his worship, does he rise to a true, permanent, historical religion expressing itself in a formal cult. The sun, for example, becomes the object of a true cult only when it is worshiped not for its radiance—for that aspect which merely strikes the eye—but as the supreme principle of agriculture, as the measure of time, as the source of natural and civil order, as the manifest and intelligible ground of human life, in short, for its necessity, its beneficence.[4]

Only when the importance of an object for the development of civilization is recognized, does religion or a branch of it become a characteristic historical factor, an object of interest to the student of history and religion. This is also true of the animal cults. Though in a religion worship may extend to other animals without importance for the history of civilization, the worship of those animals which are significant for the growth of civilization is the characteristic factor, or at least the factor which it is reasonable to stress. Still, the motives for which other animals, other objects and properties than those that condition and ground the existence and civilization of man are worshiped are, as we have shown, not excluded from the cult of objects worthy to be worshiped on human grounds. All the most necessary, most influential objects of nature, those which most eminently awaken man's feeling of dependency on them, also have the qualities that strike the eye and the soul, that arouse astonishment, admiration, and all the related emotions and moods.

In his address to Zeus, to the god, the cause of the celestial phenomena, Aratus (*Phaemonena*) accordingly writes: "Hail to thee, Father, thou great wonder [i. e., thou great awakener of astonishment and admiration], thou great blessing of men." Here we have the two elements of which we were just speaking united in a single object. The object of religion, however, is not the *thauma,* the wonder, but the *oneiar,* the blessing, i. e., the god as an object not of astonishment, but of fear and hope; he is worshiped, he is the object of a cult, not because of those attributes that arouse astonishment and admiration, but because of those that establish and preserve human existence, that appeal to man's sense of dependency.

This is also true of animal cults, regardless of how many animal gods may owe their existence merely to the *thauma,* to uncritical gaping, to stupid amazement, to arbitrary and unrestrained religious superstition. Thus we need not be surprised or ashamed that man should have worshiped animals, for in them man loved and worshiped *only himself;* at least where the animal cult is a factor in the history of civilization, he worshiped animals only because of their services to mankind, in other words, for his own sake, not for bestial but for human reasons.

Our examples of the importance man still attaches to animals show that in worshiping animals man worships himself. The hunter prizes only those animals having to do with the hunt, the peasant only those connected with agriculture; in animals the hunter prizes the hunt, which is his own being, the peasant only his farm, which is his own soul and practical godhead. Thus the animal cults also provide proof and illustration of our contention that religion is a mere projection of man's own essence. At least among those peoples who have figured in the history of civilization, the animals to which men have devoted their principal cults are as divergent as men themselves, with their needs and essential, characteristic attitudes. The nature of the animals that have served as objects of worship can therefore guide us to an understanding of the men who worshiped them.

Thus, as Rohde notes, "the Persians, who initially lived exclusively by cattle raising, looked upon the dog as their mainstay in their struggle against the Ahrimanian animal world, that is, the wolves and other beasts of prey; consequently, anyone who had killed a serviceable dog or a pregnant bitch was punished by death. The Egyptian peasant had no need to fear either wolves or other beasts of prey. Rats and mice were the instrument of Typhon that harmed him; here accordingly the cat played the role which was allotted to the dog among the Zend people."* But the cult of animals, of nature in general, expresses not only a people's practical civilization, but also its theoretical essence, its spiritual attitude in general; for the man who worships animals and plants is not yet a man like ourselves; he identifies himself with animals and plants, which he looks upon as in part human, in part superhuman beings. In the *Zend Avesta,* for example, dogs are like men subject to law. "The first time he bites a domestic animal or a man, his right ear is cut off in punishment, the second time, his left ear, the third time, his right foot, the fourth time, his left foot and the fifth time his tail." According to Diodorus, the troglodytes called bull and cow, ram and sheep *father* and *mother,* because they received their daily fare from them and not from their natural parents. Both the Indians of Guatemala and African Negroes believe, as Meiners reports, that the life of each man is inseparably bound up with the life of a certain animal and that if the brother animal is killed the man too must die. And Sakuntala says to the flowers: "I feel the love of a *sister* for these plants."

An anecdote told by W. Jones provides a striking illustration of the difference between a human being at the stage of Oriental nature worship and a human being at our level. Once he had a lotus blossom on his desk, meaning to examine it. A stranger from Nepal came to see him; catching sight of the flower, he sank to the floor in awe. What a difference between a man who prostrates himself before a flower in worship, and one who considers the flower solely from the standpoint of botany!

* Erwin Rohde, *Die heilige Sage und das gesammte Religionssystem der alten Baktrier, Meder und Parsen oder des Zendvolkes.*

Seventh Lecture

I HAVE CONTENDED that man worships himself in animals and have shown that this contention is not invalidated by those animal cults which cannot be accounted for by any rational or historical considerations, which owe their existence exclusively to fear or to special accidents or idiosyncrasies; for where man worships a being for no reason, he merely projects his own folly upon that being. With this contention, we come to the heart of the paragraph, the statement that man deifies the being or thing upon which he knows or believes his life to depend, that accordingly this *object* of worship manifests nothing other than the *value* man sets upon his life and person, and that the worship of God reflects the worship of man. This statement, to be sure, is merely an anticipation of what I shall be saying in the present lectures. But because it already occurs in this paragraph, because it is of the utmost importance for my entire development and interpretation of religion, it seems worth mentioning on this occasion, that is, in connection with animal worship which, insofar as it has a rational foundation, confirms and illustrates this same statement.

To recapitulate: where animal worship becomes a cultural factor, a noteworthy element in the history of religion, it has a human or *egoistic* foundation. Yes, to the horror of hypocritical theologians and philosophical fantasts, I use the word *egoism* to designate the ground and essence of religion. In their sublime wisdom, uncritical critics who cling to words have put two and two together and concluded that my "philosophy" culminates in egoism and that I have therefore failed to get to the essence of religion. But when I use the word egoism—as a philosophical or universal principle, mind you—I do not mean egoism in the common sense of the word, as anyone with an ounce of critical faculty can gather from the connections, the context, the argument in which I employ it: for I employ the word in arguing against theology or theism, which, in their strict and consistent form, regard every love that does not have God as its aim and object, even the love of other men, as egoism.

Accordingly I am not referring to moral egoism, the egoism of man toward man, nor to the egoism of those who in all their actions, even in what they seemingly do for others, have only their own advantage in mind, nor to the egoism that is the hallmark of the Philistine and bourgeois, namely, the direct opposite of all candor in thought and action, of all spontaneity or love. By egoism I mean the self-assertion of man in accordance with his nature and consequently with his reason—for man's reason is nothing other than his conscious nature—in opposition to all the unnatural and inhuman demands which theological hypocrisy, religious and speculative fancy, political brutality and despotism make upon man. By egoism I mean the necessary, indispensable egoism—not moral but metaphysical, i. e., grounded in man's essence without his knowledge or will—the egoism without which man cannot live, for in order to live I must continuously acquire what is useful to me and avoid what is harmful; the egoism that is inherent in the very organism, which appropriates those substances that are assimilable and excretes those that are not. By egoism I mean man's love *for himself,* that is, love of the *human essence,* the love that spurs him on to satisfy and develop all the impulses and tendencies without whose satisfaction and development he neither is nor can be a true, complete man. By egoism I mean the individual's love for his fellow men—for what am I without them, what am I without my love of my fellows?—his love of himself only insofar as every love of an object or being is an indirect self-love, for I can love only what is in keeping with my ideal, my feeling, my essence.

In short, I mean by egoism the instinct of self-preservation thanks to which man refuses to sacrifice himself, his intelligence, his mind, his body—I draw my examples from the subject we have just been discussing, from animal worship—to clerical donkeys and sheep, political wolves and tigers, philosophical maggots and bookworms; that rational instinct which tells man that it is sheer folly to let lice, fleas, and bedbugs suck the blood from his body and the intelligence from his head, or let himself be poisoned by snakes and otters or devoured by tigers and wolves, out of religious self-denial; that rational instinct which, *even* when, as sometimes happens, man errs or abases himself to the point of worshiping animals, calls out to him: honor only those animals in which you honor yourself—even when you honor certain animals without rational ground, it is only because you at least believe or imagine that their cult is useful to you.

Here, however, I wish to repeat what is said in the complementary remarks to my *Essence of Religion,* namely, that "useful" is a popular term unsuited to and incompatible with a discussion of religion. For a thing that is not only useful, but also a god, an object of religious worship, is not a thing but a being. "Useful" is a passive term, signifying that something can be put to use, while activity, life, as Plutarch has said before us, is an essential attribute of the gods. The religious term and concept for usefulness is beneficence; for only beneficence and not usefulness awakens feelings of gratitude, worship, and love, and these feelings alone are religious in their nature and effects. Nature in general, plants and animals in particular, are worshiped in religious or poetic terms for their beneficence; in irreligious, popular, or prosaic terms for their usefulness; in philosophical terms for their necessity, that is, because man cannot exist without them.

Consequently animal worship, at least where it has a rational religious basis, has its *principle* in common with every other cult; the ground of animal worship among men who are in some degree reflective, the foundation of their cult, is the same as the ground of any other cult, regardless of its object. And this ground is, precisely, utility or beneficence. Men's gods differ only according to the different benefits they confer on man, according to the different human drives and needs that they satisfy; the objects of religion differ only according to the *different human faculties or powers* to which they relate. Apollo, for example, is the physician of man's psychic, moral disorders, Asklepios of his physical ailments. But the ground of their cult, the principle of their divinity, what makes them into gods, is their relation to man, their utility, their beneficence, it is *human egoism;* for unless I first love and worship myself, how can I love and worship what is useful and beneficial to me? How can I love a physician unless I love health? or a teacher unless I am eager to acquire knowledge? How can I worship the light unless I have eyes that seek the light and need it? How shall I praise my author or primal source if I despise myself? Or worship and recognize an *objectively* supreme being if I have no *subjectively* supreme being within me? How shall I assume the existence of a God outside me—though of course in a different way—unless I am God to myself? How shall I believe in an *outward* God unless I have an inner, subjective God?

But what is this supreme being in man, on whom all other supreme beings, all gods outside him depend? It is the aggregate of all his human drives, needs, predispositions, it is his existence, his life, which encompasses all the rest. Man makes a god or divine being of what his life depends on only because to him his life is a divine being, a divine possession or thing. Men have been known to say that "life is not the highest good"; but only where life is taken in a secondary sense, where man is in a state of unhappiness, of conflict, and his life is not normal. Then, to be sure, he rejects and despises life, but only because his life lacks qualities or advantages that are essential to normal life, only because it has *ceased* to be life. When, for example, a man is deprived of freedom, when he is a slave to arbitrary power, he can and should despise life, but only because it is then a deficient, meaningless life, lacking in the most essential condition and attribute of human life, which is freedom of movement and freedom to exercise his own will. This is also the cause of suicide. A man who kills himself does not take his life, it has already been taken from him. That is why he kills himself; he destroys only a semblance of himself; what he casts away is a mere shell whose kernel, whether by his fault or not, has long since been eaten away. But a healthy normal life—if life is taken to mean the aggregate of the properties pertaining to man—is and should be man's highest good, his supreme being.

Because I cite empirical, historical examples in support of all my statements and principles, because I only wish to state and clarify what others, what men in general, think and feel, I cite (in the "Additions and Explanations" to my *Essence of Religion*) a few passages from Aristotle, Plutarch, Homer, and Luther in support of my contention. Of course I do not pretend, as absurd, uncritical critics accuse me of doing, to demonstrate the truth of an assertion by a few quotations. I am a lover of brevity; I say in a few words what others say in volumes. Still, there is no doubt that most scholars and philosophers are impressed by the weight of an argument only if it is set before them in several fat tomes or at least in a good thick book. These few passages stand for many, they are of universal import and might be substantiated by thousands and thousands of learned quotations, which, however, qualitatively at least, would say no more than these few passages.

What is worth infinitely more than learned quotations is practice, life itself. And at every step we take, at every glance we cast at it, life confirms the truth of my contention that to men life is the supreme good. It is also confirmed by religion and its history; for while philosophy in the last analysis is merely the art of thought, religion is merely the art of life and simply expresses the forces and drives which directly govern the life of man. This truth is the universal, all-embracing principle of all religions. It is only because man cannot help unconsciously and involuntarily looking upon life as a divine possession and being that he *consciously,* in religion, makes a god of what, whether really or in his imagination, determines the origin and continuity of that divine possession. The gratification of any drive, whether higher or lower, physical or spiritual, practical or theoretical, is for man a divine enjoyment, and it is for this reason alone that he reveres the objects or beings on whom this satisfaction depends as glorious, divine beings.

A people which has no spiritual drives also has no spiritual gods. A people to whom reason as a *subject,* i. e., as human power and activity, is not a divine being, will never take a rational being as the object of its worship, a god. How can I make Minerva a goddess of wisdom if wisdom in itself is not a divine being for me? And in general how shall I deify the being on which my life depends unless I look upon life itself as divine? Only the differences between human drives, needs, capacities, and their relative rank determine the differences between, and the relative rank of, the various gods and religions. Thus man has in himself the measure, the *criterion of divinity* and for this very reason the *source of the gods.* What corresponds to this criterion is a god, what goes counter to it is not. And this criterion is *egoism* in the fully developed sense of the word.

The significance of an object for man, the gratification of a need, indispensability, beneficence—these are the reasons why man makes an object into a god. For man, unbeknownst to him, the absolute being is man himself. The so-called absolute beings, the gods, are relative beings *dependent* on man; they are gods only insofar as they serve his being, as they are useful, helpful, appropriate to it, in short, beneficent. Why did the Greeks laugh at the gods of the Egyptians, their crocodiles, cats, and ibises? Because the gods of the Egyptians did not fall in with the character, the needs of the Greeks. If the Greeks regarded only the Greek gods as gods, is the reason to be sought in the gods themselves? Of course not; it is to be sought in the Greeks, and only indirectly in the gods insofar as they reflected the character of the Greeks.[5] And why did the Christians reject the pagan, the Greek and Roman gods? Because their religious taste had changed, because the pagan gods did not give them what they wanted. Why then is only *their God* God? Because He is their very essence and likeness, because He falls in with their needs, their desires, their ideas.

Starting from the most common and universal phenomena of religion, we passed on to the feeling of dependency; but now we have gone still further and discovered the *ultimate subjective ground* of religion in human egoism as defined above (though it is true that egoism in the most common and ordinary sense of the word plays no mean role in religion, but this I shall disregard). The question is only whether this explanation of the ground and essence of religion and its objects, the gods, this explanation so absolutely at variance with the usual supersensory and superhuman, i. e., fantastic, explanations, is *in keeping with the truth,* whether with *this word* I have hit the nail on the head and correctly expressed what man really intends to worship when he worships gods. True, I have already cited examples enough, but since the matter is so important, since scholars can be bested only with their own weapons, namely quotations, I shall cite some more.

"The plant, the tree, whose fruits were eaten," says Rohde (*op.*

cit.) in reference to the religion of the ancient Indians and Persians, "were worshiped and entreated to supply still more fruit in the future. The animal whose milk and meat had been enjoyed was worshiped for that reason; water, because it makes the earth fertile; fire because it gives warmth and light, and the sun and all the other heavenly bodies because their beneficent influence on all life cannot escape even the dullest mind." The author of *De l'Origine des principes religieux* quotes the following from the *Histoire des Yncas du Pérou par Garcillaso de la Vega,* a book which I have unfortunately been unable to lay hands on: "The inhabitants of Chincha said to the Ynca that they would recognize neither the Ynca as their king nor the sun as their god, that they already had one whom they worshiped, that the god of their community was the *sea,* which is something very different from the sun, because it gave them an abundance of fish for food, while the sun did them no good, that its intense heat was merely a torment to them, and that consequently they saw no need to make a fuss over it."

Thus, by their own admission, they worshiped the sea because it was for them a source of food; like the Greek writer of comedies they thought, "My god is what feeds me." The popular saying, *"Whose bread I eat, his song I sing,"* is perfectly applicable to religion. Language itself tells us as much. *Almus,* for example, means "nourishing"; primarily an epithet for Ceres, it carries for that very reason the derived meanings "dear," "precious," "glorious," and "holy." "Of all the gods recorded in mythology," write Diodorus, "none is so highly revered among men as those two who served mankind so excellently with the most beneficial of inventions, Dionysos by introducing the most cherished of beverages and Demeter by her gift of the most excellent solid food." Commenting on the ancient proverb, "To men man is God," Erasmus remarks in his *Adagia*: "The ancients believed that *to be God* meant to be *useful to mortals."*

The philologist Johann von Meyen makes the same remark in a note on Vergil's *Aeneid.* The ancients, he says, paid divine honor after death to those who had made useful inventions, for they believed that a god was nothing other than what benefits mortals. "For what reason," asks Ovid in his letters from exile, "should we revere the gods if we strip them of their will to be useful to us or help us? If Jupiter is deaf to my prayers, why should I sacrifice a beast at his temple? If the sea gives me no peace on my voyage, why should I scatter incense for Neptune to no purpose? If Ceres does not fulfill the desires of the hard-working farmer, why should she receive the entrails of a gravid sow?" Thus it is only *utility* and helpful actions that *glorify men and gods*. "To mortal men," says Pliny the Elder, "a god is he who helps mortal man." According to Aulus Gellius, even Jupiter has his name of Jove from *juvare,* to help or benefit, in contrast to *nocere,* to harm.

Cicero writes in his *De officiis:* "After the gods, the most useful beings to man are men"; in other words, the gods are foremost among the beings who are useful to man. Likewise Erasmus says in his *Adagia,* "The saying: 'one God but many friends' admonishes us to make as many friends as possible, because after the gods it is they who can help us most." In his treatise *De natura deorum,* Cicero (or perhaps the Epicurean Velleius, but here that is immaterial) ridicules Perseus' assertion that useful and salutary things were looked upon as gods and, because Prodicus had said the same thing, accuses him of having destroyed religion; but in the same breath he accuses Epicurus of having exterminated religion, root and branch, by denying the most magnificent attribute of divinity, namely kindness and beneficence. For how, says Cicero, can he revere the gods if he neither receives nor can expect anything useful from them? Piety is justice toward the gods, but how can one owe any service to those from whom one receives nothing?

In the gods, says Quintilian in his *De institutione oratoria,* we revere first the majesty of their nature, secondly the particular power of each one and the inventions with which he has benefited mankind. Quintilian here distinguishes the power and majesty of the gods from the benefits they confer, but such a distinction cannot stand up to closer scrutiny; for the more majestic and powerful a being is, the greater its capacity to benefit others, and conversely. The highest power coincides with the greatest benefits. Among nearly all peoples the god of the heavenly powers and elements is therefore the highest, most sublime, most majestic, the god above all gods, because the actions and benefits of the heavens exceed all other actions and benefits and are the most universal, all-embracing, grandiose, and necessary. Among the Romans, for example, Jupiter is known as *Optimus* and *Maximus,* signifying, as Cicero himself remarks, "because of his benefits the best or kindest," but "because of his power," or might, "the greatest or highest." In Plutarch's *Amatorius* we find a distinction similar to that of Quintilian. "The praise of the gods is based principally on their *dynamis,* power, and *opheleia,* utility or helpfulness"; but as we have seen, the two concepts reduce themselves to one, for the greater a being is in itself, the more it can be to others. The greater it is, the more it can help—or harm—others. And that is why Plutarch himself says in his *Symposiakon:* "Men tend most to deify things of universal, all-encompassing utility, such as water, light, the seasons."

Eighth Lecture

When the last vestiges of pagan religion were destroyed, or at least divested of their political significance and dignity, when the statue of the goddess of victory was to be removed from the place where it had hitherto stood, Symmachus wrote a treatise in defense of the old historical religion, including the victory cult. Among his reasons for defending Victoria, he cited *utilitas* as the most reliable hallmark of a deity. No one will deny, he says, that what he professes to yearn for should be worshiped. In other words, only objects of human desire are objects of religion, but what do men desire if not the good, the useful, the beneficent? The more cultivated among classical pagans, the Greeks in particular, therefore regarded helpfulness, kindness, *philanthropeia,* as the essential attribute and condition of divinity. "No god," says Socrates in Plato's *Theaetetus,* "is hostile to men." "What," says Seneca in his letters, "is the ground of the gods' beneficence? Their nature. It is absurd to suppose that they wish to do harm; they are not even capable of doing so." "God," he goes on to say, "needs no servants; *He himself serves the human race.*" "It is no more absurd," says Plutarch in one of his essays directed against the Stoics, "to deny the immortality of the gods than to deny their providence and love of mankind, or beneficence." "By God," says Antipater of Tarsis, cited by Plutarch in the same work, "we mean a happy, imperishable being, *who benefits mankind.*" Among the Greeks, the gods, or at least the best of them, were therefore termed "givers of the good" and *sōteres,* saviors. Indeed, the Greek religion has no specifically evil god comparable to the Typhon of the Egyptians and the Ahriman of the Persians.

The Church Fathers scoffed at the heathen for making beneficent and useful things and beings objects of worship and religion. The frivolous Greeks, says Julius Firmicus for example, regard as gods all beings who confer or have conferred a benefit upon them. The Penates, he points out, are derived from the word *penus,* which signifies nothing more than food. Because they desired nothing else in life than the freedom to eat and drink, the pagans, he declared, had made foodstuffs into gods. Vesta, he goes on, is nothing other than the hearth fire used for preparing meals and ought to have cooks rather than virgins as her priests. But although the Church Fathers and Christians in general never wearied of condemning and ridiculing the pagans for their worship of useful things, fire, water, the sun, the moon, it was not the principle of this worship that they condemned, but only its object; if they found fault with the pagans, it was not because they made beneficence and utility the foundation of religion, but because they did not take the *right* being as the object of their religion, because they did not worship the One Being who alone can help man and make him happy, namely God, a spiritual, invisible, omnipotent being, author or creator of nature, but himself distinct from nature. With their non-sensuous abstract thinking, the Christians concentrated the power to injure or help, to confer good and harm, sickness and health, life and death in One Being, while the pagans, in accordance with their sensuous view, had distributed it among many different things.

To the Christians this One Being, whom they call God, is the only powerful and terrible being, the only being who confers benefits and is worthy to be loved. To recapitulate: if we posit beneficence as the one essential attribute of God, the pagans distributed the various benefits among different benefactors while the Christians impute them all to One Being. Thus for the Christians God is the aggregate of all gods. But in their definition and concept of divinity itself, in their view of its principle, its essence or ground, they do not differ from the pagans. Whenever, in the Old as well as the New Testament, God says: "I will be their God" or, employs the possessive as in "I am the God of Abraham," the meaning is "*benefactor.*" In the fourth book of the *City of God,* Augustine says: "If happiness is a goddess as the Romans suppose, why do they not worship her alone, why do they not flock to her temple alone? For who is there who would not like to be happy? Who desires anything if not for the sake of happiness? Who wants to obtain anything other than happiness from a god? But happiness is not a goddess, it is a gift of God. Seek therefore the God who can confer it." In the same work Augustine speaks of the Platonic daemons: "Whatever immortals or blessed beings there may be in the heavenly dwelling places, if they do not love us and wish us to be happy, they are not worthy to be worshiped."

Only a being who loves man and desires his happiness is an object of human worship, of religion. In his exegesis of certain chapters of Deuteronomy Luther writes:

> Thus reason describes God as what is helpful, useful and beneficial to man. That is what the heathen did. . . . The Romans set up many gods in connection with a variety of needs and assistance. . . . The gods chosen by men were as numerous as the afflictions, goods and benefits on earth, to the point that they even made plants and garlic into gods. . . . Under the papacy we made gods in the same way, *each ailment or affliction had its own helper and god.* When pregnant women were in distress, they called on St. Margaret, she was their goddess . . . St. Christopher was supposed to help the dying. Each man gives the name of God to that from which he expects the greatest good . . . I therefore say once again: reason knows dimly that God can and should help, but it cannot find the right God. . . . In the Scriptures the true God is called a *helper in affliction* and the *bestower of all good.*

In another passage he says of the heathen: "Although because of their idolatry they err as to the person of God (i. e., turn to false gods instead of the true God), nevertheless the cult due to the true God is present, that is, they call out to Him and expect *all good things* and *all help* from Him." In other words, the subjective principle of the pagans is perfectly sound, they are subjectively right insofar as they mean by God something that is exclusively good and beneficent, but objectively (in respect of the object) they are mistaken.

The Christians were especially hostile to the gods of pagan philosophy, and above all to the God of the Stoics, Epicureans, and Aristotelians, because explicitly or implicitly they belied Providence, because they omitted the attributes which alone, as I have said above, supplied the ground of religion, those attributes which relate to human welfare. Mosheim, a learned theologian of the eighteenth century, says for example in his notes to Cudworth's *Intellectual System,** a theologico-philosophical attack on atheism, that the Aristotelian God

> . . . is neither useful nor harmful to the human race and is therefore not worthy of any cult. Aristotle believed the world, the earth and the heavens, to be as necessary and eternal as God. Hence he also held the heavens to be as immutable as God. From this it would follow that God is not free, so that it is useless to entreat Him; for if the world moves in accordance with an eternal law and its course cannot in any way be modified, I fail to see what help we can expect from God. [This example, be it remarked in passing, makes it clear that, as we shall see in the following, the belief in God is identical with the belief in miracles, which modern rationalism has discredited.] It is only in words that Aristotle recognized the existence of God; in fact he abolished Him. The Aristotelian, like the Epicurean, God is idle, his energy, i. e. activity, consists solely in immortal existence and contemplation or speculation. *But what need have we for a God who lives only for Himself and whose essence consists solely in thought!* For how can man hope for comfort and protection from such a God?

The statements thus far cited are not merely the religious or theological views of individuals; they express the attitude of theologians and Christians, of Christian religion and theology itself; similar statements might be quoted ad infinitum. But why bore you with tedious repetition? I shall merely add that the pious pagans, even the philosophers among them, had already raised the same arguments against the useless philosophical gods, the Platonists for example against the Stoic God, the Stoics, who compared to the Epicureans were pious pagans, against the Epicurean God. Thus in Cicero's *De natura deorum,* the Stoic says: "Even the barbarians, even the Egyptians who have been so much ridiculed, worship no animal except for its beneficence; but no benefits, indeed, no action whatsoever can be cited in connection with your idle god. He is therefore a God only in name."

But if the passages thus far cited have universal significance, if the attitude they express pervades all religions and theologies, who

* Ralph Cudworth (1617-1688), *The True Intellectual System of the Universe.*

can deny that human egoism is the fundamental principle of religion and theology? For if a being's worthiness to be worshiped, hence his divine dignity, depends solely on his relation to human welfare, if only a being beneficial and useful to man is divine, then the ground of divinity is to be sought solely in human egoism, which relates everything to itself and evaluates it solely in accordance with this relationship. And moreover, in calling egoism the ground and essence of religion, I am not finding fault with religion, not in principle at least, not as a whole. I find fault with religion only where the egoism it reflects is utterly base, as in teleology, where religion turns the relation that an object, and nature in particular, has to man, into the very essence of that object, and of nature, and where for that very reason religion takes an unboundedly egoistic, contemptuous attitude toward nature; or where, as in the Christian belief in miracles and immortality, it is an unnatural, supernatural, and chimerical egoism, exceeding the limits of necessary, natural egoism.

Against this, my conception and explanation of religion, the theological hypocrites and speculative fantasts, who consider things and people only from the standpoint of their self-made concepts and imaginings, who never step down from their pulpits or lecture platforms, those artificial shrines of their spiritual and speculative conceit, to examine things close at hand—they argue that I, who in direct contrast to these spiritual and speculative gentlemen, am in the habit of first identifying myself with things, of familiarizing myself with them and getting to know them before judging them—argue that I take particular, i. e., secondary, contingent aspects of religion as its essence. The essence or religion, such is the contention of these hypocrites, fantasts, and speculative theorizers who have never cast a glance at the true essence of man, is the exact opposite of what I call the essence of religion; it is not self-assertion, not egoism, but the self-dissolution of the individual into the absolute, infinite, divine, or whatever the empty term may be; it is self-denial, self-abnegation, self-sacrifice.

There are indeed plenty of religious phenomena which seem at least to confute my conception and to justify the opposite view. These are the refusal to satisfy the most natural and powerful instincts, the mortification of the flesh and its evil lusts, as the Christians call them, the spiritual and bodily castration, the self-torture and flagellation, the penance and self-chastisement which play a part in nearly all religions. We have already seen that the fanatical snake worshipers of India let themselves be bitten by snakes, that the fanatical and ecstatic Indian and Tibetan animal worshipers allow bedbugs, lice, and fleas to suck the blood from their own or other people's bodies and the reason from their brains.

It is with no pleasure that I adduce still other examples, to furnish my adversaries with weapons against me. The Egyptians sacrificed the welfare of men to the welfare of their sacred animals. When a fire broke out, they were more concerned with saving cats than with extinguishing the blaze—which reminds me in spite of myself of the royal Prussian police commissioner who one Sunday some years ago, with true Prussian-Christian denial of humanity, forbade his fellow citizens to put out a fire during church services. And Diodorus tells us: "Once when the Egyptians were hard pressed by famine, many, it is said, saw themselves obliged *to eat each other,* but no one was ever accused of eating one of the sacred animals." How pious, how divine! Men eating each other out of bestiality hallowed by religion! In his eighth dissertation, Maximus of Tyre tells of an Egyptian woman who, having raised a young crocodile along with her son, did not mourn her son when the crocodile grew up and devoured him, but esteemed him fortunate to have been a victim of the household god; and Herodotus tells the story of an Egyptian woman who went so far as to marry a billy goat.[6] And now I ask the philosophers and theologians, who of course do not reject human self-love as the principle of religion, ethics, and philosophy, in practice but only in theory: can anyone carry self-contempt and self-denial any further than those Egyptian women? An English traveler to India tells the following story: Suddenly a tiger sprang from a thicket and seized a little boy who started screaming with all his might. The Englishman was beside himself with fear and horror; his Hindu companion remained perfectly calm. How, asked the Englishman, can you people be so unfeeling? The Hindu replied: "It was the Great God's will."* Can there be any greater resignation than to stand by inactive and unmoved, while a child is being throttled by a tiger—confident that whatever happens is

* Related in the notes to Hüttner, *Hindu Gesetzbuch oder Menu's Verordnungen.*

the work of God and that whatever God does is for the best? We all know that in times of distress and danger the Carthaginians sacrificed what was dearest to them, their own children, to their god Moloch.

The relevancy of such examples cannot be questioned on the ground that religious self-abnegation implies that a man should sacrifice not others but himself; for assuredly it would be far easier for many fathers and mothers to sacrifice themselves than to sacrifice their children. The Carthaginians were not lacking in love for their children; as Diodorus tells us, they tried for a time to sacrifice foreign children instead of their own. Undoubtedly this attempt to humanize the cult of Moloch was feeble in the extreme; and yet the priests of Moloch were as strongly opposed to it as are our present-day speculative and religious supporters of divine inhumanity to any attempt to humanize religion. "There are worshipers of the godhead," say the Indians, "by sacrifice, by self-castigation, by zealous devotion, by study of scripture, by the checking of passion and by ascetic living. Some sacrifice their breath and by violence divert it downward from its natural course, others force the lower wind upward with their breath, and some, who hold both these powers in high esteem, close the door on both."* What self-abnegation, to make what is bottommost in the human body uppermost and to repress the natural, though of course egotistical, human impulse for openness and freedom from all pressure!

No people has so distinguished itself by such self-torment and penance, none has performed such masterpieces of religious gymnastics as the Hindus. "Some [Indian penitents]," relates Sonnerat, mangle their bodies by incessant flagellation or have themselves chained to a tree trunk, where they remain until death. Others vow to remain all their lives in a painful position, for example, to keep their fists clenched, so that in time their nails, which they never cut, grow through their hands. Still others keep their arms crossed over their chests or outstretched above their heads until they can no longer move them. Many bury themselves alive, leaving only a small opening for air."† Indeed,

* *Ibid.*

† *Reise nach Ostindien und China.*

Indians who have attained the highest degree of religious perfection have been known to lie down "on railroad tracks to be crushed by a car which on feast days carries the colossal statue of the destroying god [Siva]." Can we ask for more? And yet we egoistic Europeans would sooner consent to such torments than to the religious self-abnegation of those Indians who drink a cow's urine as a purge for their sins and regard it as meritorious to commit suicide by letting themselves be covered with cow dung and so burned.

But what interests us most as Christians is the self-tortures, the self-denials to which the earliest Christians submitted. Simeon Stylites spent no less than thirty years on top of a column, St. Anthony lived for a time in a tomb, and such was the religious intransigeance with which he repressed the human will and every selfish impulse of the flesh that he never removed the vermin from his body and never washed himself. It is related of St. Silvania, whose interesting acquaintance, I must own, I owe only to Kolb's *Culturgeschichte,* that "at the age of sixty this pure soul had never washed her hands, her face, or any other part of her body except the fingertips when she received holy Communion!" What heroic supranaturalism and suprahumanism it requires to overcome the natural inclination to cleanliness, to renounce the pleasant, though to be sure egotistical, feeling that comes of ridding the body of all filth! I hold up these examples to the religious absolutists; these they cannot reject as aberrations and absurdities.

True, these examples are products of religious folly and madness, but madness, folly, lunacy are just as much a part of the philosophy of religion as they are of psychology and anthropology, for the forces, causes, grounds that operate and are objectified in religion are no different from those that underline anthropology in general. Religious man expressly regards diseases, physical as well as mental, as miraculous, divine phenomena. In our day, Russian superstition, as Lichtenstädt tells us in his book on infant mortality, looks upon many pathological states in children, especially those involving convulsions, as sacred and intangible.* Madmen and idiots are still regarded among many peoples as saints, inspired by God. Moreover, absurd as these types of human

* *Ursachen der grossen Sterblichkeit der Kinder des ersten Lebensjahres.*

self-denial may be, they are necessary consequences of the principle which our theologians, philosophers, and believers in general continue to uphold. Once self-denial or dissolution into the ethereal essence of religion and theology is established as a principle, what reason can I have for not repressing the natural impulse to move from one place to another, the impulse to remove filth from my body, to walk erect rather than to crawl on all fours as did many saints; why should I not deny these impulses as much as any other? From the theological point of view all these impulses are egoistic; for their satisfaction involves pleasure and self-satisfaction. In fact, the impulse to walk erect has no other source than human pride and arrogance and is therefore in direct contradiction to the subservience that theology expects of us.

All those who banish the principle of egoism—in the fully developed sense of the word, as I must persist in repeating—from religion are religious fanatics in the depth of their being, though they gloss over the reality with philosophical phrases; intellectually if not physically they still take the attitude of the early Christian stylites; theoretically, though not in practice, they still sacrifice man to their gods after the manner of primitive, earthy peoples; by reason of religious prejudice and superstition they still neglect to wash the dirt out of their eyes and heads, though unlike St. Silvania, their ideal, they do, out of inconsistency and common egoism (for dirt in the eye, the spiritual eye at least, is less tangible and therefore less troublesome than on other parts of the body)—they do wash. If they had washed their eyes clear in the cold water of nature and reality, they would recognize that for all its religious importance self-denial is not the essence of religion and that they have merely been looking on man and therefore religion as well through clouded eyes. From the exalted vantage point of their pulpit or lecture platform, they overlook the egoistic purpose underlying this self-abnegation, they forget that in practice men in general are more intelligent than theologians in their pulpits and professors on their platforms and that consequently, even in matters of religion, they live not by a philosophy of religion but by their own instinctive reason, which safeguards them against the folly of religious self-abnegation and which, even where they succumb to such folly, injects a human meaning and purpose into it.

Why does man deny himself in religion? In order to gain the favor of his gods who grant him everything he desires. By severe penance "a man can compel the gods to grant every plea and even to fulfill his *dreams* instantly."* Thus man does not practice self-abnegation for its own sake—where such self-abnegation occurs, it is pure religious madness. At least where man has preserved his human sanity, the purpose of his self-abnegation is self-affirmation. Self-abnegation is only a form, a means, of self-affirmation, of self-love. The aspect of religion in which this stands out most clearly is *sacrifice*.

* Bohlen, *Das Alte Indien.*

Ninth Lecture

THE ELEMENT of religion which makes it obvious that self-abnegation in religion is only a means, only an indirect form and mode of self-affirmation, is *sacrifice*. Sacrifice is the gift of a possession valuable to man. But in the eyes of man the highest and most precious possession is life, and only the highest can be sacrificed to the Highest, for that alone will show Him due honor. The sacrifice in which the principle underlying it is wholly fulfilled is, therefore, the negation, the destruction of a living being, or more specifically, since the highest of living beings is man, the negation of man. Here again, regardless of the purpose of human sacrifice, which we shall discuss in a moment, we have proof that man values nothing more than life, that he ranks life with the gods; for, generally speaking, "like attracts like" is the fundamental principle of sacrifice. To the gods man sacrifices only what he puts on an equal footing with them; he consequently sacrifices life to the gods only because in the eyes of both men and gods life is the highest, most precious, most divine possession, hence a sacrifice which the gods cannot resist, which subjects the will of the gods to the will of man.

But the negation or destruction involved in sacrifice is not an end in itself; it has a very definite, egoistic purpose and basis. Man sacrifices man—the highest being—only when he wishes to give thanks for what he esteems to be supreme good fortune, or to avert a real or merely anticipated misfortune, for a propitiatory sacrifice has *no independent purpose or meaning*. Man propitiates the gods only because they are the beings upon whom all fortune and misfortune depend; to avert the anger of the gods means nothing else than to avert misfortune from oneself, to gain their good will means simply to acquire all that is good and desirable.

And now a few examples by way of confirming both the fact of human sacrifice and the explanation I have adduced. I shall begin with the Germans and the peoples closest to us, although German scholars like to imagine that the *Germani* practiced only the mildest form of human sacrifice and maintain that with them human sacrifice was restricted to the execution of criminals, serving at once to punish the evildoer and to propitiate the gods whom the criminal's misdeeds had offended. Where other forms of human sacrifice are registered among the *Germani,* these scholars claim, they were merely the results of error and corruption. But even assuming—for there is no proof—that originally criminals alone were sacrificed, it seems reasonable to expect far worse barbarities, and human sacrifices of a very different kind, from a barbaric god who delighted in the tortures suffered by a criminal, from a "prince of the gallows," as Odin was called. Accordingly, if the Germans, who to this day conceal a considerable portion of barbarity beneath the halo of their Christian faith, are alleged to have been an exception among the peoples of their time, the reason must be sought in the patriotic egoism of German scholars.

But let us get back to our subject. According to a Norwegian saga, there was

> . . . *dearth* and *famine* in Sweden under King Domald. The Swedes sacrificed many oxen, but to no avail. Then they decided to bring back *fertility* and *good times* by sacrificing their king to Odin. They slaughtered and sacrificed him and daubed all the walls and chairs in the idol's house with his blood, and after that there were better times in the land.

Most costly in human lives were the sacrifices in fulfillment of oaths, sworn at the onset of war, to recompense the gods *for victory.* To the Goths, and the Scandinavians in general, the finest sacrifice was the first man they captured in a war. The Saxons, Franks, and *Heruli* also believed that human sacrifices appeased their gods. The Saxons employed excruciating tortures in providing the gods with victims, and the

Thulites [Scandinavians] sacrificed their first prisoners of war to the war god, putting them to death with studied cruelty.*

The Gauls, as Caesar relates, sacrificed human beings in times of grave disease or war peril, in the belief that the gods could be propitiated only if one man's life was sacrificed in exchange for another's. Our eastern neighbors as well, the Estonians, for example, "offered human sacrifices to the terrible gods. They purchased the human victims from merchants and carefully examined them to make sure they had no physical blemish that might make them unfit for sacrifice."† And the Slavs, those of the Baltic at least, "sacrificed a Christian once a year and in addition on extraordinary occasions" to Swantowit, their principal god, "because the priest who performed the sacrifice said that he and the other Slavic gods delighted especially in Christian blood."‡ Even the Romans and Greeks soiled themselves with the blood of human sacrifices. Before the battle of Salamis, as Plutarch relates, Themistocles sacrificed three noble Persian youths to Bacchos Oinestes—reluctantly to be sure, his hand forced by Euphranditos the soothsayer, who promised the Greeks victory but only on condition that this sacrifice should be performed. And in Rome, as late as the day of Pliny the Elder, several prisoners were buried alive in the cattle market. The Orientals sacrificed even their own sons and daughters—the beings for whose lives, as Justinus remarks in connection with the human sacrifices of the Carthaginians, people ordinarily entreat the gods most fervently.

Even the Israelites "shed innocent blood," as the Bible has it, "even the blood of their sons and their daughters whom they sacrificed unto the idols of Canaan." But not only to idols; Jephthah sacrificed his daughter to the Lord Himself, though by mistake as it were, because he had rashly sworn an oath that if he conquered, he would make a burnt offering of what should first come toward him from the door of his house and unfortunately that proved to be his own child, his daughter. Yet how, as numerous scholars

* F. Wachter in Ersch und Gruber, *Encyclopädie,* s.v. "Opfer."

† K. Eckermann, *Lehrbuch der Religionsgeschichte,* Vol. 4, Religion des Tschudischen Stammes."

‡ Wachter, *loc. cit.*

have already observed, could it have occurred to him to sacrifice his daughter if human sacrifices had been condemned? But among all the religious torturers and slaughterers of humankind, it was the Aztecs who most distinguished themselves by their cruelty and the number of their victims; as many as twenty thousand were said to have been done away with in a single day.

Like almost all the religious absurdities and horrors of antiquity, human sacrifice has endured down to our own times. One morning in 1791, a beheaded Harri (a member of the lowest caste) was found in a temple of Siva; he had been executed to ward off some great misfortune.* And certain wild Mahratta tribes go so far as to fatten the most beautiful boys and girls like geese in order to sacrifice them on special feast days. In times of great misfortune, of war and famine, even the sentimental Indians, so concerned over the life of insects, hurl the most distinguished Brahmins from the roofs of their pagodas in order to appease the anger of the gods. "In Tonkin," Meiners informs us, "they poison a certain number of children each year, in order that the gods may *bless the fields* and grant a plentiful harvest, or they cut one of the children in two in order to appease the gods and move them to spare the others. In Laos they never build a temple to the gods without laying the first passers-by into the foundations and so in a manner of speaking hallowing the ground."† "Certain Negro peoples still sacrifice many hundreds and thousands of prisoners in the misguided belief that such sacrifices are the best way of gaining the favor of the gods and thereby victory over their enemies. In other regions of Africa they slaughter sometimes children, sometimes adults, in order to bring about the recovery of ailing kings or to prolong their lives" (Meiners). Once each year the Khonds of Gondwana, a newly discovered tribe of Indian aborigines, sacrifice human beings to their supreme deity, the earth god Bera Pennu, on whom in their belief the welfare of men, animals and fields depends.‡ In connection with particular disasters, when, for example, a child has been torn to pieces by a tiger, they perform additional human sacrifices in order to appease

* *Hindu Gesetzbuch,* Notes.
† *Allgemeine Geschichte der Religionen.*
‡ Reported in *Ausland* for 1849.

the angry gods. The South Sea Islanders performed human sacrifices until very recently, and some of them still do.

The Christian religion is commonly praised for having done away with human sacrifice. But it merely replaced bloody human sacrifice with sacrifice of a different, namely, psychological, spiritual order, which remains human sacrifice in fact if not in appearance.[7] Those to whom appearances are all-important believe that the Christian religion has brought forth something essentially different from pagan religion, but that is an illusion. An example: the Christian Church condemned self-emasculation, although it appears at least to be recommended in the Bible; in any event, Origen, the great Church Father, who was surely as learned as our present-day theologians, understood the Bible in such a way that he felt obliged to emasculate himself; however, the Christian Church and religion have strictly forbidden the physical self-emasculation of pagan religion. But has it forbidden spiritual self-emasculation? By no means. The Church has at all times advocated moral, spiritual, and mental self-emasculation. Even Luther still sets celibacy above the married state. But what difference is there between the physical and psychological destruction of an organ? None; in the one case I take away the physical, anatomical existence and function of an organ, in the other its spiritual existence and function. But whether I lack an organ or neglect to use it for the purpose designed by nature, whether I kill it physically or spiritually, is all one. And this difference between pagan and Christian self-emasculation is the difference between the human sacrifices of the pagans and those of the Christians.

True, the Christian religion has on its conscience no physical, anatomical human sacrifices, but its human sacrifices of a psychological order cannot be numbered. Once man takes as his ideal, an abstract being, clearly differentiated from all real being, is it not inevitable that he will shun and seek to divest himself of everything that conflicts with this ideal? For to a God who is not a sensuous being man will necessarily sacrifice his own sensuousness; for, as we shall see more fully below, a God is nothing other than man's goal, his ideal. A God who is not an ethical, practical prototype of man, who is not what man himself should be and wants to be, is a God in name only. In short, the Christian religion—taken as a religion based on theological faith—differs no more from other religions on this point than it does in general principle. Just as Christianity has replaced the visible, sensuous corporeal gods with an invisible God, so it has replaced visible, tangible human sacrifice with an invisible, nonsensuous but no less real human sacrifice.

The examples cited above make it clear that even the most absurd and horrible negation of man, *religious murder,* has a human or egoistic purpose. Even where man takes not others but himself as the victim of his religious murder, even where he renounces all earthly goods, rejects all sensuous human pleasure, his renunciation is only a means of gaining heavenly or divine beatitude. So also with Christians. A Christian sacrifices himself, negates himself only in order to acquire beatitude. "He sacrifices himself to God" means that because earthly, transient joys are not adequate to his supernaturalist tastes, he sacrifices them for the sake of heavenly bliss. The Indians do the same. "When the Brahmin begins to shun all sensuous enjoyments, he attains to beatitude in this world, which will continue after his death." "When, unbeknownst to all, the Brahmin . . . has mortified his body and achieved indifference to sorrow and fear, he will become most exalted in divine existence."* Thus the purpose of the Brahmin's self-renunciation and self-negation is to become one with God, to become God. But this morbid self-alienation also involves extreme self-satisfaction. The Brahmins are the most arrogant beings under the sun, they regard themselves as earthly gods, beside whom all other human beings are as nothing. Quite generally, religious humility, humility before God, is compensated by religious arrogance toward men.

Even the detachment from the senses, the non-seeing, non-feeling, non-smelling, for which Indians strive, brings with it intense pleasure. Bernier tells us in his memoirs that the Brahmins "sink so deep into rapture that for many hours they are without feeling; during this time, they maintain, they see God himself as a radiant indescribable light; they experience ineffable bliss and feel utter detachment from the world they despise. I heard this from one of them, who claimed that he could enter into such

* *Hindu Gesetzbuch.*

ecstasy at will." The close relation between religious cruelty and religious ecstasy is well known. But if it is clear that even the highest forms of sacrifice are motivated by human egoism, it is still more evident in connection with the lower forms.

The hunting and fishing peoples of America, Siberia, and Africa sacrifice some of their spoils to the gods or to the spirits of the slain animals; but ordinarily it is only in difficult situations, while traveling dangerous trails or streams, for example, that they sacrifice whole animals. When the Kamchatkans catch fish, their sacrifice to the gods usually consists only of the heads and tails, which they themselves do not eat.* The old Slavs threw only the inferior parts of their sacrificial animals into the fire. They ate the best pieces themselves, or gave them to the priests. The Tatar and Mongolian hordes in Siberia, in the governments of Orenburg, Kazan, and Astrakhan, give the gods only the bones and horns of the cows, sheep, reindeer, or horses they sacrifice, or at most throw in the heads or the nose, ears, hoofs, and entrails. The Negroes of Africa leave the gods nothing but the skin and horns.†

The Greeks and Romans had their *holokausta,* i. e., sacrifices in which, after removal of the skin, the entire animal was burned in honor of the gods; but ordinarily they gave the gods only a part and ate the best morsels themselves. Hesiod tells us (though the passage has been explained in different ways) how the wily Prometheus taught men to keep the meat of their sacrificial animals for themselves and to offer the gods only the bones. In seeming contrast to this niggardliness, the Greeks and Romans sometimes offered up the most lavish sacrifices to their gods. After his victory over the Lacedaemonians, Alexander offered up a hecatomb, and his mother Olympias made a practice of sacrificing 1,000 oxen. In order to gain victory or to give thanks after a victory, the Romans sacrificed hundreds of oxen or an entire season's yield of calves, lambs, kids, and young pigs. After the death of Tiberius, the Romans were so delighted with their new emperor that, as Suetonius tells us, they sacrificed over 160,000 head of cattle in the first months of Caligula's reign.

Meiners (*op. cit.*) remarks in this connection: ". . . it does the

* However, according to Stephan Krasscheninnikow, their highest sacrifice consists of rags attached to a pole.

† Meiners, *op. cit.*

Greeks and Romans no honor that they excelled all other known peoples in the numbers of animals sacrificed, and still less that, generally speaking, the periods of their greatest proficiency in art and science were marked by the most lavish sacrifices." It is quite characteristic of the recent philosophical trend that the Hegelian author of a book on nature religion should comment as follows on this passage in Meiners: ". . . but it does Meiners small honor not to have realized that the willingness to sacrifice one's property, the indifference to one's own advantage revealed by such a hecatomb, make it a ceremony most worthy of god and man alike." Of course! A most worthy ceremony from the standpoint of the modern spiritualist view of religion, which finds the entire meaning of religion in its *inanities,* and consequently finds it worthier of man to sacrifice hundreds and thousands of oxen to gods who are without needs than to make use of them for the benefit of needy human beings.

But even these sacrifices, which religious aristocratism and sybaritism cite in support of their thesis, confirm the view I have developed. The various aspects of sacrifice are fully explained by what I have said about the feeling of distress and the feeling of joy aroused by relief from distress. Great fear and great joy provoke great sacrifices; both emotions are immoderate, transcendent, extravagant; consequently they are also the psychological source of extravagant beings, the gods. Immoderate sacrifices occur only in states of immoderate fear and joy. The Greeks and Romans offered up hecatombs not to the gods of Olympus, not to extrahuman and superhuman beings, but only to the affects of *fear* and *joy*. In the usual course of events man does not rise above his usual base egoism and his sacrifices are determined by the most common egoism; but at extraordinary moments he offers up extraordinary sacrifices, not to everyday emotions but to extraordinary emotions.[8] When he is afraid, man promises everything he possesses; in the intoxication of joy, or at least in his first enthusiasm, before he has fallen back into the rut of everyday egoism, he makes good his promises. Fear and joy are *communist* affects, but communists out of egoism. Consequently foul and niggardly sacrifices do *not* differ in principle from generous, imposing sacrifices.

This, however, is not the only difference between the hecatombs of the Greeks and the fishtails, horns, claws, and bones sacrificed to the gods by primitive peoples. Religions are as varied as peoples, and sacrifices as varied as religions. In religion man does not satisfy *other beings;* he satisfies his own nature. The needs and interests of uncivilized man are all below the belt; his true god is his *stomach.* Accordingly, he leaves nothing for his false, apparent gods, the gods who exist only in his imagination, except what his stomach cannot use: fishtails and fish heads, horns, skin, and bones. Civilized man, however, has aesthetic desires and needs; he does not eat everything without distinction, content if it fills his belly and appeases his hunger; he wants choice foods; besides, he wishes to smell, see, and hear pleasant things; in short, he has an artistic sense.

Obviously a people that has artistic feelings as its gods will also offer up artistic sacrifices, sacrifices pleasing to the eyes and ears. Similarly, a people given to luxury will offer up luxurious sacrifices. A people's gods are no more demanding than that people itself. Where man's vision does not rise to the stars, he does not have heavenly bodies for gods, and where, like the Ostyaks and Samoyeds, man eats carrion without revulsion, where decayed whale meat does not spoil his appetite, his gods will be revolting, unaesthetic idols. Thus if we consider the hecatombs of the Greeks and Romans from the point of view that carries religion back to man, if we look upon them as reflecting those peoples' sensibilities and needs, then we can indeed honor the Greeks and Romans for indulging something more than base egoism and utilitarianism.

So far we have been considering strictly religious sacrifices; but the history of religion records sacrifices of another kind, which, in contradistinction to those of a strictly religious order, we may call *moral.* I have in mind voluntary self-sacrifice for the benefit of other men, of state and country. Here again, it is true, man sacrifices himself to the gods to appease their anger, but the characteristic feature of such sacrifice is still moral or patriotic heroism. Among Romans, the two Decii sacrificed themselves for their country, and among Carthaginians the two Philaeni, who had themselves buried alive on the occasion of a border dispute between Carthage and Cyrene—or so we are told—and thereby brought their country great benefit. Hamilcar threw himself into the flames to appease the gods, for which deed, like the Philaeni, he was accorded divine honors by the Carthaginians. Among the Greeks, Sperthias, Codrus, and the fabulous Menoiceus did likewise. But such sacrifices, less than any other, have their source in the insane, supernaturalist negation of man, which religious and speculative absolutists call the essence of religion; for clearly such examples of self-abnegation have as their content and purpose the affirmation of human aims and desires, except that here negation and affirmation, sacrifice and egoism, are apportioned among different persons. But the persons for whom I sacrifice myself are my fellow citizens, my compatriots. My interests are theirs; it is my own desire that my country be saved.

Thus I am not sacrificing my life to any alien, theological being distinct from myself, I am sacrificing to my own nature, my own will, my own desire to know that my country will be saved. Just as the true gods, to whom the Greeks and Romans offered up their sumptuous sacrifices, were not the extrahuman gods but these people's own artistic sensibilities, their aesthetic taste, their luxury, their love of spectacles, so the true god to whom a Codrus, a Decius, a Hamilcar, and the Philaeni sacrificed themselves was patriotism and patriotism alone. But love of country does not preclude self-love; my own welfare is intimately bound up with that of my country. Thus, as Herodotus tells us, a Persian offering a sacrifice asked for good things not only for himself, but "for all the Persians, for *all* the Persians includes him too." Thus even if I ask something only for my country, I am also asking for myself; for under normal conditions my welfare is inseparable from that of all my compatriots.

Only in instances of extraordinary misfortune must the individual sacrifice himself to the general, that is, to the majority. But it is an absurdity to make a norm of the exceptional and abnormal, to set up self-denial as an absolute, universal principle and law; as though the general and the particular differed in essence, as though the general did not consist of particulars, as though the state, the commonweal, would not be doomed if every man were to pursue the ideal of the speculative, religious, and political absolutists, namely, self-negation and suicide. It is egoism alone that holds states together; states disintegrate only where the egoism of a class or of individuals ceases to recognize the egoism of other men and other classes as equal. But even if I carry my love beyond the confines of my country, even if I extend it to all men, self-love is not excluded from my universal love of mankind; for in men I love my own being, my race; they are flesh of my flesh and blood of my blood. But if self-love is a necessary, universal principle, inseparable from all love, then religion too must confirm this principle. And so it does on every page of its history. Wherever man combats human egoism (in the highly developed sense), whether in religion or in philosophy or in politics, he succumbs to *sheer absurdity* and madness; for the design underlying all human impulses, strivings, and actions, is to satisfy the needs of human nature, human egoism.

Tenth Lecture

THE BURDEN of my lectures thus far, and of the texts on which they are based, has been that the ground and source of religion is within man, that it is man's feeling of dependency, and that as long as this feeling is not falsified by hyperphysical speculation and reflection, its object is *nature*. For it is in nature that we live, breathe, and are; nature encompasses man on every side; take away nature and man ceases to exist; he subsists through nature and is dependent on nature in all his activities, in every step he takes. It is no more possible to cut off man from nature than to cut off the eye from light, the lungs from air, the stomach from food; he is no more self-sufficient than they. And what man is dependent on, what holds the power of life and death over him and is the source of his joys and fears, is and is called his God. But since man worships nature or any other god only because of that god's beneficence or, since in cases where he worships a god for his destructive, terrifying attributes he does so only in order to avert that destructiveness, the feeling of dependency has led us to *egoism* as the ultimate hidden ground of religion. A fuller explanation of this context may serve to obviate misunderstandings.

The feeling of dependency seems to conflict with egoism; for in egoism I subordinate the object to myself, in the feeling of dependency I subordinate myself to the object; in egoism I feel significant and important, in dependency I feel my insignificance in the presence of something more powerful. But let us for the moment concentrate on fear, which is the highest degree and expression of the feeling of dependency. Why does the slave fear his master, why does primitive man fear the god of thunder and lightning? Because the master holds the slave's life in his hands and the thunder god the lives of all men. What then does man fear? The loss of his life. The sole motive of his fear is egoism, self-love, love of his life. *Where there is no egoism, there is also no feeling of dependency.* A man to whom life is indifferent attaches no importance to what his life depends on; he neither dreads nor hopes for anything it can bring; his unconcern offers no purchase or toehold to a feeling of dependency.

If, for example, I love freedom of movement, I feel dependent on the man who can provide it or take it away, who can lock me in or let me go out; I should like to take a walk but cannot, because a more powerful being prevents me from doing so; but if it is all the same to me whether I am confined or free, in my room or out of doors, I do not feel dependent on the person who keeps me locked in, for neither by granting nor by denying me freedom of movement does he exert a pleasing or terrifying power that would give rise to a feeling of dependency; he exerts no such power, because within myself there is no power that impels me to go for a walk. Thus outward power presupposes an inner, psychological power, a selfish motive and interest, without which it means nothing to me, exerts no power over me, gives rise to no feelings of dependency within me. Dependency on another being is in reality a dependency on my own being, my own drives, desires, interests. Consequently, the feeling of dependency is merely an indirect, inverted or negative feeling of egoism, not an immediate egoism, however, but one mediated by and derived from the object on which I feel dependent.

I am dependent only on beings whom I need for the furtherance of my existence, without whom I cannot do what I should like to do; who have the power to grant me what I wish, what I need, but have not the power to secure for myself. *Where there is no need, there is no feeling of dependency;* if man did not need nature for his existence, he would not feel dependent on it, and accordingly he would not make it into an object of worship. The more I need something and the more dependent I feel on it, the more power it has over me; but *this power of the object* is itself a derived power, resulting from *the power of my need.* The need is at once the servant and the master of its object, it is at once humble and proud, I need the object, I am unhappy without it; therein lies the subservience, the devotion, the selflessness of need; but I need the object in order to gain satisfaction through it, to enjoy it and use it to my own advantage; therein lies the will to domination or egoism of my need. These contradictory qualities are also inherent in the feeling of dependency, for that feeling is simply *the known or felt need for an object*. Hunger is simply my stomach's need for food, which it communicates to my feeling and consciousness; in other words, it is nothing other than my feeling of dependency on food.

This ambivalence, this dual character of the feeling of dependency accounts for a phenomenon that has provoked a good deal of astonishment because it seemed to defy all rational explanation: namely, men's worship of animals and plants which they nonetheless destroyed and ate.* The need that impels me to eat an object is twofold in character: it subjects me to the object and at the same time subjects the object to me; it is both religious and irreligious. Or if we break down the need into its components, its "moments," as the modern philosophers say, we find on the one hand the *lack* and on the other the *enjoyment* of an object; the need for an object implies the enjoyment of that object, need is simply the need to enjoy a given object. The enjoyment of an object is of course a frivolous notion, or can be so regarded, for in the present case I enjoy the object by eating it, but the need, that is, the sense of want, the yearning, the feeling of dependency on the selfsame object is religious, humble, imaginary, and god-engendering.

As long as a thing is solely an object of longing, it is to me the highest, my imagination paints it in the most glowing colors, my need exalts it to the seventh heaven. But as soon as I have it and enjoy it, as soon as it is present, it loses all its religious charms, the illusions surrounding it are dispelled, it becomes common and ordinary; hence the common experience that in affliction, in misfortune, at times when they need something, all men, or at least those living on a crude, sensual plane, who live exclusively for momentary emotions and impressions, are full of devotion and self-sacrifice and promise everything under the sun, but that as soon as they *possess* what they lacked or desired they become un-

* And yet the Christians even eat their God.

grateful and selfish and forget their promises. Hence the saying: Need teaches us to pray; hence the fact, so distressing to the pious, that people in general are religious only in times of affliction, need, and misfortune.

Thus it is not in the least surprising that men should worship as religious objects things or beings which they also eat; on the contrary, this phenomenon serves to clarify the two aspects of the religious feeling of dependency. The difference between the Christian and the pagan feelings of dependency is merely the difference between their objects, since the object of the pagan feeling of dependency is a finite, real, and sensuous object, whereas the object of the Christian feeling—apart from the God made flesh and therefore edible—is an infinite, universal, merely cogitated or represented object and therefore not physically enjoyable or useful. But an object of enjoyment it remains, precisely because it is an object of need, of the feeling of dependency, except that for a Christian it is the object of a different kind of enjoyment, because it is also the object of a different kind of need; for what a Christian wants of his God is not so-called temporal life, but eternal life; in his God he satisfies not an immediately sensuous or physical need, but a spiritual need, a need of the soul.

Augustine writes in the *City of God:* "We use the things which we demand or seek not for their own sake but for the sake of something else, we but *enjoy* the things we relate to nothing else, which *delight us in themselves*. Thus the secular is an object of use, *usus,* but the Eternal, God, is an object of *fructus,* enjoyment." Yet even if we accept this distinction, even if we take it as a criterion by which to distinguish paganism and Christianity, defining the pagan gods as objects of use and the one Christian God as an object of enjoyment, Christianity nevertheless presents the selfsame contradictions that we have noted in connection with the nature of need and the character of the feeling of dependency, though the Christians notice these contradictions only in the pagan religions and not in their own. Even if with Augustine we regard the Christian God as an object of enjoyment as distinguished from use, He is just as much an object of egoism as the pagan object of physical enjoyment, which is also an object of religion.

Certain peoples have given touchingly naïve expression to the paradox that man accords divine honors to what he eats—a paradox which, however, as we have just shown, is also implicit in the Christian feeling of dependency, though less conspicuous because in Christianity that feeling has a different sort of object.* "Don't hold it against us," said certain North American Indians to the bear they had just killed. "You are wise and understand that our children were hungry. They love you and want to eat you. Are you not honored to be eaten by the children of the great chief?" "Charlevoix tells of others among whom the man who had killed a bear thrust a lighted pipe into the dead animal's mouth, blew into the bowl of the pipe, filled the bear's throat with smoke, and then begged the bear not to avenge himself for what had happened. During the meal at which the bear is eaten, the head, painted various colors, is given a place of honor and all the guests address prayers and hymns of praise to it."† The pre-Christian Finns sang the following song as they were dismembering a bear: "You dear vanquished, sorely wounded animal of the woods, bring to our huts health and spoils such as you love, a hundredfold, and when you come to us, minister to our needs . . . I will honor you always and expect spoils from you, in order that I may never forget my good bear son."‡ This shows that an animal which is killed and eaten can at the same time be honored, and conversely that the object of worship is at the same time an object of use; thus the religious feeling of dependency encompasses and expresses both man's selfish domination of the object when he regards it as an object of enjoyment, and his devout subservience to the object when he regards it as an object of need.

From this long discussion of egoism and the feeling of dependency, which was in no way incidental but quite necessary to the development of our subject, I now return to nature, the first object of the feeling of dependency. I have already observed that the purpose of my *Essence of Religion* and therefore of these lectures is simply to prove that the nature god, i. e., the god whom man distinguishes from himself and looks upon as the ground or

* Though here, too, it is quite conspicuous in the celebration of the Last Supper.

† Meiners, *op. cit.*

‡ Penannt, *Arctic Zoology.*

cause of his own being, is nothing other than nature itself, while the human or spiritual God, the God to whom he imputes human predicates, consciousness, and will, whom he conceives as a being similar to himself, whom he distinguishes from nature viewed as devoid of will or consciousness, is nothing other than man himself.

But I have also remarked that I do not derive my ideas from the vapors of groundless speculation, but always build them on historical, empirical phenomena, and that for this very reason I do not, or at least not primarily, develop my ideas in the abstract, but always embody them in real cases and illustrate them by real examples. In *The Essence of Religion,* especially in the first part, I aimed to show that nature is a fundamental, first and last* being which we cannot leave behind without losing ourselves in the realm of fancy and vacuous speculation; that we must stay with nature and cannot derive from nature a being distinct from nature, a spirit, a thinking being whom we place between it and ourselves; that consequently, if we produce nature out of spirit, the product will be a subjective, formal, intellectual abstraction and not a real, objective creation and being. But I developed this purpose, this idea, in connection with an actual phenomenon which is based on the idea and expresses it, and that is nature religion, the plain, simple, direct human feeling, which does not derive nature from a spiritual, unnatural and supernatural being, but looks on nature itself as the first of beings, as the divine being itself.

In nature religion man worships nature not only as the being through which he now exists or without which he cannot live or do anything else; he also worships and views nature as the being through which he originally came into being—consequently as man's alpha and omega. But where nature is viewed and worshiped as the being that created man, *nature itself is held to be not created;* for, as we shall see more fully further on, it is only where man cannot explain his own being by nature that he goes beyond nature and derives nature from something else. Thus while nature first became the object of religion on the practical ground that man cannot live without it and is indebted to it for the benefit of his present existence, at the present stage nature be-

* Last *a parte ante.*

comes the object of religion on theoretical grounds as well. From the standpoint of nature religion, man regards nature as the first being not only in practice but also in theory, in other words, it is the being from which he derives his origin. The Indians, for example, still regard the earth as their mother. They believe that they were all made in its womb and for that reason call themselves Metoktheniake, the Earth-born.*

Some of the early Indians looked upon the sea as their principal god and called it Mamacacha, their mother; others, such as the Colla, even believed that "their ancestors had risen from the great swamp on the island of Titicaca. Some thought that their first ancestor had sprung from a large well. Still others believed their forefathers had been born in certain pits and rock vaults; consequently they held these places sacred and made sacrifices to them. One nation imputed its existence to a river, and no one was permitted to kill a fish from that river, because they regarded those fish as their brothers."† And quite aptly the author remarks: "Because they looked on *different things* as the source from which they were descended, they also had *different deities* whom they worshiped." The Greenlanders believe that in the beginning a Greenlander grew out of the earth and that, after acquiring a woman he became the ancestor of all other Greenlanders."‡

Similarly the Greeks and the Germanic peoples revered the earth as the mother of mankind. Linguists even derive the word "earth" from Anglo-Saxon *ord,* meaning roughly principle or beginning and the word "Deutsch" from *tud, tit, teut, thiud, theotisc,* meaning earthy or earth-born. How untrue we Germans have become to our source, our mother, and how unlike her, thanks to Christianity which taught us that heaven is our home. Among the Greeks, it is worth noting, a good many philosophers, especially in the early period, believed that men and animals had been generated by earth or water, or by both at once, under the influence of the sun's heat, while others held that they had never come into being but were coeternal with nature and the universe. The

* Heckewelder.

† Baumgarten; *Allgemeine Geschichte der Völker und Länder von Amerika.*

‡ Bastholm, *Kenntniss des Menschen in seinem wilden und rohen Zustand.*

religions or rather mythologies, both of the Greeks and of the Norse if not of other Germanic peoples, both of which, particularly the latter, were nature religions to begin with, looked upon nature as the source not only of men but also of the gods—clear proof that gods and men are one, that the gods stand and fall with mankind. In Homer Okeanos, Ocean, is the begetter and father of the gods and of men; while in Hesiod, Earth is the mother of Uranus, Sky, and through her union with him the mother of the gods. In Sophocles Earth is called the supreme deity. Among the Norsemen the giant Ymir, "obviously the undifferentiated totality of the elements and natural powers" (Müller, *loc. cit.*) preceded the gods.

For the Romans as for the Greeks, Earth was the mother of the gods. In his *City of God,* Augustine ridicules the idea that the gods should be earth-born, and concludes that those were right who believed the gods to have been men of the earliest times. Nevertheless the gods, including Augustine's, sprang from the earth alone; they were not men as Euhemerus supposed, but neither did they precede man. With as good reason as those who called the earth the mother of the gods, Homer called sleep the tamer of gods and men, since the gods exist only for and through men. The gods do not watch over men when they sleep; when man sleeps, the gods sleep too; when man's consciousness is extinguished, the gods cease to exist.

My purpose in *The Essence of Religion* was none other than to defend and justify nature religion, or at least the truth underlying it, against the theistic explanations and derivations of nature. And I treated every aspect of the question, devoting to it no less than twenty paragraphs, Nos. 6 to 26. But before going into their content I have a preliminary remark to make. My approach to the history of religions—and this should be self-evident—goes hand in hand with my approach to psychology, philosophy, and all human development. Just as nature is for me the first object of religion, so I regard the sensuous world as the first element of psychology and of philosophy in general; but my "first" is not merely the "first" of speculative philosophy, meaning what has to be transcended; I take it in the sense of what cannot be derived, of the self-subsisting and true. I can no more derive sensibility from spirit than I can derive nature from God; for spirit is nothing outside of and without sensibility, spirit is only the essence, the sense, the spirit of the senses. And God is nothing other than spirit conceived as universal, spirit without reference to the difference between mine and thine.

I cannot derive my body from my mind—for I have to eat or to be able to eat before I can think; as the animals demonstrate, I can eat without thinking, but I cannot think without eating; I cannot derive my senses from my faculty of thought, from my reason—for reason presupposes the senses, but the senses do not presuppose reason, for we hold that the animals lack reason, but not senses. No more, or perhaps even less, can I derive nature from God. Thus the philosophy and history of religion are based on the assumption that nature is really substantial and true, just as psychology, anthropology, and philosophy in general must assume that the world of the senses is real. And no more than nature is a passing truth in the history of religion are the senses a passing truth in philosophy. Rather, the senses are an enduring foundation, even where they vanish beneath the abstractions of reason, as they do for those who lose sight of them as soon as they begin to think, forgetting that man thinks only by means of his materially existing head, that reason has an enduring material foundation in the head, the brain, which is the center of the senses.

Nature religion demonstrates that the senses do not lie to us, and philosophy, at least that philosophy which knows itself to be anthropology, demonstrates that nature religion does not lie to us. Man's first belief is his belief in the truth of the senses, not a belief in conflict with the senses, such as theistic and Christian belief. Belief in a God, in a disembodied being who rejects and negates every trace of the sensuous as profane, is far from being an immediate certainty, as theists have so often maintained. The *first* beings of whom man had immediate certainty and consequently his first gods were sensuous objects. Speaking of the religion of the Germans, Caesar said: they worship only beings whom they *see* and from whom they derive visible benefits. These words, which have been so much carped at, apply to all nature religions. Originally man believed in the existence only of what demonstrated its existence by physical, perceptible effects and signs. The first gospels, the first and most reliable documents of human religion, unfalsified by clerical fraud, are man's senses. *Or rather, man's senses were themselves his first gods;* for belief in the outward, bodily gods is contingent only on belief in the truth and divinity of the senses; in the gods, who are sensuous beings, man deifies only his senses.

When I worship Light as a divine being, I am merely expressing, though indirectly and unconsciously, the divinity of the eye. Light, sun or moon, is a god only to the eye, not to the nose; the cult of the nose is the cult of heavenly perfumes. The eye makes the gods into luminous, radiant apparitions, it deifies only visible things: the stars, the sun, and the moon have no other existence for man than in his eyes; to the other senses they do not exist. The eye, in short, deifies only itself; to the eye the gods of the other senses are idols, or rather, they do not exist at all. Man's sense of smell, on the other hand, deifies fragrance. Long ago Scaliger, arguing against Cardan in his *Exercitationes,* wrote: "Smell is a divine thing—*Odor divina res est*—and the ancients showed that this is so by their ceremonies, for they believed that by the burning of incense the air and certain places could be made fit to receive the gods." The pagans believed, and still believe in part, that the gods live on the fragrance of sacrifices, that perfumes are the ingredients of the gods, that the gods consist solely of fragrant vapors. In any case a man possessing no other organ than the organ of smell would conceive of divinity as consisting solely of fragrance, in disregard of all other properties perceived by the other senses. Accordingly each sense deifies itself alone.

In short, the truth of nature religion is based on the truth of the senses. Thus *The Principles of Philosophy** confirms *The Essence of Religion.* But though I defend nature religion because and insofar as it is based on the truth of the senses, I by no means defend the way in which it makes use of the senses, the way in which it looks at and worships nature. Nature religion has no other foundation than sensory impressions, or rather, the impression which sensations makes on man's mind and imagination. Hence the belief of the peoples of antiquity that their country was the world or the center of the world, that the sun moved, that the earth stood still, that the earth was as flat as a plate, surrounded by ocean.

* Cf. Vol. 2, "Toward a Reform of Philosophy."

Eleventh Lecture

As I have already said, the paragraphs underlying the present lectures merely provide scientific justification and proof of the insight which, from antiquity to the present day, naïve primitive peoples have expressed, though not consciously, in their worship of nature as a divine being, namely, the insight that nature is primary and fundamental, and cannot be derived from anything else. But before going any further, I must counter two objections.

First, it may be argued: Come now, you unbeliever—do you really mean to justify nature religion? You who have been so merciless in your criticism of the philosophers who justify the Christian dogma? Are you not putting yourself in their position, with the sole difference that the dogma you are setting out to justify is that of nature religion? I reply: I do not look upon nature as an origin because nature religion worships it as such; rather, I start from the fact that nature is the ultimate and immediate origin, and infer that it *must* also have appeared as such to primitive peoples, who were close to the origin and hence to nature. In other words, the fact that men deified nature does not demonstrate the truth of the underlying idea; but it does, to my mind, confirm the impression that nature makes on me as a sensuous being; it strengthens the reasons that impel me as an intellectual, philosophical, civilized being to ascribe to nature not the same significance as that ascribed to it by nature religion—for I deify nature no more than I deify anything else—but a similar significance, corrected only by the natural sciences and philosophy.

Yes, I sympathize with the religious worshipers of nature; I passionately admire and revere nature; not through books, not on the strength of learned proofs, but by my own immediate observations and impressions of nature, I understand how the ancient peoples and even certain peoples of our own day have been able to worship nature as a god. I still find grounds for this divinity or deification not only in my heart, with its power to be moved by nature, but in my mind as well. From this I infer—since the worshipers of sun, fire, and the stars are as human as I—that they deified nature on grounds similar to mine, though differing in accordance with their historical situation. I do not, like the historians, draw inferences from the past to the present, I do the opposite. Unlike them I regard the present as the key to the past, not the past as the key to the present, for the simple reason that, though often unconsciously and involuntarily, I always appraise, judge, know the past in accordance with my present situation. That is why each epoch creates a different history of an inherently dead and immutable past. Consequently I acknowledge the value of nature religion, not because I take it as an external authority, but solely because even today I find *within myself* the motives of nature religion, motives which, if they were not countered by culture, science, and philosophy, would still make me a nature worshiper today. Such a statement may smack of arrogance; but what a man does not know by his own lights, he does not know at all. Anyone whose own feeling does not make it clear to him why it was possible for men to deify the moon, plants, and animals will also be unable to understand the historical fact of nature worship, regardless of how many books he may read and write about nature religion.

The second objection is this: You speak of nature without giving us a definition of nature, without telling us what you mean by nature. Spinoza speaks of "nature, or God" as synonymous. Do you too take the word in this indefinite sense, which makes it child's play to prove that nature is the origin, since by nature you mean nothing other than God? I reply in few words: By nature I mean the sum of all the sensuous forces, things, and beings which man distinguishes from himself as other than human; in general, as I said in one of the first lectures, I argue with Spinoza in defining nature, not as a supernatural God, a being acting with will and reason, but as a being which acts only in accordance with its inner necessity. But unlike Spinoza, I do not look on nature as a God, as supernatural, supersensual, remote, recondite, and One; it is a manifold, public, actual being which can be perceived with all the senses.

Or in practical terms: nature is everything which man, notwithstanding the supernaturalist whisperings of theistic faith, experiences directly and sensuously as the ground and substance of his life. Nature is light, electricity, magnetism, air, water, fire, earth, animals, plants; nature is man, insofar as he is a being who acts instinctively and unconsciously—and I claim nothing more; there is nothing mystical, nothing nebulous, nothing theological in my use of the word. In my use of the word, I appeal to the senses. Jupiter, said one of the ancients, is everything you see; nature, say I, is every visible thing that is not the product of human hand or human thought. Or, if we wish to enter into the anatomy of nature, nature is the being, or the sum of beings and things, whose manifestations, expressions, or effects, in which its existence and essence consist and are revealed, have their ground not in thoughts or purposes or acts of will, but in astronomical or cosmic, mechanical, chemical, physical, physiological, or organic forces or causes.

Paragraphs six and seven, which will serve as the text of the present lecture, are a defense and justification of paganism against the polemics of the Christians, and tie in with an earlier assertion of mine, to the effect that the Christian religion does not differ from pagan religion in asserting the existence of a divine being, but only in the fact that its God is not a particular object in nature or even nature as a whole, but a being distinct from nature. The Christians, at least the more reasonable among them, condemned the pagans not for delighting in the beauty and utility of nature, but for finding the cause of these benefits in nature itself, for worshiping earth, water, fire, the sun, and the moon for their beneficial properties which, in the Christian view, stem from the author of nature, who should therefore alone be honored, feared and praised. True, the Christian critics went on, sun, earth, water bring forth the animals and plants that men live on, but they are only secondary causes which are themselves caused; the true cause is the *first* cause.

In defending the pagans against this argument, I start by questioning the existence of a first cause such as that posited by the Christians, basing my argument on an example, or rather a parable, drawn from the Christian tradition. Adam is the first man; in the series of men he holds the place occupied by the first cause in the series of natural causes or things; my parents, grandparents, etc., are children of Adam, just as the causes in nature are effects of the first cause; Adam alone has no father, only the first cause has no cause. Yet I do not honor and love Adam as my father; Adam encompasses all men; in him all individuality is effaced. Adam is equally the father of Negro and white, Slav and Norseman, Frenchman and German; but I am not a man in general; my existence, my being, is individual, I am a member of the Caucasian race, and within this race of a particular people, the German people. Therefore the cause of my being is necessarily an individual, definite cause; that cause is my parents and grandparents, in short, the generations of people that are closest to me.

If I go further back, I lose all trace of my existence; I find no characteristics from which I can derive my own. A man of the seventeenth century could never, even apart from the time interval, be the father of a man of the nineteenth century, because the qualitative distance, the distance between customs, habits, ideas, attitudes—and these leave even a physical imprint—is too great. Just as man in revering the authors of his existence stops with his immediate ancestors and does not go back to the first ancestor, because in him he does not find his own inalienable individuality, so in considering the causes of his existence he stops at the sensuous beings of nature. I am what I am only in this nature, in nature as it is now, as it has been within the memory of man. It is only to the beings I see and feel—or which, if I myself do not see and feel them, are at least inherently visible, tangible, or otherwise sensuous beings—that I, a sensuous being who without senses would sink into nothingness, owe my existence. Even though this nature is the outcome of change, even though it was preceded by a nature of a different kind, I owe my existence only to a nature of the kind in which I live, the nature with which my nature is compatible. Even if there is a first cause as posited by theology, nevertheless sun, earth, water, in short all nature, had to be, and had to be as they are before I could come into being; for without sun, without earth, I myself am nothing; I presuppose nature.

Why then should I go *beyond* nature? That would be justified only if I myself were above and beyond nature. But far from being supernatural, I am not even supraterrestrial; for the earth is the absolute measure of my being. Not only do I stand on the earth; the earth and the position it occupies in the universe also determine the way in which I think and feel. True, I raise my eyes to the remotest heavens; but I see all things in the light and measure of the earth. In short, I am an earthly being, not an inhabitant of Venus, Mercury, or Uranus, and this, as the philosophers say, constitutes my substance, my fundamental being. Even though the earth too has an origin, I owe my own origin to it alone, to its origin; for the existence of the earth is the sole ground of human existence, its being is the sole ground of human being. The earth is a planet, man is a planetary being, a being whose career is possible and real only within the career of a planet. But the earth *differs* from other planets. It has its own special character, its individuality, and this individuality is the salt of the earth.

Even if we justifiably assume that all the planets originated in the same cause, force, or substance, nevertheless the force that produced the earth was different from the force that produced Mercury or Uranus, a force so peculiarly constituted that it gave rise to this planet and no other. Man owes his existence to this *individual* cause, inseparable from the character of the earth. The revolutionary impact which released the earth from its mystical immersion in the matter common to the sun, the planets, the comets—a revolution which, as Kant puts it in his magnificent *Theory of the Heavens,* had its ground in the "diversity of the elements"—to this break or impact we can still trace the movement of our blood and the vibrations of our nerves. The first cause is the universal cause, the cause of all things without distinction; but in reality the cause that makes everything without distinction makes nothing at all, it is a mere concept, a figment of thought; it has only logical and metaphysical, but no physical significance; I, this individual being, simply cannot be derived from it. Those who speak of the first cause—first in the theological sense, I hasten to add—do so in order to cut short the infinite series of causes. This endless chain of causes can best be elucidated by the above-cited example of the origin of man. The cause of my existence is my father, the cause of his existence is his father, and so on. But can I carry on this chain ad infinitum? Has man always given existence to man? Does such a series solve the problem of man's origin? Or am I not, by proceeding from father to father, simply postponing the answer? Must I not come to a first man or a first human couple? And where do they come from?

But the same applies to all the things and beings that make up this sensuous world. One presupposes another; one depends on another; all are finite, all came into being, one originating in another. But where, the theist asks, does the first member of the series come from? Accordingly we must effect a leap out of the series to a First which, itself without beginning, is the beginning of all originated beings, itself endless or infinite, the ground of all finite beings. This is one of the most common proofs of the existence of God; it is called the *cosmological* proof and variously formulated. For example: everything that is, the world, is subject to change, temporal, originated, contingent; but the contingent presupposes the necessary, the finite the infinite, the temporal the eternal; this infinite, eternal being is God. Or in another form: everything that is, everything sensuous and real, is a cause of certain effects, but a cause which is itself an effect and which itself has a cause, and so on; hence it is necessary, our reason demands it, to stop at a cause which no longer has any cause over it, which is not itself caused, which, as some philosophers put it, is self-caused or *self-created*. The ancient philosophers and theologians accordingly defined the finite, the not-divine, as that which exists through something else, and the infinite, or God, as that which is self-caused or self-created.

But against this inference the following can be argued. Even though reason rebels against tracing back causes ad infinitum in connection with man or even the earth, even though we cannot derive the present state of the earth from a previous state, but must eventually come to a point where man originates in nature and the earth in the planetary mass or whatever we choose to call its original substance—nevertheless, in its application to nature or the universe as a whole, such an endless series is by no means incompatible with a reason formed by observation of the world. It is only the limitations of man's thinking, his taste for convenience, that replace time by eternity, the endless chain from cause to cause by infinity, dynamic nature by a stable Godhead, eternal motion by eternal rest. True, for me, a man living in the present, it is unreasonable, unprofitable, tedious, in fact impossible, to think or even imagine that the world has no beginning and no end; but *this need of mine* to break off the endless series is no proof of a real break in the series, of a real beginning and end.

Even in the area of human consciousness, even in the realm of history, of things produced by man himself, we see how, partly out of ignorance to be sure, but partly out of the mere tendency to abbreviate and make things easy for ourselves, we break off our historical investigations and substitute One Cause, One Name for the many names, the many causes which it would be too complicated, too tedious to track down, and which in fact often escape man altogether. Just as man attaches the name of one individual to an invention, to the founding of a state, the building of a city, the rise of a nation, although any number of unknown names and individuals have played a part, so he attaches the name of God to the universe—and indeed all inventors, all founders of cities and states have been looked upon as gods. Most of the ancient names of historical or mythical men, heroes, and gods were collective names, which subsequently became individual names. Even the word "God," like all names as a matter of fact, was originally not a proper name but a general or generic term.[9] Even in the Bible, the Greek word *Theos* and the Hebrew word *Elohim* are used for other objects than God. The principalities and powers are called gods, the Devil is called the God of this world, and even the belly is termed the God of mankind or at least of some men—a passage which horrified Luther. "Who ever heard such language?" he says. "Who ever heard it said that the belly is God? It would not be fitting for me to talk in this way if Paul had not done so, for I can think of no more disgraceful way of talking. Is it not deplorable that the shameful, stinking, filthy belly should be called a God?"

Even when used in accordance with the philosophical definition that God is the most real, that is, the most perfect being, the epitome of all perfections, "God" is essentially no more than a collective name; for when I stop to consider the diversity of the attributes that are encompassed in God, I cannot dispel the impression that they are different things or beings, and I find that the word God is just such a collective or generic term as, for example, the words fruit, grain, or people.

Each of God's attributes, as theology or theological philosophy tells us, is God Himself, each of God's attributes can stand for God Himself. Even in everyday life people say Divine Providence, Divine Wisdom, Divine Omnipotence in place of God. But God's attributes are very different and even conflicting in character. Let us confine ourselves to His most popular attributes. How different are power, wisdom, lovingkindness, justice! One can be powerful without wisdom, wise without power, kind without justice and just without kindness. *Fiat justitia pereat mundus,* let the world perish if only justice prevails, is a motto of jurisprudence, of justice; but in this characteristic expression of justice there is certainly no spark of kindness or even of wisdom; for man does not exist for the sake of justice, justice exists for the sake of man. Accordingly as I think of God's power, the power which can destroy me if it so wishes, or as I think of God's justice as characterized in the motto I have just cited, I conceive of very different beings under the name of God. And again I have a very different God than if I think only of His kindness.

Thus the difference between polytheism and monotheism is not so great as it appears. In consequence of the multiplicity and diversity of His attributes, there are many Gods in the One God. The difference is at most that between a collective term and a generic term. Or rather, this is the difference: in polytheism God is manifest and visible, a mere collective noun; in monotheism the sensuous characteristics vanish, the appearances of polytheism are dropped, but the essence, the thing itself, remains. That is why the various attributes of the One God among Christians have waged just as many wars with one another, and not only dogmatic but also bloody wars, as the many gods of Homer's Olympus.

The early theologians, philosophers, and mystics said that God encompassed everything in the world, but that what in the world is multiple, dispersed, disjoined, sensuous, distributed among different beings, is in God simple, nonsensuous, and united. Here we have a clear statement that in God man concentrates the essential attributes of the many different things and beings in One Being, One Name, that in God man did not originally or truly conceive a being different from the world, but merely represented the world in a mode differing from sense perception; what man conceived of in the world or in sensuous reality as extensive, temporal, and corporeal he conceived of in God as without extension, atemporal, and incorporeal. In eternity he merely sums up the infinite temporal series, the full extension of which cannot be conceived, and in omnipresence he merely sums up the infinity of space in an abbreviated generic term or concept; for sound subjective reasons, he makes use of eternity as a means of breaking off endless series of numbers and the infinitely tedious reckoning it entails. But neither this break, nor the tediousness of series of times and spaces progressing ad infinitum, nor even the contradictions connected in our minds or in the abstract with the concept of infinite time or infinite space, allow us to infer the necessity of a real beginning or end of the world, of space, or of time.

The very nature of thought and speech, the requirements of life itself oblige us to make use of abbreviations on every hand, to substitute concepts for intuitions, signs for objects, in a word, the abstract for the concrete, the one for the many, and accordingly one cause for many different causes, one individual for different individuals as their representative. In this sense it is perfectly right to say that reason, at least as long as reason, not yet disciplined by observation of the world, regards itself uncritically as the essence of the world, as the objective absolute essence, leads necessarily to the idea of divinity. But we must not single out this necessity, this idea, we must not isolate it from other phenomena, ideas, and representations which are equally necessary but which we nevertheless recognize as subjective, that is, based only on the peculiar nature of representation, thought, and speech, and to which we ascribe no objective validity and existence, no existence outside of ourselves.

The same necessity that impelled man to substitute the name of *one* individual for a series of individuals, indeed for whole generations and peoples, that impelled him to substitute number for intuitable quantities and letters for numbers, that impelled him to say fruit instead of pear, apple, and cherry, to say money instead of dollars and cents, shillings and pounds, to say give me that thing, instead of give me that knife or book—the same necessity also impelled him, where he believed in an originated world, to replace the many causes contributing to the genesis and preservation of the world with One Being, One Name. But for that very reason this One is just as much a subjective being, that is, a being grounded and existing only in man, in the nature of man's representation, thought, and speech, as thing, money, or fruit. And the fact that the idea or concept of God in its metaphysical significance rests on the same grounds as the idea or concept "thing" or "fruit" proves at the very least that the gods of polytheism are nothing other than collective or class names and concepts represented as beings.

The Romans, to stay with the examples already cited, had a goddess of money, Pecunia; they even made the chief kinds or classes of money, bronze money and silver money, into gods. They had a *Deus Aesculanus* or *Aerinus,* i. e., bronze or copper god, a *Deus Argentinus,* a silver-god. They also had a fruit-god, *Pomona.* If we do not find all the class names and concepts as gods among the Greeks and Romans, it is solely because the egoistic, bigoted Romans, in particular, deified only things connected with human egoism. Why, the Romans even worshiped a dung-god, a *Deus Stercutius,* in order that fertilizer might prosper their fields! But dung is a generic concept; there are many kinds of dung, pigeon dung, horse dung, cow dung, etc.

Now to another argument against the usual inference of a first, uncaused cause. Everything that is, is dependent, or, as others put it, has the ground of its existence outside of itself; since it does not subsist by and through itself, it presupposes a being that is not dependent on others, that *is because it is.* In refutation of this proof, I again adduce the example of man; for ultimately it is man alone that man takes as his starting point, man whose dependence and origin he takes as a model for the dependence and origin of all sensuous things. True, I am dependent on my parents, grand-parents, etc.; if others had not existed before me, I would not exist; but nevertheless I am an independent being, different from my parents; I am what I am not only thanks to others, but also thanks to myself; true, I stand on the shoulders of my ancestors, but even on their shoulders I stand *on my own feet;* true, I was begotten and conceived without my knowledge or will; but I did not come into the world without a drive, unconscious to be sure at the time, toward independence and freedom, toward emancipation from my dependence on the womb.

In short, I was begotten, I am or was dependent on my parents; but I myself am also a father and a man, and the fact that I came into being, that I was once a child, that I was once physically and mentally dependent on my parents, lies far behind my present self-awareness. This much is certain: despite the enormous conscious and unconscious influence of my parents, I do not live in the past. At present I have father and mother in myself alone, no other being, not even a God, will help me unless I help myself; I stand and fall by my own resources. The swaddling clothes in which parental providence once swathed me have long since rotted away; why then should my mind endure bonds that my feet long ago kicked off?

Twelfth Lecture

IN THE LAST LECTURE I elucidated by the example of man one of the first and most common proofs of the existence of God, the so-called cosmological proof, to the effect that everything in the world is finite and dependent and therefore presupposes something infinite and independent. My conclusion was that although man was originally a child, he is at the same time a father, that although he is effect he is also cause, that though dependent he is also independent. But, obvious differences aside, what is true of man is also true of other beings. For all its dependency on other beings, each being is an independent self; each being has the ground of its existence in itself—to what purpose would it otherwise exist? Every being has come into existence under conditions and through causes—regardless of their nature—which could have given rise to no other being; each being owes its existence to a set of causes which would not be operative without it. Every being is both effect and cause. Without water there would be no fish, but without fish, or some other animals capable of living in water, there would also be no water. The fish are dependent on water; they cannot exist without it; they presuppose it; but the ground of their dependence is in themselves, in their individual nature, which precisely makes water their need, their element.

Nature has no beginning and no end. Everything in it acts upon everything else, everything in it is relative, everything is at once effect and cause, acting and reacting on all sides. Nature does not culminate in a monarchic summit; it is a republic. Those who are accustomed to a monarchy cannot conceive of a human society without a prince, and likewise those who have grown up with the idea of a Father in Heaven find it hard to conceive of nature without a God. But it is just as possible to conceive of nature without a God, without an extranatural and supernatural being, as of a state or nation without a royal idol situated outside and above it. Indeed, just as the republic is the historical task, the practical goal of man, so his theoretical goal is to recognize the republican constitution of nature, not to situate the governing principle of nature outside it, but to find it grounded in nature. Nothing is more absurd than to regard nature as a single effect and to give it a *single cause* in an extra-natural being who is the effect of no other being. If I cannot refrain from spinning out fantasies, from looking further and further afield, if I am unable to stop with nature and content my intellectual need for causes with the universal action and interaction of nature, what is to prevent me from going beyond God? What is to prevent me from looking for a ground and cause of God as well? Do we not in God find the same situation as in the concatenation of natural causes and effects, the very situation that I wished to remedy by positing the existence of a God?

If I conceive of God as the cause of the world, is He not dependent on the world? Is there any cause without an effect? What is left of God if I omit or think away the world? What becomes of His power if He does nothing; of His wisdom, if there is no world for Him to govern? Where is His goodness if there is nothing for Him to be good to—where His infinity, if there is nothing finite? For He is infinite only in contrast to finiteness. Thus if I omit the world, nothing remains of God. Why then should we not confine ourselves to the world, since in any case we cannot go above or outside it, since even the idea and hypothesis of God throws us back on the world, since if we take away nature, we deprive the world of all reality and consequently negate even the reality of God insofar as He is conceived as the cause of the world?

Thus the difficulties arising from the question of the beginning of the world are only postponed or thrust aside or glossed over by the notion of a God, a being outside the world; they are *not solved.* Is it not then more reasonable to assume that the world always was and always will be, and consequently that it has the ground of its existence within itself. "We cannot dispel but neither can we endure the thought," says Kant in his *Lectures on the Philosophy of Religion,* "that a being whom we conceive of as the highest of all possible beings says to himself as it were: I am from eternity to eternity; outside of me there is nothing except for that which is something through my will; but *whence then am I?*" In other words, where does God come from? What obliges me to stop at God? Nothing; I cannot help inquiring into His origin. And that is no secret: the cause of what for the theists, theologians, and so-called speculative philosophers is the first and universal cause of all things—is the human intellect. The intellect rises from the individual and particular to the universal, from the concrete to the abstract, from the determined to the undetermined. It also rises from real, definite, particular causes, and goes on rising until it comes to the concept of *cause as such, the* cause that produces no real, definite, particular effects.

God is not, at least not directly as the theists suppose, the cause of thunder and lightning, of rain and sunshine, of fire and water, sun and moon; all these things and phenomena have only particular, special, sensuous causes; He is merely the universal first cause, the cause of causes; He is the cause that is not a definite, sensuous real cause, the cause that is abstracted from all sensuous matter, from all special determinations. In other words, He is *cause as such,* the concept of cause personified as an independent being. Just as the intellect personifies as one being the concept of being, abstracted from all the definite properties of being, so it personifies the concept of cause abstracted from all the characteristics of real, determinate causality in a First Cause. Just as man, operating on the plane of reason disengaged from the senses, subjectively and quite logically sets the species above individuals, color above colors, mankind above men, so he sets "cause" above causes. "God is the ground of the world" means: "*cause*" is the ground of causes; without "cause" there can be no causes; the *first* in logic, in the intellectual order, is "cause"; the second and subordinate term is causes or *kinds* of cause; in short, the first cause reduces itself to the concept of cause and the concept of cause is a product of the intellect, which abstracts the universal from particular real things and then, in accordance with its own nature, sets this abstracted universal over them as the First.

But for that very reason, because the First Cause is a mere intellectual concept or entity without objective existence, it also is not the cause of my life and existence. *This* cause is of no use to me; the cause of my life is the sum of *many different, definite* causes; the cause, for example, of my breathing is subjectively my lungs, objectively the air; the cause of my vision is objectively the light, subjectively my eyes. In short, the First Cause is an unprofitable abstraction. From this first cause that causes nothing I therefore turn back to the more profitable theme of nature, the sum of real causes, and try once again to prove that we must confine ourselves to nature as the ultimate ground of our existence; that all derivations from nature which transcend nature to arrive at a nonnatural being are mere fantasies and delusions. The proofs are both direct and indirect; the direct proofs are drawn from nature and relate to it directly; the indirect ones show the contradictions involved in the contrary assumption and the absurd consequences that follow from it.

Our world—not only our political and social world, but our learned, intellectual world as well—is a world upside down. The great achievement of our education, of our culture, our science, our erudition has been, above all, to stray as far as possible from nature, from the simple palpable truth. It is a universal principle of this upside-down world that God manifests Himself in nature, whereas we should say the opposite, namely, that originally at least nature manifests itself to man as a God, that nature makes on man an impression which he calls God, which he becomes conscious of and objectifies under the name of God. It is a universal doctrine in our upside-down world that nature sprang from God, whereas we should say the opposite, namely, that God was abstracted from nature and is merely a concept derived from it; for all the predicates, all the attributes or determinations, all the realities, as the philosophers say, that is, all the essences or perfections which are summed up in God, or whose totality is, or is called, God—in short all those divine predicates that are not borrowed from man, are derived from nature, so that they objectify, represent, illustrate nothing other than the essence of nature, or nature pure and simple. The difference is only that God is an abstraction, that is, a mere notion, while nature is concrete, that is, real; but the essence, the substance, the content are the same; God is nature in the abstract, that is, removed from physical perception, transformed into an object or concept of the intellect; nature itself is sensuous, real nature as directly revealed and communicated to us by the senses.

If we now consider the attributes of the Godhead, we shall find that they are all rooted in nature, that they are meaningful only if we relate them to nature. One attribute of God is power: He is a powerful being, the most powerful of beings; according to late conceptions, He is all-powerful. Power is the first predicate of the Godhead or rather, it is the first god. But what is this power? What does it express? Nothing other than the power of natural phenomena. As we have seen in the first lectures, thunder and lightning, the phenomena that make the most powerful, most terrible impression on man, are the effects of the highest, most powerful god, or they are one with him. Even in the Old Testament, thunder is the voice of God, and in many passages lightning is "the face of God." But what is a God whose voice is thunder, whose face is lightning, other than the essence of nature, or of thunder and lightning? Even Christian theists identify the power of their God, for all His spirituality, purely and simply with the sensuous power of nature. The Christian poet Triller, for example, writes in his "poetic reflections":

> Is it not so, confess,
> That your heart trembles in your breast,
> When with shattering power the thunder
> Rolls and roars and crashes?
> What can be the cause of your fear,
> What else, if not that your mind
> Tells you that with the might of His thunder
> And with the sulphurous flames of His lightning
> God might suddenly snatch you from the earth?
> Thus there can be no doubt
> *That thunder and lightning are a sign*
> *Of God's being and God's omnipotence.**

And even in Christian views that do not make the power of nature so palpably evident as the divine Triller makes the thunder and lightning, it remains the underlying factor. The Christian theists,

* On Triller cf. Note 1 on fourth lecture below, p. 287-288.

whose guiding principle is abstraction, hence remoteness from the truth of nature, who look upon nature as dead, inert matter, regard God's power or omnipotence as the cause of motion in nature. God, they say, has conferred, implanted, impressed motion upon matter, and they marvel at God's vast power, which has enabled Him to set this enormous mass or machine in motion. But this power by which God set body or matter in motion—is it not abstracted from the force or power by which one body imparts its motion to another? The diplomatic theists deny, to be sure, that God moved matter by means of a thrust, or any immediate contact; as a spirit, they claim, He did so by His will alone. But they do not really conceive God as pure spirit—at the same time they conceive of Him as a material and sensuous, or better still, cryptomaterial and cryptosensuous being. And by that same token He did not induce motion by sheer force of will. Will is nothing without power, without a positive material capacity. The theists themselves expressly distinguish God's, power from His will and reason. But what is this power distinguished from will and reason if not the power of nature?

The notion of power as a divine predicate or god springs chiefly from a comparison of the works of nature with the works of man. Man cannot produce plants and trees, he cannot make storms, thunder, and lightning. Vergil therefore calls Jupiter's thunderbolt "inimitable," and in Greek mythology Salmoneus is struck by Zeus' lightning for his presumption in trying to make thunder and lightning. Such works of nature are beyond man's strength, they are not in his power. That is why the being who produces such effects and phenomena is *superhuman* and therefore divine. But all these effects and phenomena express nothing other than the *power of nature*. Christian theists, to be sure, attribute these effects *indirectly,* or in their ultimate source, to God, to a being distinct from nature and endowed with will, reason, and consciousness; but this is only an explanation, and what concerns us here is not whether a spirit is or is not, can or cannot be, the source of these phenomena, but solely the fact that the natural phenomena, the natural forces which even a Christian, at least a rational enlightened Christian, does not look upon as immediate actions of God, but, in accordance with the real facts, as effects of nature, are the model from which man originally derived the notion and concept of a superhuman divine power.

An example: If a man is struck down by lightning, a Christian says or thinks that this has not happened by chance or simply in the course of nature; he attributes it to a divine decision; for "God's eye is on the sparrow." God wanted the man to die, and to die in just this way. His will is the cause, the last or first cause of the man's death; the immediate cause is the lightning, or as the ancients believed, the lightning is the instrument with which God Himself killed the man, or according to modern faith, the instrumental cause which by God's will, at least with His permission or consent, brought about the man's death. But this shattering, killing, searing power is the power of lightning itself, just as the power or effect of the arsenic with which I poison somebody is not an effect of my will, of my power, but the power and effect inherent in the arsenic itself. Thus from the theist or Christian standpoint we distinguish the power of *things* from the power or rather the will of God. We do not regard the effects and hence the properties—for we know the properties of things only by their effects—of electricity, of magnetism, of air, water, and fire as the properties and effects of God; we do not say: God burns and gives warmth, we do not say or think that God makes something wet; we say that water makes it wet; we do not say that God is thundering and lightning, no, we say: *it* is thundering and lightning, etc. But it is precisely from these phenomena, properties, and effects of nature, incompatible with the spiritual God conceived by Christians, that man derives his conception of divine, superhuman power, and because of which, so long as he remains faithful to his original, ingenuous view and does not split nature into God and the world, he worships nature itself as God.

Apropos of the word superhuman, I cannot refrain from a digression. One of the most frequent laments heard from the religious and learned bewailers of atheism is that it destroys or ignores an essential need of man, the need to revere something higher than himself, and therefore turns man into a presumptuous egoist. But in annulling what is Above Man theologically, atheism does not annul what is ethically and naturally Higher. The ethically Higher is the ideal that every man must pursue if he is to make anything worthwhile of himself; but this ideal is and must be a human ideal and aim. The naturally Higher is nature itself, and in particular, the celestial powers on which our existence, our earth depend; for the earth itself is only a part of the "celestial powers" and is what it is only by virtue of the position it occupies in our solar system. Even the supraterrestrial and superhuman God owes His origin only to the physical, optical being-above-us of the sky and the heavenly bodies. According to Cyril, Julian proved the divinity of the stars by pointing out that everyone raises his hands to heaven when he prays or swears or in any way invokes the name of the Godhead. Even Christians put their "spiritual, omnipresent" God in the sky; and they put Him there for the same reasons which originally caused the sky itself to be regarded as God. Aristo of Chios, a pupil of Zeno, founder of Stoicism, said expressly: "Over us is [or goes] the Physical [nature], for it is impossible to know, and brings us no benefit." But this Physical is mainly the celestial. More than anything else it was the objects of astronomy and meteorology that aroused the interest of the first scientists and natural philosophers. Socrates rejected physics as something beyond the powers of man and directed men's minds from physics to ethics; but by physics he meant chiefly astronomy and meteorology, hence the well-known saying that he brought philosophy down from heaven to earth; and this is also why he spoke of all philosophizing that exceeded the powers and vocation of man as *meteorologein* (i. e., concern with celestial, supraterrestrial things).

But just as The Power, the superhuman, the highest or higher being above us—among the Romans the gods were called *Superi*—was originally a predicate of nature, so were eternity and infinity also predicates of nature. In Homer, for example, "infinite" is an epithet for the sea and the earth, in the philosopher Anaximenes for the air; in the Zend Avesta eternity and immortality are predicates of the sun and stars. Even Aristotle, the greatest philosopher of antiquity, imputes immutability and eternity to the heavens and the heavenly bodies in contrast to the transience and mutability of earthly things. And even a Christian infers (that is, derives) the greatness and infinity of God from the greatness and infinity of the world or nature, though he immediately proceeds (for a reason that is readily understood but need not be discussed here) to make nature disappear behind God. In agreement with innumerable other Christians, Scheuchzer, for example, writes: "Not only the unfathomable greatness of the world and of the heavenly bodies but even the tiniest grain of dust, is a sign of His infinite greatness."* And elsewhere the same scholar and pious naturalist writes: "The Creator's *infinite* wisdom and power shine forth not only from the *infinite magna,* from the mass of the universe and from the great bodies that float free in the heavens . . . but also from the *infinite parva,* from the grains of dust and tiny organisms. . . . Each grain of dust contains an infinite number of infinitesimal worlds."† The concept of infinity coincides with the concept of all-embracing universality.

God is no particular and hence finite being, He is not confined to this or that nation or locality, but neither is nature. Sun, moon, sky, earth, and sea, said a Greek philosopher, are common to all, and a Roman poet (Ovid) said that nature gave no one exclusive possession of sun, air, or water. God is "no respecter of persons," but neither is nature. The earth brings forth its fruits not for this or that chosen person or nation; the sun shines not only on Christian or Jew, but illumines all men without distinction. Precisely because of this infinity and universality of nature the ancient Jews, who regarded themselves as the chosen people and believed that the world had been created for their sake, could not understand why the good things of life had not been made available to them alone, but to idolaters as well. When asked why God did not destroy idolatry, Jewish scholars therefore answered that He would destroy the idolaters if they did not worship things that were necessary to the world; but that since they worshiped the sun, the moon, the stars, water, and fire, why should He destroy the world for the sake of a few fools? In other words: God must spare the causes and objects of idolatry, because without them the Jews could not endure.[10]

Here we have an interesting illustration of certain essential features of religion. First of all, an illustration of the contradiction between theory and practice, faith and life, implicit in every religion. This natural sharing of earth, light, and water with idolaters

* Scheuchzer, *Die Naturwissenschaft Hiob's.*

† Scheuchzer, *Physika oder Naturwissenschaft.*

was diametrically opposed to the theory and faith of the Jews; since they wished to have nothing in common with the heathen and their religion forbade it, they should not have shared the blessings of life with them. If they had been consistent, they should have excluded either the heathen or themselves from the enjoyment of these blessings. Secondly, we have here an illustration of the fact that nature is far more liberal than the God of the religions, that man's natural view is far more universal than his religious view which separates man from man, Christian from Jew, Jew from heathen, and that consequently the unity of the human race, the love that embraces all men, is by no means grounded on the concept of the heavenly father or, as modern philosophers say, on the concept of Spirit, but far more on nature, which originally was indeed its sole foundation. The universal love of man is by no means of Christian origin. It was already taught by the pagan philosophers; but the God of the pagan philosophers was nothing other than the world, or nature.

Christians, on the contrary, held the same belief as the Jews; they too believed and said that the world was created and preserved *for their sake alone*. They were as consistently incapable as the Jews of finding an explanation for the existence of infidels and of heathen in general. For if the world exists only for the sake of Christians, why and to what end are there other people who are not Christians and do not believe in the Christian God? The Christian God accounts for the existence only of Christians, and not of pagans and infidels. The God whose sun shines on the just and the unjust, believers and unbelievers, Christians and pagans alike is indifferent to such religious distinctions, He knows nothing of them; this God, in truth, is nothing other than nature.[11] Thus the Biblical words that God makes His sun shine on good and evil alike, contain a vestige or evidence of a nature religion, or else the good and the evil are taken as men who may differ from one another morally but not dogmatically, for the dogmatic, Biblical God strictly distinguishes the sheep from the goats, Christians from Jews and heathen, believers from unbelievers; to the goats He promises hell, to the sheep heaven. He condemns the sheep to bliss and eternal life, and the goats to eternal misery and death. But this is precisely why the existence of such men condemned to nothingness cannot be derived from Him; there is no way of explaining the thousands and thousands of contradictions, perplexities, difficulties, and inconsistencies in which religious belief involves us, unless we acknowledge that the original God was a being abstracted from nature and accordingly replace the mystical, ambiguous name and being of God with the name and being of nature.

Thirteenth Lecture

WHAT I SAID in yesterday's lecture about God's power, His eternity, superhumanity, infinity, and universality—namely, that they are abstracted from nature and originally expressed nothing other than attributes of nature—is also true of His moral attributes. God's goodness is merely abstracted from those beings and phenomena in nature which are useful, good, and helpful to man, which give him the feeling or consciousness that life, existence, is a good thing, a blessing. God's goodness is merely the utility of nature, ennobled by the imagination, by the poetry of man's emotions, personified and transformed into an active force. But because nature is also the cause of effects that are hostile and harmful to man, he personifies and deifies this cause in an *evil* God. Such an opposition is to be found in almost all religions, but it is most conspicuous in the Persian religion, whose world is governed by two mutually antagonistic gods: Ormuzd, who is the god or cause of all beings helpful to man, of useful animals, of pleasant phenomena, such as light, warmth, day; and Ahriman, who is the god or cause of darkness, of searing heat, and of harmful animals.

In reality the Christian religion, whose doctrines stem almost entirely from Persian and other Oriental views of the world, also has two gods, only one of whom, however, is usually or exclusively called God, while the other is termed Satan or the Devil. And even where the evil, destructive effects of nature are not derived from an independent, personal cause, that is, the Devil, they are derived from God's *anger*. The angry God, however, is simply the *evil* God. Here we have one more example to show that there is no essential difference between polytheism and monotheism. The polytheist believes in good and evil gods, the monotheist replaces the evil gods with God's wrath and the good ones with His mercy; he believes in one God, but this one God is a good *and* evil, or angry, God, a God with conflicting attributes. But God's wrath is nothing other than His *punitive justice* looked upon as an affect or passion. Anger is also a basic trait in man; essentially it is nothing else than a passionate desire for justice or vengeance. Man becomes angry when—whether in reality or only in his imagination—a wrong, an injustice, has been done him. Anger is a man's revolt against the despotic encroachments of another being. Just as God's goodness is originally derived from the good effects of nature, so justice is originally abstracted from its harmful, destructive effects. Thus the notion of punitive justice is a product of reflection. Man is an egoist; he is infinitely fond of himself, he believes that all things exist for his sole benefit and that there neither should nor can be evils. But he runs into facts that conflict with this self-centered faith; he therefore supposes that evil befalls him only when he transgresses against the being or beings from whom he derives everything that is good and helpful, so arousing their anger. He explains the evils of nature as punishments that God metes out to man because of some transgression or injustice committed against Him.

This also accounts for the Christian belief that nature was once a paradise, in which there was nothing hostile or harmful to man, but that this paradise was lost through sin, which aroused God's anger. But this explanation is a theological inversion. Originally God's wrath or punitive justice, as opposed to His mercy, was merely derived and abstracted from the harmful and destructive phenomena of nature. A man was not killed by lightning because God punishes, because He is just and angry, but the other way around: because this man was killed by lightning, the cause of his death is an angry, punishing, evil being. That was the original sequence of man's thoughts.[12] But just as God's goodness and justice are derived and abstracted from the good and evil phenomena of nature, so also is wisdom derived from nature, and specifically from the order governing the phenomena of nature, from the fabric of natural causes and effects.

Thus God's physical or metaphysical and moral attributes derived from nature. And the same is true of His negative, or less clearly defined attributes. God is not visible; but neither is the air. For this very reason nearly all those peoples who developed some degree of spiritual life identified the spirit with air or breath. Nor do they distinguish God Himself from the spirit, that is, from the air as the being which, in the undeveloped materialistic view, conditions, or rather causes and maintains, the life of man. From the commandment: Thou shalt not make unto thee any graven image or any likeness (of God), it should not be inferred that God was taken as a spirit in our modern sense of a being endowed with thought, will, and knowledge. Who can make an image of the air?

In answer to the heathen argument that the Christian God could neither be displayed nor seen, Minucius Felix said: Do not marvel that you cannot see God; wind and air are also invisible, although they buffet all things to and fro, move and shatter them. God is not palpable. But is the air palpable, although physicists can weigh it, or is light? Can images be made of light or air, can they be represented in an individual corporeal form? Is it then not absurd to conclude that because certain peoples make no images, no statues of their gods or God and therefore have no temples, they worship a spiritual being in our sense of the term? They worship nature, either as a whole or in its parts; they have not yet anthropomorphized it, not yet reduced it to a definite human form and figure, and that is why they have no human images and statues of the objects of their religious worship.

I cannot encompass God in limited forms, images, concepts; but can I encompass the world, the universe, in such forms? Who can make an image of nature, that is, an image that reflects its being? All images represent mere parts of the world; how can I expect a part to supply an adequate representation of the whole? God is not limited in space and time; but is the universe? Is the universe in this place, in this time? Is it not in all places, at all times? Is the universe in time, or is not more correct to say that time is in the universe? Is not time merely a form of the universe, the mode in which the particular beings and effects of the universe follow one another? How then can I ascribe a temporal beginning to the universe? Does the universe presuppose time, or should we not say that time presupposes the universe?

The universe is the water, time is the motion of the water; but is the water not anterior to its own motion? Does not the motion of water presuppose water? Is not its motion a consequence of its peculiar nature and essence? Is it not therefore as foolish to suppose that the world originated in time as it is to suppose that the essence of a thing originated in its consequences? Is it not just as absurd to conceive of a point in time as the beginning of the world as to conceive of the flow of water as the origin of water? And is it not clear from what has been said so far that the essence and attributes of the world and the essence and attributes of God are the same, that God is not distinct from the world, that God is only a concept abstracted from the world, that God is only the world in thought, whereas the world is only God in reality, or the real God, that God's infinity is merely abstracted and derived from the infinity of the world, His eternity from the eternity of the world, His power and glory from the power and glory of the world?

The difference between God and world is merely the difference between spirit and sensibility, between thought and perception; the world as object of the senses, especially the common sense of touch, is the world that we actually call the world, while the world as object of thought, of the thinking which abstracts the universal from the things of sense perception, is God. But just as the universal which the intellect abstracts from sensuous things is itself a sensuous thing—though only mediately—sensuous in content if not in form (for the concept of man is sensuous through the mediation of men, the concept of tree is sensuous through the mediation of the trees which my senses show me), so God Himself, though He is only the reflected, abstracted essence of the world, is mediately a sensuous being. Of course God is not a sensuous being like some visibly or tangibly limited body, like a stone, a plant, an animal, but if we were to deny the sensuousness of God for that reason alone, we should also have to deny the sensuous nature of the air or light. Even where man supposes that he is rising above nature with his concept of God, where, like the Christians, especially the so-called rational Christians, he conceives or imagines God as a disembodied being without sensuous attributes, even there the sensuous representation supplies at least the *substrate* of the spiritual God. Who can think of something as a being without at the same time thinking of it as a sensuous being, even if he suppresses all the limitations and properties of a tangible sensuous being? The difference between God's being and the being of sensuous things is merely the difference between genus and species or individuals.

God is no more a particular being than color is a particular color, than man is an individual man; for in the generic concept of man I disregard all the differences between races or individuals; in the concept of color I disregard all particular colors. Similarly in conceiving of God's being I disregard the properties of the various sensuous beings and the differences between them; I conceive of Him only universally as a being; but precisely because the concept of God is merely abstracted from the sensuous beings contained in the world, because He is only a generic concept, we always extrapolate the images of sensuous beings when we think this universal concept, we represent God sometimes as nature as a whole, sometimes as light, fire, or man, particularly as a venerable old man, just as in thinking any other generic concept we visualize the images of the individuals from which we have abstracted it. Obviously what is true of God's essence is also true of His existence, for existence cannot be dissociated from essence. Even where God is conceived as a being who, because He is spirit, exists only for man's spirit, who becomes an object for man only where man rises above the senses and abstracts Him as spirit from sensuous things, even there God's existence is grounded in the truth of sensuous existence, the truth of nature.

God is believed to exist not only in thought, in the spirit or mind, but also outside and independently of our ideas and representations. The utmost importance is attached to His independent, objective existence, His existence outside of and apart from man. But is this not tantamount to admitting the truth of sensuous being even in God, who is supposed to be above and beyond the sensuous world? Is it not an admission that there is no being apart from sensuous being? For what indication, what criterion of existence outside ourselves do we have, other than sense? Is a nonsensuous existence not mere thought, a mere ghost existence? The existence of

God, or the existence attributed to God, differs from the existence of the sensuous beings around us only as His essence, in accordance with the above analysis, differs from their essences. The existence attributed to God is existence as a universal, the generic concept of existence, existence abstracted from all particular properties or determinations. This existence, to be sure, is spiritual, that is, intellectual and abstract, as is every concept; yet it is nothing other than the idea of sensuous existence in general.

The existence of God has always been a source of difficulties to philosophers and theologians, as its so-called proofs indicate. Here we have the answer to these difficulties, the resolution of the contradictions raised by the various explanations and conceptions of God's existence. Now we can understand why on the one hand a spiritual existence is attributed to God, while on the other hand this spiritual existence is given sensuous trappings and even localized in heaven. In short, the contradiction, the conflict between spirit and sense in the conception of divine existence, the ambiguity and mystical vagueness of this existence, are explained by the simple fact that God's existence is abstracted from the sensuous existence of real things and beings, but that for this same reason an image of sensuous existence is necessarily injected into this abstract existence, just as sensuous characteristics are necessarily injected into the essence of God.

But if, as we have seen, all the features or attributes that add up to the essence of God are derived from nature, if the essence, the existence, the attributes of nature are the original from which man has taken his image of God; or if, to go into the matter more deeply, God and world or nature differ only as a class differs from individuals, so that the nature which is the object of sense perception is true nature, whereas the nature which, abstracted from its materiality and corporeality, is an object of thought, of the spirit or mind, is God; then it is proved, then it becomes self-evident, that nature did not spring from God, that the real, corporeal, material being did not spring from the abstract, spiritual being. To derive nature from God is tantamount to deriving the original from its image or copy, to deriving a thing from its concept.

For all its absurdity, this inversion is the secret of theology.

In theology things are not thought and willed because they exist, they exist because they are thought and willed. The world exists, because God thought and willed it, because He still thinks and wills it. The idea, the thought, is not abstracted from the object, thought is the author, the cause of the thought object. But this docrine—the core of Christian theology and philosophy—is an inversion in which the order of nature is stood on its head. How then did man arrive at such an inversion? In speaking of the first cause, I have already said that man, quite rightly so from a subjective point of view—or quite rightly at least so long as he has not understood his own nature—sets the class or class concept before the species and individuals, the abstract before the concrete. This explains and resolves all the difficulties and contradictions arising from attempts to explain the world as God's creation.

Thanks to his faculty of abstraction, man finds common factors in nature or reality; these he abstracts from things of like or similar nature and makes them into an independent being, *distinct from things.* For example: from physical things man abstracts space and time as universal concepts or forms, common to them all, since all things are extensive and subject to change, dispersed and successive. Thus every point in the earth is outside of every other and follows the other in the motion of the earth; where one point is now, the other will be in a moment. But although man has abstracted space and time from spatial and temporal things, he posits them as the first grounds and conditions of these same things. Accordingly, he conceives of the world, i.e., the sum of real things, the matter and content of the world, as having originated in space and time. Even for Hegel matter not only originates in space and time, but springs from them. Precisely because man sets space and time before real things, in philosophy as universals, in polytheistic religion as gods, and in monotheistic religion as God's attributes, he also made gods of space and time or identified them with God.

The famous Christian mathematician and astronomer Newton still spoke of space as God's immensity, or even as God's sensorium, i.e., the organ whereby God is present to all things and perceives all things. Newton also regarded space and time "as consequences of the existence of God, for the Infinite Being is present in all places, hence this immeasurable space exists; the Eternal Being has existed from all eternity, hence an eternal time exists." And there is indeed no reason why time, separated from all sensuous things, should not be identified with God; for abstract time, in which there is no difference between Now and Then (for the different content is lacking), cannot be distinguished from dead, stable eternity. For eternity itself is nothing other than the concept of time, abstract time, time disjoined from temporal differences. Thus it is not to be wondered at that religion should have made time into an attribute of God or into an independent god. In the *Bhagavad-Gita* the Hindu god Krishna takes time as one of his predicates, that is, titles of honor, though of course he has many more. "I am time," he says, "time which preserves all things and destroys all things."[13] Among the Greeks and Romans time was deified under the names of Kronos and Saturn. The Persian religion goes so far as to make Zaruanoakarana, i. e., *uncreated time,* the first and uppermost being, the pinnacle of its edifice. Similarly among the Babylonians and Phoenicians the god of time, the lord of time, or the king of eternity as he is also called, was the supreme god.

This example shows that man, in keeping with the nature of the activity by which he abstracts and forms universal concepts, but in contradiction with the nature of real things, presupposes representations or intuitions of space and time, as Kant calls them, prior to sensuous things, and regards space and time as the conditions, or rather as the first grounds and elements, of the existence of real things, forgetting that in reality the exact opposite is true, that things do not presuppose space and time, but rather that space and time presuppose things, for space or extension presupposes something that is extensive, and time, or motion—for time is merely a concept abstracted from motion—presupposes something that moves. Everything is spatial and temporal; everything is extensive and moved; so far so good; but extension and motion are as diverse as extensive and moved things. All the planets move around the sun; but each has its own motion, the orbit of one requires more time than the orbit of another, the farther removed the planet is from the sun, the more time is needed.

All animals move, though all do not change their location; but how infinitely diverse their movement is! Each variety of motion corresponds to a particular structure and mode of life, in short, to the nature of each individual. How can I expect to derive such diversity from space and time or explain it on the basis of mere extension and motion? Extension and motion, on the contrary, are dependent on the body or being that is extensive and moved. Accordingly, what is first for man, or at least for his faculty of abstraction, is last for or in nature; but because man turns the subjective into the objective, because he transforms what is first *for him* into the first *as such* or in nature, he regards space and time as the first foundations of nature, and since the universal, that is, the abstract, has thus become the foundation of the real, man comes to regard the being who is nothing but a bundle of universal concepts, the thinking, spiritual being, as the first being, as the being who precedes all other beings not only in rank but also in time, who is indeed the ground and cause of all being and the Creator of all beings.

The question of whether a God created the world, the whole question of God's relation to the world, is the question of the relation between spirit and sense, between the universal or abstract and the real, between the class and the individual. It cannot be solved unless these other questions are solved; for God is nothing other than the sum of generic concepts. I have just discussed this question on the basis of the concepts of space and time, but it requires further examination. It is among the most important and also the most difficult of all the questions bearing on human knowledge and philosophy. Indeed, the whole history of philosophy revolves around it; it has been the crux of all the controversies between Stoics and Epicureans, Platonists and Aristotelians, sceptics and dogmatists in ancient philosophy, between Nominalists and Realists in the Middle Ages, and in modern times between idealists and realists or empiricists. And it is one of the most difficult questions, not only because philosophers, the more recent philosophers in particular, have introduced endless confusion by the most arbitrary use of words, but also because we are hampered and misled by the nature of language and of thought itself, which is inseparable from language, in short, because every word is a universal, so that language in itself, with its inability to express the particular, is often taken as proof that the sensuous particular is nonexistent.

Finally, in dealing with this question, men have been critically influenced by their diversity of mind, occupation, inclinations, and even temperament. Men, for example, who are more concerned with life than with study, who spend more of their time out of doors than in libraries, whose occupations and temperaments lead them to observe real beings, will always answer this question in the spirit of the Nominalists, who attribute to universals only a subjective existence in man's language and thought, whereas men of contrary occupation and disposition will answer with the Realists, who endow univerals with an existence of their own, independent of man's thought and speech.

Fourteenth Lecture

AT THE END of the last lecture I said that the relation between God and world reduces itself to the mere difference between generic concept and individual, that to ask whether there is a God is equivalent to asking whether the universal has an existence *of its own.* This is not only one of the most difficult, but also one of the most important of questions, for it alone determines the existence or nonexistence of a God. There are many whose belief in God hinges entirely on this question, for they look upon God as the indispensable foundation of generic concepts or universals. If there were no God, they say, no universal concept would be true, there would be no wisdom, no virtue, no justice, no law, no community; everything would be pure chance, the world would fall back into chaos and even nothingness. But in answer to this view it may be observed at the outset that if there were no wisdom, no justice, no virtue in the theological sense, it would by no means follow that these would cease to exist in a rational, human sense. In order to recognize the importance of universal concepts, it is not necessary to deify them and make them into independent beings distinct from particular, individual beings. In order to detest a vice, I have no need to hypostatize it as a devil after the fashion of the early Christian theologians, who had a special devil for each vice, a demon of drunkenness, gluttony, envy, avarice, gambling, and so on, and at one time even dreamed up a special sartorial demon in honor of a new style of breeches. Nor in order to love virtue, wisdom, or justice is there any need to look upon them as gods, or what amounts to the same thing, as attributes of a God.

If I set myself an ideal, if, for example, I take the virtue of constancy or perseverance as my goal, must I, in order to keep my attention fixed on it, build altars or temples to it after the manner of the Romans, who made virtue into a goddess and even deified particular virtues? Must virtue be an independent being in order to influence me, in order to mean something to me? Has it no value simply as a human quality? I myself wish to be constant; I no longer wish to be buffeted by the shifting impulses provoked by impressionability and weakness; my own weakness, impressionability, inconstancy, and moodiness repel me; my goal is therefore to become a constant man. True, insofar as I am not yet constant, I draw a distinction between constancy and myself, I look up to it as an ideal, I personify it; perhaps I even address it in solitary monologues as a separate being; in other words, I treat it as a Christian treats his God, or a Roman his goddess of virtue. But I know what I am doing. I know that I am personifying it, and yet it does not lose its value for me, for I have a personal interest in it, an interest rooted in myself; my egoism, my striving for happiness, my sense of honor, with which my weakness in the face of impressions and vicissitudes conflicts, give me reason enough to become constant.

The same is true of other human virtues and faculties, such as reason, will, or wisdom, whose value and reality for me are not lost or in any way diminished if I regard them simply as human traits instead of deifying and hypostatizing them. What I have said of human virtues and faculties applies to all universals and class concepts; they do not exist outside of things and beings, they are not distinct from, or independent of, the individuals from which we have abstracted them. The subject, that is, the existing being, is always the individual, the class is only a predicate or attribute. But it is precisely this predicate, this attribute of the individual, that nonsensuous thinking abstracts from the individual and makes into an independent object. This abstraction is then held to be the essence of the individuals in question, while the differences between them are disposed of as "merely individual," that is, contingent, secondary, nonessential. Thus thought reduces all individuals to a single individual, or rather concept, and claims all substance for itself, leaving only the empty shell for the sense perception which shows us individuals as individuals in their multiplicity, diversity, individuality, and concrete existence. In other words thought transforms what is in reality the subject, the essence, into a predicate, an attribute, a mere mode of the class concept, and conversely, turns what is in reality mere attribute or predicate into essence.

For the sake of greater clarity, let us choose still another example, this one of a sensuous nature. Every man has a head, a human head of course, that is, a head with human properties; for animals too have heads, although the head is not characteristic of the concept animal, because there are animals without any true, fully developed head, and even among the higher animals the head serves only the lower needs and has no independent dignity or function, so that in them the head is less characteristic than the mouth. Thus the head is a feature common to all men, a universal, an essential characteristic or predicate of man; an infant who comes forth from the womb without arms or legs is still human, a headless being is not. But does it follow that all mankind has only *one* head? And yet the *unity of the head* is a necessary consequence of the unity of the genus as hypostatized by man in his abstract, i. e., nonsensuous thinking. Do my senses not show me that every man has his own head, that there are as many heads as men, and consequently that there is no such thing as a general or universal head, but only individual heads? That the head, the head as generic concept, the head from which I have removed all individual traits and variations exists only in my head, but that outside of my head only heads exist? But what is essential about this head of mine? That it is a head as such, or that it is this particular head?

The essential is that it is this particular head, for if you take away this one head, I shall have no head at all. And it is not the head in general, but only the real individual head that functions, that thinks. The word "individual," to be sure, is ambiguous; for we also apply it to the unimportant, fortuitous peculiarities which often distinguish one man from others. In order to grasp what is meant here by individuality, we must compare man with an animal or, to stay with our example, man's head with an animal's head; then we perceive the individuality of the human head. But when we compare human heads with human heads, individual differences prove to be nonessential, the essential is that each man has his own head, this particular, sensuous, visible, individual head. Thus to use the word "head" as a generic concept, as a universal attribute or characteristic of all men, is merely to say that *every* man has a head and that in this respect all men are alike.

If I nevertheless deny that men in their totality have only one head—though the unity of the head is a necessary consequence of the belief that the genus as a unit has an independent existence while individuals do not, and in particular of the belief that men in their totality have only One Reason—if I contend that there are as many heads as individuals, if I identify the head with the individual and refuse to differentiate, not to say separate, the one from the other, does it follow that I deny the significance and existence of the head, that I make man into a headless being? On the contrary: instead of one head, I now have *many,* and just as four eyes see more than two, so do many heads accomplish infinitely more than *one* head; I have lost nothing, but only gained. If then I deny the distinction between class and individuals, if I say that it exists only in the differentiation and abstraction of thought, this does not mean that I deny the significance of the class concept; I merely maintain that the class exists only in the individual, or as the predicate of an individual.[14]

To go back to my previous examples, I do not deny the existence of wisdom, goodness, beauty; I deny only that these class concepts are independent beings, either as gods, or as attributes of God, or as Platonic Ideas, or as self-positing Hegelian concepts; I merely maintain that they exist only in wise, good, beautiful individuals, or as I said before, that they are attributes of individual beings, that they are not beings in themselves, but characteristics or determinations of individuality. I merely say that these universal concepts presuppose individuality, and not the other way around.[15]

But theists—and this is the foundation of their doctrine—take class concepts, or at least the totality of class concepts, which they call God, as the ground and source of real things; they hold not that the universal had its source in individuals but, on the contrary, that individuals sprang from the universal. But the universal as such, the class concept, exists in thought and for thought; that is why man conceived the idea and belief that the world originated in ideas, in the thoughts of a spiritual being. And from the standpoint of the thinking that disregards the senses, this seems perfectly natural; for the abstract, the spiritual, the purely cogitated, is closer than the sensuous to the intellect that abstracts concepts from sense perceptions; regarding the spiritual world as earlier and higher than the world of the senses, this abstract intellect finds it perfectly natural that sensibility should originate in spirit, reality in mere thought. We even find this conception in modern speculative philosophers. Like the Christian God they still, to this day, create the world out of their heads.

In addition, however, to the development we have just described, which may be called philosophical or speculative, the idea or belief that the world, or nature, was engendered by a thinking or spiritual being, has yet another, popular foundation: the works of man are based on a preconceived plan or concept; they respond to an underlying aim or purpose. When a man builds a house, he has in mind an idea, an image which he transposes into an objective reality of stone or wood; and he pursues an aim, namely, to provide himself with a dwelling, a place of amusement, a factory; in short, he builds a house for one purpose or another. And this purpose determines the idea of the house that I form in my mind; for the house that I conceive for one purpose differs from the house I conceive for another purpose. In general man is a purposive being, he does nothing without a purpose. But purpose implies will, it is not a mere representation, but an idea that demands to be carried out; I carry it out by means of the implements my body affords.

In short, man produces works with, though not out of, his mind, with, though not out of, ideas, and that is why these works, even in their outward form, bear the stamp of planning and purposiveness. But man sees the world in terms of himself; he transfers his view of his own works to the works or effects of nature; he looks upon the world as a dwelling, a workshop, a clock, in short, as a human artifact. But since he draws no essential distinction, but at most specific distinctions, between the products of nature and his own artifacts, he finds the cause of nature's products in a *human,* purposive, thinking being. And since the products of nature infinitely exceed those of man, he conceives this essentially *human* cause as a *superhuman* being, a being having the same attributes as man, having the intelligence, will, and strength required to carry out his projects, but in a degree infinitely exceeding the powers and capacities of man. This being he calls God.

The proof of the existence of God based on this view of nature is known as the *physico-theological* or *teleological* proof, that is, the proof drawn from purpose; for it is based chiefly on the so-called purposes of nature. Purposes presuppose intelligence, intention, and consciousness; but, so the proof goes, since nature, the world, or matter is blind, devoid of intelligence and consciousness, it presupposes a spiritual being who created it, or who at least guides it in accordance with aims and purposes. This proof was already adduced by the ancient religious philosophers, the Platonists and Stoics; it has been repeated *ad nauseam* in Christian times. It is the most popular and from a certain standpoint most plausible proof, the proof of the naïve human mind—that is, the uneducated mind, knowing nothing of nature. Consequently it is the only, or at least the only theoretical, foundation of popular theism.

The first thing to be said against this proof is that although the idea of purpose reflects something objective or real in nature, the term and concept of purpose is not appropriate. What man interprets as the purposiveness of nature is in reality nothing other than the unity of the world, the harmony of its causes and effects, and in general the all-embracing order of things in nature. Just as words have meaning only if they stand in a necessary relationship to one another, so too it is only the necessary relationship of natural things or phenomena to one another that gives man the impression of wisdom and purposiveness in nature. In the proofs by which the Stoics sought to demonstrate an intelligent cause of the world and to controvert the patently irrational notion that the world owes its existence to chance, to the fortuitous clashes between atoms (i. e., infinitely small, stable, and indivisible bodies), they argued that to uphold such a theory was tantamount to explaining the genesis of a literary work, the *Annales* of Ennius, for example, by a chance combination of letters.

But though the world does not owe its existence to any accident, we need not for that reason suppose it to have had a man or someone similar to a man for its author. Sensuous things are not letters which stand in no necessary relation to each other and therefore have to be put in place by a printer; things in nature attract each other, they need and desire each other, for one cannot be without the rest; they enter into relationships of their own accord, they combine by their own power; oxygen, for example, combines with hydrogen to form water or with nitrogen to form air, so establishing the admirable structure which men, who have not yet examined nature and who measure everything by man, explain as the work of a being who creates in accordance with plans and purposes. They found proof of an intelligent or spiritual author of the world not only in the so-called inner organic purposiveness which supposedly caused the organs of the body to be shaped in accordance with their functions, but also and above all in the so-called outward purposiveness which caused inorganic nature to be so constituted, or so ordered as the theists say, that animals and men are able to live in it most pleasantly and comfortably.

If the earth were nearer to or farther away from the sun, if its mean temperature rose to the boiling point of water or fell to the freezing point, everything would be dried out by the heat or congealed with cold. How wisely God figured out how far the earth must be from the sun, in order that animals and men might be able to live on it! And with what solicitude He provided for the needs of living things! Even in the most dismal, most barren, coldest regions there are always mosses or lichens, shrubs and certain animals that provide man with food. And how visible, how manifest are God's wisdom and kindness in the luxuriance of the warmer countries! How generously He has provided for the needs of man's palate! What tasty morsels grow on trees and bushes! Here sugar cane, there rice, on which in China alone at least a hundred million people are said to live, elsewhere ginger, pineapple, coffee, tea, pepper; the cacao bean which is made into chocolate; nutmeg, cloves, vanilla. And consider the coconut palm, whose bark, as a pious popular botanist has observed, "Providence has provided with semicircular protuberances which make it easier for man to climb the tree and obtain the delicious fruit and the refreshing milk it offers."

But here certain observations are in order. Let us start with the first point. Organic life did not come to earth and move in with inorganic nature by accident; organic and inorganic nature go hand in hand. What am I, a product of organic life, without the outside world? Just as my lungs are part of me, so is the air; just as my eyes are part of me, so is the light; for what are lungs without air or eyes without light? The light does not exist in order to be seen by the eye, the eye exists because there is light; similarly, the air does not exist in order to be breathed; rather, because there is air and because without it there could be no life, the air is breathed. There is a necessary relationship between the organic and the inorganic. This relationship is indeed the ground, the essence of life.

Thus there is no reason to suppose that if man had more senses or organs he would know more properties or things of nature. Nothing more exists in the outside world, in inorganic nature, than in organic nature. Man has exactly as many senses as he needs to apprehend the world in its totality. Man, the organism, did not, as the ancients believed, spring from water or from the earth, or from any one element or even from any class of objects corresponding only to one sense or another; he owes his existence and origin to the interrelation of all nature. And likewise his senses are not restricted to any particular classes or types of physical qualities or forces, but encompass all nature. Nature does not hide; with all her energies, brazenly as it were, she forces herself upon man. Just as the air presses in upon us through our mouths and noses and all our pores, so the things or properties of nature which supposedly we do not perceive with our present senses would, if they existed, impress themselves upon us by appropriate senses. But back to our discussion.

It is true that life on earth, or at least this present life on earth, would cease if the earth should take the position of Mercury, but then too the earth would no longer be the earth, that is, this individual planet distinct from other planets. The earth is what it is only because of the place it occupies in the solar system, and it was not so placed in order that man and animals might be able to live on it, but the other way around. Because it occupies this position by necessity, in accordance with its fundamental nature, in short, because it is as it now is, such organic beings as are found on earth came into being on it and live on it. On the earth itself we observe how particular countries and regions produce particular animals and plants, how warm countries produce the most fiery temperaments, beverages, and spices, how organic and inorganic nature go inseparably hand in hand and are indeed essentially one.

Thus it is not to be wondered at that the earth provides suitable food and living conditions for men and animals, for the individuality of our being corresponds fundamentally to the individuality of the earth; we are not children of Saturn or Mercury, but creatures of the earth. The monkey-bread tree, the monkey, and the Negro owe their origin and existence to the same earth, the same sun, the same climate. A temperature in which water can exist not as vapor or ice but as water, where there is water that men can drink and plants absorb, air that can be breathed, light of an intensity compatible with the eyes of men and animals—there we have the elements, the first grounds and origins of animal and plant life, and where they are present it is natural, necessary in fact, that there should be plants suited to the animal and human organisms, and serving as food. If we wish to marvel at something, we should marvel at the very existence of the earth and confine our theological wonderment and proofs to the original characteristics of the earth, its so-called astronomical characteristics; for once these are present, once we have the earth as this individual, independent planet distinct from other heavenly bodies, this individuality provides the condition, or rather the source, of organic individuals as well; for individuality and individuality alone, is the principle, the ground of life.

But what is the ground of the earth's individuality? The attraction or repulsion which are inherent in matter, in the elements of nature, and which are abstracted from them only in human reason. By attracting one another and repelling other things, certain material bodies or particles form a distinct whole. The original elements, the matter of which the world is made, should not be conceived of as a uniform, undifferentiated mass; such matter is a mere human abstraction, a chimera; nature—that is, matter—is as such differentiated, for only what is determinate, differentiated, individual can be active. Just as it is meaningless to ask why there is anything at all, so it is meaningless to ask why this particular thing is as it is and not otherwise; why, for example, oxygen is odorless, tasteless, and heavier than the atmospheric air, why it becomes incandescent under pressure, why even under extreme pressure it does not liquify, why its atomic weight is expressed by the number eight, why it combines with hydrogen only in proportions, measured by weight, of eight to one? These properties define the individuality of oxygen, that is, its determinateness, its special nature, its essence.

If I take away the properties that distinguish it from other elements, I take away its existence. Consequently, to ask why oxygen is thus and not otherwise is to ask why oxygen is. But why then is it? To this I reply: it is because it is; it is an intrinsic part of nature; it does not exist for the sake of combustion and the respiration of living things; on the contrary, because it is, fire and life exist. Where the condition and ground of a thing are given, the consequence is inevitable; where the substance, the matter of life is given, life cannot be absent; just as combustion necessarily ensues once oxygen and an inflammable body are present.

Fifteenth Lecture

IN THE LAST LECTURE I offered a few hints as to how natural phenomena, which theists explain by the presence of a conscious being who conceives and pursues purposes, may be explained in physical, or natural terms. I am well aware that these few superficial remarks do not explain the origin and nature of organic life. We are far from the stage of scientific development that will enable us to solve this problem. But this much we can know for certain: that just as we now are born and kept alive in a natural way, man came into being by a natural process, and that theological explanations explain nothing. But even apart from the crucial question as to the origin of life, there are many strange and striking phenomena in nature, which the theists pounce upon with singular glee. "Here," they cry out to those who hold that nature developed naturally, "here you have clear proof of a divine Providence and purpose!" But these natural phenomena are no different from those facts of human life, discussed in my notes on *The Essence of Religion,* in which theists find proof positive that a divine Providence watches over man. These facts are always related to human egoism, and although there are other, equally remarkable phenomena to which we do not hesitate to ascribe a natural cause, we single out the phenemona that have a bearing on human egoism, overlook their similarity to others upon which we look with indifference, and take them as proofs of a special Providence conscious of its designs, as natural miracles, so to speak.

In low temperatures [says Liebig] we exhale more carbon than in higher temperatures, and must in the same proportion consume more carbon in our food, in Sweden more than in Sicily, in our latitudes a good eighth more in winter than in summer. Even though we consume the same quantities of food, measured by weight, in cold and in warm regions, an infinite wisdom has seen to it that these foods differ radically in carbon content. When fresh, the fruit eaten by southerners does not contain more than 12 per cent of carbon, whereas the blubber and fish oil consumed by the inhabitants of the polar regions have a carbon content of from 66 to 80 per cent.

But what manner of infinite wisdom and power is it that merely palliates the consequence of an evil or deficiency? Why does it not prevent the evil itself? Why does it not prevent the cause? If the carriage I am riding in collapses, but I break no bones, should I attribute my good fortune to divine Providence? Why couldn't it have prevented the carriage from collapsing? Why do the divine wisdom and goodness not prevent the polar cold, which makes the very rocks crack? Is a God unable to create a paradise? What good is a divine being who comes to our help only after the harm is done? Isn't life in the polar regions wretched in the extreme despite all the carbon-rich blubber and fish oil? How, in view of such phenomena, can one take refuge in the religious conception of divine wisdom and goodness, when even religion, faced with the contradictions between the world as it is and divine goodness and wisdom, does not claim that God made the world as it is, but prefers to suppose that this world has been corrupted by sin and the Devil, and therefore holds out the prospect of a better, divine world?

Is it not possible to find a natural ground for this phenomenon? Why not? True, the unfortunate dweller in the polar regions, the Greenlander, for example, who is sometimes reduced to sustaining his wretched life with old tent furs and shoe soles, does not eat tropical fruits and other good things characteristic of warm countries, but only for the simple reason that they do not grow in his climes. If he is largely dependent on the blubber and oil of the seal and whale, it is out of grim necessity; but blubber and fish oil are by no means confined to the polar regions. Only persecution by man has driven the whale to the far north, and the sea lion, which is much in demand because of its abundant oil, is also to be found on the coasts of Chile. But even if it should be true that carbon-rich foods are particularly abundant at the North Pole, we find an analogous phenomenon in the fact that wood felled in the winter is denser, heavier, and hence richer in combustible or carbon than wood felled in the spring or summer, for the obvious reason that in the summer, under the influence of heat and light, the plant consumes carbon, that is, assimilates it and gives off oxygen, and moreover that budding, flowering, and fecundation use up carbon, so that in sugar cane, as J. Dumas observes, the sugar stored in the stalk is totally used up by the time the plant has blossomed and been fertilized.* I might add that the same Liebig who finds proofs of divine wisdom in the blubber and oil of the unfortunate inhabitants of the polar regions, attributes other equally remarkable phenomena, which also can be, and have been, explained theologically, to very simple natural causes.

It is much marveled at [he writes], that the varieties of grass whose seeds serve as food, should follow man like domestic animals. They follow man for reasons similar to those which make halophytes follow beaches and salt pits and chenopods rubbish heaps; just as the dung beetles are dependent on the excrement of animals, the halophytes require salt and the goose grasses require ammonium and nitrates. None of our grain plants can produce the fully-developed seeds that provide flour, unless it finds an abundant supply of magnesium phosphate and ammonium. Such seeds develop only in soil where these ingredients are present, and nowhere is the soil richer in them than in places where animals and people live domestically; plants follow their urine and excrement, because without the ingredients of urine and excrement they cannot grow seed.

In the foregoing we have considered two kindred and equally striking phenomena. One is of the utmost importance to man, the kind of phenomenon that a theist, as long as he is ignorant of its natural cause, can throw up to a naturalist as the most striking proof of a divine Providence, while the other is of no importance to man (for apart from one species whose leaves are used for soothing poultices, the chenopods, found chiefly near human dwellings, are useless to man and domestic animals alike). We have explained both phenomena—the presence of useful as well as of useless plants in the vicinity of human habitations—by the link

* J. Dumas, *Versuch einer chemischen Statik der organischen Wesen.*

between these classes of plants and animal excrement. Let me cite another example of the same kind of relationship. "The most widely distributed salts," says Mulder in his book on the chemistry of physiology, "are those which . . . are as necessary to life as are the four organic elements. . . . Most of these salts are indispensable to the blood and are present both in drinking water and in the juices of the plants that serve both men and animals as food. This indicates that the two realms of nature which scientists are too much inclined to treat separately are closely linked."* And though there are numerous phenomena in nature whose physical, natural ground we have not yet discovered, it is absurd to resort to theology for that reason. What we do not know, posterity will find out.

How many things that our ancestors could explain only through God and His purposes we have derived from the workings of nature! There was a time when even the simplest, most natural, most necessary things were explained exclusively by teleology and theology. Why, an early theologian asked, are men not alike? Why do they have different faces? And he replied: God made men with different faces in order that they might be distinguished, lest one be mistaken for another. Here we have a superb example of the teleological method. On the one hand man's ignorance, on the other his egoist tendency to explain everything with reference to himself, to think the world in his own image, lead him to transform the involuntary into the voluntary, the natural into the intentional, the necessary into the arbitrary. The fact that a man differs from others is a necessary, natural consequence of his individual existence; for if he were not different, he would not be an independent, individual being, and if he were not an individual, he would not exist. No two leaves on one and the same tree, said Leibniz quite correctly, are exactly alike; infinite diversity is a basic principle of life; likeness would annul the necessity of existence; if I cannot distinguish myself from others, it makes no difference whether I exist or not, I am interchangeable; in short, I am because I am different, and I am different because I am. I differ from others, if for no other reason, because of the impenetrability of matter, for the place that I occupy cannot be occupied by another, I exclude all others from this place of mine. In short, every man has a face of

* Mulder, *Physiologische Chemie*.

his own, because he has his own life, because he is a distinct being. And the same applies to countless other phenomena that man explains teleologically, except that in other instances the superficiality, ignorance, and absurdity of teleology are not as obvious as in this example, which, however, is far from unique.

As I have just said, I do not claim, with these remarks, to have explained the natural phenomena which theists explain teleologically. I will go further and contend that, even if natural phenomena could be explained only teleologically, this would by no means justify the consequences drawn by theology. Let us concede for the moment that the eye can be accounted for by the hypothesis of a being who in forming or creating the eye had in mind the purpose of vision; that the eye does not see because it is constructed as it is, but was so constructed in order that it might see. But even if all this is conceded to the teleologists, I still deny the need to infer the existence of a being who can plausibly bear the name of God; in other words, I deny that my concession carries us beyond nature. The means and purposes in nature are always natural means and purposes; why then should they refer us to a supernatural and extranatural being? You say that you cannot explain the world to your own satisfaction without assuming a personal, spiritual being to be its author. Very well. But will you then kindly explain how a world can spring from God, how spirit, mind, thought—for what does a mind produce but thought?—can engender flesh and blood? I am willing to concede that purpose as such, purpose as you conceive it in your minds, purpose disjoined from its content, object, or matter, points to a God, a mind; but I contend that this purpose and its author, the being who acts in accordance with purposes, exist solely in your heads, just as the first cause of theism is solely the personified concept of cause, just as God's essence is merely the abstracted (i. e., abstracted from all particular determinations) essence of particular things, and just as the existence of God is merely the concept of existence.

For purposes are as different and *as material as are the organs of these purposes*; how can you, how do you propose to sever the purposes from their organs? How, for example, will you dissociate the purpose of the eye, namely, vision, from the sclera, the retina, the iris, the aqueous fluid, the vitreous humor, and the other elements requisite to vision? But if you cannot dissociate the purpose of the eye from the material means and organs that serve it, how are you going to dissociate the being who produced the purpose of the eye from the being who produced the various materials through which the purpose is carried out? But can a being who is not material or corporeal be the cause of purposes that are exclusively the consequence of material, corporeal instrumentalities and organs? How, from purposes that are dependent solely on material, corporeal conditions and means, can you infer an immaterial, incorporeal being as their cause? A being which carries out purposes by material means alone must necessarily be a material being. How then can the works of nature be proofs and works of a God?

A God, as we shall see later on, is merely the *hypostatized and objectified essence of the human imagination.* A God has all the wonders of the imagination at his command; a God can do everything; like man's desires, like man's fancy, He is unrestricted; He can make men out of stones; He even creates the world out of nothingness. And just as everything God does is a miracle, so He himself is in essence a miracle. A God sees without eyes, hears without ears, thinks without a head, in short, He is and does everything without employing or even having the means and organs requisite to His activities. Nature, on the other hand, hears only with ears, sees only through eyes; how then can nature be derived from God? How can we derive the organ of hearing from a being who hears without ears; how can we derive the conditions and laws of nature, which govern all its phenomena and workings, from a *being who is bound by no conditions or laws?* In short, the works of a God are mere miracles, *not works of nature*. Nature is not all-powerful. It cannot do everything; it can only do things for which the conditions are present; nature, the earth for example, cannot make trees blossom and bear fruit in winter, for the necessary warmth is lacking. But a God can do so with ease. "God," says Luther, "can make the leather of your purse into *gold* and make dust into *pure grain* and the air into a *cellar full of wine*." Nature cannot make a man unless two different human organisms, a male and a female, are present and cooperate; but a God brings forth a man from a virgin's womb without the help of a male. "Is any thing too hard for the Lord?" In short, nature is a republic, the outcome of beings and forces that need and engender each other, that work together, and all of which enjoy equal rights. The entire animal organism, which may serve as an illustration of nature, can be reduced to nerves and blood. But a nerve is nothing without blood, blood is nothing without nerves; thus in nature it is impossible to tell who is the lord and who the vassal, because all things are equally important, equally essential; here there are no privileges; the lowest is as important, as necessary as the highest; my optic nerve may be ever so admirably constituted, but if some fluid, some membrane is lacking, my eye will be unable to see. And this very fact that the organism is a republican community, that it owes its existence to cooperation among equal beings, is the source of material evil, of struggle, illness, and death; but the cause of death is also the cause of life, the cause of evil is also the cause of good.

A God, on the other hand, is a monarch, an absolute, unrestrained monarch who does what he pleases, who is "above the law," but makes his arbitrary commandments into laws for his subjects, regardless of how contrary such laws may be to the subjects' needs. As in a republic the only laws are those that express the will of the people, so in nature the only laws are those that are appropriate to nature itself. It is a law of nature, for example, at least among the more highly organized animals, that generation and reproduction require the cooperation of two individuals of different sex. But this is not a despotic law; sexual differentiation is inherent in the nature of the higher organisms, and because of it each member of the species develops into an independent individual, different from all others; whence it follows that the higher animals reproduce in a more difficult, less direct way than lower organisms, such as the polyps, which reproduce simply by fission. And although we can give no reason for a natural law, analogy leads us to the belief, or rather the certainty, that the law has a natural cause. But a God gives a virgin the privilege of giving birth without benefit of a man, commands fire not to burn but to behave like water, and water to behave like fire, in other words, He tells them all to produce effects that are contrary to their nature and essence, just as the commands of a despot are contrary to the nature of his subjects. In short, a God imposes His will on nature, His rule is absolute and arbitrary, just as a despot expects unnatural things of men. It is specified, for example, in Emperor Frederick II's decree on heretics: "Since lèse-majesté against God is a greater crime than against men, and since God visits the sins of the fathers on the children, the children of heretics shall be deemed unfit for all public offices and posts of honor, with *the exception of those children who have denounced their fathers.*" Can any decree or exception be more contrary to human nature? One of William the Conqueror's many tyrannical laws was that in the towns all gatherings should disband, and that fire and light should be extinguished, when the bells rang at seven o'clock in the evening. Can there be a more unnatural restriction of human freedom, a restriction more unworthy of man? As a matter of fact, we ourselves, only a few years ago, incurred similar regulations in our principalities. Thomas Paine relates that a soldier from Brunswick who had been taken prisoner in the American Revolution said to him: "Ah, America is a beautiful, free country, worthy that a people should fight for it; I know the difference, because I know my country. In my country when the prince says *eat straw, we eat straw.*" Can we conceive of an order more unnatural, more contrary to the nature of man, than the order to eat straw? Does not a monarch, or at least an absolute monarch, perform just such miracles in the realm of politics as God in the realm of nature?

But is such a regime compatible with nature? Where in nature, where everything is natural and in harmony with the essence of natural things, do we find any such miraculous regime? To infer the existence of a God, that is, of a supernatural, wonder-working being from nature, is no less absurd, shows no less ignorance not only of the essence of nature but also of the essence of God, than if I were to maintain, by some mental sleight-of-hand, that a republican chief of state is a prince, king, or emperor as in our German states, and from this conclude that no state can exist without a prince. A president stems from the blood of the people; in all his being he is one with the people, he is merely the personified will of the people; he cannot do what he likes, but merely executes the laws made by the people. A prince, on the other hand, is explicitly set apart from the people, he is different in kind, as is God from the world. He is of royal blood, he does not rule over the people as the personified will of the people, but as a special being, separate from the people, just as God rules over nature as a separate supernatural being. The actions of God and king are therefore nothing more than arbitrary decrees and miracles.

But in nature, as we have said, there is only one regime, and that regime is republican. My head may be the president of my life, but it is not an absolute monarch, king by divine right; for the head is just as much a thing of flesh and blood as is the stomach or the heart; it issued from the same substance, the same basic organic matter as the other organs. True, it is over the other organs; it is the *caput*, the first being; but it does not differ from them in kind, in race; it does not exert despotic power; it directs the other parts of the body to perform only such actions as are in keeping with their nature; and it is not irresponsible but is punished, stripped of its command if it tries to play the prince and make unnatural demands on the stomach, the heart, or any other organ. In short, just as a republic, at least the democratic republic I have in mind, is governed not by princes but by representatives of the people, so nature is not governed by gods, but only by natural forces, natural laws, and natural elements or beings. Accordingly, it is just as absurd, just as unreasonable to derive a God from the power that governs nature as it would be to sniff out a prince or monarch in the president of a republic.

Sixteenth Lecture

THE BELIEF or idea that God is the author, preserver, and ruler of the world—an idea which man has derived from his own political regime and transferred to nature—rests on ignorance of nature; thought it has endured down to our own day, it harks back to the infancy of mankind and is appropriate, reflecting an at least subjective truth, only at the stage where man, in his religious simplicity and ignorance, attributes all the phenomena or effects of nature to God. It was natural, says Bretschneider, a modern rationalistic theologian,

> that in the earliest times religious feeling should have regarded all or most natural changes as direct actions of the gods or of God. For the less people knew of nature and its laws, the more inevitably they attributed all change to supernatural causes, that is, to the will of the gods. Thus among the Greeks it was Zeus who sent storms and hurled thunderbolts right and left. The religious feeling of the Israelites as well related everything, or almost everything, to God as its immediate cause. According to the Old Testament, it was Jehovah who made the seed sprout, protected the harvest, provided grain, oil and wine, sent fertile or barren years, diseases and plagues; it was He who incited foreign nations to make war, rewarded the virtuous with long life, riches, good health and other blessings, punished the wicked with sickness, early death, etc.; who put the sun, the moon and the stars into the sky and guided all nature and the destinies of nations and individuals according to His will.*

But in answer to this rationalist, it must be observed that the conception he describes is grounded in the essence of religion, that

* Bretschneider, *Die religiöse Glaubenlehre nach der Vernunft und der Offenbarung.*

the belief in God is true and vital only where everything is explained exclusively in terms of theology, and not of the sciences. We find such a conception not only among the peoples of antiquity but also among the early Christians and to this day among all pious Christians who have preserved the old, that is, the authentic religion and faith, in whom the discipline of reason has not yet triumphed over religious imagination—which clearly demonstrates that this is the true religious conception. Thus we also meet with it among our religious reformers. In their view the difference between miracles and the normal course of nature is only that in miracles God's action is strikingly evident, whereas the normal course of nature, though it reflects an equal activity on the part of God, does not, precisely because it is normal, strike the average man as miraculous. In the opinion of our religious reformers, everything that happens in nature is an act of God; the only difference between a miracle and a natural happening is that in the miracle God's action is contrary to nature, while in the natural process His action appears at least to be in harmony with nature.

Not bread [says Luther] but the word of God feeds the body naturally, just as it creates and preserves all things. When there is bread, God is behind it and feeds men through it, in such a way that they do not see what is happening, and suppose the bread is feeding them. And where there is none, He feeds men without bread by the Word alone, as He does behind the bread. Conclusion: All creatures are masks and mummery of God [or "feeble shadows" of God, as Luther says elsewhere], which He allows to work with Him and help Him to do all manner of things, though He can and does do the same things without their help.

Calvin speaks in the same way in his *Institutes of the Christian Religion*: "Divine Providence does not come to meet us naked, but often clothes itself in natural instrumentalities; sometimes it helps us through a man or a dumb creature, but it also helps us without any natural instrumentality or even in a manner contrary to nature," that is, in a conspicuously miraculous way. In other words, all happenings in nature are acts of God, all things are instruments of God. And moreover, unlike the instrument of nature which sees only through the instrumentality of the eye and not of the ear or nose, they are interchangeable instruments. By the mere force of His will, God can produce any effects He pleases with any of them, just as He can produce the same effects without them.

"God," says Luther in a sermon, "could perfectly well engender children without father and mother. . . . But since He created men for this purpose, He engenders and rears children through their parents, their fathers and mothers. He could also, if He wished, make day without the sun, for were not the first three days of the Creation day and night although neither sun, nor moon, nor stars had then been created? God could do all these things . . . if He wished; but He does not wish to do so." A strange restriction indeed, a strange But: He does not wish to do what He is *capable* of doing.

In these utterances of the genuine old-time believers, we see that theology cannot be reconciled with physics or physiology, and that even those phenomena which rationalist theists interpret as divine purposes and invoke as proofs of God's existence, cannot be derived from a God. In nature there is a *necessary connection* between the eye, the means of vision, and its purpose, the act of vision; the nature or organism of the eye is such that it can do what no other organ is capable of doing, that is, it can see. But in theology God's will breaks off this necessary connection; if God wills, He can make man see without eyes or through some entirely different organ, even a senseless one, through the anus if need be. Calvin says explicitly that God in the Old Testament created light before the sun, in order that men might see that the beneficent effects of light were not necessarily connected with the sun, that even without the sun God is capable of doing what He now, in the customary but by no means necessary course of nature, does by means of the sun.

Here we have also one of the most convincing proofs that nature negates the existence of a God and that conversely the existence of a God negates nature. If there is a God, why the world, why nature? If there is a perfect being such as God is conceived to be, why should there be an imperfect one? Doesn't the existence of a perfect being annul the ground and necessity of an imperfect being? Imperfection may need perfection; but how can perfection need imperfection? The meaning of imperfection lies in perfection; the imperfect strives to become perfect, a boy tends to become a man, a girl tends to become a woman; the lower strives upward. But how, if I am in my right mind, can I derive a lower being from the highest being? How, in my right mind, can I derive mindless beings from a mind? How can a spirit produce spiritless beings? If I conceive of a God and want Him to produce something—though the idea of God seems to imply unproductivity—what, if I reason soundly, can I let Him produce but beings similar to Himself, that is, gods? And if there is a God, a being who sees without eyes and hears, that is, learns about everything that is going on, without ears, how can I derive eyes and ears from Him? The meaning, the purpose, the essence, the necessity of eyes and ears are sight and hearing; but if there is already a being who sees without eyes, what can be the purpose of the eye? Isn't the reason for its existence done away with? "He who has made the ear, how should he not hear? He who has made the eye, how should he not see?" But what need has He who already sees to make an eye? The eye exists because without it there would be no seeing being; not *because* there is a seeing being. The eye springs from nature's striving to see, from the desire for light, from the vital need, at least among the higher organisms, for eyes.

It has often been said that the world is inexplicable without a God; but the exact opposite is true: if there is a God, the existence of a world becomes inexplicable; for then the world is utterly superfluous. The world or nature is explicable, we find a rational ground for its existence (if we insist on looking for one) only if we recognize that there is no existence outside of nature, that there is no other existence than a bodily, natural, sensuous existence, only if we take nature as its own ground and recognize that the question as to the ground of nature is one with the question as to the ground of existence. But the question why is there anything at all, is absurd. Far from having its ground in God, as the theists say, the world loses its ground if there is a God. Nothing follows from a God; everything beside Him is superfluous, futile, meaningless; why then should I try to derive the world from God as its ground?

But the reverse is also true. If there is a world, if this world is a truth and its truth guarantees its existence, then God is a dream, a being imagined by man and existing only in his imagination. But which of these inferences shall we adopt as ours? The latter, for the world, or nature, is an immediate, sensuous, indubitable certainty. To infer the necessity and reality of an object from its existence is assuredly far more reasonable than to infer the existence of a being from His necessity; for such necessity, a necessity that is not grounded in existence, can only be a subjective, imaginary necessity. But there can be no man, no human life without water, light, warmth, sun, bread, in short, the means of life. Thus we are perfectly justified in inferring the necessity of these things from their existence, justified in concluding that if life cannot exist without them, without inorganic nature, it exists only thanks to them.

We feel, we know, that without water we parch, we die of thirst; that without food we starve. We feel, we know, that the special power of water and food, grounded in their individual nature, is the source of these benefits. Why then should we wish to take this power away from nature and give it to a being distinct from nature, to a God? Why should we wish to deny what our senses and our reason tell us so plainly, namely, that we owe our existence only to these forces, these things in nature; that without them we should not exist, that they are the necessary elements or grounds of our existence, that a God does not preserve us through the instrumentality of these things, but rather that these things preserve us by their own power, without God. For why would a God need such common, profane instrumentalities as bread and water; and on the other hand, why would bread and water need a God in order to produce the effects that are inherent in their own material nature? But we have digressed enough.

In God's *modus operandi,* His method of ruling the world, we may distinguish three different stages. The first may be termed patriarchal; the second may be characterized as despotism or absolute monarchy; and the third as constitutional monarchy. At the first stage God is essentially an expression of emotion, of wonderment, a poetic name for everything in nature that makes a particular impression on man; instead of saying: it is thundering, or it is raining, man says: God is thundering, God is raining, but in so doing he does not distinguish God from nature and natural phenomena, for at this stage man knows nothing of nature and its workings. There are no miracles, in our strict sense of something apart from the lawful or usual course of nature, because *everything* seems miraculous to man. I call this view of the world patriarchal, because it is the oldest and simplest, the most natural to childlike, uncivilized man and because the patriarchal form of government is that in which the ruler is related to the ruled as a father to his children, from whom he does not differ in kind, but only in age, power, and intelligence, just as, at this stage, the ruler of nature and of mankind does not yet differ essentially from nature.

Zeus is the god from whom come thunder and lightning, wind and hail, snow and rain. He is the lord, that is, the personified cause of these natural phenomena, which he commands as he sees fit; to this extent, to be sure—though only from *our* point of view—he is differentiated from them; but that distinction vanishes in the blue haze of the sky. Zeus is and remains the sky, the ether, the air. The poets even speak of cold Zeus or damp Zeus instead of cold or damp air. That distinction turns to water with every drop of rain that falls from heaven to earth and dwindles to a meteor with every flash of lightning. Pliny sometimes calls lightning the *work* of Jupiter and sometimes a *part* of Jupiter. The Romans spoke of holy lightning, of sacred fire, to them lightning was divine. At least in their original forms, the gods of antiquity were virtually indistinguishable from natural phenomena; their persons merged with nature; and indeed, as we look more deeply into the ancient religions, we find that they deified natural phenomena which we should find it impossible to represent as personal beings. The Persians, for example, deified the day and the times of day, morning, noon, afternoon, and midnight; the Egyptians even deified the hours; the Greeks deified the *kairos,* the propitious moment, the motion of the air, the winds.* What an unstable, evanescent god! And who can distinguish the wind god from the wind? The Greek and Roman history books are full of miraculous tales, but these miracles are still very different from the miracles of monotheism, or at least of highly developed monotheism; products of naturalistic rather than theological superstition, they are more poetic and naïve than the doctrinaire, calculated miracles of the monotheistic religions.†

Although God was originally nothing other than the essence of nature or the world abstracted from its sensuous content, in monotheism, He is conceived of as differentiated from the world. The poetic naïveté and patriarchal coziness of polytheism are lost,

* So did the Persians, but that is of no importance here.
† Here we take no account of priestly skulduggery.

and reflection steps in. Radically distinguished from nature, God becomes a despot, ruling over the world, over nature. Deprived of all autonomy, of all will of their own, the things of nature incline to the will of Him, who by a mere command has called the world into existence. "For He spake, and it was done," says the Bible, "He commanded, and it stood fast." "He commandeth and it is done." "He can make what He willeth." Later in this same stage, man, because he differentiates between nature and God, comes to distinguish between their *modus operandi*. Special actions of God are distinguished from natural happenings and called miracles.

At this stage, however, as long as man's religious outlook is unrestricted by reason and unbelief, as long as he lives in strong, undivided faith, the works of nature remain works of God. We need only consider Luther's example of bread. If God sustains people without food, without bread, that is a patent miracle; if He sustains them with bread, this is no less a miracle or act of God, for the agent is still God, though He hides *beneath the appearance* of bread; it is not the power of the bread that feeds and sustains the people, but God's power. Natural beings are only masks, shadows, behind which God acts. At this stage, then, the difference between natural action and divine action is already recognized, but at bottom all actions are miracles or acts of God; for nature only appears to act, the usual workings and phenomena of nature are merely hidden, masked acts of God, whereas miracles in the strict sense are God's unmasked, overt acts. In the one case God acts *incognito,* in the other He acts in His divine majesty. To recapitulate: in the patriarchal or polytheistic stage, God loses Himself in nature, the distinction between God and nature vanishes; here, in the theistic or monotheistic stage, nature is lost, for God has deprived it of all spontaneity and independence.

Now God alone is real; He alone acts. Mohammedanism expressed this thought with all the force and fire of the Oriental imagination. An Arabic poet says, for example: "Everything that is not God, is nothing." And in al-Senusi's *Principles of Mohammedan Faith,* we read: "It is impossible that anything other than God should act independently." In opposition to certain Mohammedan philosophers who had held that God does not at every moment act and create anew, that the world sustains itself through the energy which God once put into it, al-Senusi argues: "Nothing has active power except for God, and if the causal nexus we observe in the world leads us to infer an autonomous activity of the world, we are mistaken; this, too, is only an indication of God's eternally active power." There were even Mohammedan philosophers who followed religion in this rigorous, and from the religious point of view logical, denial of the independent activity of nature.

The orthodox Islamic philosophers and theologians, the Mutakallimun, believed and taught "that the world is forever created anew and is therefore an enduring miracle, that things are not immutable in essence and that there is no necessary relation between ground and consequence, cause and effect." These contentions are a necessary consequence of God's omnipotent will and miraculous action; for if God can do everything, there can be no necessary relation between cause and effect. Thus these orthodox Moslems maintained, quite correctly from the standpoint of theology, that it is "no contradiction if a thing undergoes a change that is contrary to its nature, for what we ordinarily call the nature of things is merely their customary behavior, from which God's will can deviate. It is not impossible that fire should exert a cooling effect, that the terrestrial sphere should be turned into a celestial sphere, that a flea should be as large as an elephant and an elephant as small as a flea; each thing might be otherwise than it is." And yet, as Ritter, from whose book on Arabic philosophy these passages are drawn,* remarks, the only reason they cite these examples is to support their contention that "God might have pleased to create a different world and hence a different order of nature." But actually this notion that everything might be different from what it is, that there is no necessary order of nature, is merely the consequence of the belief that God can do everything, that everything is possible for God, that in view of God's will there is no natural necessity. But many Christian theologians and philosophers as well have also held that in the light of God's will there is no such thing as natural necessity, and have recognized no causality, no spontaneity or independence in things apart from God.

But though consistent with the tenets of religion, this strictly religious view is so contrary to man's natural common sense, to his

* *Über unsere Kenntniss der arabischen Philosophie.*

experience and his feeling for the independent power of nature, that men or at least those men who gave ear to reason and experience, were obliged to abandon it and to recognize the autonomous action of nature. But because God, a being distinct from nature, is to him a real and active being, there are now two actions, that of God and that of nature. The latter is immediate and close at hand, while the former is mediated and remote. In this view, God produces no immediate effects, but acts through subordinate, instrumental causes, which are the things of nature. They are termed subordinate or second causes because the first cause is God, or instrumental causes because they are the instruments through which God acts. However, they are no longer, as in the old faith, the arbitrary interchangeable instruments of God's omnipotence, but instruments in the same sense as the eye, for example, which may be called the instrument of vision; necessary instruments, each possessing its own nature and power.

In this view, God not only does not act directly, without recourse to natural causes, but moreover acts only in conformity with the workings of nature; He does not act as an unrestricted, absolute monarch who manipulates things as he pleases, who is capable of transforming a thing into something contrary to its nature, fire into water, dust into grain, leather into gold, but governs wholly in accordance with the laws of nature; in other words, He governs as a *constitutional monarch*. The king, according to constitutional law—and it is English law that I have specifically in mind—*must govern in accordance with the laws of the land;* and from the standpoint of rationalism—for the standpoint we are now considering is none other than so-called rationalism, taken in the broadest sense of the word—God governs entirely in accordance with natural laws. Constitutionalism, as the German doctrines of political law put it, sets up barriers "against the abuse of state power," and rationalism sets up barriers against the abuse of divine omnipotence, of God's arbitrary miraculous power. The only difference between constitutionalism and rationalism in this respect is that the rational or constitutional God *can* perform miracles—for rationalists do not deny His ability to work wonders—but refrains from doing so, whereas a constitutional monarch or sovereign not only can abuse his power, but also does so whenever he pleases. An unlimited monarch governs and administers, or at least takes a hand in the administration whenever he pleases; a constitutional monarch governs but does not administer; similarly, the constitutional or rational God governs, but does not, like the absolutist God, take a direct hand in the operation of the world.

Just as constitutional monarchy is monarchy attentuated by democracy or democratic institutions, so rationalism is theism attenuated by atheism or naturalism or cosmism, in short, by elements opposed to theism. In other words: just as constitutional monarchy is a limited and restricted democracy, which, if it develops, can lead only to true and complete democracy, so modern rationalistic theism is only a limited, restricted, and incomplete atheism or naturalism. For what is a God who acts only in accordance with natural laws, whose actions are exclusively the actions of nature? He is a God only in name; in content He does not differ from nature. Such a God is contrary to the concept of a God; for only an unlimited, wonder-working God, bound by no laws, a God who, at least in man's faith and imagination, can save us from all trouble and affliction, is truly a God. But a God who helps me only through doctors and medicines when I am sick, a God who is no more powerful than doctors and medicines, is an utterly superfluous, unnecesssary God, whose existence gives me nothing that nature alone would not give me, and whom I can therefore well afford to lose. The choice is between no monarchy and absolute monarchy, between no God and an absolute God like the God of our fathers. A God who, like the God of our constitutionalists and rationalists, bows to the laws of nature and adapts himself to the world as it is—such a God is an absurdity.[16]

Seventeenth Lecture

THE MATTER TREATED in the last lectures calls for certain explanations and observations. Man starts from what is closest to him, from the present, and from it draws inferences concerning what is further away; this procedure is common to atheist and theist alike. The difference between atheism or naturalism, the doctrine which interprets nature on the basis of nature or of a natural principle, and theism, the doctrine which derives nature from a heterogeneous, alien being distinct from nature, is merely that the theist takes man as his starting point and proceeds to draw inferences about nature, whereas the atheist or naturalist takes nature as his starting point and goes on to the study of man. The atheist takes a natural, the theist an unnatural course. The atheist puts nature before art. The theist puts art before nature; in his view, nature is a product of God's art, or, what amounts to the same thing, of divine art. The atheist puts the end after the beginning; he starts with what is earlier in the course of nature; whereas the theist starts at the end, with what came last in nature. The first, in the theist's view, is not the natural, unconscious operation of nature, but the conscious artistry of man. His mistake, which we have already pointed out, is to derive the unconscious from consciousness, rather than consciousness from the unconscious. For the theist, as we have already seen in appraising the teleological proof of the existence of God, looks upon nature, or the world, as a house, a clock, or some other mechanical artifact, and therefore infers the existence of an architect or artisan or artist as its author. Thus he makes art the original of nature, taking the works of man as the models for the works of nature; and goes on to infer that the works of nature must have been produced by a personal being, an artificer, a creator after the manner of man.

This, we have seen, is the inference or proof that seems clearest to men, at least at a certain stage in their development. Accordingly missionaries use it in teaching primitive peoples to believe in God, just as Christian teachers and parents use it on children. This proof is regarded as not only the clearest and easiest to understand, but also as the most reliable, as the proof which leaves no room for doubt as to the existence of God. Believers even assure us that God implanted the questions—Who made the stars? Who made the flowers?—in the hearts of little children, precisely in order to call their attention to His existence. But we cannot help asking: does this question rise spontaneously in little children, or is it not inculcated by their parents? At all events, there are many peoples and innumerable individuals who do not ask where we came from, but where shall we find food, what shall we have to live on? When asked how heaven and earth came into existence, the Greenlanders replied that they came into existence "by themselves," or that such matters were of no concern to them provided they had plenty of fish and seals.

Similarly the Indians of California "had not the slightest notion of an author of nature. When asked if they had never wondered who had made the sun, the moon, or, what they prize most, the *pitahaya,* they invariably answered *vara,* no."* But aside from these considerations, even if this question really originates in the depths of the child's mind, it has a perfectly naïve and childlike or childish motivation which hardly lends itself to Christian theological inferences. A child asks who made the stars because he does not know what they are, because he does not distinguish the stars from the lights in his parents' living room, which were made by the candlemaker; he asks who made flowers, because he does not distinguish them from other colored objects in his environment, which are the work of human hands. And moreover, even if the answer—God made them—satisfies the child mind, it by no means follows that this is the true answer, any more than the usual answer to the children's question of who brings Christmas

* Zimmermann, *Taschenbuch der Reisen.*

presents (i. e., Santa Claus) or where their little brothers or sisters came from (i. e., that the stork brought them) is the true answer, although children are satisfied with it.

How then should we respond to the curiosity of children? As long as they are really children, as long as the question is a childlike question, we can only give a childlike answer, for they are incapable of understanding the true answer. Or if such answers repel us, we must say that they will be able to understand such things only when they are older and have learned something. But when children have grown older, when their minds have developed to the point where they no longer believe that babies are drawn from wells, or that Santa Claus brings the Christmas presents, we must try to give them an idea, a conception of nature—and the same goes for the grown-up children who look upon God as the cause of all things. And we must not start our explanation with man, or if we do, we should consider him not as an artist or artisan—for his works always presuppose nature—but as himself a product and part of nature. The first point we must drive home to the child or uneducated adult is the difference between art and life—for primitive peoples look upon works of art as living beings, while the more advanced peoples who believe in a God look upon living beings as works of art and upon the world as a machine; we must show them by examples how a ship differs from a fish, a puppet from a man, clockwork from the living organism of man or animal. Then we must look into the origins of things: you see the plant growing from a seed, the animal developing from an egg, the one from vegetable matter, the other from animal matter which, however, is not yet an animal.

Once we have acquainted our pupil with the generation, the reproduction of animals and plants, we can encourage him to draw inferences about what is further away. The evident facts of reproduction will enable him to envisage and accept the idea that the first plants and animals were not made, not created, but developed from natural substances and causes, that in general all things and creatures in the world owe their origin not to a being outside and distinct from the world, but to nature, to the world itself. And if he should find this incomprehensible and unbelievable, we must point out that if man did not know from experience that children are engendered in a natural way, this too would strike him as unbelievable; he would be convinced that God made children, that they came directly from God.

Actually men have regarded the reproductive process, i. e., the way in which man produces man as no less inexplicable and incomprehensible than the first emergence of man from nature, and have resorted to God in one case as in the other. But comprehensible or not, the reproductive process remains a natural process; not although, but because it is incomprehensible—for precisely what is most natural is most incomprehensible to those men who consider everything in terms of themselves and have no mind for nature. Why, men cannot even understand men: the miser fails to understand the openhanded man, the respectable citizen the criminal, the Philistine the genius; how much more baffling must nature be to him! Each man understands only what is similar or akin to him. But just as a man who is incomprehensible to certain of his fellow men remains a man, so nature, which we do not understand because it conflicts with our limited ideas of it, is still nature and not something supernatural. The supernatural exists only in the imagination, or else it is that part of nature itself which surpasses the limited ideas man has formed of nature. How absurd it is therefore to draw theological conclusions from the incomprehensible aspects of nature, let alone try to solve the problem by theology! Even today there are numerous phenomena in organic and inorganic nature that physicists and physiologists are unable to explain. But does it follow that these phenomena are any less the result of physical and physiological causes than other phenomena which we can explain? Is one part of nature physical and another hyperphysical? Or shall we not say that nature in all its parts is one, a natural unity?

And now to our second observation. The main reason why man derives the world from God, from a spirit, is that he cannot account for his own spirit on the basis of the world or nature. Where, says the theist in his arguments with the atheist, does the spirit come from? Spirit can only come from spirit. But this difficulty in deriving the spirit, or mind, from nature has arisen only because men have formed too disparaging a conception of nature and too lofty a conception of the spirit. If we call the spirit God, of course its origin can only be divine. To say that the spirit or mind cannot be derived from nature is merely an indirect way of saying that the spirit is an unnatural being, outside and above the world, divine. And indeed, the spirit as conceived of by the theists cannot be explained by nature; for this spirit is a very late product, a product of human imagination and abstraction, which, accordingly can no more be derived directly from nature than a lieutenant, a professor, a cabinet minister, can be directly explained on the basis of nature, though man as such can. But if we cease to overestimate the spirit, or mind, if we cease to consider it as an abstraction, distinct from man, we shall no longer find it so impossible to envisage its natural origin. The mind develops with the body, with the senses, with the whole man; it is bound up with the senses, the head, the bodily organs in general; are we to suppose that the head as a physical organ, that is, the skull and the brain, originated in nature, but that the mind within the head, that is, the activity of the brain, owes its origin to a product of our thought and imagination, a God? What inconsistency, what wrongheadedness! The source of the skull and the brain is also the source of the mind; the source of the organ is also the source of its function; for how can the two be separated? Consequently, if the brain and the skull are a product of nature, so is the mind.

In language we distinguish the activity of the brain as psychic from the other functions which we call physical. We limit the words bodily or sensory to particular kinds of bodily or sensory activity, and, as I have shown in my books, make the activity that differs from these into an activity of an entirely different class, a spiritual, that is, absolutely nonsensuous and disembodied activity. But the spirit and its activity—for what is the spirit but mental activity, hypostatized and personified by human imagination and language?—are also physical activity, the activity of the brain, which differs from other activities only insofar as it is the activity of a *different* organ, namely, the brain. But because the activity of the brain is an activity of a special kind, which cannot be compared with any other, because the organ underlying it is not an immediate object of man's feeling and consciousness—unlike the mouth and stomach whose emptiness or fullness we feel when we eat, or the eye which we are aware of when we see, or the hands and arms, which we are conscious of when we perform manual labor; because the activity of the brain is the most hidden, withdrawn, soundless, and imperceptible activity, man has come to look upon this activity as an absolutely *disembodied,* inorganic, abstract being, to which he has given the name of spirit. But since this being owes its existence solely to man's ignorance of the organic conditions of thought and to the imagination with which he compensates for his ignorance; since this "spirit" is therefore merely a personification of man's ignorance and imagination, all the difficulties it involved are dispelled. If the mind or spirit is an activity of man and not an independent being, if it is not without organs, not separable from the body, then it can only be derived from nature, and not from God, for the God or divine spirit from which the human spirit supposedly derives is itself nothing other than intellectual activity which human thought has abstracted from the body and all bodily organs, and has set up as an independent being.

The mind, to be sure, is the highest part of man; it is man's badge of nobility, which distinguishes him from the animals; but first in man is not first in nature. On the contrary, what is highest and most perfect is the last and latest. Thus to make mind or spirit into the beginning, the origin, is to reverse the order of nature. But it pleases men, in their vanity, self-love, and ignorance, to believe that what is qualitatively first preceded everything else also in time. Man's tendency to derive his mind from God, that is, from mind, to accord a primordial existence, a preexistence, an existence before nature, to mind or spirit, is consequently identical with the tendency of noble families of antiquity, and of the ancient peoples in general—for each people regarded itself as noble in contradistinction to other peoples—and of many peoples even today, to identify the beginning of history, the beginning of existence, with the beginning of their own history and existence, and to claim divine origin. After a missionary had made every effort to convince them that someone must have made the world, the Greenlanders replied: "Well, in that case it must have been a Greenlander." This notion strikes us as absurd, and rightly so. And yet it springs from the same tendency that leads a thinking people, a people which looks upon intelligence as its badge of nobility, to ascribe a divine, primordial existence to the mind and to regard a mind or spirit as the source of the world.

Now to our third observation. Since it is too patently impossible that a corporeal world should have sprung from a spiritual God or being, since moreover a disembodied spirit is an obvious abstraction of the human mind, a few modern theist thinkers or philosophers of religion abandoned the old doctrine of a *creatio ex nihilo,* which is a necessary consequence of the notion that the world sprang from the spirit—for where is this spirit to derive matter, the material substances, if not from nothingness?—and transformed God Himself into a material, corporeal being, precisely in order to explain the world through Him. In short, they ceased to regard God as pure spirit; instead of deifying only that part of man which he calls mind or spirit, they also deified the other part of man, which is body; their God now consisted of body and mind, like man himself. Schelling and Franz Baader have argued this doctrine. But it originated with certain older mystics, notably Jakob Böhme, who was born in 1575 in Oberlausitz and died in 1624. A shoemaker by trade, Böhme was undoubtedly a most extraordinary thinker. He distinguished positive and negative attributes in God, light or fire and darkness, good and evil, mildness and severity, love and wrath, in short, spirit and matter, soul and body. Once he had taken this step, it was, or seemed to be, a simple matter to derive the world from God, since all the forces, qualities or phenomena of nature such as hot and cold, bitter and acrid, solid and liquid, were now encompassed in God. The extraordinary thing is that because there is in his system no light without darkness, no spirit without matter or nature, he makes God's nature precede His spirit, which is the true God, although sometimes, because of his Christian habits of thought, Böhme contradicts this view, or attenuates it by saying that the genesis or development of the spirit from nature or matter is not temporal and therefore not real.

Up to a certain point this is a rational doctrine; like atheism or naturalism it starts with nature and only then proceeds to man, it lets spirit develop from nature—an order which is confirmed by nature and thus by experience, for all of us are materialists before we become idealists, we all serve the body, the lower needs and senses, before we rise to spiritual needs and sensibilities; the infant sucks, sleeps, and stares vacantly at the world before it learns to see. But Böhme's doctrine is also irrational in that it cloaks the natural process of development in the mystical darkness of theology, it *identifies elements antagonistic to the God-concept with God* and *attributes unnatural properties to nature;* for nature is corporeal, material, and sensuous, but the divine nature that is a component of God is supposed to be none of these. Nature in God, or divine nature, to be sure, contains everything that is contained in profane, sensuous nature, but divine nature contains all this in a nonsensuous, immaterial way; for despite His materiality God is, or is supposed to be, a spirit. Ultimately this brings us back to the same old difficulty: the impossibility of explaining how real, corporeal nature can have sprung from immaterial, spiritual nature.

This difficulty disappears only if we replace divine nature with real nature, nature as it is; only if we ascribe the origin of corporeal beings to a real corporeal being, and not to a merely imagined one. But just as the notion of divine nature contradicts the concept and reality of nature, so Jakob Böhme's God contradicts the concept of divinity; for a God who rises up from darkness to light, who starts out as a nonspiritual being and develops into a spiritual one, is no God. A God is essentially an abstract, complete, perfect being, from whom every motive or need for development is excluded; for only natural beings are subject to development. True, as we have seen, this development is said to be atemporal, but how can development be dissociated from time? In short, this is a mystical doctrine, a doctrine of nature which is supposed to be at the same time a doctrine of God, consequently a welter of contradiction and confusion, a theistic atheism, at once an affirmation and denial of God, a supernatural naturalism. The study of such a doctrine compels us to leave the realm of fantasy and mysticism, in which it has its home and root, to step out into the light of reality; to discard immaterial nature for material nature, divine history for real, secular history, and in general theology for anthropology.

Jakob Böhme's doctrine once again confirms our contention that God is nothing other than a concept abstracted from nature; what distinguishes it from the usual theist view is merely that his God is abstracted not only from the real or imaginary purposes of nature, that is, from the natural phenomena which man explains by predicating the existence of a purposive, thinking being, but also from the matter, the substances underlying these purposes (which, it must be admitted, are all concerned with very material things); Jakob Böhme thus deifies not only God but matter as well. To say that "God is a spirit" presupposes that the spirit is God, or a divine being; and similarly, to say that "God is not only spirit, but body as well," presupposes that matter, or body, is divine; or rather, the latter statement contains the true meaning and explanation of the former. But if the God who is a spirit is only a personified expression of the divinity of the spirit, the God who is body, matter, is also nothing other than the personified divinity, or in philosophical terms the essence and truth of nature or matter. Thus it becomes clear that the doctrine which demonstrates the divinity of matter in God is a mystical, inverted doctrine, and that the true, rational doctrine, in which the mystical doctrine first finds its meaning, is the atheist doctrine which considers mind and matter as such, without God.

If God is a material, bodily being, as the followers of Jakob Böhme maintain, the true proof of this bodily nature is that God is also an object of our *bodily senses*. What is a body that cannot be perceived by the body? Only the bodily impressions we have of a body allow us to infer that it is indeed a body. But this of course our materialistic theists do not admit; they do not let their God sink into matter to the point of becoming tangible and visible; that would be too profane, too ungodly for them.

And moreover such a transference to the profane, material world would cost Him His existence, for where the eyes and hands begin, the gods cease to be. The Greenlanders even believe that a gust of wind, or mere contact with a dog, would be fatal to Tornasuk, one of the mightiest of their gods. But precisely because of this dread of experimental physics, the body of Jakob Böhme's God is only a fancied, imaginary body. In short, his doctrine, like all theological doctrines, is an inversion, a contradiction. It deifies nature, matter, yet disregards, in fact denies, what would make this matter into real matter. If you wish to know the truth about matter, make use of your senses, recognize the truth of the senses. But you recognize only the truth of the imagination, of mystical, immaterial thinking; consequently you are forced to admit that despite the materiality and corporeity of your God, all you are deifying in Him is your own imagination. What I perceive is determined by my organs of perception. If I deny the senses, I deny the existence of a sensuous being, and whatever remains can only be a spiritual or imaginary being.

Eighteenth Lecture

To the observations made in the last lecture I have the following to add. I have said that in the rationalist view we have God *and* nature, two beings, two causes and modes of action, the one direct, which is ascribed to real and natural beings, the other indirect, which is ascribed to God, just as in constitutionalism two powers, people and prince, govern or dispute the government, while in naturalism only nature and in genuine theism only God rules; that accordingly rationalism, like constitutionalism, is a hybrid system, characterized by contradiction, indecision, and pusillanimity. I must observe, however, that even religious absolutism, the cult of the one God who is absolute monarch, presents a glaring contradiction: God alone is said to be active, yet an autonomous activity is attributed to things other than God. And to a certain degree this same contradiction is also to be found in polytheism—one has only to read the Roman and Greek historians and poets, who amalgamate divine and human activity in the most naïve way.

The reason for this inconsistency is very simple: for all his extravagant faith, man is unable to repress or relinquish his natural human reason, which tells him that extradivine things or beings act independently. This is particularly true of the Germanic and other Occidental peoples, whose highest ideals are autonomy, freedom and independence, qualities to which they could not lay claim if God alone were capable of autonomous action. Western man's innate leaning toward rational, independent action prevents him from drawing the full consequences; the Oriental, on the other hand, opposes no barriers to the consequences of his belief in God;

renouncing his freedom and his reason, he submits wholly to the divine decree, so demonstrating that God is not only the *first* cause, as the clever, self-centered, rationalistic Occidentals suppose, but the *sole* cause, the sole being capable of autonomous action. In the lecture before last I cited a few examples from the Islamic sphere; there are, to be sure, Mohammedan and other Oriental philosophers and theologians who hold that things other than God act independently, but the contrary is the dominant and characteristic view. God, says the orthodox Mohemmedan philosopher al-Ghazzali, "is the only effective cause in all nature; thanks to this cause, it is just as possible that fire should touch tinder without burning it as that tinder should burn without contact with fire. There is no such thing as natural process or natural law; the difference between miracles and natural happenings is nonexistent."

Thus, even in the most orthodox minds, Western theology labors under this contradiction. It is inherent in the nature of theology; for if there is a God, a world is unnecessary, and conversely. And if God and world are mutually exclusive, how can their respective activities be reconciled? The activity of God negates the activity of the world, and conversely. If I have done a certain thing, God has not done it; and if God has done it, I have not; one possibility precludes the other. But what of the notion of means, of instrumentality; what of the idea that God acts through me? No autonomous activity is compatible with the idea of instrumentality. In short, any attempt to make God and world coexist and cooperate leads to the most absurd contradictions and calls forth the most preposterous sophisms and mental gymnastics, as theology has amply shown throughout its history with its doctrine of the so-called *Concursus Dei,* i. e., of God's participation in the free actions of men. An example. In his *Institutes of the Christian Religion,* Calvin, whose extreme rigor in matters of faith gives him exemplary status, writes:

Since a Christian is absolutely certain that nothing happens by chance, that everything occurs in accordance with God's decree, he will always direct his gaze upon God as the most eminent or first cause of things, but he will also accord due recognition to the subordinate causes. He will not doubt that a special Providence, encompassing every detail, watches over him, permitting nothing that does not redound to his welfare and salvation. Consequently, he will relate everything that happens for the best, in accordance with his heart's desires, to God and regard God alone as its cause, even if he has experienced God's benefaction through the service of man or received help from soulless creatures. For in his heart he will think: Surely it is the Lord who has inclined their souls toward me, in order that they might be the instruments of His benevolence toward me. Thus when he receives something good from man, he will honor and praise God as the principal author; but he will honor men as God's servants and recognize that he is obligated by God's will to those by whose hands God wished to do him good.

In this passage the entire wretchedness of this theological view is brought home to us. If God is the most eminent or principal cause, or rather the one and only cause, of the good things done to me by men—for only the first cause is truly a cause—how can I honor men, how can I feel obligated to those through whom God has favored me? They deserve no credit; not their own heart, their own being, but God has inclined them in my favor; God might just as well have helped me through other men, even through men who were ill-disposed toward me, or through nonhuman beings; actually He could have helped me Himself, without intermediary. The intermediary is quite irrelevant and meaningless, no more capable of arousing sentiments of gratitude, veneration, or love than the vessel in which I am handed a drink of water when I am parched with thirst. And let no one say that my metaphor is ill chosen, for the Bible itself says that men are to God as pots to the potter. By this example we see how theology, in contradiction to its faith in God as the omnipotent cause of all things, compromises with man's natural feeling and common sense, which lead him to regard the beings from whom he receives favors as their causes and consider himself bound to them in gratitude, love, and veneration. We see how God and nature, the love of God and the love of man, are in contradiction, how the activity of God on the one hand and that of man and nature on the other cannot be reconciled except by sophistry. Either God or nature! There is no third, middle term combining the two.

Two courses are open to you: The first is to profess God and deny nature; or if that exceeds your powers, because you cannot help recognizing the existence of nature, which your senses impress upon you in spite of your faith, you can at least deny nature all causality, all substantiality, and call it mere appearance, a mere mask. Or else: Profess nature and deny that there is a God concealed behind it and acting through it. And if you look on God as the true cause or purely and simply as *the* cause of the good—for only the first cause is the true cause—then do not deny that God is also the cause of the evil that is done men by other men or beings. But theism is inconsistent; it denies this consequence. The same Calvin who regards men who do good as mere instruments of God, calls it godless and absurd to infer that a murderer, for example, who kills a righteous man, is a mere instrument carrying out the decision or will of God, that all crimes are therefore committed by God's decree or will. And yet this is a necessary consequence of his doctrine. If real, natural beings are mere means, mere instruments in the hands of God, they remain so whether they do good or evil. If you deny that man does good by his own resources, out of his own heart, you must also deny that he does evil out of his own heart; if you refuse to honor man as a benefactor, you must also refuse to condemn him as an evildoer; for to do evil requires as much strength and power as to do good, and sometimes more; but according to you, all strength, all power, are God's. How absurd, and indeed how malicious, to deny man's autonomy in one case and to recognize it in another, to dispose of the good a man does as the grace of God, but to hold man guilty of the evil he does.

But that is the nature of theology. Its personification, the theologian, is an angel in his dealings with God, a devil in his dealings with man; he imputes good to God and evil to man, the creature, and nature. True, the good a man does is not due to him alone, it is not exclusively the work of his own will, but also the result of the natural and social conditions, relations and circumstances under which he is begotten and conceived, brought up and educated. Only the crudest, most superstitious and abject egoism can suppose that these conditions, relations, and circumstances, and the inclinations and attitudes they have engendered in me, have their ground in the purposes and decisions of a God. Just as the purposiveness of nature is simply a human, or rather, theological expression for the profound and all-embracing coherence of nature, so the divine will or decision which supposedly endows each of us with certain inclinations, impulses, predispositions, and capacities is merely an anthropomorphism, a popular term for the context in which man has become what he is.

This is the only rational meaning behind the belief or doctrine that man becomes what he is not through his own will, but by the will or grace of God. The grace of God is personified chance or personified necessity, the personified context in which men develop and live. I am a child of the nineteenth century, a part of nature as it is in this century, and this alone makes me what I am; for nature also changes, which is why each century has its own ailments; and it was not by my will that I was born into this century. But no more than I can dissociate my being from this century, no more than I can suppose that I exist outside it and independently of it, can I dissociate my will from the century. And explicitly or not, consciously or not, I accept this fate, I accept the necessity of being a part of my time; what I am by nature, without having willed it, I also will; I cannot wish to be something other than what I am, i. e., than what I essentially am. I may wish to modify certain secondary, accidental traits, but not my essential nature; my will is dependent on my nature and not the other way around; *whether I like it or not, whether I know it or not,* my will conforms to my nature; try as I may, my nature—that is, the essence of my individuality—does not conform to my will.

And yet, though a man's nature cannot be dissociated from his times, it is not uncommon to hear someone say: Ah, if only I had been born in Athens in the days of Phidias and Pericles! But such desires are mere fantasies, and even so they are determined by the character of the times in which I was born and educated, by the nature of the man I *am,* which remains unchanged even when my fancy migrates to other times and places. For such a desire can arise only in a period that understands and appreciates the life of ancient Athens, and only in a man who by his own nature feels drawn to that life.

And even if I remove to Athens in my thoughts, this does not remove me from my century, from my own nature; that is impossible. For I picture Athens in my own way, which conforms to the thinking of my own century; this Athens is merely a reflection of my own being, for every age sees the past in terms of itself. In short, man's will is also contained in his essential being; he cannot break with his nature; even the wish fantasies which depart from it are determined by it; they may seem to go far afield, yet they always fall back on it, just as a stone thrown into the air falls back on the ground. In other words: much as I may owe to my own activity, my work, the exertion of my will, I have become what I am only in the context of this people, this country, this place, this century, this nature—only in the context of the environment, conditions, circumstances, and events that constitute my biography. This is the only rational meaning underlying the belief that man owes what he is not to his own merit or efforts alone, but to God. But this goes for the bad as well as the good; it is not my fault, or at least not mine alone, but also the fault of conditions, of the people with whom I have come into contact, of the times in which I was born and raised, that I have certain faults, certain weaknesses. Just as every century has its ailments, so every century has its dominant vices, that is, dominant inclinations toward one thing and another, which are not bad in themselves but become evils or vices only through their preponderance, their tendency to repress other, equally justified inclinations or impulses.

This does not negate human freedom, or at least not the rational freedom grounded in nature, that freedom which manifests and maintains itself as independent activity, diligence, education, self-mastery, and effort; for the century, the circumstances and conditions amid which I have developed, are not all-powerful gods. Nature throws man upon his own resources; it does not help him unless he helps himself; it lets him sink if he cannot swim, whereas a God prevents me from sinking even if I am unable to stay above water by my own strength and ability. Even the ancients knew the proverb: "If God wills, you can float on a reed." Even an animal has to work hard and exert all its powers to find food; what infinite pains it often costs a caterpillar to find the right leaf, or a bird to catch an insect or another bird! But a God relieves men and even animals of the need to act on their own; He cares for them; He is active, they are merely passive and receptive. At the Lord's behest the ravens brought Elijah "bread and flesh in the morning, and bread and flesh in the evening." But "who provideth for the raven his food?" We find the answer in the Psalms and the Book of Job: God, who "giveth to the beast his food, and to the young ravens which cry." Thus the rational freedom, independence, and autonomous activity of men and all other beings are compatible with nature, but not with the existence of an all-powerful God who knowingly and purposively determines everything in advance.This incompatibility between the independent activity of creatures and God as the sole or principal active being has always confronted theology with the most perplexing and heartbreaking contradictions. But they will vanish, or at least lend themselves to a solution, as soon as God is replaced by nature.

Just as theists blame man for ethical evil and derive only the good from man, so they put the blame for physical evil, for evil in nature, directly or indirectly, explicitly or tacitly, on matter or on the unswerving necessity of nature. But without this evil, they say, there would also be no good; if man did not experience hunger, he would not enjoy food, or be impelled to eat; if he were unable to break his leg, he would have no bones and would be unable to walk; if he felt no pain when wounded, he would have no impulse to protect himself, which explains why superficial wounds are far more painful than deep ones. Thus it is absurd, they say, that atheists should cite the evils, sufferings, and pain of life as arguments against the existence of a kindly, wise, and all-powerful Creator. It is, indeed, perfectly true that without certain evils, certain good things would not be possible; but this necessity is applicable only to nature and not to God. God, in the theist view, is characterized by good without evil, by perfection without imperfection. From this it *necessarily* follows that He is capable of creating good without evil, a world without sufferings and deficiencies.

For this reason Christians believe in a future world in which this will really be the case, a world from which all the features which atheists adduce as arguments that the world is not of divine origin are eliminated. The old orthodox Christians had such a world in Paradise. If Adam had persevered in the state of innocence, of perfection, in which he issued from God's hands, his body would have remained indestructible and invulnerable, and nature in general would have been spared all its present evils and deficiencies. All the arguments with which theists justify the evils of the world (I am speaking here of natural, not social evils) are valid only if nature is taken as the ground of the existence of things, as the first cause, but not if a God is presumed to be the author of the world. All theodicies, all justifications of God, are therefore, consciously or unconsciously, based on the idea of an autonomous nature; in them God's activity and omnipotence are limited by the existence and action of nature; God's freedom, which would have enabled him to make the world entirely different from what it is, is limited by the idea of necessity, which springs solely from nature and applies only to nature. This is made especially clear by the prevailing views of divine Providence. Before the election of a new pope in 1846, the Archbishop of Paris issued a circular calling on the faithful to pray "that *no alien influences would obstruct God's merciful intentions.*" And in a recent order to the army (January 1849), the King of Prussia declared: "In the past year, when *without God's help* Prussia would have succumbed to seduction and high treason, my army preserved and renewed its ancient glory."

But what a sickly God, whose merciful purposes can be frustrated by alien influences! What an odd Providence that cannot help man without bayonets and shrapnel! What weird omnipotence that has to be bolstered up by military power! Does a true God share His glory with the royal Prussian army? Therefore I say: Either honor God alone after the manner of the earlier theists and Christians, who believed that God can help without bayonets and shrapnel, that we can defeat our enemies by prayers alone, that prayer, in other words religion or God, is all-powerful; or frankly admit that brute, material force has helped you.

These examples, which might be multiplied ad infinitum, for they are to be found in any newspaper, show how godless men are today, even those who nominally believe in God, how for all their lip service to their God our modern theists actually abjure and belittle Him by ascribing independent power and efficacy to matter, to the world, and to man, and casting their God in the mere role of an idle observer or inspector, who at most springs into the breach in extreme emergencies. Even the standard phrases—divine help, divine succor—point up this ugly conflict between God and nature; for someone who helps me, who comes to my assistance, does not annul my activity; he merely sustains me, he only takes on a part of the work or burden. And yet, in one who believes in God, how unseemly it is to deny His omnipotence at least in practice, to put Him into partnership with the power of nature and of man, which alone is really relied upon. If there is an eye watching over me, why do I need an eye of my own, why should I look out for myself? If a God provides for me, why should I provide for myself? If there is a good and all-powerful being, why should I require the limited power of natural means and forces?

Let us not, however, find fault with Western man for not drawing the practical consequences of his religious faith, for highhandedly ignoring the implications of his faith and in reality, in practice, abjuring it; for it is solely to this inconsistency, this practical unbelief, this instinctive atheism and egoism that we owe all progress, all the inventions which distinguish Christians from Mohammedans, and Occidentals in general from Orientals. Those who rely on God's omnipotence, who believe that whatever happens and is, happens and is by the will of God, will never cast about for means to remedy the evils of the world, either those natural evils that can be remedied—for there is no cure for death—or the evils of human society. "To each man," says Calvin in his *Institutes,* "God assigns his situation and position. In his proverb—'The lot is cast into the lap; but the whole disposing thereof is of the Lord'—Solomon therefore admonishes the poor to patience, for those who are not content with their lot are seeking to shake off a burden imposed on them by God. And another prophet, the Psalmist, condemns the godless persons who put it down to human intelligence or fortune that some achieve posts of honor while others remain lowly."

Where theism has not become purely theoretical, inactive, and unbelieving, but is still a true, practical faith, this is its inescapable consequence. Some of the Church Fathers even regarded the shaving of the beard as godless criticism of God's works. And rightly so! The beard owes its existence to God's will and purpose, which extend to every slightest detail; by having my beard cut off, I am expressing dissatisfaction, indirectly finding fault with the author of my beard; I am rebelling against His will; for in making my beard grow, God has said: Let there be a beard, whereas in cutting it off, I say: Let it not be. Leave everything as it is! That is the necessary consequence of the belief that a God governs the world, that everything happens and is by God's will. Any change which man, on his own authority, makes in the existing order of things, is rebellion against God. Just as in absolute monarchy the government monopolizes all political activity and leaves none for the people, so also in religion God, as long as He remains an absolute, unlimited God, leaves nothing for man to do. "Therefore," says Luther in his exegesis of Ecclesiastes, "it is the best and highest wisdom to let God order and command all things . . . to let God reign and rule, and entrust all injustice and all the suffering of the pious to the hands of God, who in the end will judge all things exactly and justly. . . . Therefore if you desire joy, peace and happy days, wait until God provides them." But fortunately for them and for us, the Christians, in conformity with the spirit and character of the Western and especially the Germanic peoples, have asserted autonomous human activity in opposition to the consequences of the religious dogmas and doctrines derived from the Orient. In so doing, it is true, they have transformed their religion, their theology—to which, in theory at least, they have clung fast to this day—into a fabric of the most absurd contradictions, half-statements, and sophisms, into a revolting, insipid mishmash of belief and unbelief, theism and atheism.

Nineteenth Lecture

THE KAMCHADALS, as theistic travelers tell us, have a supreme God, whom they call Kutka and regard as the creator of heaven and earth. He is, they say, the source and maker of all things. But they consider themselves far cleverer than God, and believe that no one is sillier and more stupid than their Kutka. If he had been intelligent, they say, he would have made the world much better, he would not have put so many impassable mountains and cliffs in it, he would not have made so many raging torrents and persistent gales. Accordingly, when they cross a high mountain in the winter, they cannot refrain from reviling Kutka in the most intemperate terms. "We were properly shocked by such absurdities," a rationalist author remarks. I, for my part, am not the least bit shocked; on the contrary, I am surprised that Christians should have so little self-knowledge and fail to realize that fundamentally they do not differ from the Kamchadals. The only difference is that instead of venting their irritation at the crudeness and brutality of nature in curses like the Kamchadals, the Christians do so in deeds.

The Christians level mountains or at least build roads over them; they dam the raging torrents, or cut channels around them; in short, they do their best to modify nature for their own convenience. But every such action implies a criticism of nature; I do not level a mountain unless I am annoyed at its existence, unless I curse it; by leveling the mountain I transform my curse into action. Against the persistent gales, whose author the Kamchadals feel justified in cursing, Christians, it is true, have still found no direct remedy, and generally speaking the atmosphere is the province of nature that is least understood and mastered; but Christians have other means, provided by civilization, of defending themselves against the rigors of the climate. The Bible admonishes us: "Dwell in the land, and verily thou shalt be fed"; yet this does not prevent Christians, if "Providence" gives them the wherewithal, from going off to watering places or even to foreign countries where they find a better, more propitious climate. But when I leave a place, I am in fact cursing it; I think and sometimes even say: the climate here is abominable; I can't stand it here any longer; this place will be the death of me, and so on. When a Christian leaves his country, however, whether temporarily or permanently, he is in practice abjuring his faith in divine Providence; for it is divine Providence that has put him in this place, because in spite, or perhaps because of its unpleasant and unhealthful climate, Providence has singled it out as the right place for him.

For Providence extends to every least detail; a Providence such as that of the rationalist theists, which concerns itself only with the species, the universal, the general laws of nature, is a Providence only in name. Therefore, if I leave this place in which Providence has put me, if I level this mountain which it obviously put in this exact place and made exactly so high on purpose, if I dam this torrent, which obviously derived its power from God's will and power, I am by my practical activity negating, denying, the religious theory and dogma that everything God does is well done, that everything God makes is wisely made, excellent, and without blemish, for God not only fashioned the general scheme of things, but is responsible for every infinitesimal detail. How then can I effect a radical change, how can I subordinate God's purposes to my human purposes, how can I oppose human power to God's power as manifested in the power of this raging torrent and the enormity of this mountain? I cannot if I wish my actions to confirm my faith. When, as Herodotus tells us, the people of Cnidos wished to dig a trench through a small neck of land in order to make their country a true island, the Pythia objected, saying:

> Do not fortify the isthmus and do not cut it through,
> *Zeus would have made an island had he wished.*

And when the Romans, as Tacitus tells us in his *Annals,* thought of preventing the Tiber from flooding by diverting its tributaries, the Reatines opposed the project, saying that nature (which in this case clearly means the same as God) had made the best possible provision for human interests in establishing the sources, courses, and mouths of rivers.

Every step toward civilization, everything man has invented in order to protect himself against the inclemencies of nature—the lightning rod, for example—has therefore been condemned by strict believers as an interference in the affairs of God, and inconceivable as it may seem, this has been true even in our own day. When sulphuric ether was first used as an anaesthetic, the theologians of a Protestant university (Erlangen) condemned its use in difficult deliveries, invoking, so I am told on good authority, the words of the Bible: "In sorrow shalt thou bring forth children." In other words, God decreed that childbirth must be painful. For theological faith makes people both stupid and cruel. But we have spoken enough of Protestant theologians and universities. Let us get back to the Kamchadals, who have a good deal more sense; for they are perfectly right in regarding the creator of steep mountains, inaccessible to human civilization, of raging torrents that destroy fields and meadows and of persistent gales, as a being devoid of intelligence. Nature is indeed blind and without understanding; it is what it is and does what it does, not intentionally, not with knowledge and will, but of necessity; or if, as we should, we include man in nature—for he too is a natural being or creature—its only reason is human reason. It is man alone who by his devices and creations sets the stamp of consciousness and intelligence on nature; it is man alone who little by little, in the course of time, has transformed the earth into a rational dwelling place suitable for man, and who will one day make it an even more human and rational dwelling place than it is today. Human civilization even modifies the climate. Consider what Germany is today and what it was in olden times, even as late as Caesar's day. But how can the radical transformations effected by man be reconciled with belief in a supernatural, divine Providence, which created all things and concerning which it is written: "And God saw every thing that he had made, and, behold, it was very good."

There is still another point to which I must devote a few words. As I have said, most attempts to demonstrate the existence of Providence have been based on those natural phenomena which attenuate or forestall the consequences of an existing or necessary evil. The weapons with which animals defend themselves against their enemies and the defenses with which certain organs of the human and animal body are equipped have been looked upon as proofs of a special Providence. Thus "the eye is protected by the eyelashes against foreign particles, by the eyebrows against the sweat that runs down from the forehead, and by the bones surrounding it from injury; and it can be covered by the eyelid." But why is the eye not protected against the disastrous consequences of a blow with the fist, of a flying stone, or other dangers capable of destroying the eye or at least the power of vision? Precisely because the being which formed the eye is not omnipotent and omniscient, precisely because it is not a God.

If an *all*-seeing eye and an *all*-powerful hand had made the eye, it would be protected against *all* possible dangers. But the being that made the eye was not thinking of stones or fists or innumerable other destructive forces, for the simple reason that nature does not think and consequently does not, like a God, know in advance of the dangers that can beset an organ or being. Every being, every organ, is protected only against particular dangers and effects, and this protection is one with the *specific character,* the existence, of this organ or being, which consequently could not exist without it. If something is to exist, it must have the means of existence; if a being is to live and want to live, it must be capable of asserting its life, of defending it against attacks. Life is a struggle, a battle; the weapons by which it is to be preserved are provided along with life itself.

Thus it is absurd to stress the weapons, the defenses, as things apart, and to put them down as proofs of a Providence. If life is necessary, the means of preserving it are also necessary. If there is war, there are also weapons; without weapons there can be no war. Consequently, if we wish to wonder at the defenses of an organ or an animal, we must wonder at its existence. All these defenses are *limited* and inseparable from the character of the organ or animal. Because they are one with the nature of the organ or animal, they are not proofs of the existence of a being who creates intentionally or arbitrarily, and because they are limited, they are not proofs of the existence of an omnipotent and omniscient God, for a God protects a being or organ against every possible danger. Every being has developed under conditions which yielded *no more* than was necessary for the production of this particular being; every being asserts itself *to the best of its powers,* preserves itself *as well as possible,* as well as its *limited* nature permits; every being has an instinct of self-preservation. And no omnipotent or omniscient God, but precisely this instinct of self-preservation, which is one with the individual nature of an organ or being, is the source of its weapons and defenses.

Finally, I must mention an argument raised by believers against the early atheists or naturalists who held that men and animals originated in nature without benefit of a God, though, it must be admitted, their account of how this came about was unsatisfactory. If nature once brought forth animals and men by spontaneous generation (there being as yet no animals or men), why does this no longer happen? I reply: because everything in nature has its time, because nature can act only when the necessary conditions are present; if things no longer happen that did happen once, there must have been conditions which are no longer present. But a time may come when nature does the same thing again, when the old varieties of animals and men pass away and new men, new animals come into being.

To ask why this no longer happens, it seems to me, is tantamount to asking why a tree bears fruit only in the fall and blossoms only in the spring, why it does not blossom and bear fruit continuously, without interruption. Or why is a certain animal in heat only at a particular time? Why are heat and gestation not continuous? Individuality, uniqueness, is the salt of the earth; individuality is the principle of generation and creation; only very individual conditions of the earth, geological upheavals such as have not taken place since, produced organic beings, at least those of them that have existed on earth in the most recent geological era. Even man, even the human mind, does not produce original works at all times; no!—a single period in the life of a man is always the most favorable, the most fruitful; there are events, moments, conditions, which will never occur again, which will never be repeated, not at least in their pristine freshness; and only in such moments does a man create original works; at most other times he merely repeats himself, mechanically reproduces his original creations.

With this observation I conclude my remarks on nature. I have thereby completed the first half of my task, which was to prove that man must look for his source not in heaven but on earth, not in God, but in nature; that his life and thinking begin with nature; that nature is not the work of a being distinct from it, but, as the philosophers say, the cause of itself; that it is not a creature, not created and certainly not created from nothing, but an independent entity which can be understood only in terms of itself and derived only from itself; that the origin of organic beings, the origin of the earth, and even of the sun if we conceive of it as having come into being, was never anything but a natural process; that in trying to visualize and understand this origin, we must not take man, the artist, the artisan, the thinker, who builds the world out of his thoughts, as our starting point, but nature—just as the ancient peoples, whose sound natural instinct led them, at least in their religious and philosophical cosmogonies, to take the reproductive process as the model and prototype of world creation; that, just as plants spring from seeds, animals from animals, man from man, so everything in nature originated in a natural being, related to it in substance or essence; that nature cannot be derived from spirit, cannot be explained on the basis of a God, because all those attributes of God that are not patently human are derived and abstracted from nature alone.

But obvious as it may seem that sensuous, bodily nature cannot be derived from a spiritual, that is, abstract being, still, so it is argued, there is something in us that makes such a derivation credible, that makes it appear natural or even necessary, an element in our make-up that refuses to regard sensuous, bodily nature as the first, primordial being and gives rise to the belief, the idea, that the world and nature are a product of the spirit, that they even were created *ex nihilo*. But I have already disposed of this argument and explained it by showing that man first abstracts the universal from the sensuous and then proceeds to posit the former as the ground of the latter. Consequently it is the human faculty of abstraction and the related imagination (for it is only thanks to his imagination that man hypostatizes abstract, universal concepts and comes to conceive of them as entities, as Ideas) that lead him to look outside the sensuous world and to derive it from a nonsensuous, abstract being. But it is absurd to transform a subjective human necessity of this kind into an objective necessity; it is absurd to suppose that because man rises from the sensuous to the suprasensory, to abstract, universal ideas, that because he then descends from the universal and abstract to the concrete and derives the latter from the former—it is absurd to suppose therefore that the abstract is really the source of the concrete.

The absurdity of this procedure is made patent by the fact that those who wish to make the bodily and material originate in the spirit are inevitably driven to take refuge in the hollow, extravagant conception of a *creatio ex nihilo*. When I say: The world was created from nothing, I am saying nothing at all; this *nihil* is a mere evasion, a means of side-stepping the question: Where did the spirit get the nonspiritual, material, corporeal substances of which the world consists? Though it was once an article of faith as sacrosanct as the existence of God, this *nihil* is merely one of the innumerable theological or clerical skulduggeries that have benighted mankind for centuries. And we are merely begging the question if instead of saying: God created the world from nothing, we say with Jakob Böhme and Hegel: He created it *out of Himself*, out of spiritual matter. This, as I have already shown, does not get me anywhere at all, for how does real matter issue from spiritual matter, from God? Whatever theological and speculative stratagems may be designed to derive the world from a God, this much is certain: what makes the world world, what makes body body and matter matter, is something that cannot be theologically or philosophically deduced from anything else; it cannot be derived, but simply is, and can be understood only in terms of itself.

Having completed the first part of my task, I now proceed to the second and last part, which is to prove that the God differentiated from nature is nothing other than man's own essence, just as in the first part I set out to demonstrate that the God differentiated from man was nothing other than nature, or the essence of nature. In other words: in the first part I aimed to prove that the essence of nature religion is nature, that in nature and nature religion nothing else is expressed or revealed than nature; now it is up to me to prove that in spiritual religion nothing else is expressed or revealed than the essence of the human mind or spirit. Early in the present series of lectures I stated my intention to disregard secondary distinctions between religions and to concentrate on the central distinction between nature religion and human or spiritual religion, between paganism and Christianity. Accordingly I now pass from the essence of nature religion or paganism to the essence of Christianity.

But before going into the subject itself, I must briefly indicate the transitional stages between the two types of religion and the factors which draw man away from nature and guide him back to himself, which lead man to seek his salvation not outside but within himself. In so doing, I shall have to deal with certain elements which are vital to the understanding of religion and common to all religion, to nature religion as well as spiritual religion, but which I can treat fully only now. The order I follow in my exposition is that followed by the evolution of human language and thought. The transition from nature religion to true theism or monotheism is dealt with in paragraphs 26–41 of *The Essence of Religion.*

Nature is the first concern of religion, but where natural objects are worshiped, they are not natural phenomena as they are for us, but anthropomorphic or, rather, human beings. In nature religion, man worships the sun because he sees that everything is dependent on it, that no plant, no animal, no man can exist without it; nevertheless, he would not worship the sun if he did not conceive of it as a being which like man moves of its own volition, if he did not conceive of the sun's gifts as voluntary gifts, which it bestows on the earth out of sheer benevolence. If man had seen nature as what it is, if he had seen it with our eyes, there would have been no motive for religious worship. The feeling that drives a man to worship an object presupposes the belief that this object is not insensible to worship, that it has feeling, that it has a heart and, what is more, a human heart which takes an interest in human affairs. In the Persian Wars the Greeks entreated the winds with sacrifices, but only because they regarded them as their allies against the Persians. The Athenians especially revered Boreas, the North Wind, and prayed for his help, but they also, as Herodotus tells us, regarded him as a friendly, kindred being, for the daughter of their King Erechtheus was his wife.

But what is it that transforms a natural phenomenon into a human being? The imagination. It is the imagination that makes an object appear to us differently from what it really is; it is man's imagination that bathed nature in the enchanting, dazzling light for which human language has coined the term divinity, godhead, god. In short, it is the imagination that creates man's gods. I have already said that originally the word god or godhead was not a proper name but a class name, that it orginally expressed not a subject but only a predicate, not a being but a qualification which applies, or is applied to, every object which in the light of man's imagination appears to him as a divine being; which makes, as it were, a divine impression upon man. Thus any object can become a god, or what amounts to the same thing, an object of religious worship. I say "amounts to the same thing," because religous worship is the only touchstone of divinity: a god is what is worshiped. But an object is worshiped only if, and insofar as, it is seized upon by the imagination.

Twentieth Lecture

All manner of objects not only can but actually have been worshiped by man as gods—or, what amounts to the same thing, as objects of religion. This occurs at the stage of so-called fetishism, in which man indiscriminately makes gods of all possible objects and things, artificial or natural, natural or man-made. The Negroes of Sierra Leone, for example, choose horns, crab claws, nails, pebbles, snail shells, bird's heads, and roots as their gods; they carry them in a bag suspended from their necks and decorated with glass beads and other ornaments.* "The Tahitians worshiped the flags and pennants of the European ships, the Malagasy looked upon mathematical instruments as gods, the Ostyaks made a god of a bear-shaped Nuremberg clock."† But what impels men to make gods of snail shells, crab claws, flags, and pennants? Their imagination, whose power is proportional to their ignorance. Savages do not know what a clock, a flag, a mathematical instrument is; they consequently imagine that these things are something other than they really are, and make them into fantastic beings, fetishes, gods. The theoretical cause or source of religion and of its object, God, is therefore the imagination.

Christians designate the theoretical religious faculty by the word *faith* or *belief*. To their mind, belief is synonymous with religion, unbelief with irreligion or godlessness. But on closer scrutiny the words mean nothing other than imagination. Faith, says Luther, the foremost authority on the matter, the greatest German hero

* Bastholm, *op. cit.*
† Meiners, *op. cit.*

of faith, the German St. Paul as he has been called—"Faith," he says in his commentary on Genesis, "is in truth *all-powerful* . . . to the believer all things are possible. For faith brings into being what is not, and makes possible things that are impossible." But this omnipotence of faith is simply the omnipotence of the imagination. The symbols of Christian faith, at least according to Lutheran doctrine, are baptism and Communion. The substance, the matter, of baptism is water, the matter of Communion is bread and wine, but for faith the natural water of baptism is a spiritual water, as Luther calls it, and the bread and wine of Communion are the Lord's flesh and blood. In other words, it is the imagination that transforms wine into blood and bread into flesh. Faith believes in miracles, faith and belief in miracles are one; faith is not bound by the laws of nature; it is free and unrestricted; it believes whatever it pleases. "Is any thing too hard for the Lord?" But this power of faith or God, unhampered by the laws of nature, is precisely the power of the imagination, to which nothing is impossible.

Faith sees the invisible; faith is not of "things which are seen," says the Bible, but of "things not seen." And the imagination, as well, is not of things which are seen but of things which are not seen. The imagination concerns itself exclusively with things and beings which are no longer or not yet, or which at least are not present. "Faith," says Luther in the above-mentioned commentary, "grasps at a thing that is still pure nothingness and waits for it to become everything." And in another passage, quoted in my book on Luther: "In truth, faith has only to do with the future, not with the present."* That is why a believer does not lose heart if the present is dark; he hopes for a better future. The main field of the imagination is indeed the future. We are less interested, less concerned with the past, though it too occupies the imagination; for it is far behind us, it is unchangeable, it is over and done with. Why worry about the past?

But it is a very different matter with the future, which still lies ahead of us. And in this respect Luther is perfectly right in deploring men's lack of faith in the future, in finding fault with those

* *The Essence of Faith According to Luther,* Melvin Cherno, trans. (New York: Harper & Row, 1967).

who despair because they see no hope at the present moment; for today is not the Day of Judgment, the present is not the end of history. Dismal as the present outlook may be, everything can change, tomorrow may present an entirely different picture. This is especially true in social and political affairs, in matters that concern mankind as a whole; for there is no doubt that an individual can find himself in a situation so dark that all hope of improvement or even of change is lost and "despair becomes a duty."

God, say the Christians, is not an object of sense perception; He cannot be seen or felt. But no more, at least according to orthodox Christians, is He an object of reason; for reason is grounded in sense perception; the existence of God cannot be demonstrated, it can only be believed. In other words, God does not exist in sense perception or in reason but only in faith, that is, imagination. Luther writes in one of his sermons: "I have often said that the way in which God appears to a man depends on that man's frame of mind; *as you think and believe, so you have Him.* If in your heart you paint Him merciful or angry, sweet or sour, that is how you will have Him. If you think He is angry at you and wants none of you, that is how He will treat you. But if you can say: I know that He wants to be my merciful father, and so on, that is how you will have Him." And in one of Luther's sermons on Genesis, "As we feel Him, so He is to us. If you think He is angry and ill-disposed, He is ill-disposed." Or in the commentary on the Second Epistle of Peter, "If you regard Him as a God, He will behave as a God toward you." Which means: God is as I believe Him to be, as I imagine Him; the nature of God depends on the nature of my imagination. But what is true of God's nature is also true of His existence. If I believe that God is, then He is, at least for me. In short, a God is an imaginary being, a product of fantasy; and because fantasy is the essential form or organ of poetry, it may also be said that religion is poetry, that a God is a poetic being.

If religion is taken as poetry, may it not be inferred that to abolish religion, to break it down into its basic components, is to do away with poetry and all art? Such an inference has indeed been drawn from my elucidation of the essence of religion. My adversaries throw up their hands in horror at the hideous desolation to which my doctrine would reduce human life, since in their opinion it would destroy poetry along with religion and so deprive mankind of all poetic drive. But I should have to be out of my mind to deny religion in the sense my adversaries suppose. I do not deny religion, I do not deny the subjective, human foundations of religion, namely, feeling and imagination and man's impulse to objectify and personify his inner life, an impulse which lies in the very nature of speech and emotion; I do not deny man's need to lend nature a human aspect, provided that his view of it is compatible with its character as known to us through science, I do not deny his need to contemplate nature in poetic, philosophical, and religious terms. I merely deny the object of religion, or rather of religion as it has been up to now; I should merely like man to stop setting his heart on things which are no longer in keeping with his nature and needs, and which he therefore can believe and worship only by coming into conflict with himself.

True, there are many people for whom poetry and imagination attach only to the objects of traditional religion, and who, if deprived of these objects, will lose all imagination. But many are not all; a necessity for many is not an absolute necessity, and what is necessary now will not be necessary forever. Do not human life, history, nature provide sufficient material for poetry? Will painting be without subject matter if it ceases to concern itself with the objects of Christian religion? Far from annulling art, poetry, imagination, I deny religion only insofar as it is *not* poetry, but common prose. And this brings us to an essential limitation of the statement that religion is poetry. In a sense it is poetry, but with one important difference: poetry and art in general do not represent their creations as anything but what they are, namely products of art, whereas religion represents its imaginary beings as *real* beings. An artist does not expect me to regard a landscape painting as a real landscape, a portrait of a man as the man himself, but religion expects me to take an image for a real being. From a purely artistic point of view, I regard the ancients' statues of gods as mere works of art; but pagan believers looked upon these works of art, these statues, as real, living beings and treated them as they would have treated real beings whom they honored and loved. They chained such statues of gods to prevent them from running away, they dressed them and decorated them, they served them choice food and drink; they even laid them down on soft dining couches—the male deities, that is, for goddesses were no more permitted to recline at table than were the Roman ladies of the time; they bathed and anointed them, provided them with all the accessories of human vanity—mirrors, towels, massage brushes, footmen, and lady's maids—paid their respects to them in the morning as to eminent mortals, organized plays and other entertainment for their pleasure. Seneca, quoted by Augustine, even tells of a seedy old comedian who put on an act every day in the Capitol, as though to show that even if human audiences wanted none of him he could still amuse the gods. Precisely because the statues of gods were regarded as gods, sculptors and painters were called *theopoioi,* godmakers, and sculpture was known as the art of making gods.[17]

What we find even among the most cultivated peoples of antiquity is still to be met with today among primitive peoples, except that their gods and idols are not masterpieces of human art like those of the Greeks and Romans. The idols of the Ostyaks,* for example, are wooden dolls. "They provide these idols with snuff and also with a little bast, in the belief that after taking snuff the idol would stuff his nose with bast in the Ostyak manner. When Russians passing by in the night steal the tobacco, the Ostyaks are amazed in the morning that the idol can have taken so much snuff."† And not only pagans, but Christians as well, have been and still are image worshipers; they too looked upon, and in part still look upon, religious pictures or statues as the real beings they represent. Learned Christians, it is true, distinguished the image from the subject it represented, saying that they worshiped the subject through the image and not the image itself; but the common people ignored such subtle distinctions. In the Greek Church Christians were at sword's point for two centuries on the question of image worship, which finally triumphed. Among Christians, our eastern neighbors, the Russians, are especially distinguished for their image worship.

Every Russian . . . ordinarily has a copper image of St. Nicholas or some other saint in his pocket. He takes it with him wherever he goes.

* Most of them, however, are Christians today.

† Bastholm, *op. cit.*

One sometimes sees a soldier or peasant take his copper god out of his pocket, spit on it, clean and polish it with his hand, sit down in front of it, cross himself a thousand times, fling himself on the ground with great sighs, and cry out forty times: *Gospodi pomiluy,* that is, God have mercy on me. Then he puts his god back in his pocket and goes his way. Every Russian also has several icons in his house, in front of which he places candles. Before going to bed with his wife, a man covers the icons with a cloth. Russian prostitutes are also full of reverence for the saints. When they receive visitors, the first thing they do is to cover their icons and put out the candles.*

This example, be it said in passing, shows how easily religion—commonly regarded as the sole support of morality, which is thought to be quite incapable of standing on its own feet—composes with immorality. A religious person need only cover the image of his god; or if he is less crude than a Russian prostitute or peasant, he need only hang the cloak of Christian love, of divine grace, over God's punitive justice and proceed to do anything he pleases.

I have cited these examples of image worship only by way of indicating the difference between art and religion. Both create images, a poet in words, a painter in colors, a sculptor in wood, stone, or metal. But unless religion enters in, an artist merely expects his images to be faithful and beautiful; he does not claim that a semblance of reality is reality itself. Religion, on the other hand, deceives people, or rather people deceive themselves in religion; for it does claim that the semblance of reality is reality, that an image is a living being. But this being lives only in the imagination; in reality the image is only an image—a being who, precisely because he is an image, is called a divine being. For a god as such is an imagined, unreal, fantastic being, which however *is supposed to be* a real being. Thus religion does not, like art, demand that its images be faithful representations of their model and beautiful—on the contrary, the truly religious images are the ugliest and most monstrous. As long as art serves religion and is not its own master, it produces works, as the history of Greek and Christian art demonstrates, that can make no claim to being works of art.

What religion demands of images is that they be *useful* to man,

* Stäudlin, *Magazin für Religionsgeschichte.*

that they help him in distress; and for this reason it endows its images with life—for only living beings can help—and, specifically, human life, not only with the appearance, the outer form of life as the artist does, but also with actual life, with human feeling, human needs and passions, and even offers them food and drink. Absurd as it is that the Ostyak should expect help from an idol who owes everything he is to the Ostyak's own good nature, imagination, and ignorance, or for man in general to expect help from pictures and statues, even such nonsense has an underlying meaning. It is a way of saying that man can expect help only from men, that a god who is supposed to help man must have human feelings and hence human needs, for otherwise he would have no feeling for human affliction. One who has never experienced hunger will not help a hungry man. But one who has the power to help also has the power to injure. Consequently religion, unlike art, regards the images it makes as objects of the feeling of dependency, as beings who have the power to help and to harm, as beings to whom man therefore brings his devotions and sacrifices, before whom he kneels, and whom he worships in order to gain their favor.

But I have not cited these examples of image worship in order to show the difference between art and religion in connection with the so-called idolatrous religions alone; I have cited them because they concretely illustrate the nature of all religion, hence also of the Christian religion. Man must always start from the concrete, from what is simplest, clearest, most undeniable, namely the sensuous object, and only then proceed to the more complicated, to abstractions that the eye cannot see. The difference between pagan and Christian religion is merely that the images of the Christian religion, at least where it upholds its distinction from paganism, where it does not relapse into paganism, are not images of stone, metal, wood or color, but *spiritual* images. The Christian religion is not based on the *senses,* but as I remarked a number of times in the first lectures, on the word—the word of God, as the older, truly believing Christians called the Bible, which they regard as God's special revelation and oppose to nature; it is not, like the religion of the pagans—who attributed existence, the creation of the world, to the power of physical love and fertility—based on the power of sensuous nature, but on the power of the word. God said: "Let there be light, and there was light"; let there be a world, and there was a world. "Thus the word of God," says Luther, "is a precious and costly gift, which God holds in such high esteem that He looks even upon heaven and earth, the sun, the moon and the stars, as nothing compared to these words, for through the word have all creatures been created." "*Heaven and earth shall pass away,* but my words *shall not pass away.*"

Or since the word (subjective for man) is communicated by the ear, we may say, as I have already remarked in passing, that the Christian religion was also based on sense, but only on the sense of hearing. "Take away the word," says Calvin in his *Institutes of the Christian Religion,* "and no faith is left." And "although man should earnestly turn his eyes to the contemplation of God's works [i. e., nature], he must above all direct his *ears* toward the Word, for the image of God impressed on the glorious form of the world is not effective enough." Thus Calvin fulminated against all corporeal images of God because His majesty cannot be apprehended by the eye, and condemned the doctrine formulated by the second Council of Nicaea to the effect that "God is known not only by the hearing of the Word, but also by the contemplation of images."

In his book on the uncertainty and vanity of the sciences, Cornelius Agrippa von Nettesheim wrote: "We [Christians] must not learn from the forbidden book of images, but from the book of God, which is the book of the Holy Scriptures. Hence anyone who wishes to know God should not look for Him in the images of the painters and sculptors, but, as St. John says, in Scripture, for it bears witness to Him. And those who cannot read should listen to the word of Scripture, for their faith, as St. Paul says, comes from hearing. And Christ says, in the Gospel of St. John: *'My sheep hear my voice.'* " "The word of God," says Luther in his commentary on the Eighteenth Psalm, "is such a word that unless we seal all our senses and apprehend it with our hearing alone, and lend it belief, we cannot grasp it."

Thus the Christian religion rejects all the senses but hearing and ignores them in its worship. A pagan god, by contrast, is apprehended also by the other, even by the lower senses; a pagan god who lives, and reveals himself to man, in images of wood, stone, and color can even be grasped with the hands, but for the same reason he can also be shattered and destroyed—the pagans themselves often smashed their gods and threw them down into the mud in fury, because, having obtained no help from them, they thought the gods had deceived them. In short, the pagan god is a physical thing, exposed to all the perils of nature and the human world. The Church Fathers ridiculed the heathen for worshiping beings or things for which the very swallows felt so little respect that they soiled them with their droppings.

The Christian God, on the other hand, is not, like the stone or wooden gods of the heathen, a fragile destructible being, restricted to one place, shut up, or capable of being shut up, in a temple; for He is mere Word and Mind. I cannot smash the word, I cannot shut it up in a temple, see it with my eyes, or grasp it with my hands; the word is an incorporeal, spiritual being. The word is a universal; the word tree signifies and embraces all trees, birches, beeches, pines, oaks, without distinction, without limitation; but the bodily, sensuous thing that the pagan worships, this particular tree, this stone statue, is an individual thing; it is limited, it is only in this place, not in other places. The Christian God is therefore a universal, omnipresent, unlimited, infinite being; but all these attributes apply equally to the word. In short, the essence of the Christian, spiritual God, of the being who is not apprehended by the senses, who reveals His true essence not in nature or in art but in Holy Scripture, represents nothing but the essence of the word.

In other words: the differences between the Christian God and the pagan god reduce themselves to the differences between the word and the sensuous matter of which the pagan god consists. Strictly speaking, therefore, no art stems from the Christian or Jewish God—for all art is sensuous—in any case not painting or sculpture, but at most poetry, the art that expresses itself in words alone. Our lawgiver, wrote the learned Jew Josephus, forbade us to make images, because he held the art of making images to be beneficial neither to God nor to man. But where man's God may not and cannot be represented sensuously, in images, where sensibility is excluded from what is venerable, divine, supreme, art cannot attain its supreme possibilities, it cannot thrive, or can thrive only in violation of the religious principle. And yet the Christian God is also a product of the imagination; like the pagan god, He is an image, with the sole difference that He, like the word, is a spiritual, all-embracing image. A word or name is a product of the imagination—operating of course with intelligence and on the basis of sense impressions; it is the image of an object. In speech man imitates nature; the sound made by an object is consequently the first thing that man seizes upon in nature; it becomes the characteristic or sign by which he represents and names the object. But that does not concern us here. Christianity, then, is concerned with the word as an expression, an image, not of outward things, but of the inner life.

Thus the Christian God reveals and expresses Himself not in images of stone or wood, and not directly in nature, but only in the word; He is not a bodily, sensuous God, but a spiritual God, a God of the mind. Moreover, the word too is an image. It follows that the Christian God, and even the God of the rationalists, is an image of the imagination and that, if image worship is idolatry, Christian worship of the spiritual God is also idolatry. The Christians accused the pagans, the Protestants accused the Catholics, and the rationalists today accuse orthodox Protestants of idolatry, in each case for the same reason, for worshiping a man, an image of God (for man is made in God's image) as God, instead of worshiping the original, God himself. But I go still further and say: rationalism itself, in fact every religion that takes an unreal being, abstracted and differentiated from real nature or real man, as its supreme being and worships him, is an image cult and consequently idolatry, since, as we have seen, all worship of images is idolatry. For God did not, as the Bible says, make man in His image; on the contrary man, as I have shown in *The Essence of Christianity,* made God in his image.

And even the rationalist, the devotee of the so-called religion of thought and reason, creates the God he worships in his own image; the living prototype, the original of the rationalist god, is rationalist man. Every God is a *creature* of the imagination, an image, and specifically *an image of man,* but He is an image which man places outside himself and conceives of as an independent being.[18] For man does not invent gods for the pleasure of producing poetry;

his religious poetry or fantasy is not disinterested, nor is it without law and measure; its law and measure is man. A man's imagination is molded by his nature; a gloomy, fearful man imagines terrifying beings, terrible gods; a serene, happy man imagines serene, friendly gods. Men's gods, the creatures of their imaginations, are as diverse as are men themselves; or, *ex post facto,* we can reverse the order and say that men are as diverse as their gods.

Twenty-first Lecture

Before I go on with the topic broached in the last lecture, I must counter a possible misunderstanding, which I did not deal with yesterday for fear of breaking the line of my argument. I have said that the objects of Christian faith, like the pagan gods, are products of the imagination. From this it might be inferred, and some people actually have inferred, that Biblical history, as related both in the Old and the New Testament, is pure invention. But such an inference is unjustified, for I only maintain that the objects of religion, *as* objects of religion, are imaginations; I have not denied the reality of these same objects *as such.* We say that the sun as represented in pagan religion, namely, as a personal, divine being, a sun-god, is an imaginary being; but this does not imply that the sun itself is imaginary. Similarly, when we say that Moses, as represented in the religious history of the Jews, or Jesus as represented in the religion and religious history of the Christians, is a product of the imagination, this does not imply that Moses and Jesus were not, as such, historical individuals. For between an historical person and a religious person there is the same difference as between a natural object *as such* and the same object as represented by religion.

The imagination creates nothing out of itself—if it did, we should have to believe in a *creatio ex nihilo;* the fire of the imagination feeds on natural and historical materials. The imagination no more produces religious or poetic figures without material than oxygen without fuel produces the fire that delights the eye.[19] But an historical person *as* object of religion is no longer an historical person; he is a person transformed by the imagination. Consequently I do not deny that Jesus lived, that he was an historical person to whom the Christian religion owes its origin; I do not deny that he suffered for his teachings. But I do deny that Jesus was a Christ, a God or son of God, a wonder-worker, born of a virgin, that he healed the sick by a mere word, quelled storms by a mere command, awakened dead men who had begun to rot, and that he himself was raised from the dead; in short, I deny that he was *as* the Bible represents him; for in the Bible Jesus is a subject not of straightforward historical narrative, but of religion, hence no longer an historical but a religious person, that is, a creature transformed by the imagination. And any attempt to sift the historical truth from the additions, distortions, and exaggerations of the imagination is absurd, or at all events, fruitless. We lack the historical tools. The Christ who has come down to us in the Bible—and we know of no other—is and remains a product of the human imagination.

At first, however, the imagination which makes men's gods worked only with nature; as I showed in the first lectures, those phenomena of nature on which man feels and knows himself to be most dependent are also those that make the greatest impression on his imagination. What is life without water, fire, earth, sun, moon? And what a powerful impression these objects make on man's theoretical faculty, his imagination! And the eye with which man first contemplates nature is not the intelligence that makes experiments and observations, but solely the imagination, the poetic faculty. But what does the imagination do? It fashions everything in man's image; it transforms nature into an image of man. "Wherever there is motion," Benjamin Constant says aptly in his book on religion, "the savage sees life; a rolling stone seems to him either to be fleeing or pursuing; a raging torrent flings itself upon him; some offended spirit lives in the frothing waterfall; the howling wind is an expression of suffering or menace; an echo in the mountains prophesies or gives answer, and when a European shows the savage a magnetic needle, he regards it as a being ravished from its country, which turns in fear and longing toward the objects of its desire."

Thus man's only way of deifying nature is to humanize it; he deifies himself by deifying nature. Nature merely provides the raw material for the gods; but the soul which transforms this raw material into a manlike and hence divine being is the imagination. The only difference between paganism and Christianity, polytheism and monotheism, is that the polytheist makes gods of the various forms and bodies in nature, and for this very reason, though unconsciously, takes sensuous, real, individual man as the model and standard according to which his imagination humanizes and deifies the things of nature. Just as man is a *bodily individual,* so the polytheist's gods are bodily individuals; that is why he has innumerable gods; he has as many gods as he observes different kinds of things in nature. And he goes still further: he even deifies specific differences. This deification, this religious scholasticism, to be sure, attaches chiefly to the things that have the greatest reality for human egoism; for it is in such objects that man observes every detail, noting the most trifling differences and then, through his imagination, deifying them. Of this the Romans provide a priceless example. For every stage in the growth of the plants most useful to man, the grain-producing plants, for example, they had special deities, one for germinating, one for sprouting, one for the stage at which the stalk forms its first knot, in short, for every perceptible stage and distinction. They also had any number of gods connected with the growth of children—Natio, goddess of birth, Educa, goddess of children's eating and Potina of their drinking, a god Vagitanus for screaming and weeping children, a goddess Cunina for infants in the cradle, and another, Rumia for suckling babes.

A monotheist, however, does not start from the real, sensuous human being, who is a living individual, but from the inside, from man's mind or spirit, which manifests itself through the word, which produces effects by the mere word, whose mere word has the power to create. The man who is lord over others, whom they obey, governs millions by his mere word; he need only command, and through his underlings his will is done. Thus the monotheist starts from the mind and will of man, and in particular the mind and will of the despot, which act through the mere word; this is the model from which his imagination works. The polytheist deifies the human mind and imagination indirectly—for it is through the imagination alone that the things of nature become gods for him—the monotheist does so directly.

Accordingly—and this is what we set out to prove—the monotheistic or Christian God is just as much a product of the human imagination, just as much an image of man as the polytheistic god, except that the man according to whom the Christian thinks and makes his God is not a tangible, perceptible being that can be represented within the limits of a statue or picture. It is not possible to make an image of the Christian and Jewish God; but who can make a corporeal image of the mind, the spirit, the will, the word? A further difference between monotheism and polytheism is that polytheism has as its starting point and foundation sense perception, which shows us the world in all its multiplicity, while monotheism starts from the coherence, the unity of the world, from a world which man, by his thought and imagination, has shaped into a unified whole. There is only one world, says St. Ambrose, and consequently only one God. The many gods are creatures of the imagination working directly with sense perception; the One God is a creature of imagination abstracted from sense perception, of the faculty of abstraction.

The more man is dominated by his imagination, the more sensuous is his god, and this also applies to the One God; the more familiar man becomes with abstract concepts, the less sensuous, the more abstract, the more sophisticated becomes his God. The difference between the Christian God of the rationalists, of those whose faith is tempered by thought, and the Christian God of the older total believers, is merely that the rationalists' God is more sophisticated, more abstract, and less sensuous than the God of the mystics or orthodox believers, that the rationalists' faculty of abstraction restricts their imagination, whereas the old believer's imagination is stronger than his powers of conceptual thinking. In other words: the rationalists's faith is determined, or rather limited, by reason—for reason is the name we ordinarily give to the faculty of forming abstract concepts—whereas the orthodox believer's reason is dominated by his faith. The orthodox God *can do anything* and actually does things that conflict with reason; he can do everything that seems possible to the unrestricted imagination of faith—and to the imagination nothing is impossible. The orthodox God, in other words, accomplishes what the believer imagines; He is only the embodied, hypostatized, unrestricted imagination of the total believer. The rationalist God, on the other hand, can do nothing and does nothing that conflicts with the rationalist's reason, or rather with his faith and imagination restricted by rationalist reason.

Nevertheless, rationalism too is image worship and idolatry—if the two may be equated; for just as the true, sensuous idolater takes an image, in his case a sensuous image, for God, for a real being, so the rationalist also takes an image, namely, his God, the creature of his faith, imagination, and reason, for a *real* being existing outside of man. He flies into a rage and relapses into the fanaticism of the old faith if anyone contests the existence of a God or, what amounts to the same thing, of *his* God—for everyone regards only his own God as God—or if anyone tries to prove that his God is only a subjective, that is, imagined, represented, being, a product of thought, a reflection of his own rationalistic thinking, which limits imagination by the faculty of abstraction, and faith by reason. But enough for the present about the difference between rationalism and orthodox belief. We shall have more to say of it later on.

At this point I must make a brief digression. In my comparison between paganism and Christianity, polytheism and monotheism, I made no distinction between natural and artificial objects of worship in pagan religion. I lumped the two together, saying: the pagan god is this natural phenomenon, this statue, this tree. I said that the imagination transforms natural objects, the sun, moon, and stars, plants, fire, and water into human, personal beings, personifying them in different ways according to their manifestations and the impressions they make upon man. The sky, for example, fertilizes the earth with rain, lights and warms it by means of the sun. Accordingly, the human imagination saw the earth as a woman, acted upon and conceiving, and the sky as a man, active and fecundating. And religious art has no other aim than to provide sensuous, visual representations of natural phenomena or their causes as seen by the religious imagination; it has no other aim than to embody religious imaginings. Man wishes to see as an outward reality the inward imagining that he believes. Through art—religious art, that is—man tries to confer existence on something that has *no* existence; religious art is a self-deception on the part of man.

Through it he wishes to assure himself that what exists only in our heads—regardless of all the elaborate proofs with which theist philosophers try to demonstrate that a God exists—has real existence outside us.

For what is it exactly that this art aims to bring into existence? Is it the sun, is it the earth, the sky, the air as the cause of thunder and lightning? No, these already exist, and what interest would man—religious man, that is—have in representing the sun as it appears to our senses? None. Religious art aims to represent not the sun, but the sun-god, not the sky but the sky-god; it sets out to represent only something that the imagination injects into the sensuous object, something that consequently *has no sensuous existence;* its sole aim is to represent, to lend sensuous existence to the sky or the sun insofar as it is conceived of as a personal being, in other words, to represent the imagination, to represent the sun not as a sensuous object but as an object of the imagination. The principal element in the artistic representation of a god is his person, his anthropomorphic character as created by the imagination; nature is secondary. Although the god is originally a mere personification of the natural object, the object serves in religious art only as a means of identifying the god, and is appended to the god as an attribute. Thus, though in Greek religion as in all nature religions, the sky and thunder god was originally one with the thunder and lightning, in Greek religious art Zeus is shown holding his royal scepter or a flaming thunderbolt. Nature, the original essence of the thunder-god, is reduced to a mere attribute of his person. Nevertheless, the sky as a natural being and the sky-god represented in a work of art are alike or identical in one respect: both are sensuous, corporeal beings—the sky-god, to be sure, only in the imagination—so that, at least in comparison with a god who is not a sensuous being, the difference between art object and natural object becomes insignificant. And that is why it seemed unnecessary to stress this distinction. But back to our subject.

I have maintained that the imagination is the principal organ of religion, that a god is an imaginary being, an image, and specifically an image of man, and that natural objects as well, when viewed religiously, become manlike beings, hence images of man, and that the spiritual God of the Christians is also an image of man, created by the human imagination and projected outside of man as a real, independent being; that accordingly the objects of religion—considered, it goes without saying, *as* objects of religion—have no existence outside the imagination. Believers, and especially theologians, have declaimed and vituperated against this contention: how is it possible, they say, that something that has provided millions with so much consolation, for which millions have laid down their lives, can be mere imagination? But that is no proof at all of the reality and truth of such objects. The pagans also regarded their gods as real beings, they offered up hetacombs of bulls to them, they sacrificed human lives to them, their own or those of other men; but this does not prevent Christians from recognizing today that those gods were imaginary beings whom the pagans themselves had made. What the present regards as reality, the future recognizes to be imagination. Some day it will be universally recognized that the objects of Christian religion, like the pagan gods, were mere imagination. It is only man's egoism that leads him to look upon his own God as the true God, and upon the gods of other peoples as products of the imagination. Where sense perception and reason provide no counterweight to the imagination, man invariably accepts its products as realities.

A few examples from the life of so-called savages may serve to illustrate the power of the imagination over man. "The savages of America and Siberia undertake no campaign, barter no goods, conclude no treaty, unless they have been encouraged to do so by *dreams*. In reliance on a dream, they give up their most precious possession, something they would not hesitate to defend with their lives. A Kamchadal woman gives herself without resistance to a man who tells her he has slept with her in a dream. After dreaming that his arm had been cut off, an Iroquois cut his arm off; another dreamt he had killed his friend, and on waking killed him."* Can the power of the imagination be carried any further than this, that the loss of an arm in a dream should impel a man to lose it in reality, that the killing of a friend, imagined in a dream, should lead a man to kill him in reality, that a man should sacrifice his body, his arm, and even his friend to a mere dream?[20]

Like the savages of today, the ancient peoples looked upon

* Benjamin Constant, *op. cit.*

dream figures as divine beings, revelations, manifestations of God. In part, even Christians look upon dreams as divine messages. But the medium in which a God appears is nothing other than that God's own essence. Consequently, the essence of a God who reveals himself in a dream is nothing other than dream. But what is a dream? It is the imagination unchecked by the laws of reason and sense perception. True, Christians let themselves be persecuted for the objects of their faith and sacrificed their blood and possessions to them; but does it follow that these objects were true and real? Not at all; no more than dreams are realities because an Iroquois chops his arm off for their sake, or because a man who lets himself be governed by dreams sacrifices the truth of sense perception to them.

I have mentioned dreams only as striking examples of the religious power of the imagination over men. But I have also maintained that the religious imagination is not the free imagination of the artist, but has a practical egoistic purpose, or in other words, that the religious imagination is rooted in the feeling of dependency and attaches chiefly to objects that arouse it. But man's feeling of dependency is not aroused only by particular objects. Just as the heart is always in motion and never ceases to beat and throb, so the feeling of dependency never rests in man, especially in a man dominated by his imagination; for at every step he takes, some harm may befall him, every object, however trifling, threatens injury and even death. This feeling of anxiety, of uncertainty, this fear of harm that always accompanies man, is the root of the religious imagination; and since religious man ascribes every evil he encounters to wicked beings or spirits, the fear of ghosts and spooks is, at least in uneducated persons and peoples, the essence of the religious imagination. Man's imagination transforms what he fears, what frightens him, into an evil being, or conversely, he fears what his imagination represents as an evil being, and tries to win its favor or neutralize it by religious means.

Among the Chiquitos of Paraguay, for example, Charlevoix tells us in his history of Paraguay, he "found no clear indication of religion, but they feared demons, who, as they said, appeared to them in the most hideous forms. They began their feasts and banquets with an appeal to the demons *not to disturb their re-*

joicing." The Tahitians believed that if a man stubbed his toe on a stone and it hurt, this was the work of an *eatua,* i. e., god. Indeed, as we read in Cook's third and last voyage, "they can, *in their religious system,* be said literally to *walk always on enchanted ground.*" The Ashantis of Africa believe that when they stumble over a stone at night, an evil spirit has hidden in the stone in order to harm them.* Thus the imagination transforms a stone over which a man absentmindedly stumbles into a spirit or god. But how easy it is for a man to stumble! The same misfortune can overtake him at every step. And so, men dominated by feeling and imagination always think that evil spirits are hovering around them. When a North American Indian has a toothache or headache, the people around him say: "The gods are displeased and want to be propitiated."† Fear of ghosts and spirits is especially prevalent among the peoples of northern Asia, the devotees of so-called shamanism, a religion that consists in nothing other than "fear of spirits and the conjuring of spirits"; they live in a continuous battle "with the hostile spirits who wander around in the desert and over the broad snow fields."‡ But it is not true, as Stuhr says in his book, that shamanism is the only religion rooted in the belief in spirits; the same is true of the religions of all peoples. Heckewelder writes: "Great and powerful as the Indian conceives himself to be, firm and undaunted as he really is . . . the American Indian has one weak side, which sinks him down to the level of the most fearful and timid being. . . . It is incredible to what a degree the Indians' superstitious belief in witchcraft operates upon their minds; the moment that their imagination is struck with the idea that they are bewitched, they are no longer themselves; their fancy is constantly at work in creating the most horrid and distressing images."

The fear of witchcraft is simply the fear of being injured by an evil being in some supernatural, magical way. And such is the power of this superstitious imagination over the Indians that "often they actually die because of the mere imagining that an evil is

* *Ausland.* May 1849.

† (Rev.) John Heckewelder, *An Account of the History, Manners, and Customs of the Indian Nations* . . . (Philadelphia: Abraham Small, 1819).

‡ Stuhr, *Religionssystem der heidnischen Völker des Orients.*

being done them, that they are bewitched."[21] In his book on North America, Volney speaks of the North American savages in very much the same terms as Heckewelder: "The fear of evil spirits is one of their dominant and most tormenting notions; their most fearless warriors are like women and children in this respect; they are terrified by a dream, a nocturnal apparition in the woods, a harsh cry."* But among Christians we also meet with the most grotesque accounts of the evils and mortal perils which pursue man on the pathways of life, which their religious imagination represents as the works of the Devil or some other evil being or spirit hostile to man, and which are counteracted only by the efforts of a good and all-powerful God well disposed toward man.

Thus the gods are creatures of the imagination, but of an imagination fired by man's feeling of dependency, his afflictions and egoism; they are creatures not only of the imagination but also of emotion, especially the emotions of hope and fear. As I have already pointed out in connection with image worship, man demands that the gods help him if he conceives of them as good, and that they refrain from injuring him, or at least from interfering with his plans and pleasures, if he looks upon them as evil. Thus religion has its source not only in imagination and feeling, but also in desire, in man's striving and desire to put aside unpleasant feelings and to create pleasant feelings for himself, to acquire what he does not but would like to possess, or to eliminate certain evils or deficiencies. It springs from man's longing to be free from the evils he has or fears, and to obtain real or imaginary benefits. In short, it springs from the so-called *striving for happiness.*

* Constantin François de Chassebœuf, Comte de Volney, *Recherches nouvelles sur l'Amérique ancienne* (1814).

Twenty-second Lecture

MAN BELIEVES IN GODS not only because he has imagination and feeling, but also because he has the striving to be happy. He believes in the existence of happy beings, not only because he has a conception of happiness, but because he himself wishes to be happy; he believes in a perfect being because he himself wishes to be perfect; he believes in an immortal being because he himself does not wish to die. What he himself is not but would like to be, he conceives of as existing in his gods; the gods are men's desires conceived as realities, transformed into real beings. A god is man's striving for happiness, fulfilled in his imagination. For all man's imagination and feeling, he would have no gods if he had no desires. Gods are as varied as desires, and desires as varied as men. Men who desire neither wisdom nor intelligence, have no goddess of wisdom in their pantheon.

At this point it may be useful to recall a remark I made in one of the first lectures; to gain an understanding of religion, we must not account for it by any single cause, or rather, we must assign each cause its proper place. Insofar as the gods are powers (initially natural powers) which the human imagination has transformed into manlike beings, man flings himself into the dust before them; in their presence he feels his insignificance; expressions of his feeling of nullity, of his fear, veneration, amazement or admiration, they are terrible or grandiose and majestic beings who make a profound impression on him because they are endowed with all the magical powers of the imagination; but insofar as they are powers that satisfy man's desires, that give man what he wishes and needs, they are expressions of human egoism. In short, religion has essentially a practical aim and foundation; the drive that gives rise to religion, its ultimate foundation, is the striving for happiness, and if this is an egoistic drive, it follows that the ultimate foundation of religion is egoism. Anyone who denies this or fails to understand it is blind; for the history of religion confirms it at every turn, at the lowest and at the highest levels. We need only recall the passages cited from Christian, Greek, and Roman authors in an earlier lecture. Both from a practical and from a theoretical point of view, this is the most important factor; for once it is proved that God owes His existence exclusively to man's striving for happiness, but that religion satisfies this striving only in the imagination, it necessarily follows that man can seek to satisfy this striving by other than religious ways and means.

I have already attempted to prove that human egoism is the *ultimate ground* of religion. But now I wish to demonstrate more specifically that religion has human happiness as its *aim,* that man reveres and worships the gods only in order that they may fulfill his wishes and thereby make him happy. I shall therefore cite a few examples. "Ask and it shall be given to you," says the Bible . . . "For every one that asketh receiveth. . . . Or what man is there of you, whom, if his son ask bread, will he give him a stone? . . . If ye then, being evil, know how to give good gifts unto your children, how much more shall your Father which is in heaven give good things to them that ask him?" "Therefore," says Luther in one of his sermons, "if any man could be mindful enough of God and himself to conceive such a vision of God and boldness toward Him as to say with all his heart: Thou art my beloved father, what could he not ask of Him? And what could God deny him? his *own heart will tell him that whatever he asks for will be given.*" Thus God is represented as a being who fulfills desires, who hears man's pleas. Men pray in order to receive good things, in order to be saved "from perils, from afflictions and from all trouble." But the greater the affliction, the danger, the fear, the more powerful becomes the instinct of self-preservation; the keener the desire to be saved, the more fervent becomes the prayer. At the approach of a storm the Indians, as Heckewelder tells us, pray to the Manitou of the air (i. e., the god of the air, the air represented as a personal being) to divert all danger from them; the Chippewas by the lakes of Canada pray to the Manitou of the waters to prevent the waves from rising too high while they are crossing the lake.* Similarly, the Romans sacrificed to the storms and waves before going to sea, and to Vulcan, the fire-god, whenever they were endangered, or fear to be endangered, by fire. Heckewelder tells us that when the Lenape go to war they pray and sing the following verses:

O poor me!
Who am going out to fight the enemy,
And know not whether I shall return again,
To enjoy the embraces of my children
And my wife.
O poor creature!
Whose life is not in his own hands,
Who has no power over his own body,
But tries to do his duty
For the welfare of his nation.
O! thou Great Spirit above!
Take pity on my children
And on my wife!
Prevent their mourning on my account!
Grant that I may be successful in this attempt—

That I may slay my enemy,
And bring home the trophies of war
To my dear family and friends,
That we may rejoice together.
O! take pity on me!
Give me strength and courage to meet my enemy,
Suffer me to return again to my children,
To my wife
And to my relations!
Take pity on me and preserve my life
And I will make to thee a sacrifice.

In this simple, moving prayer we have all the elements of religion.

Man does not hold the success of his undertaking in his own hands. Between the desire and its fulfillment, between the purpose and its execution, lies a great gulf of difficulties and eventualities

* Heckewelder, *op. cit.*

that may frustrate his designs. However excellent his plan of battle may be, all manner of natural or human happenings, a cloudburst, a broken leg, the accidental delay of a relief column, can reduce it to nothing. Man's imagination fills in this gap between purpose and execution, between wishes and reality, with a being on whose will he supposes all these circumstances to depend and whose favor he need only implore in order to be assured, so he imagines, that his plans will prosper and his wishes be fulfilled.[22] Man does not have his life in his own hand, or at least not entirely; some outward or inward circumstance, if only the bursting of a tiny blood vessel in my brain, can suddenly end my life, can remove me against my will from my wife and children, friends and relatives. But man wants to live; life is his most precious possession. Impelled by his instinct of self-preservation, his love of life, he instinctively transforms this desire into a being capable of granting it, a being with human eyes to see his tears, with human ears to hear his complaints. For nature cannot grant this desire; nature, in reality, is not a personal being; it has no heart, it is blind and deaf to the desires and complaints of man.

What good is the sea to me if I conceive of it as a mere mass of water, in short, as what it really, objectively is? I can entreat the sea not to swallow me up only if I see it as a personal being whose will governs the motion of the waters, whose favor I can gain by gifts and worship, in other words, if I conceive of it as a god. Thus it is not only his own obtuseness which makes a man see all things in terms of himself, not only his ignorance of nature, and not only his imagination, that lead him to personify everything; his temperament as well, his *self-love,* his *egoism* or *striving for happiness* is still another reason why he attributes the actions and phenomena of nature to thinking, personal beings who live and will like men—regardless of whether, as in polytheism, he finds many gods, many personal causes in nature, or as in monotheism only one God, one cause operating with will and consciousness. For only by making nature dependent on a God does man make nature dependent *on himself,* does he subject nature to his power. "Jupiter's lightning," writes Ovid in the *Fasti,* "can be propitiated; the terrible one's anger can be guided." If a thing in nature, the sea, for example, is a god; if the storms and sea currents that so imperil man are dependent on his will, but the sea-god's will can be inclined toward men by the prayers and sacrifices of his worshipers —"presents force the hand even of the gods"—then indirectly the movements of the sea depend on man; man dominates nature through, or with the help of, God. A vestal virgin who had unjustly been accused of murder, picked up a sieve and invoked Vesta with the words: "Vesta! If I have always served you with chaste hands, enable me to gather water with this sieve and carry it to your temple"—and *nature itself,* as Valerius Maximus has it, obeyed the priestess' rash and unreflecting plea. In other words, the water forgot its nature and stayed in the sieve. In the Old Testament the sun stands still in response to Joshua's prayer or command. Actually there is no essential difference between prayer and command. *Overcome* (or conquer) Juno's anger with *humble prayers,* says the divine Tiber to Vergil's Aeneas; and Helenus also says to him: Overcome the mighty queen with humble gifts.

Prayer is only a humble command, a command in religious form. Modern theologians, to be sure, have abrogated the miracle of the sun standing still, explaining the Bible passage as a poetic figure or something of the sort, I've forgotten exactly what. But since there are still plenty of equally tall miracles in the Bible, it makes little difference whether belief preserves this particular miracle or unbelief does away with it. Elijah's prayer brought rain. "The prayer of a righteous man availeth much," says the New Testament. "Elijah . . . prayed earnestly that it might not rain; and it rained not on the earth by the space of three years and six months. And he prayed again, and the heaven gave rain." And the psalmist says: "He will fulfill the desire of them that fear Him."

Referring to this passage in his exegesis of Exodus, Luther writes: *"God does the will of him who believes."* And to this day, in times of prolonged drought, Christians pray for rain, or in times of protracted rain for sunshine; thus, even if they deny it in theory, they believe that the will of God, on which they conceive of everything as depending, can be moved to provide rain or sunshine even in opposition to the course of nature; for if they believed that rain and sunshine occurred only in accordance with natural process, they would not pray—such prayer would be an absurdity!—no, they believe that nature can be governed by prayer, that nature can be subordinated to human desires and needs. For this very reason men, or at least men with religious habits of mind, regard the doctrine that nature can only be understood in terms of nature, that nature is not dependent on the will of a God, of an anthropomorphic being friendly to man, as *depressing* and *therefore* untrue; for although in theory the theists place truth above good cheer, in practice the power to provide consolation is their sole criterion of truth or untruth; they reject a doctrine as untrue because it provides no consolation, because it is not as comforting and comfortable, as flattering to human egoism, as the opposite doctrine which derives nature from a personal being who guides the course of nature in accordance with the prayers and desires of man.

"The Epicureans," wrote Plutarch, himself a lover of moral comfort, in his treatise on the impossibility of living happily according to the precepts of Epicurus, "are punished by the very fact that they deny Providence, for this deprives them of the joy conferred by belief in a divine Providence." And in the same work Plutarch quotes Hermogenes as saying; "What comfort, what joy there is in the thought that omniscient and omnipotent beings are so benevolently inclined toward me, so concerned for me, that their eyes watch over me by day and night, regardless of what I may do, and that, in order to reveal to me the outcome of every undertaking, they give me all manner of signs." "To live without God," says Cudworth, an English theologian, in the same vein, "is to live without hope. For what hope or trust can a man repose in lifeless and insensible nature?" Whereupon he quotes Linus, the Greek poet: "There is reason to hope for everything (to despair of nothing), for God accomplishes all things with ease; nothing is an obstacle to him."

A belief, a conception which, in practice if not in so many words, is adhered to only because it is comforting and easy to live with, because it flatters man's egoism and self-love, can only have sprung from man's egoism and self-love. The source of a doctrine can be inferred with certainty from the impression it makes upon man. What a thing, in this case an imaginary thing, acts upon is also its source. What leaves the heart cold and indifferent is not grounded in any heartfelt, egoistic interest of man. Man's self-love is moved by the notion that nature does not operate with unswerving necessity but it is governed by a manlike being who loves man, a being endowed with will and intelligence who guides and governs nature to suit the needs of man, who takes man under his special protection, protects him from the dangers with which blind and ruthless nature threatens him at every turn.

I step out of the house; at that very moment a stone falls from the sky; according to natural necessity it falls on my head and kills me, for I have just entered the path of its fall, and the force of gravity which causes the stone to fall is no respecter of persons, however distinguished, however brilliant. But a God inhibits the force of gravity, suspends its action in order to save me, because God has more respect for the life of man than for the laws of nature, or at least, if He feels inclined to perform a miracle, He knows how to twist the circumstances so cleverly, so artfully and rationalistically, that without infringing on the laws of nature, which rationalists hold in the greatest esteem, the stone does me no harm. How comforting it is to spend one's life under the protection of heaven, how gruesome and depressing to expose oneself directly, as unbelievers do, to nature's impertinent meteors, hailstones, cloudbursts, and sunstrokes!

But here I find it necessary to digress. Because of their appeal to man's self-love, the idea of divine Providence and similar religious notions may indeed be said to spring from his heart, from human egoism; but this is true only as long as the heart is dominated by the imagination and consequently finds its only comfort in religious conceptions. For as soon as man opens his eyes, as soon as he ceases to be beclouded by religious ideas and sees reality for what it is, his heart revolts against the notion of Providence, repelled by its partisanship, by the way in which it saves one man and lets another go to his doom, destines one man to happiness and prosperity and others to abject misery, or at all events by the cruelty and inactivity with which it has allowed millions of men to suffer the most terrible torments. Who can reconcile the horrors of despotism, of the political and religious hierarchy, of religious belief and superstition, of Christian and pagan penal justice, such natural horrors as the Black Death, plague, and cholera, with belief in a divine Providence? Pious theologians and philosophers have racked their brains trying to think away the obvious contradictions between reality and the religious fantasy of a divine Providence; but it is far more compatible with a truth-loving heart, and even with the honor of God to deny His existence than to give Him a precarious lease on life by means of the shameful and silly sophisms and tricks which pious theologians and philosophers have hatched and spawned to justify divine Providence. It is better to fall with honor than to stand without honor. The atheist allows God to fall with honor, the rationalist believer makes Him live on without honor, *à tout prix*.

Twenty-third Lecture

RELIGION, THEN, has a practical purpose. By transforming the forces of nature into the deliberate actions of one or more personal, manlike beings, and its products into gifts bestowed by these same beings, it strives to put nature into the hands of man, to harness it to man's striving for happiness. As I have said in *The Essence of Religion,* man's dependence on nature is therefore the ground and beginning of religion, while freedom from his dependence, in both a rational and an irrational sense, is the ultimate aim of religion. Or in other words: the divinity of nature is indeed the *foundation* of religion, but the *divinity of man is* its *ultimate end.* What civilized man strives to achieve by molding and cultivating nature, namely, a beautiful, happy existence, sheltered from the brutalities and blind accidents of nature, uncivilized man tries to achieve by religion. At the dawn of history religion was man's only means of bending nature to his aims and desires. In his helplessness and perplexity, he had no other recourse than the prayers and gifts or sacrifices with which he tried to gain the favor of the thing he feared, felt threatened by, or dependent on; he had no other recourse except perhaps through magic, which is only an irreligious form of religion; for religious man merely projects magic—that is, the real or alleged power of magicians to control nature by mere words, by sheer force of will—into beings outside of man. Moreover, prayer often contains an element of magic, some prayers are simply formulas of magic or exorcism, whereby the gods are compelled willy-nilly to fulfill the desires of man. Even among pious Christians prayer is not always characterized by religious humility, but often carries a note of command. "When we are in distress and temptation," Luther writes in his commentary on Genesis, "we are none too respectful of [God's] sublime majesty, but blurt out: now help me, God! God, have mercy! We make no long preambles."

Thus prayer and sacrifice are means whereby man in his helplessness and perplexity tries to combat difficulties and force the hand of nature. Sonnerat tells us that during storms at sea, in a situation calling above all for energy and skill, the Chinese pray to the compass and go to the bottom with the object of their prayer; during epidemics, the Tungus pray fervently and with much ceremonial bowing, imploring the disease to pass their huts by; when smallpox breaks out, the Khonds offer the blood of oxen, sheep, and pigs to the pox-god; and in times of plague the inhabitants of Amboina, one of the so-called Spice Islands in the East Indies "collect all manner of gifts and sacrifices, load them into a ship, and push it out to sea, in the hope that the plague will be propitiated and leave the island in pursuit of the gifts and sacrifices."* Thus, instead of attacking or condemning a source of evil, the so-called idolaters often try to win it over with pious prayers. This, I own, a Christian does not do; but like polytheists and idolaters he tries to overcome the evils of nature, to bend nature to his will, not by activity, not by direct effort, not by his own intelligence, but by praying to the almighty God.

Here of course we must call attention to the difference between the uncivilized older Christians and modern educated Christians: the older Christians put all their trust in the power of prayer, that is, the power of God; modern, educated Christians continue, it is true, to pray: deliver us from evil, protect us against the ravages of fire! In practice, however, they put little reliance in the power of prayer, but prefer to take out fire insurance. Still, lest there be any misunderstanding, I had better add that, unlike religious faith or religious imagination, civilization is not all-powerful. No more than nature can make gold out of leather after the manner of God, can civilization, which masters nature only through nature—that is, by natural means, perform miracles.

By the use of natural means, civilization, human activity, has

* Meiners, *op. cit.*

eliminated or at least attenuated innumerable evils which man formerly tried in vain to combat by religious methods. Religion is the childhood of man. Or better still, in religion man is a child. Unable to satisfy his desires by his own resources, a child turns to his parents, the beings on whom he feels and knows himself to be dependent, in the hope of obtaining what he wishes through them. Religion has its origin, its true position and significance, in the childhood stage of mankind. But the childhood stage is also the stage of ignorance and inexperience, the uneducated, uncivilized stage. Those religions that arose in later periods, such as Christianity, which has been called a "new" religion, were not essentially new. They were critical religions; they merely reformed and spiritualized religious conceptions stemming from the earliest ages of mankind and adapted them to a more advanced stage in human development.

Or even if we concede that the later religions were essentially new, the period in which these new religions arose was still a period of childhood in relation to later times. Let us go back to the most recent of these periods, the period in which Protestantism came into being. What ignorance, what superstition, what bestiality! What childish, crude, vulgar, superstitious notions prevailed even among our God-illumined Reformers! And precisely for this reason, they had nothing more in mind than a *religious* reformation; they, and Luther in particular, were wholly engrossed in religious interests.

Religion arises solely in the night of ignorance, in times of misery, helplessness, and rudimentary culture,* when for this very reason the imagination overshadows all man's other powers, where man entertains the wildest and most extravagent ideas. Yet it also springs from man's need of light, of culture, or at least of the products of culture; it is indeed the first, still crude and vulgar form of human culture; and that is why every epoch, every important stage in the history of human civilization, begins with religion. Everything which later became a field of independent human activity, of culture, was originally an aspect of religion: all the arts, all the sciences, or rather, the *first beginnings,* the

* Even today, in all matters of profound human concern, *ignorant, uncivilized* governments try to combat the misery of the world by means of religion rather than by positive measures or education.

first elements—for as soon as an art or science achieves a high state of development, it ceases to be religion—were originally the concern of religion and its representatives, the priests. Philosophy, poetry, astronomy, politics, jurisprudence—or at least the power to judge difficult cases and to determine innocence and guilt—and medicine as well, were formerly the affair and concern of religion. Among the ancient Egyptians, for example, medicine "was religious and astrological in character. Like every part of the year, every organ of the human body was under the influence of a particular star-god. . . . No legal disputation or cure could be undertaken without consultation of the stars."* And even today among savages the magicians or sorcerers who are in contact with the spirits or gods—hence the clergy, the priests of the savages—are also their physicians.

Among Christians as well, the art or at least the power of healing was also a matter of religion or faith. In the Bible, healing power attaches even to the clothing of the saints, the heroes of faith, the men of God. Here I shall mention only the garment of Christ, the hem of which one only had to touch in order to be healed, the handkerchiefs and aprons of the Apostle Paul, which, according to the Book of Acts, had only to be held over a sick man and the plagues and evil spirts "went out of him." But religious medicine was not limited to the use of supernatural means, to exorcism, prayer, the power of faith or of God; it also included *natural remedies*. At the beginning of human development, however, these natural remedies had a religious significance. The Egyptians, among whom as we have just seen medicine was an aspect of religion, also had natural remedies; how, indeed, could man have been expected to content himself with religious devices, with prayer and magical spells! Even undeveloped and stultified by faith, his intelligence told him to look for medicines appropriate to their purposes; but the "books in which the medicines and medical treatments of the Egyptians were recorded were counted among the *sacred* books, and consequently *all innovations* were absolutely forbidden; a physician who made use of a new medicine and was so unfortunate as not to save his patient, was punished by death."

Thus, as the Egyptian sanctification of traditional medicines

* E. Röth, *Die ägyptische und die zoroastrische Glaubenslehre.*

clearly illustrates, the first elements of civilization or culture were *sacraments*. Among us Christians water, wine and bread are sacraments only indirectly; but originally water was a sacrament, i. e., something sacred, divine, because of the beneficial effects and properties which had been discovered in it and which contributed to the civilization and welfare of mankind. Among the ancient peoples washing and bathing were a religious duty.[23] They made it a point of conscience not to pollute their bodies of water. The ancient Persians never spat or passed water into a river. Among the Greeks it was forbidden to enter a river with unwashed hands, or to pass water in the source or mouth of a river. Even holier than water were bread and wine, because their invention required a more advanced civilization than that needed to discover the beneficial properties of water, which are known even to animals. The "sacred bread" was among the mysteries of the Greek religion. Even among us, as Hüllmann quite soundly remarks, "there prevails a *certain religious feeling* for bread and grain, which, for example, causes us to regard usurious dealings in grain as the most detestable form of usury and leads a common man, who sees grain going to ruin, to cry out: 'Oh, the good bread! Oh, the good grain!' "* The invention both of bread and wine was attributed to gods, because both bread and wine were regarded as sacred. Even in the Bible it is written that wine "maketh glad the heart of man."

But to the ancients, as we have seen by the examples of bread and wine, all beneficial, useful, pleasant things, all the things that embellish and ennoble man's life, were divine, sacred, religious. The more ignorant men were, the less equipped they were to procure pleasures, to provide themselves with an existence worthy of man, to protect themselves against the cruelties of nature, the more they revered the inventors of such good things, and the more sacred they held the things themselves. To the thoughtful Greeks, everything that makes man a man was a god: fire, for example, because it gathers men around the hearth, because it brings man closer to man, in short, because it benefits man. But precisely because man made sacraments of the first medicines, of the first elements of human civilization and well-being, religion always became, in the course of development, the antithesis of true civilization, an ob-

* Hüllmann, *Theogonie, Untersuchungen über den Ursprung der Religion des Alterthums* (Berlin, 1804).

stacle to progress; for it opposed every innovation, every change in the old traditional ways.

Christianity came into the world long after the invention of bread, wine, and other elements of civilization, at a time when it was too late to deify their inventors, when these inventions had long since lost their religious significance. Christianity introduced another element of civilization: morality. Christianity wished to provide a cure not for physical or political evils, but for moral evils, for sin. Let us go back to our example of wine in order to clarify the difference between Christianity and paganism, that is, common popular paganism. How, said the Christians to the heathen, can you deify wine? What sort of benefit is it? Consumed immoderately, it brings death and ruin. It is a benefit only when consumed in moderation, with wisdom, that is, when drunk in a moral way; thus the utility or harmfulness of a thing depends not on the thing itself, but on the moral use that is made of it. In this the Christians were right. But Christianity made morality into a religion, it made the moral law into a divine commandment; it transformed a matter of autonomous human activity into a matter of faith.

In Christianity faith is the principle, the foundation of the moral law: *"From faith come good works."* Christianity has no wine god, no goddess of bread or grain, no Ceres, no Poseidon, god of the sea and of navigation; it knows no god of the smithy, no Vulcan; yet it has a general God, or rather, a *moral* God, a God of the art of becoming moral and attaining beatitude. And with this God the Christians to this day oppose all radical, all thoroughgoing civilization, for a Christian can conceive of no morality, no ethical human life, without God; he therefore derives morality from God, just as the pagan poet derived the laws and types of poetry from the gods and goddesses of poetry, just as the pagan smith derived the tricks of his trade from the god Vulcan. But just as today smiths and metalworkers in general know their trade without having any particular god as their patron, so men will some day master the art of leading moral and happy lives without a God. Indeed, they will be truly moral and happy only when they no longer have a God, when they no longer need religion; for as long as an art is still imperfect, as long as it is in its swaddling clothes, it requires the protection of religion. For through religion man compensates for the deficiencies in his culture; and it is only from lack of culture that, like the Egyptian priest who makes sacraments of his rudimentary medicines, he makes sacraments of his moral remedies, makes sacred dogmas of his rudimentary ideas, and makes divine commandments and revelations of his own thoughts and emotions.

In short, religion and culture are incompatible, although culture, insofar as religion is the first and oldest form of it, can be termed *the true and perfect religion,* so that only *a truly cultivated man is truly religious.* This statement, however, is an abuse of words, for superstitious and inhuman notions are always bound up with the word "religious"; by its very nature religion comprises anticultural elements; for it strives to perpetuate ideas, customs, inventions that man made in his childhood, and to impose them as the laws of his adult age. Where man needs a God to tell him how to behave—as He commanded the Israelites to relieve themselves in a place apart—man is at the religious stage, but also at a profoundly uncivilized stage. Where man behaves properly of his own accord, because his own nature, his own reason and inclination tell him to, the need for religion ceases and culture takes its place. And just as it now seems ridiculous and incredible that the most natural rule of decency should once have been a religious commandment, so one day, when man has progressed beyond our present pseudo culture, beyond the age of religious barbarism, he will find it hard to believe that, in order to practice the laws of morality and brotherly love, he once had to regard them as the commandments of a God who rewarded observance and punished nonobservance. As Luther says:

> If you want to live like swine
> As Epicurus laid down the line,
> Abjure belief in man and God above,
> Who sees and judges every move.
> Say that this life is the end
> Although your heart cries out: Forfend!
> Say you were born for yourself alone,
> Swill and gobble till you groan.
> Live like a sow, eat, drink, spit, shit,
> Think only of your private benefit.

These lines show strikingly that religion is the barbarian's culture, but that this culture itself is still sheer barbarism. A religious man eschews gluttony and drunkenness, not because they are distasteful to him, not because he finds them repellent, bestial, contrary to human nature, but for fear of the punishments that a heavenly judge may mete out to him in this life or the next, or for love of his Lord, in short, for religious reasons. Religion prevents him from behaving like an animal, it is the barrier between humanity and bestiality; in other words, bestiality is *inside him,* humanity is *outside and above him.* The sole foundation of his humanity, the only thing that deters him from gluttony and drunkenness is a God, a being who, or so at least he thinks, is distinct from, and outside himself. If there were no God—this is the meaning of Luther's verses—I should be a beast; the ground and essence of my humanity are outside me. But a man whose humanity rests on a being outside him, on a being who, or at least so he believes, is not human—where a man is human not for human but for religious reasons, he is not yet a truly human being. I am a man only if I act humanly of my own accord, if I recognize and practice humanity as a trait of my nature, as a necessary consequence of my own being.

Religion merely suppresses the symptoms of evil, not its causes; it prevents bestiality and barbarism from erupting but leaves their roots intact; it is not a radical cure. Only where the actions of mankind flow from causes inherent in the nature of man can there be harmony between principle and practice, cause and effect; only then can man be complete and whole. And such a man is the product or goal of culture. Religion is supposed to take the place of culture, but cannot; culture, on the other hand, really takes the place of religion, rendering it superfluous. A man who has science, said Goethe, has no need of religion. Instead of science, I prefer to say culture, or education, because education embraces the whole man, though in view of what passes for education today, this word too can provoke objections. But what word is without taint?

The paramount task of our time is not to make men religious but to educate them, to disseminate education in all classes and walks of life. All history down to our own times demonstrates that the greatest horrors are compatible with religion, but not with education. Every religion built on theological foundations—and this is the only kind of religion that comes our way—involves superstition. And superstition is capable of every kind of cruelty and inhumanity. There is no point in drawing a distinction here between false religion and true religion. True religion, from which all evil and cruelty are banished, is simply religion restricted and illumined by education and reason. Hence, even if both in theory and in practice, in word and in deed, people who profess such religion do in fact reject human sacrifice, the persecution of heretics, witch burnings, death penalties inflicted on "poor sinners," and other such atrocities, their change of heart cannot be accredited to religion, but only to their education, reason, kindness, and humanity, which they naturally take with them even into their religion.

In opposition to our statement that religion has originated only in the earliest periods of mankind, or more specifically in barbarous, uncivilized times, that consequently religion shows its full freshness and vitality only in such times, and that religion and civilization are contraries, it may be argued that the wisest, most cultivated and learned men have been supremely religious. But such phenomena can be explained on many grounds. I shall not go into those already put forward in these lectures, for at the moment we are speaking of the opposition between religion and the culture derived from education—an opposition which no one can or will deny, for it is possible to have religion without culture and culture without religion. Here it suffices to observe that the greatest and most irreconcilable contradictions are often found in man. Of this fact the history of mankind, and especially the history of religion, provide the most striking examples, and not only in individuals but in whole nations as well.

Consider the most cultivated peoples of antiquity, whose books are still the foundation of our scholarly culture and education, the artistic and keen-minded Greeks and the practical, energetic Romans—what ridiculous, senseless superstitions they had even in their best periods! The very foundation of the Roman state was augury,* which derived its wisdom from the entrails of sacrificial animals, from lightning and other common or uncommon phenom-

* That is, religious deception, which, by the way, is still the foundation of the Christian throne and altar. Is it not, for example, an obvious swindle still to represent the Bible to the people as the word of God after all the theologians themselves have found out about it in their investigations?

ena of nature, from the song, flight, and eating habits of birds. For the Romans embarked on no important undertaking, war for example, if their sacred chickens had lost their appetite. In many of their religious usages and conceptions the Greeks and Romans did not differ from the most barbarous, uncultured peoples. Thus it is perfectly possible for a man to be cultivated and intelligent in a certain sphere and yet, in matters of religion, to be subject to the most absurd superstition.

This contradiction is especially frequent at the beginning of the modern era. The reformers of philosophy and of science in general were at once freethinking and superstitious. They lived in the midst of a disastrous conflict between state and Church, the secular and the religious, the human and the divine. They subjected the so-called secular world to their critique; but in ecclesiastical and religious matters they were as credulous as women and children, humbly submitting their reason to the most preposterous and fantastic ideas and articles of faith. This repugnant state of affairs is easily accounted for. Religion sanctifies its beliefs and usages, makes man's salvation dependent on them, burdens man's conscience with them. The consequence is that they are handed down unchanged from generation to generation. In religious Egypt, as Plato observes in the *Laws,* the art works of his time and those fashioned thousands of years before were in every way alike, because all innovation was condemned. In East India, according to Paulinus a S. Bartholomäo, no painter or sculptor was permitted to fashion a religious work that differed from the ancient works in the temples.*

In all other fields man progresses; in religious matters he remains stone-blind, stone-deaf, and rooted to the spot. Religious institutions, customs and articles of faith continue to be held sacred even when they stand in the most glaring contradiction to man's more advanced reason and ennobled feelings; even when the original justification and meaning of these same institutions and conceptions are long forgotten. We ourselves are living amid this same repugnant contradiction between religion and culture; our religious doctrines and usages also stand in the most glaring contradiction to our present cultural and material situation; our task

* *Brahmanensystem,* 1795.

today is to do away with this loathsome and disastrous contradiction. Its elimination is the indispensable condition for the rebirth of mankind, the one and only condition for the appearance of a new mankind, as it were, and for the coming of a new era. Without it, all political and social reforms are meaningless and futile. A new era also requires a new view of the first elements and foundations of human existence; it requires—if we wish to retain the word—a *new religion!*

Twenty-fourth Lecture

THE OBSERVATION that intelligence in certain spheres of life can exist side by side with the most unintelligent superstition, political freedom with religious servitude, scientific, industrial progress with religious stagnation and even bigotry, has led some to the superficial view and contention that religion is without bearing on life, and especially on public, political life, and that consequently our only goal in this connection should be absolute freedom to believe what we wish. To this I reply that a state of affairs in which political freedom is combined with religious prejudice and bigotry is not satisfactory. I for my part don't care a farthing for a political freedom that leaves me enslaved to my religious prejudices and imaginings. True freedom is present only where man is also free from religion; true culture is present only where man has become master over his religious prejudices and imaginations. But the state can have no other aim than to form complete, authentic men, though of course this is not meant here in any Utopian sense; consequently a state whose citizens, while enjoying free political institutions, are not free in a religious sense, cannot be a truly human and free state. The state does not make men, men make the state. As men are, so is their state. Once a state exists, to be sure, the individuals who by birth or immigration become its citizens, are molded by it; but what is a state in relation to the individuals who come to it if not the sum and combination of the people who already constitute it, who through the means at their disposal, through the institutions they have created, mold newcomers to their spirit and will? Thus, where men are politically free but unfree in religion, the state is not perfect or not yet complete.

As to the second point, freedom of faith and conscience, the first condition of a free state is indeed that "every man may be saved in his own way," that every man may believe what he likes. But this is a secondary and empty freedom; for it means nothing more than each man's freedom or right to be a fool in his own way. True, the state, in the present sense of the word, can do no more than refrain from all intervention in the field of faith—than grant unrestricted freedom in this respect. But man's task in the state is not only to believe what he wishes, but to believe what is reasonable, not only to believe, but to know what he can and must know if he is to be a free and cultivated man. Here no barrier to human knowledge can excuse us. In the realm of nature, to be sure, there are still many things we do not understand; but the secrets of religion spring from man himself, and he is capable of knowing them down to their remotest depths. And because he can know them, he ought to know them. Finally, it is an utterly superficial notion, refuted every day by history and even by daily life, to suppose that religion is without influence on public life. This view has originated only in our own day, when religious faith has ceased to be anything more than a chimera. Obviously, where religious faith has ceased to be a truth in man, it can have no practical consequences, it no longer inspires deeds of world-shaking importance. But where this is the case, where faith has become a mere lie, man is involved in the ugliest contradiction with himself and the consequences of faith are at least *morally* disastrous. Modern theism is just such a lie. The elimination of this lie is the condition for a new, energetic mankind.

The above-mentioned observation that piety in the common sense of the word is often combined with diametrically opposed traits, has led many to suppose that man has a special organ of religion, a specific religious feeling. We should be more justified in assuming the existence of a specific organ of superstition. Religion, that is, the belief in gods, in spirits, in so-called higher invisible beings who rule over man, has been said to be as innate in man as his other senses. Translated into the language of honesty and reason, this would only mean that, as Spinoza has already maintained, superstition is innate in man. But the source and strength of superstition are the power of ignorance and stupidity, which is the greatest power on earth, the power of fear and the feeling of dependency, and finally the power of the imagination. For out of every evil whose cause is unknown to man, out of every phenomenon, even some passing atmospheric effect, the appearance of some gas which frightens a man because he does not know what it is, the imagination makes an evil spirit or god; while out of every stroke of good fortune, every discovery, every good thing that chances his way, it makes a good spirit or god, or at least the work of a spirit or god. The Caribs believe, for example, than an evil spirit is at work in a gun, that in a lunar eclipse an evil spirit swallows the moon, that a *bad smell* indicates the presence of *the evil spirit* in person. And in Homer, contrariwise, where chance suddenly brings a man something he has been wishing for, a god is said to have brought it. Belief in the Devil is just as innate or natural to man as belief in God, so that, if we predicate the existence of a special feeling or organ for God, we must also predicate the existence of a special feeling or organ for the Devil.

Indeed, down to the most recent times the two beliefs were inseparable; as late as the eighteenth century a man who denied the *existence of the Devil* was held to be just as *godless* as a man who denied the existence of a good God. In those days the doctors of religion defended the belief in the Devil as astutely as our present-day doctors defend the belief in God. In the eighteenth century even Protestant theologians were just as highhanded in terming the denial of the Devil an absurdity as are our present theologians in disposing of atheism. I refer you to the passages from Walch's *Philosophical Lexicon,* cited in the notes to my *Bayle.* It was modern rationalism, with its characteristic flabbiness and halfway methods, that first decided to retain one half of religious faith and to drop the other, to sever the bond between the belief in good spirits and gods and the belief in bad spirits and gods. Consequently, if we resort to religion, that is, the belief in God, on the ground that it is human, that almost all men have believed in a God, that it is necessary to mankind to conceive of a "free," that is, human, cause of nature, then we must be consistent and honorable enough to resort, on the same grounds, to devils and witches, in short to man's superstition, ignorance and stupidity; for nothing is more human or more widespread than stupidity, nothing is more natural and innate in man than ignorance.

The negative theoretical cause, or at least condition, of all gods is indeed man's ignorance, his inability to consider nature as nature; and the more ignorant, stupid, and barbarous a man is, the more he projects himself into nature and the less able he is to dissociate nature from himself. When the Peruvians saw a solar eclipse, they thought the sun was *angry at them* for some wrong they had done. They believed the eclipse to be the consequence of a free cause, that is, the sun's displeasure or ill-humor. And when the moon was eclipsed, they thought it was *sick* and were alarmed lest it die, fall from the sky, crush them all, and bring about the end of the world. When the light returned to the moon, they rejoiced, taking the moon's brightening as a sign of *recovery*. Thus at the religious level, the level in which belief in God is rooted, man transfers even his own ailments to the heavenly bodies! The Indians of the Orinoco even regard the sun, moon, and stars as living creatures. One of them once said to Salvator Gilii: "They up there are people just like us." The Patagonians believe that the stars are former Indians and that the Milky Way is a field in which they are hunting ostriches; similarly the Greenlanders believe that sun, moon, and stars are their ancestors, who on some special occasion were moved to the heavens; other peoples have believed that the stars were the dwellings or even the souls of the great dead, who because of their glorious deeds were removed to the sky, where they shine forever.

When a comet appeared in the sky after Caesar's death, the Romans, as Suetonius tells us, believed it to be Caesar's soul. Can man's presumption and ignorance, his tendency to make a man of nature and subject it to a free cause, namely, the human imagination and will, be carried any further than by those Romans who looked upon the stars as their colleagues or ancestors, or as medals with which men are decorated after death for their achievements? Modern theists smile at such conceptions, but they fail to realize that their own belief in God rests on the same foundations. The only difference is that in their view the first principle of nature, or rather the spook lurking in the background, is not a man of flesh and bone, not—as I have set forth above*—man as a bodily individual, but the abstract essence of man. But fundamentally it

* Cf. the eleventh and twenty-first lectures, in reference to polytheism and monotheism.

makes no difference whether like the Patagonians I derive celestial phenomena from emotional states and intentions of the will, the light of the sun from its friendliness and good nature, and its darkening from its displeasure with man, or whether like a Christian, a theist, I derive all nature from the free cause or will of a personal being—for only a personal being has a will.

Where belief in God is still genuine, not slovenly and undecided as in modern religion, but consistent, all of a piece, there everything is determined by God's free choice, there are no physical laws, nature has no power of its own, the terrifying and calamitous manifestations of nature are derived from God's anger or—what amounts to the same thing—from the Devil, and the contrary phenomena are attributed to God's goodness. But this derivation of natural necessity from a free cause is grounded exclusively in the ignorance and imagination of man. Accordingly, when men had acquired some knowledge of the more commonplace natural phenomena, they began to find signs and proofs of an arbitrary or free cause chiefly in the unusual and unknown manifestations, in other words, in the manifestations of human ignorance. That was the case with the comets, for example. Because they appeared rarely, because people did not know what to make of them, even the academic rabble looked upon them as late as the beginning of the eighteenth century as *arbitrary* signs, demonstrations which God staged at will for the betterment or chastisement of men.

The rationalists, however, shifted the arbitrary free cause back to the beginning of the world; from then on, they explain everything naturally, without God; they are too lazy, too slovenly, too superficial to go back to the beginning, to the fundamental principles of their natural view and method of explanation; they are too lazy to ask themselves whether the question of how the world began is a rational question to begin with, or mere childishness rooted in man's ignorance and stupidity; they know they cannot answer the question rationally, and so they fill in the vacuum in their heads with the fantasy of a "free cause." But such is their inconsistency that they directly abandon this free cause and replace freedom by natural necessity, whereas in the old faith the first freedom breeds an unbroken chain of freedoms, of arbitrary actions or miracles.

Only unconscionably dishonest, half-hearted thinking can attempt to combine theism with nature and natural science. If I believe in God, in a "free cause," I must also believe that the will of God is the only necessity in nature, that if water makes things wet it is not because that is its nature, but by the will of God, that accordingly, if God wills, it may at any moment take on the nature of fire and burn. That I believe in God means: I believe there is no nature, no necessity. Let the rationalists drop their belief in God, or let them drop physics, astronomy, and physiology. No man can serve two masters. And if they defend the belief in God, let them also defend the belief in the Devil, in ghosts and witches. Not only because they are equally widespread, but also because they are identical in character and cause; these two beliefs are inseparable. God is the mind of nature, that is, the personified impression of nature upon the mind of man, or man's mental image of nature, which however he differentiates from nature and conceives of as an independent being. Similarly a man's spirit, or ghost, that walks after his death, is nothing other than an image of the deceased, which lives on in other men's minds and which they personify as a being distinct from the real, living bodily man. Consequently, let those who profess belief in the one spirit or ghost of nature, the great ghost, also profess belief in that other spirit or ghost, the ghost of man.

But I have digressed. I merely wished to say that if we are going to assume the existence in man of a special organ for religion, we must also and above all assume the existence of a special organ for superstition, ignorance, and mental laziness. But some people who are in certain respects rationalistic and unbelieving are in other respects superstitious, because they have not attained clarity about certain things, because certain influences and motivations, of which they are often quite unaware, prevent them from advancing beyond a certain limit. If we wished to explain such contradictions organically, we should have to assume the existence in one and the same man of two diametrically opposed organs or senses. There are in point of fact men who in practice deny, reject, and ridicule what in their minds they profess, or conversely deny with their minds what they profess in their hearts; who, for example, are afraid of ghosts though they deny the existence of such beings, and who feel quite ashamed and annoyed with themselves for having in the darkness mistaken a shirt for a ghost or specter. If, in trying to explain such a state of affairs, we were to resort to the notion of a special sense or organ, we should have to endow such people with a special organ for the sacred world of spirits and for fear of ghosts, and another special organ with which to deny the existence of ghosts. True, nothing is more convenient than to single out a special cause for a striking phenomenon; but precisely because they are so convenient such explanations are suspect. And as for religion in particular, our whole foregoing argument makes it plain that there is no justification whatever for deriving it from a special feeling, sense, or organ.

For the sake of still greater clarity, I appeal to the senses. We can know a thing only by its manifestations, its effects, its action on the senses, and this is also true of religion. The most important act of religion, the act that is most striking and also most indicative of its essence, is prayer or worship; for worship is prayer as perceived by the senses, prayer expressed in sensuous gestures and signs. Thus, if we consider the different modes of worship among men at large, we find that man's religious feelings are no different from his feelings in situations that have nothing to do with religion in the strict sense. In Meiners, who has collected the most important material on this point as on many others, we read the following:

The most universal, most natural expression of abasement before higher beings and absolute rulers was the prostration of the whole body. Though not as common as the prostration of the whole body, kneeling has also been very frequent among the most diverse peoples. The Egyptians honored their gods as well as their king and his intimates by kneeling. The Jews, like the Mohammedans of today, were not permitted to sit down while praying, because in the Orient the laws of propriety have always forbidden subjects to sit in the presence of their rulers, clients in the presence of the patrons, women, children, or servants in the presence of their husbands, fathers or masters. In the ancient Orient, as in ancient Greece and Italy, subjects expressed their veneration and submission toward rulers, servants toward masters, women and children toward husbands and fathers, by kissing either their hands or their knees, the hem of their garment or their feet. As subordinates behaved toward their superiors, men in general behaved toward their gods. They kissed either the hands, knees, or feet of the divine images. The free Greeks and Romans even took the liberty of kissing the statues of their gods on the chin or mouth.

We see by these examples that men express their feelings and attitudes toward divine beings by the same means as toward human beings. This shows that they have identical attitudes and feelings toward nonreligious objects and toward religious objects, or gods. Thus no special feelings are involved in religion, and indeed there is no such thing as a specifically religious feeling. Man throws himself on his knees before his gods; but he does the same before his rulers and in general before those who hold his life in their hands; he humbly entreats them from mercy; in short he shows men the same veneration as gods. The Romans revered country, blood relatives, and parents with the same piety as they showed the gods. Piety, as Cicero said, is justice toward the gods, but it is also, as the same author says in another passage, justice toward one's parents.[24] Hence among the Romans, as Valerius Maximus observes, offenses against the gods and against parents incurred the same penalty. But though parents stood on an equal footing with the gods, the majesty of the *patria,* as the same author tells us, enjoyed still higher esteem; in other words, the supreme god of the Romans was Rome. In India one of the five great religious ceremonies or sacraments which, according to the Hindu Code of Manu the head of a family is expected to observe each day, is the "sacrament of man," the sacrament of hospitality, the honoring of guests.

But, especially in the Orient, the veneration of princes has been carried to the highest degree of religious servility. In China, for example, all subjects, even tributary chiefs of state, must kneel three times and touch their foreheads to the ground nine times before the Emperor; on certain days of the month the most distinguished mandarins appear before the Emperor, and even if he himself is not present, they perform the same acts of obeisance before his *empty throne.* Indeed, the emperor's subjects must even kneel and touch their heads to the ground nine times in the presence of an imperial missive. The Japanese regard their emperor as so exalted that "only the nobles of the first class enjoy the privilege of seeing the *emperor's feet,* though they are not permitted to look higher." Precisely because man, and especially Oriental man, feels the highest possible reverence for his rulers, his imagination has made them into gods and endowed them with all the attributes and titles of divinity. The hyperbolic titles of the sultans and of the emperors of China are generally known. But even a petty East Indian prince is called "king of kings, brother of the sun, moon and stars, lord of the ocean's ebb and flow." Among the Egyptians as well, kingship was identified with divinity, to such a degree that king Ramses is represented *worshiping himself as a god.*

From the Orientals the Christians have inherited not only religion, but also this deification of princes. The first Christian emperors assumed the same attributes or titles of divinity as the pagan emperors. And to this day Christians address their princes with as much servility as anyone has ever shown a god. To this day the titles of Christian princes are fully as hyperbolic and fantastic as the titles with which religious flattery has from time immemorial tried to glorify the gods. To this day the distinctions between titles of divine power and titles of royal power indicate mere differences of diplomatic precedence, not of essence. For there is no special religious feeling, no special religious sense, and consequently no special religious object with an exclusive claim to religious worship. It follows that the worship of God and idolatry, religion, and superstition stem ultimately from a common root in the nature of man.

Twenty-fifth Lecture

IDOLATRY and the worship of God, as I said at the end of the previous lecture, are both rooted in the nature of man. There is no special organ for either the one or the other. And if we wished to assert the existence of such an organ for religion, we should also have to make the same claim for superstition. But what then is the source of the difference between idolatry and the belief in God? The sole basis of this difference is that feelings and marks of veneration which ought to be reserved exclusively for an object regarded as "holy," can also be directed toward another object, either of a natural and sensuous, or of a spiritual character. The religion which manifests itself in public professions of faith, in certain forms of worship, is, as I say in *The Essence of Christianity,* a public declaration of love.

As object of his love, man chooses the woman who exerts the highest power over him, who in his eyes is the highest and best of women, who for this reason inspires him with a feeling of dependency, the feeling that he cannot live or be happy without her; at least and as long as he does not possess her, as long as she is merely an object of his desires and imaginings, he accords her the highest veneration and offers her the same sacrifices and tokens of devotion, as a religious man offers his God. The same holds good in religion—and love too is religion. A religious man worships a tree, yet not just any tree, but only the tallest, the most sublime; a river, but only the most powerful and beneficent, such as the Nile in Egypt and the Ganges in India; a spring, yet not every spring, but only a spring distinguished by particular qualities, such as the salt springs worshiped by the early Germans; the heavenly luminaries, yet not all, but only the most eminent, the sun, the moon, the planets, or certain conspicuous stars.

Or he worships the human essence, yet not in just any man, but only in the person of a beautiful human being—as among the Greeks, the Aegestans, for example, worshiped Philip of Crotona even though he had invaded their country, because he was the most beautiful of men—or, after the manner of Orientals, in the person of a prince, a despot, or, like the Greeks and Romans, in the person of a hero who has done their country outstanding services; or else he worships the human essence as such, man's spirit or reason, because he regards it as that which is highest, most glorious, and most excellent. But just as I can transfer my love and esteem for one woman to another, I can honor one tree as well as another—the Germans worshiped the oak, the Slavs worshiped the lime tree; instead of revering the spirit, the abstracted essence of man, I can equally well revere a real individual man; instead of worshiping the abstracted essence of nature and the Creator-God whom I conceive to be its cause, I can equally well worship sensuous nature, the creature; for the sensuous being, the creature, *appeals* to all man's senses, while the nonsensuous essence *eludes* all his senses and therefore exerts much less power over man.

This is the source of jealousy in religion, of God's jealousy. I am a jealous God, says Jehovah in the Old Testament. Both Jews and Christians have repeated these words in a thousand variations. But why is God jealous, or thought to be jealous? Because the feelings or attitudes of devotion, love, veneration, trust, or fear, which He claims for Himself alone, can just as well be transferred to another object, to other gods or beings, such as men or the things of nature. Thus the distinction between idolatry and the worship of God owes its origin to positive, that is, arbitrary laws. You shall not trust men, but me alone; you shall not fear natural phenomena, but me alone; you shall not worship the stars as the source of your salvation, but me who made the stars to serve you—so speaks the God Jehovah, so speaks every monotheistic God to his servants in order to deter them from idolatry. But *if there were a specific religious feeling or organ,* He would have had no need to speak in such terms, no need to command men to trust and serve Him alone. No more than I have to command my eye: Thou shalt not hear, or my ear: Thou shalt not see, thou shalt not dance attendance on the light, no more would the object of religion have to say to man: Thou shalt serve me alone—if there were a special religious organ; for such an organ would no more turn to another religious object than the ear turns to the light or the eye to sound. And God could no more be, or be thought to be, jealous of men or natural beings if there were an exclusively religious or divine organ, attuned to Him alone, than the eye is jealous of the ear, or fears that the ear will abduct and appropriate its object.

The organs of religion are feeling, imagination, the desire or striving to be happy, but these organs are not restricted to particular objects, to the objects designated as religious (supposing such objects to exist), for every object, every force, every human or natural phenomenon can become an object of religion. But an object of imagination, feeling, or the striving for happiness becomes an object of religion, or at least of religion in the strict sense, only under the special conditions we have set forth. And the first such condition is a stage of human development at which, for lack of education, science, and critique, for lack of ability to distinguish between the subjective and the objective, man sees an object not as it really is, not as an object of intelligence and sensibility, but only as a product of the feeling, imagination, or striving for happiness.

Even to a believer in natural process, to be sure, nature is an object of the striving for happiness, for who can be happy in a dungeon without space, air or light? Even to a scientific thinker it is an object of imagination and of feeling, even of the feeling of dependency, but only on the basis of its real, objective character; he is not so hoodwinked by his feeling or so overwhelmed by his imagination as to take a subjective view of nature, to regard it as a personal, arbitrary, friendly or unfriendly being, who metes out punishments and rewards and who, because he is what he is, is automatically entitled to sacrifice and penance, hymns of praise and thanksgiving, devout prayers and genuflections, who is, in other words, a religious object. A humanist or naturalist, to cite still another example, still honors the dead, but not in a religious way, not as gods, because he does not, like the religious imagination, transform beings who are present only in his thoughts into real, living persons, because he does not transfer to an object the feelings with which the dead inspire him and does not look upon the dead as terrible beings or beings of some other kind, who still have the will and power to injure or help him and who must therefore be honored, feared, besought, and appeased like real beings.

But back to our main theme. I have attributed the transition from paganism to Christianity, from nature religion to the religion of the spirit or of man, to the imagination. First I showed that God is an image, a creature of the imagination: concurrently I pointed out the difference between the Christian or monotheistic God and the pagan or polytheistic god, namely that the pagan god is a material, bodily, individual image, whereas the Christian God is a mental image, the word, and that accordingly, in order to know the essence of the Christian God, one need only understand the essence of the word. Then, however, I put a restriction on my derivation of religion from imagination, by distinguishing between the products of religious imagination and mere poetic imaginings or fictions, and by showing that the religious imagination operates only in conjunction with the feeling of dependency, that the gods are creatures not only of the imagination, but also of human emotion, of feelings which seize upon man in the most crucial moments of his life, in fortune and misfortune, that because man strives to obtain what is good and pleasant and to avoid what is harmful and unpleasant, the gods are also products of the striving for happiness.

This point brought us to the difference between religion and civilization, between prayer and work: religion resembles education, civilization, and work insofar as it has the same aims; it differs from them insofar as it strives to realize these aims without the tools of civilization. Having pointed out this difference, I return to religion as a product of the striving for happiness. In this connection I uttered the daring phrase: the gods are the fulfillment of man's desires, or man's desires conceived of as real beings; a god is nothing other than man's striving for happiness fulfilled in his imagination. I observed, however, that the gods are as varied as men and peoples, for although all men wish to be happy, different men embody their idea of happiness in different objects. Because the pagans have different desires from Christians, they also have different gods. Or in other words: the difference between the Christian God and the pagan god resides in the difference between Christian desires and pagan desires. "As your heart is, so is your God," says Luther. "Down to the founding of Christianity," Meiners writes, "all peoples prayed to the gods only for temporal goods and for the diversion of temporal evils.[25] Savage fishing and hunting peoples prayed to the gods to favor their fishing and hunting, cattle-raising peoples to smile on their pastures and herds, agricultural nations to prosper their gardens and fields. All without exception prayed for health and long life for themselves and their families, for wealth, favorable weather, and victory over their enemies." In other words, the pagans had limited, sensuous, material desires, or in the language of the Christians, earthly, carnal desires. They therefore had material, sensuous, limited gods, and as many gods as there are material benefits. They had a god of riches, a god of health, a god of happiness, of good fortune, etc., and since the desires of men depend on their occupations, each trade, among the Greeks and Romans, had its own special gods, the shepherd had shepherd gods, the tiller of the soil had agricultural gods, and the merchant had his Mercury, to whom he prayed for profit.[26]

The objects of pagan desires are not "immoral"; it is not immoral to wish for health, on the contrary, it is a perfectly reasonable wish; nor is it immoral to wish to be rich—even pious Christions thank their God when they receive a rich inheritance or other financial blessing. The pagan's wishes or prayers for wealth were immoral or rather inhuman—for only the inhuman is immoral—only when he prayed to the gods to kill off his parents, relatives, and the like in the hope of inheriting their possessions. The pagan desires were desires which did not exceed the nature of man, the limits of this life, of this real sensuous world. And for this very reason their gods were no such unlimited and supernatural beings as the Christian God. No! like the pagans' desires, their gods were not outside or above the world; they were one with the world, worldly beings. The Christian God does what He pleases with the world; He even makes it out of nothing, because to Him the world is nothing, for He Himself was when the world was still nothing.

But in all his actions, the pagan god is bound up with matter; even those pagan philosophers who came closest to the ideas of

Christianity believed in the eternity of matter, of the substance of the world; they regarded their god as the mere architect of the world, not as its creator. The god of the pagans was bound up with matter, because the pagan's desires and thoughts were restricted to matter, the content of the real world. The pagan did not break away from the world, from nature; he could conceive of himself only as a part of it, and consequently he had no god differentiated and removed from nature. To him the world was a divine, glorious being, or rather, the highest, most beautiful thing he could conceive of. Accordingly, the pagan theist philosophers used the words god, world, and nature synonymously. As man is, so is his god; the pagan god is the image of pagan man, or as I put it in *The Essence of Christianity,* he is the objectified essence of pagan man, represented as an independent being. The common or identical element in the different gods or religions is simply the element common to all human nature. For all the differences between them, all men are men, and this identity and unity of the human race, of the human constitution, is the basis of the similarity among gods; the Ethiopian paints his God black like himself, and the Caucasian paints his God white; but all give their gods human form or character.

Actually it is superficial to disregard the differences among gods; to the pagan only the *pagan* god is *the* god, who is one with what makes this particular pagan different from other men and nations; to the Christian only the *Christian God* is *God.* Many orthodox Christians have therefore gone so far as to term the pagans atheists, on the ground that the gods of the pagans are no gods in the Christian sense, since if nothing else their multiplicity is contrary to the Christian concept of divinity. But the Christian God is simply the essence of Christian man, personified or objectified, and represented by the imagination as an autonomous being. The Christian has unearthly, suprasensory, and superhuman desires. A Christian, at least a true Christian, who is not part pagan like modern secular, lip-service Christians, desires neither wealth, nor posts of honor, nor long life, nor health.

What is health in the eyes of a Christian? Why, this whole life is nothing but a sickness; only in eternal life, as St. Augustine says, is there true health. What is long life to a Christian? In comparison with the eternity that a Christian carries around with him in his head, the longest life is only a vanishing moment. What are earthly glory and fame? In comparison with heavenly glory they are no more than a will-o'-the-wisp compared to the light of the sun. And precisely because of these desires, the Christian also has an unearthly, superhuman God, situated outside and above the world. The Christian does not, like the pagan, look upon himself as a part of nature, as a part of the world. We "have no certain dwelling place," says the Bible; "we seek the dwelling place" to come. Our life (that is, our citizenship) is in heaven. Man, says the Church Father Lactantius expressly, is not a product of the world, nor is he a part of the world. And man, says Ambrose, is "above the world." "One soul," says Luther, "is better than the whole world."

The Christian has a free cause of nature, a lord of nature, whose will and word nature obeys, a God who is not bound by the so-called causal nexus, by necessity or by the chain which links effect to cause and cause to cause, whereas the pagan god is bound by natural necessity and cannot even save his favorites from the necessity of death. But the Christian has a free cause because his desires are not limited by the structure, the necessity, of nature. He desires and believes in an existence, a life, in which he will be removed from all the needs and necessities of nature; in which he will live without having to breathe, sleep, eat, drink, beget, or conceive, whereas among the pagans even a god is subject to the necessity of sleeping, loving, eating and drinking, precisely because the pagan did not tear himself away from the necessity of nature and could not conceive of an existence without natural needs. Thus the Christian embodies his desire to be free from all natural needs and necessities in a being who is really free from nature, who can and in the end actually will eliminate all barriers to the realization of these Christian desires. For the only real barrier to human desires is nature. The barrier to the desire to fly like an angel, or to arrive at some distant place this very second, is gravity; the barrier to the desire for a life devoted exclusively to religious meditations and emotions is my bodily needs; the barrier to the desire for a life of beatitude, free from sin,[27] is my carnal, sensuous nature; the barrier to my desire to live forever is death, the necessity of finiteness and mortality. The Christian fulfills all these desires, or provides himself with the possibility of their fulfillment, by means of a being who, in his imagination, is above and outside of nature, and in the face of whose will nature is powerless or nonexistent.

Man makes a god of what he is not but would like to be; that is his god. A Christian would like to be perfect, free from sin without senses or bodily needs, divine, immortal and blissful, but he is not; he therefore conceives of a being who is what he himself would like to be and hopes to become some day; and to this being, distinct from himself, this embodiment of his own supernatural desires, of his own mind that thinks away the barriers of nature, he gives the name of God. Thus the belief that the world originated in a free, transcendent, supernatural being is closely related to the belief in an eternal, heavenly life. For a Christian's only guarantee that his supernatural desires will be fulfilled lies in his conviction that nature itself is dependent on a supernatural being and owes its existence solely to the arbitrary exercise of this being's will. If nature stems not from a God but from itself, if it is necessary, then death too is necessary, then all the laws or natural necessities to which human nature is subject are immutable and not to be overcome. Where nature has no beginning, it also has no end. But a Christian believes in and desires the end of nature or the world; and since he believes and desires that all natural processes and necessities will cease, he must also believe in a beginning, or, more precisely, a spiritual, arbitrary beginning of nature, of physical life.

An end necessarily presupposes a beginning; belief in immortality presupposes belief in an all-powerful God, who can even awaken the dead, to whom nothing is impossible, in the face of whom there is no natural law, no necessity. Through the *creatio ex nihilo,* that masterstroke of divine omnipotence, man, I say in *The Essence of Christianity,* gains certainty, or better still, acquires the comforting belief, that the world is nothing and has no power over man. "We have a Lord," says Luther, "who is greater than the whole world; we have a Lord so mighty that He has only to speak and all things are born. Wherefore then should we *fear* if He is *graciously inclined* to us?" And in his commentary on Genesis, he writes: "Anyone who believes that God is a Creator who makes all things from what is not must necessarily draw this conclusion and say: then God can also awaken the dead." Thus belief in miracles is one with the belief in God, or at least in the Christian God.

Twenty-sixth Lecture

WE MUST NOW SAY a few words about miracles, or wonders, for nothing is more vital to an understanding of the nature of religion, particularly of the Christian religion. First of all, we must be careful not to confuse the miracles of religion with the so-called wonders of nature—the "wonders of the heavens," for example, as an astronomer has titled his book, or the "wonders of geology," to cite the title of an English work. The wonders of nature are phenomena that arouse our admiration and surprise because they exceed our limited knowledge, our immediate experience and customary ideas. We admire, for example, the petrified skeletons of animals that once lived on the earth, of those enormous lizards, the dinosaurs and megatheres, the ichthyosaurs and plesiosaurs, because they are so much larger than any of the present species of animals we are accustomed to. But religious miracles have nothing whatever in common with the dinosaurs and megatheres, the ichthyosaurs and plesiosaurs of geology.

The so-called wonders of nature are wonders for us, but not as such or for nature; regardless of whether or not we discover their underlying cause, they have their explanation in nature. Theist, religious wonders, on the other hand, exceed the *powers of nature;* far from having a ground or explanation in nature, they are contrary to nature; they are works, and proofs of the existence, of a being *differentiated from nature* and situated outside and above it. The learned Vossius writes, for example, in his book on the origin and development of paganism: "Although God prescribed the order of the heavens, He did not forgo the right to change it, for He commanded even the sun to stand still. In defiance of the order of nature, which is said to be necessary, in defiance then of natural necessity, a virgin bore a child, the blind were given sight, the dead were more than once restored to life at His command."

True, those who wished to make religious wonders seem credible have time and time again invoked the so-called miracles of nature, which are no miracles at all. This is one of the many pious dodges to which the champions of all religions have resorted down through the ages in order to pull the wool over people's eyes and reinforce their religious servitude.

One evident difference between the two kinds of wonders or miracles is that the miracles of nature are of no concern to man, whereas in a religious miracle man is an interested party, his egoism is involved. Thus religious miracles are grounded not in objective nature, but in man. A religious miracle presupposes a human *desire* or need. Religious miracles occur in time of distress, they occur only when man wishes to be saved from an evil, but cannot unless the laws of nature are suspended. The essence of religion is embodied in miracles. Like religion itself, miracles stem not only from feeling and imagination, but also from will, from the striving for happiness. In *The Essence of Christianity* I therefore define a miracle as the fulfillment, or supposed fulfillment, of a supernatural desire. I say supernatural because both in object and in content a Christian's wishes exceed the limits of nature and of the world. Actually all wishes are supernatural, at least in respect of the form, manner and means in which we would like them to be fulfilled. I wish, for example, to be at home when I am wandering about in some far country. There is nothing unnatural or supernatural about the object of my wish, for I can attain it in a natural way; I need only take the boat or train. But the essence of my wish is precisely that I would like to be home without loss of time, that I would like to be immediately and in reality where I am in my thoughts.

If we now turn to miracles, we shall find that they objectify, embody, realize nothing other than the essence of a wish. Christ heals the sick. There is nothing miraculous about healing the sick; millions of sick people get well in a natural way. But he heals them as sick people wish to be healed, instantly, not by the tedious, troublesome and costly process of applying natural remedies. As

Luther writes: "He says: Be well. And people are well. Thus he needs *no medicine,* but cures them with his *word.*" Christ heals the sick even from a distance; he need not go where the patient is in order to heal him; but neither can a sick man wait for the doctor to arrive; his wish brings the doctor by enchantment. Wishes are not subject to the barriers of space and time; they are unrestricted, unfettered, as free as a god. And Christ's healing is not limited to ailments that might have been cured in natural ways; he also heals incurable ills; he gives sight to men who were born blind.* "Since the world began was it not heard that any man opened the eyes of one that was born blind. If this man were not of God, he could do nothing."

But even this divine miraculous power merely embodies and brings home to us the power of human desires. To human desire nothing is impossible, nothing is unattainable. Christ awakens the dead, Lazarus, for instance, who had "lain in the grave four days already," who, as his sister Martha said, "by this time . . . stinketh, for he hath been dead four days." But in our wishes, in our imagination we each day awaken dead persons who were dear to us. Our wishes, to be sure, remain wishes. But a god can accomplish what man only desires; through its gods, the religious imagination realizes man's wishes. Thus the *belief in God* and the *belief in miracles* are one: the only difference between miracle and God is the difference between action and agent. Miracles are the proofs that the wonder-working being is all-powerful, capable of fulfilling all man's desires and for this very reason he is invoked and revered as a divine being. A God who has ceased to perform miracles, who fulfills no desires, hears no prayers except for those which can be fulfilled by natural process and consequently without recourse to Him, without prayer, is a useless God, who serves no purpose. Nothing is more superficial, more arbitrary, than the attitude of modern Christians, the so-called rationalists, toward miracles, which they abolish while still clinging to Christianity and the Christian God, either offering natural explanations which destroy the whole significance of miracles, or disposing of them in some other equally frivolous way.

* Medical skill can also cure the born blind, but only in cases of curable blindness; such cures, accordingly, are not miracles.

A modern rationalist whom we have already mentioned goes so far as to quote the following passage from Luther in support of his superficial and frivolous treatment of miracles: "The word is far more important that the works and acts of Christ, and if we had to forgo one or the other, it would be better to forgo the works and acts than the word and doctrine. Therefore those books are most to be praised which treat most of the word and teachings of Our Lord Jesus Christ. For even if the miracles of Christ had not taken place or we knew nothing about them, we would have enough with His word, without which we could have no life." If here and there Luther shows indifference to miracles, he is referring only to miracles represented without religious meaning, without faith, as mere historical, i. e., past and dead occurrences. What is it to other men that some Jew or other was miraculously healed, or miraculously fed? Seen as historical facts, miracles are relevant only to the time and place where they occurred; to this extent they have, as the rationalists put it, only a relative value, limited to the contemporaries who saw them and benefited by them. But to take miracles as mere historical facts is to disregard their true religious significance.

A miracle is held to be proof positive that the being who performed it is all-powerful, supernatural, and divine. We should be amazed, not at the miracle, but at the being who performed it and is capable of performing others like it, if they are required by man's affliction. The word, the teachings are more than works insofar as the works benefit only individuals and are bound to time and place, whereas the word penetrates everywhere and even in our own day does not lose its meaning. Nevertheless, if I am not mistaken, a miracle says the same thing as the word, the doctrine, except that the doctrine says in universal terms, in words, what the miracle expresses in tangible examples. The word says: "I am the resurrection and the life; he that believeth in me, though he were dead, yet shall he live. And whosoever liveth and believeth in me shall never die." But what does the miracle of Lazarus' resurrection from the dead say? What does Christ's own resurrection from the grave say? These miracles say the same thing, but in examples, in specific acts which lend sensuous confirmation to what the word says in universal terms. Thus a miracle is also a doctrine, a word, except that it is a dramatic word. Miracles, I say in *The Essence of Christianity,* have universal, exemplary significance. "These miracles," says Luther, "are written *for us* who are chosen. This act, the passing through the Red Sea, was performed as an example to show us that it would be the same for us," that is, that in similar emergencies God would perform similar miracles. Thus when Luther speaks disparagingly of miracles, it is only of miracles considered as dead historical events that are of no concern to us.

But Luther speaks just as disparagingly of other matters, indeed, of all doctrines or articles of faith that are considered only historically, that are not seen in connection with the present, with the living man, and even of God if He is regarded solely in relation to Himself and not to man. One need only consider the passages quoted in *The Essence of Faith According to Luther.** When Luther speaks disparagingly of miracles, his meaning is as follows: What does it help you to believe that Christ raised Lazarus from the dead if you do not believe that He can also awaken you, your brother, and your child from the dead if He so wills? What does it help you to believe that Christ "filled" five thousand on five barley loaves, if you do not believe that he can fill you and indeed all the hungry with as little food or none at all if He so wills? Thus Luther did not limit the power to work wonders to the early period of Christianity, when, according to the now prevailing belief, it was necessary as at no other time to perform miracles in order to propagate the Christian faith. An absurd distinction, be it said in passing. Either miracles are *always* necessary or *never* necessary. Was there ever a greater need for miracles than in a time like our own, when there are more deeply convinced unbelievers than perhaps ever before? Luther was far from restricting the power to work miracles to the early period of Christianity: "We still have the power," he says, "to give such signs," though of course, as he says elsewhere, only when they are necessary.

Hence nothing could be more arbitrary, unreasonable, and dishonest than to dissociate belief in God from belief in miracles, or Christian doctrine from Christian miracles. The equivalent would be to dissociate cause from effect, a rule from its application, a doctrine from the facts that confirm it, and to accept one while

* Melvin Cherno, trans. (New York: Harper & Row, 1967).

rejecting the other. If you reject miracles, you must also reject God. If you reach out beyond the world and nature and assume the existence of a God, you must also reach out beyond the manifestations of nature. If a God, a being distinct from the world and nature, is the cause of nature and world, then His existence must be demonstrated by manifestations distinct from the manifestations of nature. Such manifestations are miracles; they are the only proofs of the existence of a God. God is not only distinct from nature, He is its contrary. The world is sensuous and corporeal, God, at least according to the faith even of our rationalist believers, is nonsensuous and incorporeal; but if there is such a being, He must have manifestations, and these will necessarily be contrary to the manifestations of nature. Such manifestations contrary to nature are miracles. If I deny the existence of miracles, I have to content myself with nature, with the world, and if I nevertheless hold that nature and the world—the objects that strike my senses, the stars, the earth, the plants and animals—are caused, I can only posit a cause that is not essentially differentiated from nature. For such a cause the word God would be a misnomer. For "god" always designates an arbitrary, spiritual, fantastic being, differentiated from nature. In order to go beyond nature, to arrive at a God, I must make a leap. This leap is the belief in miracles.

The rationalists believe in a God; they believe, as the above-cited rationalist puts it, that there is "*no justification whatever* for saying that law or world order reside in *the nature of things* themselves; things cannot give laws, but only receive them." And it is true that nature gives no laws. But it also receives none. Only human rulers give laws and only human subjects receive them; neither notion is applicable to nature for the simple reason that the sun, the moon, the stars, and the substances of which they are composed are not men. It was not a legislator who commanded oxygen to combine with other elements only in definite proportions, nor did oxygen receive any such law; this property is simply a characteristic of oxygen and one with its nature and existence. A rationalist, however, assumes the existence of a God who, like a king giving laws to his subjects, gives the world laws that are not inherent in the world, in the nature of things. If he wishes to be consistent, he must therefore assume that there are proofs of the existence of such a lawgiver, proofs that what we call law or world order is not inherent in the nature of things; *these proofs* are *miracles.*

The only possible proof, for example, that no necessary law, grounded in the nature of woman, prevents her from becoming a mother without the help of a man, and that whether she does so or not depends on God's will alone, is provided when a woman becomes pregnant without the help of a man. But the rationalist does not believe in miracles, he denies them, that is to say, he denies the obviously absurd consequences of religion; but he does not question the causes of these absurdities, because they are not obvious and are discovered only by painstaking thought and investigation, and for that he is too lazy, too narrow-minded, too superficial. And yet, to be consistent, I should have to deny the cause along with the effects, or accept both cause and effects. To make nature dependent on God is to make the world order, the necessity of nature, dependent on the will; it means to put a prince, a king, a ruler at the head of nature. But just as a prince proves he is a true ruler only by his ability to make and unmake laws, so a God can only prove His divinity by His power to abolish laws, or at least to suspend them temporarily when the situation demands. The only proof that He has made the laws is that He also *unmakes* them. And such proof is provided by miracles. "God," says Bishop Nemesius in his treatise *On Human Nature,* "is not only outside of all necessity, but He is also the Lord and Maker [i. e., of necessity]; for since He is a being who can do everything He wills, nothing He does results from natural necessity or from law. All things are possible for Him [i. e., contingent], even those that are necessary. And that this might be made manifest, He once halted the course of the sun and the moon, which move with necessity and always act in the same way, in order to show that for Him nothing is necessary and that everything is possible according to His will."

Rationalist believers try to side-step the necessity of miracles by saying: "The divine will is the most perfect, as such it cannot change but must work undeviatingly toward a goal; the divine will must therefore be the most constant, it must be manifested as an unalterable law, as a fixed rule that never admits of an exception." How preposterous! A will that is not *manifested as a will,* but as an *unalterable law* is no will at all, it is only a clerical phrase and circumlocution for natural necessity, an expression of the lukewarmness and slipshodness of the rationalists, who are too much influenced by theology to see the whole truth of nature and too much influenced by science to draw the ultimate consequences from theology, and who consequently subordinate the world to an image and likeness of their own indecision, to *a will that is not a will* and a *necessity that is not a necessity*. A will that always does the same thing is not a will. If we deny that nature has free will it is only for one reason, because it always does the same thing. We say that an apple tree bears apples out of necessity and not out of free will, because it never bears anything but apples, which moreover are always of the same variety; if we deny that a bird sings with freedom, it is only because it always sings the same songs, which means that it can sing no others.

But man does not, like a tree, always produce the same fruits; he does not, like a bird, always sing the same songs; sometimes he sings one song, sometimes another, sometimes a sad one, sometimes a gay one. The manifestations of man are precisely diversity, multiplicity, variability, irregularity, unlawfulness, and the only conceivable cause of such manifestations is a being endowed with free will. Thus the unchanging, regular orbits of the planets led the Christians to infer that they were not divine free beings as the pagans believed, for if they were free in their movements, they would change their course now and then. The Christians were right: a free being proves himself only by free, inconstant actions. The river or brook that rushes by before my eyes and ears always makes the same impression on me, or at least the same kind of impression, for the current may increase or decrease as the amount of water varies. But how varied is the impression made by human song! It provokes all manner of moods and emotions; it can be in any of several keys. But a monotonous being, a being that always manifests itself in the same way, that always produces the same effect, is no more free than a stream, whose effects are always identical and unchanging, is a free human being.

It is an absurdity that the rationalist should divest God of His power to work wonders on the ground that wonder-working is a human conception. If we eliminate God's humanity or resemblance to man, we also eliminate God. What distinguishes God from man is precisely nature, it is the attributes or powers abstracted from nature, for example, the power of nature that causes the grass to grow or a child to form in the womb. If you want a being who has nothing in common with man, replace God by nature; if you want a being who has will, intelligence, consciousness, and personality like man, if you want a perfect, whole human being, do not deny that God works wonders, that He does and plans different things according to the times and circumstances, in short, that His will is as changeable as a monarch's will, as the will of man in general, for only a *changeable* will is a will. *Voluntas hominis,* say the jurists, *est ambulatoria usque ad mortem,* man's will is changeable up to his death. I have no need to will what I always, unchangeably will; "always" and "unchangeable" are the end, the death, of will. I want to walk because I have been sitting or standing, to work because I have been resting or idling, to rest because I have been working. Will occurs only where there are oppositions, inconstancies, interruptions. But in the realm of religious faith, which appoints a being endowed with will ruler over the world, this change, this interruption of the eternal monotony of nature is provided by miracles. Thus it is arbitrary in the extreme to dissociate miracles from the belief in God.

But such arbitrariness, such thinking by halves, is characteristic of our rationalists, of our modern Christians in general. One more example in support of this contention. In opposition, it is true, to certain other rationalists who explain the resurrection by saying that Christ did not really die on the cross, the rationalist author we have quoted above puts up with the resurrection, accepts it as an historical fact, but does not draw the inference that inevitably follows from acceptance of the resurrection, and moreover does not accept the circumstances attending this supposed fact in Scripture. Mark, Matthew, and Luke are unanimous in relating that when Jesus yielded up the ghost "the veil of the temple was rent in twain from the top to the bottom"; according to Matthew "the earth did quake and the rocks rent; and the graves were opened" both at the death and at the resurrection of Christ. All this our rationalist ascribes to the embroidery of the oral tradition. But if Christ really rose from the dead and did not merely awake from a cataleptic trance, his resurrection from the dead was a miracle, and indeed a very great and important miracle; for it was a victory over death, over nature's hardest and most unyielding necessity, which even the pagan gods had not been strong enough to overcome. How can such a miracle stand alone? Must it not have been attended by other miracles? If once we accept this one miracle, is it not natural, is it not necessary, to believe that all nature trembled when the chain of natural necessity, the chain that binds a dead man to death, to the grave, was forcibly sundered? Verily, our orthodox ancestors were far more rational than our present-day rationalists; for their faith was a coherent whole; they thought: if I believe this, I must believe that, whether it suits me or not; if I accept the cause, I must put up with the effect; in short, if I say A, I must also say B.

Twenty-seventh Lecture

In the preceding lecture I contended that the miraculous events attending the death of Jesus are intimately connected with the resurrection. For if Christ rose from the dead, his resurrection is a miracle, a proof of God's omnipotence, in the face of which death is nothing; but such a miracle cannot stand by itself and requires other miraculous and extraordinary events in confirmation. The resurrection would be meaningless without the preparation and support of other miracles. The circumstances attending the death of a man who is going to rise from the dead and so prove to the world that there is no death—for that is the meaning of the resurrection—cannot be as common and natural as those attending the death of some ordinary man. Consequently, if I go as far as our rationalist friend and dispose of the miracles surrounding the resurrection as legends, poetic embellishments, works of the imagination, I must necessarily take one step more and declare the resurrection itself to be the work of the religious imagination.

What man wishes, what at a given stage of development he cannot help wishing—that he believes. A wish is the desire that something which is not should be. His imagination and faith tell him that this thing exists. The Christians wished for heavenly life; they had no earthly wishes like the pagans, no interest either in the natural or the political world. To quote Theodoretus, the Greek Church Father: "Plato's definition of a true philosopher as a man who does not concern himself with political affairs, does not apply to the heathen philosophers but only to the Christians, for Socrates, the greatest of philosophers, frequented gymnasiums and workshops and even served as a soldier. But those who took up the Christian or evangelical philosophy withdrew from political turmoil and retired to secluded places where, undistracted by concern for women, children, and earthly goods, they were able to devote themselves to religious contemplation and the mode of life that goes with it." Because Christians desired a better life to come, they believed that there was such a life. Men who do not wish for another life do not believe in one. God and religion are nothing more than man's yearning for happiness, satisfied in his imagination. The Christian desire for a life of endless, deathless beatitude in heaven was fulfilled, in the religious imagination, by Christ's resurrection; for the resurrection, the immortality of every Christian depends on his resurrection; he is its exemplar.

But the belief in a resurrection is much older than Christianity; it was a dogma of the Zoroastrian or Persian religion. And it is possible to find still another historical explanation for the fulfillment, or supposed fulfillment of this wish: conceivably Christ's followers believed him to be dead and were already mourning his death, so that, when he reappeared, they supposed he had really risen from the dead. But such an attempt to trace religious facts, that exist only in faith, back to historical facts, to determine their underlying historical truth, is sheer pedantry and shows an utter misunderstanding of religion. Historical facts are not religious facts; when an historical person or event becomes an object of religion, that person or event ceases to be historical and becomes a creature of man's feeling or imagination. Thus Jesus, as presented to us in the Bible, has ceased to be an historical and has become a religious person; he is represented as a miraculous, all-powerful wonder-worker, who is able to fulfill all man's desires, at least those that are aimed at nothing evil or immoral in the Christian sense—hence as a creature of the imagination.

Another argument by which rationalist believers dispose of miracles is formulated as follows by our rationalist friend: "If miracles are to provide a scientific proof of revelation, a miracle must be defined as a physical fact which cannot be explained by the natural chain of causality and from which it can therefore be inferred that God's hand has directly intervened. But in order to be sure that a fact cannot have resulted from natural process, we should have to know all about nature and its laws. And since no man has or can have such knowledge, we can never be absolutely certain that a given fact cannot have followed from the natural order of things, and must therefore reflect an extraordinary intervention of the divine omnipotence." But precisely because man's wishes and imaginings, which represent miracles to us as realities above and outside the natural scheme of things, are above and outside natural necessity (for example, an incurably blind man's wish to see not only disregards the physical nature of blindness but actually stands in direct opposition to the natural conditions and laws which determine the possibility of fulfilling such a wish), miracles differ so obviously and unmistakably from the workings of nature that we need have no hesitation about saying that they cannot possibly have resulted from the scheme of natural things and causes. The early theologians were quite right in saying that miracles are not only above the order of nature but also contrary to it; for they reflect pure desire.

Thus we may state apodictically, as the philosophers put it, that is, with absolute certainty and conviction, that miracles cannot be explained on the basis of nature, that is, of external nature, and that they can have sprung only from the extraordinary intervention of the divine omnipotence. To which statement we need only add that this divine, superhuman power is precisely the power of human desires and imagination. In short, the essence of religion and divinity is simply the essence of desire and of the inseparably related imagination; for only in the imagination is God—and this includes the God of the rationalists and philosophical thinkers, who is nothing other than the essence of their own thinking—a being existing outside of thought. And the foregoing explanation also shows the absurdity of the question or controversy about the possibility, reality, and necessity of miracles. Such a controversy, such a question can arise only if we consider miracles *in themselves,* or confine ourselves to the outward manifestation without going into the inner psychological and human source to which alone the outward manifestation owes its existence. Moreover, the psychological or human origin of miracles is made evident by the mere fact that miracles are performed *by men,* or in the language of religious faith, by God through the instrumentality of men. And this also marks the obvious difference, which we have touched on above, between the so-called miracles of nature and religious miracles. Religious miracles are not conceivable without man; for they relate only to man. Natural miracles, the natural phenomena that arouse our admiration, occur even where there is no man to admire them. The wonders of geology, the Megatheria, Dinotheria, and Ichthyosauria, existed, at least according to the assumptions of modern geology, even before men existed; but until Joshua came along, the sun was not halted in its natural course.

At first glance it seems paradoxical to derive religion from human desires, to say that God, the supreme object of religion, is one with desire; for in religion, at least in the Christian religion, man prays: Father, not my will, but thine, be done; for religion commands man to sacrifice his desires. But a Christian—a *genuine* old Christian, it goes without saying, not a modern one—sacrifices only the desire for wealth, the desire to have children, the desire for health or long life, but not the desire for immortality, divine perfection, and beatitude. He subordinates all these desires, which to his way of thinking are temporal, earthly, and carnal, to the one fundamental and principal desire for eternal bliss; and the Christian God cannot be differentiated from this desire, from the fantasy of an eternal heavenly life. *To the true Christian, God and beatitude are therefore one.* Even a man who has no such extravagant supernatural desires as a Christian, whose desires are limited to real human life, even a man animated by normal selfish desires, must subordinate any number of secondary desires to his main desire if he wishes to satisfy it. A man whose main desire is to become rich or to remain in good health must repress innumerable other desires if he really wishes to become rich or keep his health. Much as he would like to pursue a certain pleasure at this moment, he must forgo it if he is not, by satisfying a momentary impulse, urge, or desire, to endanger the fulfillment of his main desire.

Thus when a Christian says: not my will, but thine, be done—the meaning of these words is simply: not my will, not my desire for this and that, which if fulfilled may later be my downfall, not my will for so-called temporal goods in general be done. But this does not mean that the will or striving for happiness as such, the desire for enduring eternal happiness, for heavenly bliss should not be done. In wishing or praying that the will of God be done, a Christian assumes that He wills only the welfare of man, or at least his eternal welfare and salvation.[28] Thus the religious ordinance that man should renounce certain desires is no argument against our reduction of religion and the gods to human wishes. Without man there is no religion; but without wishes, there is no man. The only difference between the wishes without which there is no religion or God and the wishes without which there is no mankind, without which man is not man, is that religion has wishes that can be fulfilled only in the imagination, in faith, whereas man as man, the man who replaces religion with culture, reason, science and replaces heaven by earth, has desires that do not exceed the limits of nature and reason and whose realization lies within the realm of natural possibility.

The apparent difference between wish and religion can also be stated as follows: man's wishes are arbitrary, lawless, and unrestrained, whereas religion imposes laws, duties, and restraints upon man. But duties are merely man's fundamental strivings, predispositions, and desires, which in uncivilized times are translated by religion or God, and in civilized times translated by man's own nature, into laws to which he is expected to subordinate certain particular desires, wishes, and passions. All religions, but especially those that have played a significant part in the history of human civilization, have been concerned solely with man's well-being. The only reason for the duties, the restrictions, they imposed on man was that without such duties and restrictions, it was thought, man would be unable to attain his main purpose, his main desire, namely, happiness. There are indeed times when man's duty comes into conflict with his striving for happiness, where a man must sacrifice even his life to duty; but such cases are tragic and in any case unusual. They cannot be cited as justification for raising the conflict between duty or morality and the striving for happiness to the level of a law, norm, or principle.

Originally and fundamentally, duty had no other purpose than the happiness and well-being of man. Man makes a law, a duty, of what he desires, what he desires before all else. Where the existence or, what amounts to the same thing, the welfare of a people —for what is existence without welfare, without happiness?—and by that same token the human individual, was bound up with agriculture, where a man could not be happy, could not be a man without agriculture—for only the happy man is a man, a free, complete, true man who feels himself to be a man—where, accordingly, man's main desire was that agriculture should prosper, there farming was a *religious duty and concern.* And where a man cannot attain his human desires and aims without destroying the wild beasts that interfere with them, it becomes a *religious* duty to destroy them; but the dog, the animal which helps man to fulfill his desires, to attain to happiness, to accomplish his human purposes, becomes a sacred, divine animal, as in the old Persian religion. In short, the opposition between duties and desires is merely deduced from certain special cases in human life, and is without universal truth or validity. On the contrary: what man desires from the bottom of his heart is the one rule and duty of his life and activity. Duty, or law, merely transforms the object of man's unconscious drives into an object of will and consciousness. If, to give an example based on the diversity of men's minds and inclinations, it is your desire—a desire justified by your capacities, mind you—your inner drive, to become an artist, then it is your duty to become one and to regulate your whole mode of life accordingly.

But how then does man come to transform his desires into gods, into beings; the desire to be rich, for example, into a god of riches, the desire for fertility into a god of fertility, the desire to be happy into a happy god, the desire not to die into an immortal being who overcomes death? What man desires, what each man in his own situation necessarily and fundamentally desires, becomes his belief; the part of his mind in which religion has its roots regards it as something real or possible; he does not doubt that it may be; his mere wish is the pledge of its possibility. Desire as such is to him a magic power. In Old German "to wish" is synonymous with "to perform magic." In the Old German language and religion, one of the names for the supreme deity was *Wish,* with which word, as Jacob Grimm writes in his *German Mythology,* the old language expressed the "summit of salvation and happiness, the fulfillment of all gifts." And he expresses the belief that the German word "*Wunsch*" derives from "*Wunjo,*" meaning joy, bliss, or perfection of all kinds. Certain thirteenth-century poets personify Wish as a mighty, creative being. This Grimm regards as a vestige of the old pagan usage and observes that in most such passages the name Wish might be replaced by the word God.

Though he distinguishes the meaning of wish in later usage, where it means the striving for the gifts and perfections that God possesses, from the original meaning, it is nonetheless evident that originally, both for language and for religion, the wish and its *object* were one. What I wish to have I already possess in my imagination, what I wish to be—healthy, rich, perfect—I really am in my imagination; for in wishing for health, I imagine myself to be healthy. And for this very reason Wish is a divine being, a supernatural, magical power, which from the cornucopia of the imagination showers me with all desirable powers and gifts. And the Christian blessing is the same as the pagan wish. To bless someone is equivalent to wishing him good things; thus blessing is tantamount to wish, and blessing also means the object, the good, that I wish myself and others. "In Scripture too," says Luther in his exegesis of *Blessing,* "the common manner of speaking is: *Give me a blessing. Have you not more blessings?* That means: Give me goods, bread, garments. For all things are gifts of God; it is through His blessing that we have what we have, and that is why these things are called blessings, that is, gifts of God, which He gives us by His blessing." The only difference between the divine wish or blessing and the human wish or blessing is that the divine wish is the *fulfilled, realized* human wish. If God is called Wish, it is therefore for the same reason that God can, and indeed must, be described as man's striving for happiness realized in his imagination, that *prayer* is said to be *all-powerful* and that Almighty God Himself is merely the omnipotence of human prayer and desire, transformed into an objective being.

Like poetry, religion represents as really and concretely existing what exists only in the imagination; it transforms desires, thoughts, imaginings, states of feeling into real beings, differentiated from man. The source of the belief in witchcraft and magic is precisely that men attributed a real superhuman power to wishes, believing, for example, that one man can *really harm* another by *wishing* him harm. The Romans and Greeks represented wishes of vengeance, even *curses,* as gods or rather goddesses, that is, as beings who executed curses and fulfilled wishes of vengeance. The Greeks called them Erinyes, the Romans Dirae or Furiae. And what is true of curses is true also of blessings. "In Holy Scripture," says Luther in his exegesis of the Pentateuch, "*active* blessings are not mere wish-blessings, but, as the words indicate, those which invariably bring about [what is wished for], which give it and bring it with them. . . . Thus if I were to say: would to God that your sins be forgiven you . . . that might be called a blessing of love. But the blessing of promise and faith and present gifts is as follows: I absolve you of your sins."

In other words: faith and imagination transform subjective into objective, thought into reality; they transform "Oh, if only I were" or "Oh, if only I had" into "I am," "I have"—wish into act. But as we all know, man couches his wishes, good or bad, his blessings and maledictions, in certain words and formulas, and to these formulas, words, and names he attributes objective superhuman effects, that is to say, magic powers. The religious Romans, for example, believed that through certain formulas of prayer or magic they could produce or prevent rain and storms, bewitch the fruits of the field, protect houses against fire, cure wounds and diseases, and prevent people from running away. And the Bavarians still believe that it is possible to "pray a man to death," that is, to kill him by prayer. It is also for reasons of faith or superstition that people hesitate to utter the names of things they fear, for they believe that by pronouncing the name they will summon up the object it designates. Some North American Indians are so afraid of the dead that they never say their names, and the living homonyms of the deceased take new names. They believe that the deceased—or his ghost—lives on as long as he is named and thought of, but ceases to exist as soon as he ceases to exist *for them,* that he goes out of existence when they stop thinking of him or uttering his name. The Greeks and Romans held that an omen is effective only if one pays attention to it, which is perfectly true, for it has a good or bad effect only if I put a pleasant or a gloomy interpretation on it.

Many peoples, in fact most childlike or barbarous peoples, believe that when they dream of dead persons, the dead are really present; and in general they look upon the image or thought of a being or object as the being or object itself. Uncivilized peoples even believe that in dreams the soul leaves the body and goes to the places where the dreamer's imagination has taken him in his dream; they look on such dream journeys as real journeys and take the lies and fairy tales served up to them by their imagination for truths and facts. And because in daydreams one often wanders to distant places, because the mind is not always in the same place as the body, the Greenlanders believe that even in the waking state the soul leaves the body and goes on trips.

Such notions are merely gross and glaring examples of how man transforms the subjective into the objective, how he confers objective existence on what exists only in his own thought and imagination, especially when his representation—a good thing he desires or an evil that he fears—is related to his striving for happiness, for like fear, love and yearning, too, make a man blind, so that he sees nothing but what he loves and desires, forgetting everything else. Or in other terms: man does not transform all his imaginings, thoughts, and wishes *into beings,* but chiefly those that are intimately bound up with *his own nature,* which are as real to him as his own being because they are its characteristic expression; which have a character of necessity for him precisely because they are rooted in his fundamental nature. The pagans regarded their gods as real beings because they *could conceive of no other gods,* because only those gods were consonant with their pagan being.

The Christians, on the other hand, do not doubt that the pagan gods are mere *imaginary* beings, but only because, from the standpoint of true Christians, the gifts bestowed by these gods, the wishes they fulfill are vain, futile wishes. To a true Christian, it is not necessary to be healthy; why then would he require a god of good health? It is not necessary to be rich; why then a god of riches? To him nothing is necessary except for what helps him to attain heavenly beatitude. In short, a Christian regards as *real* beings only *those* thoughts and imaginings that are consonant with, and related to, his Christian being, those thoughts and imaginings that image and embody his own nature. A Christian has no doubt about the truth and reality of immortality, of a life after death, and yet this life exists only in his thought and imagination. He does not doubt the truth of such fantasies, because they are rooted in his Christian supernaturalist essence. Man believes only in a God who expresses and reflects his own being, he regards as real only the representations or imaginings that are consonant with his most heartfelt wishes. And that is why I wrote in *The Essence of Christianity* that man's belief in God is nothing other than his belief in himself, that in his God he reveres and loves nothing other than his own being, but that for this very reason it is now necessary and incumbent on us to transform this unconscious, perverted, fantastic veneration and love of man into a conscious, straightforward, rational veneration and love.

Twenty-eighth Lecture

THUS MAN TRANSFORMS his feelings, desires, imaginings, and thoughts into beings; though what he wishes, thinks, or imagines has no other existence than in his mind, it takes on objective existence for him. "*All objects of thought*," says Kleukner (speaking of the religion of Ormazd, but what he says is equally true of every other religion, though the objects are not the same), "all objects of thought [i. e., in this context, imaginary distinctions or beings] are here regarded as *real* beings and hence also as objects of worship."* Thus man has even projected "nothing," which is a mere thought or word, into the outside world, so arriving at the preposterous notion that before the world there was nothing, that the world was even created out of nothing. But by and large, it is only the thoughts and wishes rooted in his innermost being that man transforms into beings, things, or gods. A savage, for example, transforms every painful sensation into an evil being who torments man, every product of the imagination that frightens him into a diabolical spook. Civilized man transforms his human feelings into divine beings. Among all the Greeks, according to Vossius, only the Athenians erected an altar to Compassion. And political man transforms his political wishes and ideals into gods. In Rome there was a goddess of freedom, to whom Gracchus built a temple; Concordia also had her temple; and public welfare, honor, in short every idea that is of special importance to political man, was deified.

The Christian kingdom, on the other hand, was not of this world; the Christians looked upon heaven as their home. Accord-

* Kleukner, *Zend-Avesta.*

ingly, the first Christians celebrated not a man's birthday, like the pagans, but the day of his death, because to them death was not only the end of life, but also the beginning of a new, heavenly life. This is what distinguished them from the pagans, whose whole being was immersed in the reality of the natural and political world. And the Christians hypostatized only the wishes, thoughts, and imaginings that reflected this distinction, that reflected their own essence. The pagans made a god of flesh-and-blood man, the Christians deified only the spiritual and moral essence of man. If the Christians strip their God of all sensuous attributes, passions, and needs, it is only because they think these away from their own being, because they believe that their essence, their spirit will, as they put it, cast off the bodily husk, that they will one day become beings who neither eat nor drink, but are pure spirits.

What a man is not yet in reality but hopes and believes that he will one day become, what is consequently the object of his wishes, yearnings, and strivings and by that same token not an object of sense perception, but only of imagination, is known as an *ideal,* or in plain language, a model or prototype. The god of a man or people, at least of a people which is not content to stagnate in savagery but wants to progress and for that very reason has a history (for the sole foundation of history is man's urge and striving to perfect himself, to procure a suitable existence), is nothing other than its ideal. "Be ye therefore perfect, even as your Father which is in heaven is perfect," says the New Testament. And the Old Testament: "Ye shall be holy, for I the Lord your God am holy." Thus if religion is taken to be nothing other than the cultivation of an ideal, it is perfectly right to regard the elimination of religion as inhuman, for man in his striving must set himself a goal, a model to emulate.

But the religious ideal—and that includes the Christian ideal—is not a satisfactory model. True, a god, the religious ideal, is always a human being; but he is a human being from whom numerous qualities characteristic of a real man are removed; he does not represent the whole human essence; he is only *a part* of man, torn out of the whole, an aphorism of human nature. The Christians, for example, tear spirit or soul out of man's body, and make this disembodied spirit into their God. Even the pagans, the Greeks for instance, who made flesh-and-blood man, as it were, into a god—even they deified the human form only as an object of the sense of sight, not of the sense of touch. Though in practice, in their daily life and cult, they treated the gods like real people, even serving them food and drink, their gods were, in their imagination and poetry, abstract beings, not real creatures of flesh and blood. This is still more true of the Christian God. And how can an abstracted, nonsensuous, disembodied being, a being without sensuous needs, impulses, passions, expect me, a bodily, sensuous, real being, to emulate Him? How can He be the law, the model of my life and activity? How can He give me laws? Man does not understand God, says theology, but neither, says anthropology, does God understand men. What does a God know of sensuous drives, needs, and passions?

But where, the believers cry, do the laws of morality come from if there is no God? Fools! Laws consonant with human nature originate solely with man. A law that I cannot observe, that is beyond my powers, is no law for me, no human law; and for that very reason a human law has a human origin. A God can do all possible, that is, imaginable, things, and can therefore expect all possible things of man. Just as He can say to men: You shall be as perfect and holy as I, He can say: You shall not eat and drink, for I, the Lord your God, do not eat or drink. In the eyes of a God eating and drinking are utterly disreputable, unholy, bestial. Laws that a God gives to man, that is, laws that have as their foundation and goal an abstracted being who lives only in the imagination, are consequently unfit for man, they result in the greatest hypocrisy, for I cannot be a man without denying my God, or, as the history of Christianity and similar religions has demonstrated, they result in the most unnatural actions. The necessary consequence of a spiritual, that is, abstract God, whom man makes into the law of his life, is self-mutilation and mortification.

The material misery of the Christian world consequently has its ultimate cause in its spiritual God or ideal. A spiritual God concerns himself only with the salvation of the soul, not with man's bodily well-being. Indeed, as the most pious and distinguished Christians have said, bodily welfare is incompatible with the welfare of the soul. Man must therefore replace the religious ideal with another ideal. Let our ideal not be a castrated, disembodied, abstract being but the whole, real, many-sided, fully developed man. Let our ideal imply not only the welfare of the soul, not only spiritual perfection, but also bodily perfection, welfare, and health. Here, too, the Greeks set us an example. Athletic games and exercises were a part of their religious festivals.

Moreover, religious ideals have always involved all manner of irrational and even superstitious conceptions. For religion presents its ideal as a being on whose will the fate of man depends, as a personal or at least independent being, independent of man, whom man should revere, love, and fear, toward whom, in short, he should direct all the feelings and attitudes aroused by real living beings. Man cannot conceive of an existence other than his own sensuous physical existence. Consequently, though the religious ideal is only a moral being, a figment of thought, religion represents it as a physical being. Of what is in man's mind the highest being or model it makes an objectively first being, whence all other sensuous, corporeal beings have sprung and on which their existence depends. Religion—and therein lies its absurdity—makes man's goal into the beginning of the world, the principle of nature. Because man feels and knows himself to be dependent on his ideal, because he feels that without this goal he is nothing, that to lose it would be to lose the aim and foundation of his existence, he concludes that the world cannot subsist without such a model, that without it the world would be nothing. Such thinking is the work of human vanity, which preens itself not only in the resplendent uniform of the state but also in the humble monk's or priest's robe of religion; or to use a modern word, it is the work of romanticism, which accords its religious ideal first place and honors it by neglecting everything else.

Man's attitude toward his religious ideal is that of the lover, or at least the romantic lover, who by comparison with his beloved reduces the virtues and charms of all other women to nothing, for in his eyes she is the one and only, incomparably, ineffably beautiful, the essence and epitome of all feminine virtues and charms, so that nothing is left for other women but the absence of these same charms, which she has gobbled up all by herself. In the face of the religious ideal, all other things and beings dwindle to nothingness, for it is the epitome of all virtues and perfections. Because all other things are indifferent to religious man, their existence becomes inexplicable to him, just as the existence of other women is inexplicable to the romantic lover. But since despite his religious ideal, which alone is worthy of existence, other things do somehow exist, he must discover some justification, however unsatisfactory, for their existence; and he finds such justification solely in their similarity—a very remote similarity, it is true—to his religious ideal, in the notion that they have something divine in them after all, though of course it is extremely imperfect; just as the romantic lover condescends to let other women exist side by side with the one and only, because, come to think of it, they bear her a certain resemblance. They too, after all, are women, just as other beings have at least this much in common with the divine being, that they too are beings.

For this reason—though it is not the only reason—man accords his religious ideal the first rank among all beings and believes that all other beings originated not only *after* Him but also *out of* Him. Man believes that they came into being after Him because he supposes that the being who is first in rank is first also in time, because man, especially the man of the ancient world in which religion is rooted, regards the older, earlier being as higher than the younger, newer being.* But man's reason for supposing that all other beings have their source in the first being is a purely negative, empty reason, namely, his ignorance; he just doesn't know where else they may have come from.

And one boner invites another. The first boner of religion is to make the religious ideal into a first, primordial being; the second, to make this first being the source of all others; and the second boner follows inevitably from the first. "Examine your premises!" This maxim is relevant both to religion and to politics. But though generally praised and followed in medicine, ethics, and pedagogy, it is decried in politics and religion. To cite an example from the field of religion—we are, after all, talking about religion—the rationalists take great pains to point out the obvious fallacies of religion; but these are secondary, subordinate fallacies; as for the fundamental fallacies, which have all the others as their conse-

* E.g.: "Antiquity is closer to the gods" (Cicero, *De Legibus*).

quence, the same rationalists let them stand, for they are sacred and inviolable. Consequently, when a rationalist asks an atheist what atheism is, the proper answer is: Rationalism is a half-baked, incomplete atheism; atheism is complete and thoroughgoing rationalism. Or: A rationalist is a surgeon, an atheist a physician. The surgeon cures only tangible ills; the physician cures the inner ills that cannot be grasped with fingers and forceps. But back to our main theme.

The God, the religious ideal, of the Christians, is the spirit or mind. The Christian sets aside his sensuous nature; he wants to hear nothing of the common, "bestial" urge to eat and drink, the common, "bestial" instincts of sexuality and love of young; he regards the body as a congenital taint on his nobility, a blemish on his spiritual pride, a temporarily necessary degradation and denial of his true essence, a soiled traveling garment, a vulgar incognito concealing his heavenly status. He wishes to be and to become pure spirit. The early Christians, it is true, believed in the resurrection of the flesh; in fact, the only difference between the Christian, or at least the early Christian, view and that of the pagan philosophers was that the Christians believed in the immortality not only of man's spirit, mind, and reason, but also of his body. "I wish to live not only by the soul, but also by the body," says Luther. "I want the body too." But this Christian body is in reality a heavenly, spiritual body, that is, an imaginary body which like all other religious objects is a mere reflection of human wishes and imagination. Like man's imagination, the spiritual body can remove instantly to a remote place; like thought, it passes through closed doors—for a closed door or a wall does not prevent me from imagining what is happening on the other side; the spiritual body can neither be punched nor kicked, sabered nor shot, any more than a fantasy or dream image can be punched or kicked.

Thus it is a wholly miraculous body, the fulfillment of man's supernatural wish to have a body that is free of sickness and suffering, invulnerable and immortal, and hence without needs. For the manifold needs of our body are the source of its manifold ailments; if, for example, man had no need of air and hence of lungs, he would have no pulmonary disorders, there would be one class of ailments the fewer. But the heavenly, spiritual body needs neither air, food, nor drink; it is a divine body without needs; in short, this body that is *not* a body is indistinguishable from the substance of the human imagination. This heavenly body notwithstanding, we may therefore say that the Christian's, even the early Christian's, ideal is the spirit or mind. The only difference between the different varieties of Christians is that the old believers in miracles had as their principal ideal or model the imaginative mind, a mind pregnant with sensuous, emotional images, whereas the Christian philosophers idealized the mind that derives abstract concepts from images; and the Christian rationalists and moralists chose as their ideal the practical, ethical mind that expresses itself in action.

And because the mind, the organ of feeling, thought, and will, is the Christian's supreme being and ideal, he also makes it the first being, the cause of the world. In other words, he transforms his mind into an objective being, distinct from himself and existing outside himself, and from it also derives the existing objective world. God, says the Christian, God, which means the objectified mind conceived as existing outside of man, made the world by His will and intelligence. But the Christian distinguishes this world-creative mind, which is perfect and infinite, from the human mind, which is imperfect, limited, and finite. This process of differentiation, this inference from a "finite" mind to an infinite mind, *this* proof of the existence of God, that is, of a perfect mind, is the *psychological* proof. Whereas the so-called cosmological proof starts from the world as a whole, and the physiological or teleological proof from the order, coherence, and purposiveness of nature, the psychological proof, which is the proof most characteristic of Christianity, starts from man's psyche, soul, or mind. The pagan god is a god abstracted from nature, sprung from nature; the Christian God is abstracted from the soul or mind, a product of the soul. The reasoning is briefly as follows: The human mind is; we cannot doubt its existence; there is something invisible and incorporeal in us that thinks, wills, and feels; but the knowledge, will, and ability of the human mind are deficient, restricted by the senses, dependent on the body. But the limited, finite, imperfect, and dependent presupposes something that is unlimited, infinite, and perfect; thus the finite mind presupposes an infinite mind as its source; therefore there is such a mind and this mind is God.

But are we justified in inferring the real independent existence of such a mind? Is the infinite mind not simply man's mind, which desires to be infinite and perfect? Don't man's desires play a part in the genesis of this God? Doesn't man wish to be free from the limitations of the body, does he not wish to be omniscient, omnipotent, and omnipresent? Isn't this God, this mind, therefore the fulfillment of man's wish to be an infinite mind? Have we not therefore objectified man's essence in this God as in other gods? For from man's desire to know everything, from his infinite thirst for knowledge, which is not and cannot be satisfied here below, from man's infinite striving for happiness, which no earthly possession or good fortune can satisfy, from his yearning for perfect morality, sullied by no sensuous drives, don't Christians, and even the present-day Christian rationalists, infer the necessity and reality of an infinite life and existence for man, not limited to the time of a man's life span or the space of this earth, unfettered by the body or by death? And by drawing such an inference are they not, if only indirectly, expressing the divinity of man? Is a being who endures forever, who never ends, who is attached to no time or place, who is capable of omniscience and indeed of infinite perfection, not a God or a divine being? Is then the Christians' God, their infinite mind, anything other than the model and prototype of what they wish to be some day, an image of the future unfolding of their own essence?

For what distinguishes the divine from the human mind? Solely the perfection and infinity of the divine mind; the attributes and properties are identical. According to Christian psychologists, the mind has nothing in common with matter, with the body. It is, as they put it, absolutely distinct from the senses and the body; the same is true of God. God cannot be seen, felt, touched; neither can the mind. The mind thinks, so does God. Christians, even Christian rationalists, believe that things are only the realized, materialized, embodied thoughts of God. The mind has or is consciousness, will, personality; so also God. Thus the only difference is that what is limited and finite in man, is unlimited and infinite in God. But what does this infinity of the divine attributes reveal? Nothing but the infinity or unlimitedness of human desires, of the human imagination and faculty of abstraction, of man's power or ability to abstract the universal from the individual and particular; as I, for example, abstract the universal concept *tree* from the various trees by disregarding all the differences and particularities by which individual trees are actually distinguished.

The infinite mind is nothing but the class concept of the mind that the imagination, at the behest of human wishes and strivings for happiness, embodies as an independent being. "The less definite, the more universal and abstract a word or definition is," says St. Thomas Aquinas, "the better it fits God, the more appropriate it is to Him." We have already shown this to be true in connection with the existence and nature of God in general. Now that we are dealing specifically with Christianity, the essence of which is mind or spirit, we must apply the same demonstration to the characteristics of God's mind. God, says the Bible for example, is love, that is, God is love in general. There are different kinds of human love: love of friends, love of country, sexual love, love of children and parents, an attitude of benevolence toward people in general, love of mankind; in man love is based on inclination, feeling, and the senses. But the love that is God or attributed to God is a concept abstracted from all these varieties, from all sensuous and individual specifications, love as such.

Another example is God's word, or the divine word. The older Christians, who were far more consistent in their thinking than the modern ones who have injected almost the whole of psychology and anthropology into their theology, attributed a *divine word* to the divine mind, and quite rightly so. The most spiritual, appropriate way in which the mind can express itself is in words; thought and speech (for speech need not be audible) are inseparable; take away the word, and the thought vanishes with it; destroy the name and you destroy the thing it designates; men began to think only when they began to speak, to form words. Consequently, if we attribute mind, intelligence, to God, if we speak of God's thoughts, we must also, if we are to be consistent, speak of His *words*. If we are not ashamed to suppose that the world, the sensuous, corporeal world, originated through the thought and will of a mind; if we are not ashamed to assert that things are not thought because they are, but are because they are thought, then we should also not be ashamed to say that they originated through the word—that words are not because things are, but that things exist only because of words. The mind as mind acts only through the word; only through the word does it reach out into the world, is it manifested.

In accordance with the belief that God is mind, the older theology and religion attributed the creation of the world to God's speech, to the divine word. But the Jewish or Christian religion was not alone in holding that the world came into being through the word; the Persians had held a similar view even earlier. What the Greeks termed *logos,* the Persian called *honover,* which, according to modern scholars such as Röth, simply means "the word" in the most literal sense.* But the word of God, at least in Christian theology, is nothing other than the concept of the word; the divine word is not any particular word, it is no Latin, German, Hebrew, or Greek word; no specific, individual word, no temporal word that dies away once spoken; but all these and similar specifications that theologians attach to the word of God are applicable to the concept of the word, to the word in general and as such. The religious and theological imagination hypostatizes the concept, the essence common to all the innumerable different words, as an *individual,* personal being; which itself in turn is differentiated from the word, just as it represents God as a special being, distinct from the world, although originally and in truth He is simply the essence of the world. And what is true of the word and of love, is true of the mind in general, of the intelligence, will, consciousness, and personality that are attributed to God, or deified, i. e., represented as God. In every case it is a human power, attribute, or capacity that is deified; but once it is deified, it is separated from all the specific properties attaching to the real human power, capacity, or attribute; so that, when this process of abstraction is carried to the extreme, nothing is left but a *mere word* —the word will, the word consciousness, but not consciousness or will themselves, not the specifications that constitute real consciousness and will—so that ultimately theology leads to nothing more than hollow but edifying phraseology.

* Röth, *Die Aegyptische und die Zoroastrische Glaubenslehre.*

Twenty-ninth Lecture

In discussing the psychological proof (which I termed the proof most characteristic of Christianity) I showed—and this was the crux of my exposition—that this proof of the existence of a God, or rather of an infinite mind, for that is how God is defined in Christianity, is merely an indirect, devious proof of the infiniteness of the human mind; whereas the proof of man's immortality is a direct, straightforward expression of the infiniteness of the human mind. For because there is a finite mind the Christians infer that there must be an infinite mind, and similarly from the existence of an imperfect mind which knows some things and is capable of doing some things, they infer the existence of a perfect mind which knows everything and can do everything. But they also conclude that because there is not room enough for man's mental powers and capacities within the confines of this life, this body—because in this life man cannot fulfill all his desires and potentialities—there must be an eternal, infinite life to come; they conclude that because man wants to know everything, because his thirst for knowledge is unlimited, he will inevitably know everything some day; that because man has not only an infinite capacity for perfection, but also an infinite drive toward perfection and happiness, which can never be fulfilled on this small earth, in this brief life span, in this vale of tears—therefore man, or the human mind, must some day become perfectly ethical and happy, or, as our cautious and cagey rationalists put it, perhaps not absolutely perfect, but at least progressively more perfect ad infinitum.

This makes it clear that the reasoning which arrives at a God and the reasoning which arrives at immortality are basically *one and the same,* and that consequently the idea of God and the ideal of immortality are essentially and fundamentally identical. The only difference is that God must be inferred before one can infer immortality; God is prerequisite to immortality; without God, there can be no immortality. Yet it is immortality that first provides the meaning and purpose of God's existence, or of the inference that He exists. Without God the belief in immortality has no support, no beginning, no foundation, in short, no principle. Immortality is a suprasensory, fantastic wish and thought, which contradicts the evidence of the senses that the dead are truly dead. How can I believe in the truth of such an idea, in the realization of such a wish without the support of a fantastic being above and opposed to the senses? How can I base such a belief on nature, on the world?

In nature there is no other immortality than reproduction, whereby a creature survives in others of its kind, in the species, and dead individuals are replaced by new individuals. Among the lower animals, the butterflies, for example, death is directly related to the act of mating. The butterfly dies as soon as it has brought other butterflies, or at least the eggs or germs of other butterflies, into the world. Without reproduction there would be no death; for in mating a creature exhausts its vitality; in multiplying, in bringing many creatures of its kind into the world, it annuls the uniqueness and hence the necessity of his own existence. Man, it is true, lives on for a considerable time after the loss of his reproductive power; but once this power is exhausted, old age sets in and, though slowly, the end approaches. How then can I base a belief in immortality on nature? Nature brings death, God alone confers immortality.

Once a man believes in immortality, it is true, nature provides him with countless examples and proofs to support his belief; that is, he interprets nature in line with his belief. The pagans, who did not believe in immortality, found proofs and images of their transience and mortality in the very same phenomena—the changes of the seasons, the setting and rising of the sun—which to the Christians, who believed in immortality and saw the world through the spectacles of their faith, were proofs and images of their immortality. The zephyrs melt the ice, says Horace, the summer tramples the spring, but vanishes as soon as the autumn pours forth its fruits, and immediately thereafter lifeless winter returns. But new circuits of the moon replace the sky's losses; we alone, once we go down, are dust and shadow like the pious Aeneas, like the wealthy Tullus and Ancus. How can I believe that after the visible, evident, undeniable ruin of the body, the so-called soul, the mind, the essence of man still remains, unless I believe in the existence of a soul or mind without a body, and that this disembodied mind is a supreme and all-powerful being, in comparison with whom all sensuous, bodily beings are insignificant and powerless?

Thus belief in immortality presupposes belief in God; that is to say, man thinks up a God because without a God he cannot conceive of immortality. In theory, in *doctrine, immortality* is merely a consequence of the belief in God; but in *practice,* in reality, the *belief in immortality* is the *motive* for the belief in God. Man does not believe in immortality because he believes in God, he believes in God because he believes in immortality, because without belief in God he can find no basis for his belief in immortality. In appearance, God is the first and immortality the second; but in reality *immortality is the first* and *God the second.* God is first only insofar as He is the instrument, the condition of immortality, or in other words: He is first because He is *personified, hypostatized beatitude* and *immortality,* the human future represented and embodied as a *present* being, so that the beliefs in immortality and God are not two separate beliefs or articles of faith, but one and the same.

Contrary to this assertion that the beliefs in God and immortality are one, that there is no difference between them, it can be argued that, as has been demonstrated not only by many individuals but by whole peoples, it is possible to believe in God without believing in immortality. But a God with whom one does not associate the idea or belief in human immortality is no true God, he is only a deified aspect of nature; for the divinity and eternity of a nature god, it is perfectly true, do not imply human immortality: nature is heartless, impervious to man's wishes, without concern for man. If like the ancient Parsis and other peoples I conceive of the sun, moon, and stars as eternal beings, what does this belief imply for me? Sun, moon, and stars existed before any human eye saw them; they do not exist because I see them; I see them because they exist; although they exist only for a being who sees, they do not exist for my eye without the action of what we call light—in short, my seeing them presupposes their existence; they were before I saw them, and they will be when I no longer see them, for, I should hope, they do not exist in order to be seen by me.

What does this imply for the immortality of my eye or of my being as a whole? The God from whom no immortality follows is either a natural object or, like the gods of the polytheists and notably the Greeks, a human but aristocratic individual. Among the Greeks men were known as mortals, the gods were called the immortals. Here again immortality is one with the concept of divinity; but it is a privilege of the gods and does not extend to men, because the gods are aristocrats who relinquish no part of their privileges, for they are jealous, selfish, envious beings. True, they are human through and through; they have all the vices and passions of the Greeks; but they are a special class of beings, who would not think of sharing their happiness and immortality with the common human rabble. "The gods have allotted fear and suffering to wretched mankind," says the Iliad. "They themselves live happily and without care." Actually, at least in Homer, the father or godfather of the Greek gods, the immortality of the gods does not amount to much; for though they do not really die, they *can* die.

Another type of God with whom the belief in immortality is not associated is a mere national God, the God of the early Jews, for example. The Jews did not believe in immortality, but only in the survival of the race through reproduction; they wished only for long life and progeny, wherein they resembled all the ancient peoples, especially those of the Orient, among whom it was and still is regarded as the greatest misfortune to part childless from the world. But the God Jehovah, the early one at least, was indistinguishable in character from the ancient Israelites. What the Israelite hated, his God hated; what smelled good to the Israelite was also a welcome smell to his God. On leaving the ark, Noah "offered burnt offerings on the altar. And the Lord smelled a sweet savour." Even the food that the Hebrews ate was also God's food. A national God can provide a foundation only for the idea of the nation's permanence and infinite expansion. "I will bless thee," said Jehovah to Abraham, the patriarch of the Jews, "and in multiplying I will multiply thy seed as the stars of the heaven, and as the sand which is upon the sea shore."

The God who does not give man consciousness of his immortality, in whom man finds no pledge of his eternal life, is a God only in name. Such a God in name is, for example, the God of certain so-called speculative philosophers, who deny immortality but cling to God; but they cling to Him only because there are many things that they are unable to explain without Him, because they need Him to fill in the gaps in their systems and heads; this, accordingly, is a merely theoretical, philosophical God. Such also is the God of certain rationalist scientists, who is simply nature or natural necessity, the universe or the cosmos personified. Obviously the idea of immortality is incompatible with such a God, for in viewing the cosmos man loses sight of himself, sees himself vanishing. Or else the rationalist God is the *first cause* of nature or the world. But a first cause is a far cry from a God. I can conceive of a mere force in nature as the first cause of the world. A God is essentially an object of veneration, love, and worship; I cannot love, revere, and worship a natural force. A God is not an aspect or force of nature; a God is a product of abstraction, of imagination, of the heart.

Essentially He is a creature of the heart; a God, I say in the next to last paragraph of the work underlying these lectures, my *Essence of Religion,* is not something you can find with a telescope in the astronomer's heavens, or with a magnifying glass in the botanical gardens, or with a mineralogist's hammer in the geologist's mines, or with a dissecting knife in the entrails of animals and men: you will find Him only in the faith, the imagination, the heart of man; for He himself is nothing other than the essence of the imagination, the essence of the human heart. A God is essentially a being who fulfills man's desires. And the most heartfelt desire, at least of those men whose desires are not curtailed by natural necessity, is the desire not to die, to live forever; this is indeed man's highest and ultimate desire, the desire of all desires, just as life is the epitome of all blessings, and for that very reason. Consequently a God who does not fulfill this desire, who does not annul death or at least replace it by a new life, is no God, at least no true God consonant with the concept of a God.

Without belief in God the belief in immortality is *without foundation;* and without belief in immortality the belief in God is *meaningless.* God is essentially an idea, a model of man; but a model of man does not exist *for itself,* it exists *for man;* its sole meaning and purpose is that man should become what the model represents; the model is simply the future man, personified and conceived of as an independent being. For this reason God is essentially a communist, not an aristocrat; He shares everything He is and has with man; all His attributes become attributes of man; and with full right, for they originated in man, they were abstracted from man, and in the end they are given back to him. "God is happy," says Luther, "but He does not wish to be happy for himself alone."

Religion looks upon God as an independent personal being; it therefore regards immortality and other divine attributes which man possesses or will possess, as gifts, so to speak, of God's love and goodness. But the true reason why at the end of religion—the present stage in our development—eschatological doctrine represents man as a divine being, the true reason is that God, at least the Christian God, is nothing other than the *essence of man.* And if the essence of man is a divine being, it necessarily follows that human individuals also are or will become gods. In Christianity the ideal or model, and at the same time the pledge of the divinity and immortality, not only of man as such, not only of the abstract man who is mind, reason, will, and consciousness and is deified in the invisible, intangible God, in the so-called God the Father, but also of the individual, real man, is the *God-man Christ,* in whose person it is made abundantly manifest that the divine being is not a being distinct from man. With typical halfheartedness, superficiality, and lack of discrimination, modern rationalist faith has abandoned the God-man, but clung to God; in other words, it has abandoned the consequence, the necessary corollary to belief in God, but kept the foundation. As I have already shown in another context, it has kept the *doctrine,* but rejected the *application,* the individual concrete *example* by which the doctrine is confirmed. The rationalist has kept the mind—God, says the rationalist like the old Christian, is a mind—but for all his mind and rational faith, he has lost his head; he has mind without a head, whereas the old Christian, quite reasonably and naturally, equipped the divine mind with the head of the God-man as the necessary organ and hallmark of the mind.

The rationalist has a divine will, but he lacks the indispensable conditions and organs of the will, the motor nerves and muscles, the instruments with which the Christian God, thanks to the God-man's miracles, demonstrates that He has a *real* will; the rationalist speaks of divine goodness and Providence, but he omits the God-man's human heart, without which goodness and Providence are mere words without truth. The rationalist bases immortality on the idea of God, though not alone; he also has other arguments. He speaks of the divine attributes as pledges of immortality: "As true as there is a God, we are immortal"; and yet he rejects the foundation of this inseparability or unity of divinity and immortality by rejecting the *unity of the divine and the human essence* in the God-man as idolatrous superstition. For the inference "As true as there is a God, man is immortal" is justified only if it has as its premise, or is translated into, this other statement: "As true as God is man, man is God, and consequently God's attribute of deathlessness, of exemption from the necessity of an end, is also an attribute of man."

Without the unity, that is, identity, of the divine and the human essence, there is no justification for inferring human immortality from the concept and existence of a God. Even religious faith, though representing immortality solely as a consequence of God's goodness, of God's grace or free will, also grounds it in the kinship between God and man, between the divine and the human mind. But kinship presupposes unity and equality of essence or nature; or rather, it is merely a homely expression for unity and equality. Consequently man's belief in immortality—and here I am limiting and correcting a previous statement of mine—can be founded even on an object which in itself is unfeeling and indifferent toward men, a natural phenomenon such as the sun or another heavenly body, though the immortality envisaged in such a belief is not the immortality of the Christians; but this is possible only on condition that man regards himself as one with the heavenly bodies, that he believes his essence and theirs to be one and the same. If I am a heavenly being, of heavenly origin, it goes without saying that I can no more die than the heavenly bodies—provided I conceive of them as immortal. Their immortality guarantees my own; for will a father abandon his own children and let them die? He would be combating his own flesh and blood, his own being.

Just as a heavenly being engenders only heavenly children, an immortal being engenders only immortal children or beings. Consequently, man traces his existence back to a God in order to assure himself of his divine origin and thereby of his divinity or immortality. Anyone who wishes to surmount death, the consequence of natural necessity, must also surpass its cause, nature itself. And anyone who does *not wish to end* in nature *cannot begin with nature,* but only with a God. Not nature, no!—a supernatural, divine being is my author, my cause, or in plain language: *I am a supernatural, divine being.* But the ground of my supernatural, divine nature is not my derivation from a supernatural being; on the contrary, I derive myself from such a being because in the depths of my heart I already regard myself as such and therefore cannot conceive of myself as originating in nature, in the world. "We see," says Luther in his commentary on Genesis, "that man is a creature *apart,* made to partake of divinity and immortality, for man is a *better creature than heaven and earth and all that is in them.*" "*I am a man,*" says the same Luther in another passage that I have quoted in my earlier works: "*that is a higher title than prince.* Reason: *not God but men made the prince,* but God alone made me a man."

The pagan philosopher Epictetus, who comes very close to Christianity in his doctrines and conceptions, speaks in similar terms. "If we imprint it sufficiently on our minds that we all of us have God as our principal cause, that God is the father of men [and gods], we shall surely never have a small or base opinion of ourselves. If the Emperor took you as his son, no one would be able to endure your pride. Should then the thought that you are God's son not exalt you, not make you proud?" But aren't all things and beings God's creatures? Doesn't religion tell us that He created everything? Yes, but He is not the creator of animals, plants, and stones in the same sense as He is the creator of man; His relation to men is that of a father to his sons; but He is not the father of the animals, or else Christians would look upon the animals as their brothers, just as they hold that because God is the father of all men all men are and should be brothers. "He [God]," says Luther in one of his sermons, "is your father, and *your* father alone, not the father of the birds, of the geese or ducks (or of the godless heathen)."

Similarly the Platonists, who lacked a Christology but had almost the same theology as the Christians, distinguished between God the demiurge or architect and God the Father; they called God as the author of thinking beings, of men, the Father, whereas they called God as author of the animals and inanimate beings the demiurge.* Thus the substance of the doctrine that God is the father of men, or that men are God's children, is that man is of divine origin and therefore divine, that is, immortal. God as the common father of men is simply the personified unity and equality of the human race, the generic concept in which all differences between men are annulled and effaced, but this concept is viewed as an independent being, differentiated from real men.

Thus it is quite natural and necessary that the divine attributes should become attributes of man; for what is true of the genus or class is also true of individuals; the genus is only the principle common to all individuals and comprising them. Accordingly, where men believe in a God but not in immortality, either the true meaning of divinity has not yet been found, or it has been lost. This meaning is as follows: God is the personified generic concept of man, the personified divinity and immortality of man. Thus, as I have said in *The Essence of Christianity*,† man's belief in God—that is, in a God who does not express the essence of nature—is simply man's belief in himself. A God is merely a being who fulfills man's desires; but how can I believe in a being who fulfills my desires if I do not first, or at the same time, believe in the sanctity, the justification and absolute validity of my desires? And how can I believe in the necessity of the fulfillment of my desires—which is my only reason for believing in the necessity of a fulfiller of desires, a God—unless I believe in myself, in the truth and sanctity of my being? What I desire is my heart, my being. How can I separate my being from my desires?

Hence the belief in God depends only on man's faith in the

* Plutarch, *Moralia*.

† George Eliot, trans. (New York: Harper Torchbook, 1957).

supernatural sublimity of his own being. Or in other words: in the divine being man merely objectifies his own being. To sum up briefly: in the divine omniscience man merely fulfills his own desire to know everything, or objectifies the faculty of the human mind not to be limited in its knowledge to this or that object, but to encompass all things. In divine ubiquity, he fulfills his desire not to be tied to any place, or objectifies the faculty of the human mind to be everywhere at once. In divine eternity, he merely fulfills the desire not to be restricted to any time, not to have an end, or merely objectifies the endlessness (at least if he thinks logically) and beginninglessness of the human essence, the human soul; for if man's soul cannot die, cannot end, it also, as many have quite logically held, cannot begin, or come into being. In divine omnipotence, man merely fulfills his desire to be able to do everything, a desire that is related to, or a consequence of, the desire to know everything; for, as Bacon said, knowledge is power; if you don't know how to make a thing, you can't make it; doing presupposes knowledge; so that a man who wishes to know everything also wishes to be able to do everything; or in other words: in divine omnipotence man merely objectifies and deifies his own universal powers, his unlimited capacity to do all things.

An animal, says Hugo Grotius—a Christian thinker who himself wrote about the truth of the Christian religion—can only do certain things; but man's power or ability is unlimited. In divine happiness and perfection man merely fulfills his wish to be himself happy and perfect, morally as in other respects, for without moral perfection there is no happiness: who can be happy if he is weighed down by envy and ill will, malice and vengefulness, greed and drunkenness? Thus the divine being is man, but not man in his prosaic reality; he is man according to man's poetic claims, desires, and thoughts, or rather man as he should be and some day will be. But man's most ardent, most sacred desire and thought is, or was, the thought of eternal life, the desire to be immortal. Thus man, immortalized by his own thought and desire, is God. In other words: God is nothing other than the future immortal man, differentiated from man as he exists at present in the body and flesh, and conceived of as an independent being. God is not a human but a superhuman being; but the immortal man of the future is also superior to the present, real, mortal man. God differs from man as the future or immortal man of faith differs from the real present or mortal man. In short, the unity, the identity of divinity and immortality, hence of God and man, is the solution to the riddle of religion, especially of the Christian religion. Just as nature—but nature as an object and product of human desire and imagination—is the core of nature religion, so man—but man as an object and product of man's desires, imagination, and faculty of abstraction—is the core of spiritual religion, the Christian religion.

Thirtieth Lecture

THE DEMONSTRATION that the meaning and purpose of God are immortality, that God and immortality are one, that God, starting out as an independent being, as immortality, ends up as an attribute of man, completes my task and with it this series of lectures. I have tried to prove that the god of nature religion is nature and that the God of spiritual religion, of Christianity, is the spirit or essence of man. I have been guided by the conviction that henceforth man should seek and find the determining ground of his action, the goal of his thinking, the cure for his ills and sufferings *in himself,* rather than *outside himself* like the pagan or *above himself* like the Christian. In dealing with Christianity, the religion which concerns us most closely, I have not, it goes without saying, been able to apply my demonstration to all the many Christian doctrines and views and still less have I been able, as I originally intended, to extend it to the history of Christian philosophy.

However, it is not necessary, in dealing with such a theme as ours, to go into every detail and particular. It suffices to set forth the elements, the first principles, from which the subordinate principles may be inferred. I have formulated the principles of my doctrine as clearly as possible. I own that I might have been more brief in the first lectures. But permit me to plead the extenuating circumstances that I am not an academician, that I am not accustomed to lecture, that I had no finished text before me and consequently was unable to measure my material by the yardstick of academic schedules, and organize it accordingly. However, to conclude with the proofs adduced in the last lecture would be to end my series on a discordant note; for I have left the premises or presuppositions from which Christians derive God and immortality unquestioned and intact.

God, I have said, is the fulfiller, or the reality, of the human desires for happiness, perfection, and immortality. From this it may be inferred that to deprive man of God is to tear the heart out of his breast. But I contest the premises from which religion and theology deduce the necessity and existence of God, or of immortality, which is the same thing. I maintain that desires which are fulfilled only in the imagination, or from which the existence of an imaginary being is deduced, are imaginary desires, and not the real desires of the human heart; I maintain that the limitations which the religious imagination annuls in the idea of God or immortality, are necessary determinations of the human essence, which cannot be dissociated from it, and therefore no limitations at all, except precisely in man's imagination. Man, for example, is confined by place and time, "his body chains him to the earth," as the rationalist believers say, "and so prevents him from knowing what is on the moon or on Venus." But this is not a real limitation. The gravitation that attaches me to the earth is merely an expression of my inseparable bond with the earth. What am I if I cut my bond with the earth? A phantom; for I am essentially a creature of the earth. Consequently my desire to transfer to other planets is a mere imaginary desire. If I were able to satisfy it, I should not be long in seeing that it is an absurd, extravagant desire, for I should be very uncomfortable on another planet and therefore realize—alas too late!—that it would have been better and more reasonable to remain on earth.

Man has many wishes that he does not really wish to fulfill, and it would be a misunderstanding to suppose the contrary. He wants them to remain wishes, they have value only in his imagination; their fulfillment would be a bitter disappointment to him. Such a desire is the desire for eternal life. If it were fulfilled, man would become thoroughly sick of living eternally, and yearn for death. In reality man wishes merely to avoid a premature, violent or gruesome death. Everything has its measure, says a pagan philosopher; in the end we weary of everything, even of life; a time comes when man desires death. Consequently there is nothing frightening about a normal, natural death, the death of a man who has fulfilled himself and lived out his life. Old men often long for death. The German philosopher Kant could hardly wait to die, and not in order to resuscitate, but because he longed for the end. Only an unnatural, unfortunate death, the death of a child, a youth, a man in the prime of life, makes us revolt against death and wish for a new life. Such misfortunes are bitterly painful for the survivors; and yet they do not justify belief in a hereafter, if only because such abnormal cases—and they are abnormal even if they should be more frequent than natural death—could only have an abnormal hereafter as their consequence, a hereafter for those who have died too soon or by violence; but a special hereafter of this kind is an absurdity which no one could believe.

But like the desire for eternal life, the desire for omniscience and absolute perfection is merely an imaginary desire; and, as history and daily experience prove, the supposed human striving for unlimited knowledge and perfection is a myth. Man has no desire to know everything; he only wants to know the things to which he is particularly drawn. Even a man with a universal thirst for knowledge—a rare exception—does not want to know everything without distinction; he does not like a mineralogist wish to know every single stone, or like a botanist every plant; he contents himself with general knowledge, because it fits in with his general cast of mind. Similarly, man desires the ability, not to do everything, but only to do those things toward which he feels a special inclination; he does not strive for unlimited, indeterminate perfection, which exists only in a god or in an infinite other world, but for a limited, determinate perfection, for perfection within a certain sphere.

Accordingly, we not only find individuals stopping once they have achieved a certain stage of education or perfection, but whole nations marking time for thousands of years. The Chinese, the Indians, are today at the same stage of development as thousands of years ago. How do such phenomena fit in with the rationalist's myth of an unlimited human striving for perfection, for which he can only find room in an infinite hereafter? Man has not only an impulse to progress, but also an impulse to rest once he has arrived at a stage of development corresponding to his finite nature. It is these opposing impulses that give rise to the conflict that runs through all history, including the present period. The progressives, the so-called revolutionaries, want to go forward; the conservatives want to leave everything as it is, except that their love of stability does not extend to their attitude toward death—for most of them are believers—and in order to prolong their interesting existences they are willing, in this respect, to put up with the most radical changes, the most revolutionary transformations, of their being. But even revolutionaries do not wish to progress ad infinitum, they have specific aims; once these are achieved, they halt and seek stability. Thus in each generation new young men take up the thread of history where the old progressives, having attained the goal of *their* desires and with it the limits of their being and thinking, leave off.

No more than man has an unlimited drive toward knowledge and perfection, no more has he an unlimited, insatiable lust for happiness, which the good things of this earth cannot assuage. Men, even those who believe in immortality, are perfectly content with earthly life, at least as long as all goes well, as long as they do not want for necessities, as long as no special, grave misfortune strikes them. They do not want a radically different life, they would merely like to see the evils of this life done away with. "The Greenlanders, for example, situate the abode of the blessed under the sea, because most of their food is derived from the sea. Under the sea, they say, there is good water and plenty of birds, fishes, seals, and reindeer which can be caught without difficulty or which are even found cooked alive in a great kettle." Here we have an example, a picture, of the human striving for happiness. The Greenlander's desires do not go beyond the limits of his country, his natural surroundings. He does not want anything radically different from what his country provides; he only wants the same things in *good quality* and *ample supply*. He does not want to stop catching fish and seals in the hereafter; he does not regard what he is as a limitation or burden; he does not want to exceed his species, his essential condition and occupation—he would only like to catch his fish and seals more easily in the hereafter.

What a modest desire! True, the desires of civilized man—whose mind and life, unlike those of the savage, are not restricted to any particular locality—are not so modest. He not only desires (to stay with our example) the edible flora and fauna of his country; he also aspires to the pleasures of distant lands; compared with those of the savage, his pleasures and desires are infinite; and yet they do not exceed the earth or the nature of man as such. Civilized man belongs to the same species as the savage; he wants no heavenly foods, he has no knowledge of them; he wants only the products of the earth; he does not want to abolish eating as such but only an uncivilized diet limited to the products of one particular place. In short, a reasonable and natural striving for happiness does not exceed the nature of man, it does not surpass the bounds of this life, of this earth; it aims merely at eliminating those evils and limitations that can actually be eliminated, that are not necessary, that are not an essential part of life.

Consequently, desires that exceed human nature or the human race itself, such as the desire not to eat at all, not to be subject to any bodily needs whatever, are imaginary, fantastic desires, and it follows that both the being who fulfills such desires and the life in which they are fulfilled are purely imaginary and fantastic. As to the desires that do not go beyond man and his nature, that are grounded not only in empty imagination or unnatural indulgence of the emotions, but in a real need and drive of human nature, they find their fulfillment within the human race and in the course of human history. Accordingly, we should be justified in inferring a religious or theological hereafter, a future life devoted to the perfecting of man, only if mankind always remained rooted to the same spot, if there were no history, no perfecting or betterment of the human race on earth, though even then such an inference would still not be true.

But there is a history of human civilization: why, even animals and plants change and develop so much in the course of time that we can no longer discover and demonstrate their ancestry! We *know* innumerable things and *are able* to do innumerable things, that our ancestors did not know and could not do. Copernicus—an example I have already cited in my book, *The Question of Immortality from the Standpoint of Anthropology,* but which is so much to the point that I cannot refrain from repeating it—lamented on his deathbed that for all his desires and efforts he had never in all his life seen the planet Mercury. Today astronomers with their perfected telescopes see it at high noon. Those human desires that are not imaginary and fantastic are fulfilled in the course of history, of the future. Many desires which today remain mere desires will someday be fulfilled; innumerable things which the presumptuous champions of present-day religious dogmas and institutions, present-day social and political conditions, regard as impossible, will one day be reality; innumerable things that today we do not know but would like to know, will be known to our descendants. We must therefore modify our goals and exchange divinity, in which only man's groundless and gratuitous desires are fulfilled, for the human race or human nature, religion for education, the hereafter in heaven for the hereafter on earth, that is, the *historical future*, the future of mankind.

Christianity set itself the goal of fulfilling man's unattainable desires, but for that very reason ignored his attainable desires. By promising man eternal life, it deprived him of temporal life, by teaching him to trust in God's help it took away his trust in his own powers; by giving him faith in a better life in heaven, it destroyed his faith in a better life on earth and his striving to attain such a life. Christianity gave man what his imagination desires, but for that very reason failed to give him what he really and truly desires. In his imagination, man yearns for heavenly, immoderate happiness; in reality, he desires earthly, moderate happiness. Earthly happiness, it is true, does not require wealth, luxury, splendor, glory, and empty display, but only the necessities, only the things without which man cannot carry on a human existence. But innumerable men still lack the barest necessities! For this reason the Christians call it blasphemous or inhuman to deny the existence of a hereafter and so deprive the unfortunate, the wretched of this earth, of their one consolation, the hope of a better world to come. Herein, they still believe, lies the moral significance of the hereafter, its unity with the divine; for without a hereafter there would be no retribution, no justice, no reparation in heaven for the misery of those who suffer on earth, or at least of those who suffer through no fault of their own.

But this justification of the hereafter is a mere pretext, for it would justify a hereafter or immortality only for the unfortunate and not for those who have been lucky enough to satisfy their human needs and develop their human aptitudes on earth. The above-mentioned argument would make sense only if those who have already attained the goal of human desires ceased to be after death, or if they were worse off in the next world than in this, occupying in heaven the position that their brethren occupied in this. The Kamchadals actually do believe that those who have been poor on earth will be rich in the next world, whereas the rich will be poor, and that in this way a certain equality between the two classes is achieved. But this is not what the Christian gentlemen who champion the hereafter for the above-cited reason want or believe; they are determined to live just as well in the next world as the poor and unfortunate.

This justification of the hereafter is in the same class as the argument in favor of belief in God adduced by many learned gentlemen who say that atheism is the sound view, that they themselves are atheists, but that atheism is suitable only for learned gentlemen not for men in general—that is, the public at large or the common people—and that it is therefore unfitting, impractical, and even criminal to teach atheism publicly. But the gentlemen who express this opinion are merely hiding their own wishy-washiness, their own unclarity and indecision, behind the vague and broad word "people" or "public"; to them the people are a mere pretext. When a man is truly convinced of something, he does not fear to say it in public, in fact, he must say it in public. An idea that fears the light is a feeble idea that cannot bear scrutiny. The atheism that fears the light is an unworthy and hollow atheism. Such atheists have nothing to say, and that is why they are afraid to speak out. The cryptoatheist says only in private that there is no God; his atheism is summed up in this one negative statement, which stands all alone, so that his atheism changes nothing. And it is perfectly true that if atheism were a mere negation, a denial without content, it would be unfit for the people, that is, for man or for public life; but only because such atheism is worthless. True atheism, the atheism that does not shun the light, is also an affirmation; it negates the being abstracted from man, who is and bears the name of God, but only in order to replace him by man's true being.

What is truly negative is theism, the belief in God; it negates nature, the world and mankind: *in the face of God, the world and man are nothing,* God was before world and man were; He *can exist without them*; He is the nothingness of the world and of man; at least according to strict orthodox belief, God can make the world into nothingness at any moment. For the true theist the power and beauty of nature, the virtue of man, do not exist; a believer in God takes everything away from man and from nature in order to adorn and glorify his God. "*Only God alone is to be loved,*" says St. Augustine, for example, "*this whole world* [i. e. all sensuous things] *is to be despised.*" "God," says Luther in a Latin letter, "wishes either to be *the only friend* or no friend at all." "Faith, hope, and love," he says in another letter, "are due to God alone, and that is why they are called the theological virtues." Thus theism is "negative and destructive"; it builds its faith solely on the nullity of world and man, that is, of the real man.

But God is nothing other than the abstracted, phantasmagoric essence of man and nature, hypostatized by the imagination; hence theism sacrifices the real life and nature of things and of men to a being who is a mere product of thought and imagination. Thus atheism is positive and affirmative; it gives back to nature and mankind the dignity of which theism has despoiled them; it restores life to nature and mankind, which theism had drained of their best powers. God, as we have seen, is jealous of nature and man; He wants man to honor, love, and serve Him alone; He wants everything else to be nothing and Himself alone to be something; in other words, theism is jealous of man and the world and begrudges them any good. Envy, ill will, and jealousy are destructive, negative passions. Atheism, on the other hand, is liberal, openhanded, openminded; an atheist acknowledges every being's will and talent; his heart delights in the beauty of nature and the virtue of man: joy and love do not destroy, they are life-giving, affirmative.

The same applies to the elimination of the hereafter, which is inseparable from atheism. If denying the existence of a hereafter were an empty negation, without consequence, it would be better, or at least no worse, to retain the afterlife. But the negation of the next world has as its consequence the affirmation of this world; the denial of a better life in heaven implies the demand for a better life on earth; it transforms the hope of a better future from a concern of idle, inactive faith into a duty, a matter of independent human activity. Of course it is outrageously unjust that some men should have everything while others have nothing, that some wallow in the good things of life, in the benefits of art and science, while others lack the barest necessities. But it is just as preposterous to argue the necessity of a hereafter in which reparation will be made to men for their sufferings on earth as to argue the necessity of a public justice in heaven which will correct the defects of the secret justice that prevails on earth. The necessary conclusion to be drawn from the existing injustices and evils of human life is the determination, the active striving to remedy them—not a belief in the hereafter, which only makes men fold their hands and leaves the evils intact.

But, it might be argued, granted that the evils of our social and political world can be corrected, what good does that do those who have already suffered and died as a result of these evils? How does a better future benefit the people of the past? True, it does them no good at all, but neither does the hereafter. The hereafter with its balms always comes too late; it cures an ill after it has passed, after death, when man no longer feels the evil and consequently has no need to be cured; for though death, at least as long as we are alive and thinking about it, has the disadvantage of taking away our feeling and consciousness of the good, the beautiful and the pleasant, it also has the advantage of releasing us from all evils, sufferings, and sorrows. The love that has created the hereafter, that comforts the suffering with the thought of the hereafter, is the love that heals the sick after they are dead, that slakes the thirsty and feeds the hungry after they have died of hunger and thirst.

Let us then follow the example of the pagans and let the dead rest in peace! "The pagans," I wrote in *The Question of Immortality,* "cried out to their dead loved ones: May thy bones rest gently! or: Rest in peace!—whereas the Christians shout a cheery *vivas et crescas in infinitum* into the ears of the dying, or else their pietistic healers of souls *à la* Dr. Eisenbart take advantage of their fear of death to bellow at them that only the fear of God can guarantee their eternal beatitude." Let us then leave the dead in peace and concern ourselves with the living. If we no longer *believe* in a better life but decide to *achieve* one, not each man by himself but with our united powers, we will *create* a better life, we will at least do away with the most glaring, outrageous, heartbreaking injustices and evils from which man has hitherto suffered. But in order to make such a decision and carry it through, we must replace the love of God by the love of man as the only true religion, the belief in God by the belief in man and his powers—by the belief that the fate of mankind depends not on a being outside it and above it, but on mankind itself, that man's only Devil is man, the barbarous, superstitious, self-seeking, evil man, but that man's only God is also man himself.

With these words, gentlemen, I conclude my lectures. My only wish is that I have not failed in the task I set myself and formulated in the opening lectures: to transform friends of God into friends of man, believers into thinkers, devotees of prayer into devotees of work, candidates for the hereafter into students of this world, Christians who, by their own profession and admission, are "*half animal, half angel,*" into *men,* into *whole men.*

Additions and Notes

1. When we explain religion by fear, we must, as I indicate in a later lecture, take into account not only the lowest form of fear, fear of one natural phenomenon or another, the fear that begins and ends with a storm at sea, a tempest, or an earthquake, in other words the fear that is circumscribed in time and space, but also the fear that is limited to no particular object, the perpetual, ever present fear which embraces every conceivable misfortune, in a word, the *infinite* fear of the human soul. In his letter of condolence of 1520 to Elector Frederick Luther writes:

All present evils and calamities will be alleviated and diminished if a man turns his mind to future evils and calamities which are so many, of such a nature, and so great that there can be no other response to them but the great and outstanding movement of the soul termed *fear*. . . . So much so that St. Paul said to the Romans: Be not highminded, but *fear*. And this evil is all the greater in proportion as its measure and extent are more uncertain. . . . So that every present evil or burden is nothing other than a memory of a great pain with which God honors us and does not allow us to be crushed by the abundance of evils, burdens, and adversities under which we live. For what wonder is it if a man beset by *infinite* and *innumerable* blows is in the end injured by a single blow? Indeed, it is a mercy that all the blows do not strike him.

What innumerable misfortunes [says Augustine in the *City of God*] man has to fear from without, from heat and cold, storms, cloudbursts, floods, meteors, lightning, thunder, hail, earthquakes and landslides, from the bucking, the *terror* or even malice of draft animals, from the many poisonous shrubs, waters, vapors and bugs, from the fatal or merely injurious bite of voracious beasts, from rabies! What evils we have to withstand in the course of a journey by land or sea! Where in the world can we take a step without being exposed to unexpected calamities? A man leaves the market sound of limb and, on his way home, falls, breaks his leg, and dies of the injury. What seems to be safer than sitting still? And yet the priest Heli [Eli] fell from his chair and died of his fall.

"Innumerable," says Calvin in his *Institutes of the Christian Religion,* "are the evils that beset the life of man and threaten it with innumerable fatal accidents. Embark on a ship; you are only a hand's breadth removed from death. Mount a horse; the fall of a hoof puts your life in danger. Go through the city streets; as numerous as the tiles on the roofs are the fatal accidents to which you are exposed. Pick up a knife, you are faced with naked death. Consider the wild beasts; they are all equipped with weapons for your destruction. What then can be more wretched than human life?" And the Christian poet D. W. Triller has the following to say of the matter in his "*Poetic Reflections in Reply to the Atheists and Naturalists.*"

Nearly all things beneath the sky
Are made with arms to kill us by.
The aim of all that meets the eyes
Is our demise.

Hail, fire, water, precipices,
Winds, lightning, bottomless abysses,
Smoke, poison, powder, sulphur, lead—
All leave us dead.

Knives, axes, saws and pikes of steel,
The mace, the noose, the rack, the wheel,
Oil, pitch, lime, sand—all tools of death
To halt man's breath.

An egg, an apple, a cherry pit,
A piece of glass, the merest bit
Of dust—to encompass our downfall
Nothing's too small.

A tortoise shell of medium size
Can one day kill us by surprise.
From every roof a tile can fall
Upon us all.

And though the beasts we dominate,
Hardly a one will hesitate
To claw, to bite, and if it can,
To kill a man.

Why, worms and maggots often bite
Our vital threads and quench our light.
Our mouths and ears are an open door
Through which they pour.

Man, look within and contemplate
All the disasters lying in wait,
Reminders all that death is nigh,
That soon you'll die.

Into this life we penetrate
By only one exclusive gate.
And yet a thousand gates of doom
Lead to the tomb.*

But that's enough of the divine Triller, though his poem goes on and on.

But how then does man's fear give rise to gods? In various ways. If for example a man is more alert to evil than to good, if he is too foolish or frivolous to prize the good in life, he has only evil gods; if his ideas and feelings of evil hold the balance with his ideas and feelings of the good, he has good and bad gods, equal in power; but if the ideas and feelings of the good predominate over those of evil, then he has a good God who overcomes the power of evil. In other words: fear is either the *positive* or the *negative* cause of religion or the divinity, which is tantamount to saying that religion

* He was a contemporary of Lessing, born a generation before him in Erfurt on February 10, 1695 and surviving him by a year (d. May 22, 1782 in Wittenberg). A physician by profession and a not inconsiderable philologist for his day, he also, like his friend and model, the jurist Barthold Heinrich Brockes, wrote verse in defense of orthodoxy. He filled six impressive octavo volumes, which were forgotten even before his death, after briefly serving as a butt for the attacks of the Swiss critics Bodmer and Breitinger.—Ed.

springs either from *subservience* or from *opposition* to fear. In the first case terrible gods, in the second case good gods come into being. Fear is an evil and man's response to it is either passive or active: either I accept it, resign myself to it however reluctantly, or else I react, that is, oppose it. Reaction to fear of the infinitely many evils and mortal perils which in the form of evil spirits perpetually beset man's anguished imagination gives rise to the idea of an infinitely good being, an all-powerful love, capable of doing as much good as fear can do evil, capable of safeguarding man against all evils and in his imagination actually doing so.* Divine love extends no further than human fear, for it can only do as much good as fear does harm; the heaven of love is everlasting, but equally everlasting is the hell of fear; innumerable are the hosts of angels that love has put into the world, but innumerable too are the hosts of demons created by fear; love goes back to the beginning of the world, but fear extends to the end of the world; love made the First Day, but fear made the Day of Judgment.

In short, where the *creative omnipotence* of *human* fear ceases, the omnipotence of *divine* love also ceases. We need not look for an example of how fear gives rise to religion—we have one in the genesis of Protestantism and specifically of Lutheranism, which sprang solely from terror, from fear of the inhuman, angry, jealous God whom even the Old Testament refers to as the fear and dread of Israel, who with utter indifference to human nature demands that man resemble Him, that instead of being a man, a living being, he should be a moral abstraction, a walking law. But although Luther started out as a monk and remained a cleric, he was too practical and vigorously sensuous a man to sacrifice himself by prayer, fasting, and self-immolation to this God, one of whose names—Shaddai—derives from devastation, extermination. Luther did not

* It is precisely because of this ever present fear that polytheistic belief or superstition inhabits every locality, every corner, every point in space with tutelary gods and spirits. Prudentius writes for example (*Adv. Symmachum*): "To gates, houses, baths, and stables you attribute their geniuses. You invent thousands of geniuses for every square and quarter of the city, in order that every nook and cranny may have a spook of its own." Accordingly, if, despite the many altars that men erect to Fear, the learned gentlemen do not recognize it as a god and indeed as the first god, it is only because they fail to see the forest for the trees.

wish to be an angel, but a man; he was a theologian who from within theology fought against theology; he tried to discover an effective remedy for the *evil* nature of theology, which on pretext of reconciling man with God brings him into conflict with his own nature, poisons the blood in his veins with the gall of divine jealousy, burns the brain in his head with the hell-fire of divine wrath, and condemns man to eternal death for his mere impulse to be a man.* But since he tried to discover the remedies for the bugaboos of religion or theology in theology or religion themselves, that is, to discover an antidote to the evil, inhuman God in a human God, just as the devotee of religion seeks an antidote to inhuman nature in human nature the Tungus, for example, seek a cure for a natural, inhuman epidemic in a religious human epidemic, it goes without saying that his cure was not and could not be a radical one.

This is demonstrated by Luther's letters, which are of great psychological interest, because they show the difference between Luther's public and private personalities, between the power of faith in the pulpit and the power, or rather impotence, of faith in his own home; because they show how little benefit he himself derived from the beatific effects of faith which he recommended so highly to others, how he was constantly pursued by the nightmares of his religious imagination. Fortunately, despite his servitude to theology, Luther found, *outside* of religion or theology, antidotes to the power of sin, hell, the devil or, what amounts to the same thing, the divine wrath. In a Latin letter to L. Senfel he writes that music, too, gives man what otherwise only theology can bestow, namely, a tranquil and serene mind, that the Devil, the author of all cares and emotional disturbances, takes flight at the sound of music as he does at the word of theology. And in a letter to H. Weller he goes so far as to say that to spite and foil the Devil we must sometimes drink, play, joke, and even sin, so depriving him of any

* The evil, antihuman character of Christian theology is expressed with classical sharpness in Calvin. "*All desires of the flesh*"—as though the desire for eternal life were not also a desire of the flesh—"*are sins*"; "every sin is a mortal sin"; "the law, says St. Paul, is spiritual, by which he signifies that it demands not only obedience of the soul, the mind, the will, but also *angelic purity* [*angelicam puritatem*], which, purified of all carnal taint, savors exclusively of spirit." What diabolical nonsense behind the mask of an angelic soul!

ground to plague our consciences with trifles. Truly a highly untheological, and for that very reason eminently anthropological remedy!

2.* Is the feeling or consciousness of dependency—they are inseparable, for "what people don't know won't hurt them"—the right universal term and concept for the subjective, that is, human (and here I am speaking of practice, not of theory) ground of religion?

Although I have already cited plenty of evidence in support of an affirmative answer to this question, I wish to provide still more, but only from the classical pagan writers and not from Christianity—because the dependency of the creature on the "independent cause" came to be a technical term in Christian theology and metaphysics and also because the peoples of classical antiquity did not repress or hide man's natural and original feelings or attitudes (here too Pliny's dictum: *Res Graecorum nuda est* is applicable) and did not offer sacrifices to a conventional, dogmatic concept of God, so that they provide us with the most instructive and interesting insights into the genesis of the idea of God. "All men need gods," says Homer in the *Odyssey*. And what is this need but a pathological expression of dependency? On this occasion I must observe that the opposition between the human and the divine which I took as the starting point for *The Essence of Faith* and *The Essence of Christianity*, and the feeling of dependency which I took as the starting point for *The Essence of Religion*, amount to the same thing, except that the opposition in question springs more from reflection on the feeling of dependency. If men need gods, it necessarily follows that gods have what men lack, that consequently the divine freedom from needs presents a contrast to human need—and this contrast is explicitly formulated by later Greek thought or philosophy, though already in Homer the ethereal, blissful, im-

* In this section I have gathered a number of passages which are the elements or fragments of a *separate book*. In view of the uncertainty of all undertakings in the present wretched political situation, I prefer to publish them at once, as an appendix to these lectures. Those readers who take an interest in them are requested to read them only after completing the lectures.

—The book in question was published in 1857 under the title *Theogony* and constitutes Vol. 9 both in the earlier and in the present edition.—ED.

mortal, and all-powerful character of the gods is contrasted with the arduous, wretched, mortal, impotent existence of man, if only in a highly emotional or poetic way, which reduces to nothing the antithesis between the bloodless gods and men as creatures of flesh and blood.

But back to the *Odyssey*. "From God different things come to different men. Good and evil come from Zeus, for he is all-powerful." "It is not possible for mortals to remain forever sleepless, for the gods order the measure and goal of all things for man." Thus man's dependency on sleep, the necessity of sleep is a *moira,* a divine fate. Indeed, sleep itself is a divine being, "ruler over mortals and over the immortal gods." "So the minds of mortal men change as the mighty father brings other days." On happy days man is exuberant, on unhappy days he is sad, but the days themselves depend on the father of gods and men." "The outcome of battle," we read in the *Iliad,* "depends on the immortal gods in heaven." When Odysseus and Ajax were running a race, Pallas Athena, in answer to Odysseus' plea, placed an obstacle in Ajax' path just before the goal: he fell over a pile of ox dung and Odysseus carried off the first prize. Thus it is up to the gods whether a man triumphs or is defeated, whether he slips or reaches the goal unhindered. "If you set sail at the right time," says Hesiod, "your ship will not be wrecked, nor will the sea destroy your men, unless Poseidon the earth-shaker or Zeus the immortal king has deliberately planned your ruin, for both good and evil are in their power." "From you, revered one," says the Homeric Hymn to Demeter, "come abundance of children and abundance of fruits, it is up to you [*seu d'echetai*] to *give* mortal men *life* or to *take it away;* happy is he whom you honor and love in your heart, for he has everything in superfluity."

"Pray to the gods," says Theognis, "for great is their power, and without the gods nothing befalls man, neither good nor bad." "Vain are our thoughts, we men know nothing, the gods dispose of all things as they will." "No man is the author of his profit or loss, it is the gods who give one and the other. And no man acts, discerning in his mind the outcome, whether it will be good or bad." But if everything—good and evil, fortune and misfortune, wealth and poverty, victory and defeat—depends on the gods, then obviously the feeling of dependency is the source of religion, the reason why man transforms his action into passivity, his desires and resolves into prayers, his virtues into gifts, his mistakes into punishments, in short, transforms his salvation from an object of his own activity into an object of religion. But there are more specific proofs. "All men need the gods," says Plutarch, "but all men do not need all the gods."

No, [says Varro in his work on agriculture] as a peasant I do not, like Homer and Ennius, invoke the Muses, but the twelve greater gods, and not the city-gods whose gilded statues stand in the Forum, but those twelve gods who are eminently the guides [or lords] of the peasants, first of all Jupiter and the Earth, for heaven and earth encompass all the fruits of agriculture; second the Sun and the Moon, whose times are observed when some seed is sowed and set into the earth, then Ceres and Bacchus, because their fruits are the most necessary for the preservation of life, for they are the source of food and drink, then Fire and Flora, for if Flora is favorably disposed, Fire does not destroy the grain and the trees, and they ripen at the right time; further, I honor Minerva and Venus, because the one presides over the olive tree, the other over gardens. Finally, I also pray to water and Bonus Eventus [Good Outcome], for without water a farm is dry and wretched, and without good outcome it is vain labor. As a raiser of sheep and cattle, I turn especially to the goddess Pales and entreat her, as Ovid says in his *Fasti,* to dispel diseases, to keep men, herds, and dogs in good health, to banish hunger, to provide vegetation and herbs, water for drinking and bathing, milk and cheese, lambs and wool, while as a merchant I pray Mercury for profit in commerce.

Thus men need gods, but only those on whom their natural or social existence depends, and precisely this need, this dependency of their existence, of their lot, on the gods is the source of religion, the reason why they are looked upon and worshiped as gods. Thus the *first* definition of "god," derived from *practice,* from *life,* is simply that a god is what man requires for his existence, and specifically for his physical existence, which is the foundation of his spiritual existence, so that a god is a *physical being;* or in subjective terms: man's first god is need, and specifically physical need; for whether I worship the object which satisfies my need depends on the power which this need of mine exerts on me. We have in ourselves an image of the Divine Trinity, says St. Augustine in *The City of God;* "we *are* and *know* that we are, and we *love* this being and knowledge of ours; and that is why the philosophers divide science into the spheres of natural science, logic, and ethics. The Holy Ghost is goodness, love, or their source; the second person is the word, reason, or the source of wisdom; the first person, God the Father, is being or the author of being."

In other words, the first and oldest God, the God *before and behind* the ethical and spiritual God is the *physical* God; for just as the Holy Ghost is merely the deified essence of ethics, and the son of God is merely the deified essence of logic, so God the Father is nothing other than the deified essence of physics, of nature, from which alone man has derived the abstract concept and term "being." "Some sort of natural necessity," says Augustine in this connection, "causes *mere being* to pass for a desirable thing, and for its sake alone the wretched do not wish to die; for why otherwise would they fear death and prefer even a miserable life to death, except that nature shuns nonbeing? That is why the unintelligent animals themselves desire to *be* and avoid death in every possible way, and why the unfeeling plants and even utterly inanimate bodies strive to maintain and to assert their being." This makes it clear that the abstract concept "being" has flesh and blood, truth and reality, only in nature and that consequently, just as being precedes wisdom and goodness, so the physical God precedes the spiritual and the ethical God; it also shows that man's attachment to his own being, his love of life, is the source of all gods, that Jupiter is the highest and most powerful god only because the desire to be, to live, is the highest and most powerful of man's desires, and that the satisfaction of this desire, namely, life, depends in the last analysis on Jupiter alone, so that the awe which Jupiter inspires with the tumult of his thunder is merely a *consequence of man's love of life and fear of death.*

Thus it is solely from the "angry fire," from the darkness of human desires, the chaos of human needs, that the Greek and Christian gods developed. And how indeed could man look upon bread as holy, how could he praise Ceres as a divine benefactress, without his experience of hunger as an implacable tormentor? No! Where there is no devil there also is no god, where there is no hunger there is no Ceres, where there is no thirst, there is no

Bacchus. Accordingly, nothing is more priceless than the views of the learned gentlemen who, because *to them* religion, especially that of the ancient peoples, retains only a theoretical or aesthetic interest, declare that religion itself sprang exclusively from theoretical or ideal motives, and whose preoccupation with the mythological figures and curlicues with which the imagination adorns the shield of religion makes them forget that for all this luxury of artistic trimmings, over which they are still racking their brains, the shield actually had no other purpose than to protect the life of man.

Since everything depends on the gods, but since the gods are *subjective*—i. e., personal and selfish—beings who think and feel just like men ("I am a jealous God," says Jehovah in the Old Testament—"The gods," says Venus in Euripides, "take pleasure in being honored by men"—"We are an ambitious race," say the gods in Ovid's *Fasti*), since, then, everything depends on the favor or disfavor, the love or anger of the gods, they are worshiped for reasons not only of human, but also of *divine egoism.* They are worshiped not only because they do man good, but also because they wish to be worshiped; in short, they are worshiped not only for the sake of man, but also for their own sake. We can honor a subjective or personal being only by doing for him what appeals to him, what suits his nature, hence by eliminating everything that displeases him. In honor of a distinguished guest, we banish all domestic dirt and rubbish, grief and affliction, discord and anger; we sweep away everything that might make an unaesthetic, unpleasant impression on him.

This is exactly what men do on feast days dedicated to the honor of the gods; they abstain from all business and all acts and pleasures that are at odds with the character of the gods; they forget their own joys and sorrows for the joys and sorrows of the gods, as, for example, on the feast of Demeter. But precisely this worship of the gods in keeping with their tastes and interests is at the same time in keeping with the tastes and interests of man; for it is only by such chaste, selfless worship that I win the gods' favor; and if I gain their favor, I have everything I desire, I have tapped the source of all good things. The same applies to the appeasement of the gods' anger, to the reconciliation of gods and men. Accordingly, it makes no difference whether I regard the propitiation of the gods as a means or as an end, for once their anger is appeased all evil is gone; once the cause of evil is done away with, the consequence also vanishes.

"My greatest punishment," writes Ovid in his elegies from Tomi, whither he had been banished by the anger of the earthly Jupiter, the Emperor Augustus, "is to have offended him" (namely, Augustus). If apart from the Emperor's anger no evil beset me, is the Emperor's anger not evil enough?" "For the Emperor's ill favor brings all evil with it." The same applies to the heavenly gods. To still their anger is to dam the source of all evil.

Since the gods command over life and death, fortune and misfortune, therefore ethics, the theoretical and practical distinction between good and evil, right and wrong, has been linked to them and their cult. I say linked, because inherently and originally religion and ethics—at least ethics as we view it—have nothing in common, and this for the simple and obvious reason that in ethics man confronts himself and his fellow man, while in religion he confronts another being, distinct from man. "All Holy Scripture," says Bodin in his *Démonomanie,* "abounds in testimonies to the effect that God has the greatest horror of sorcerers (that is, of those who forsake God and make a pact with the Devil), that they are far more damnable than parricides, committers of incest, and sodomites." "Even if a sorcerer should do no harm," he says later, "even if he should inflict no injury on men and cattle, he deserves to be burned alive just for forsaking God and allying himself with the Devil, so offending against the majesty of God." *"The intention of killing,"* says Luther, *"is not so great a sin as not to believe,* for murder is a sin against the *fifth commandment,* but unbelief is a *sin against the first and greatest commandment."* "There is no doubt," says Calvin, "that in the Law and the Prophets faith and what concerns divine worship occupy first place, that love comes *after* faith."

The Catholic Church has expressly condemned as heretical the doctrine that he who has faith *without* love is not a Christian, and consequently sanctioned the doctrine that a man can have faith and religion, that he can be a Christian, without love, that is, without morality. And the pious Russian, the last stronghold of desperate religious and political absolutism, is so strict about fasting that he would sooner forgive theft or murder than nonobservance of a fast.* "Armenian priests will sooner grant forgiveness for murder and other grave crimes than for a breach of the fasts. The wickedest among the Greek Christians observe the fasts no less punctiliously than the most virtuous."† The jurist Carpzov was so pious, so Biblical, so Christian, that he took Communion once a month and read the entire Bible no less than fifty-three times, and yet, or perhaps for that reason, this pious man condemned to death no less than twenty thousand malefactors, i. e., poor sinners.‡

"Le connetable Anne de Montmorenci . . . peut-être le seul chef du parti catholique qui aimât la religion pour elle-même . . . c'étoit en dsant son chapelet, si l'on en croit Brantôme, qu'il ordonnoit des supplices, des meurtres, des incendies, sans se debaucher nullement de ses paters, tant il étoit consciencieux."§

What then has faith in common with love, religion with ethics? Nothing; they have no more in common than have the God to whom man is bound by faith and the fellow man with whom he is united by love; for according to religious faith, there is the most violent opposition between man and God: God is a nonsensuous being, man a sensuous being, God is perfect, man is wretched, pitiful, worthless. How then can love flow from faith? It cannot, any more than wretchedness can spring from perfection, want from abundance. Yes, *ethics* and *religion, faith* and *love are exact opposites*. He who has once loved a God can no longer love any human being; he has lost his feeling for mankind. But the converse is also true: he who has once loved man, truly and from the bottom of his heart, can no longer love a God, he can no longer permit his living humanity to seep away in a vacuum of infinite objectlessness and unreality.

Religion, it is said, guards us against sin through its conception

* Stäudlin, *Magazin für Religionsgeschichte.*

† Meiners, *op. cit.,* II. L.

‡ Stein, *Geschichte des peinlichen Rechts.*

§ *Dictionnaire universel par Roliner Art. Ligue.* Concerning the contradiction between ethical and ecclesiastical worth, between humanity and piety, morality and fidelity to the Church, as represented in the lives of our Protestant and Catholic clergy, I prefer to keep silence, because I regard it as unnecessary and undignified to write of things that are obvious even to the dull minds of our peasants.

of an omniscient being; but the ancients have already said that we must pray to God as though *men heard us,* and that "he who does not stand in awe of men is likely to deceive God himself"; religion, it is said, punishes sinners; so it does, but it also has its stock of little devices—such as Christ's merits, certificates of indulgence, cow dung, ablutions, and so on—by which to cleanse men of their sins, or rather by which to exculpate the sinner, to whitewash the blackest Moor—for against sin itself faith can do little or nothing, as honest believers have admitted and demonstrated by their life and character. Even the pagan poet Ovid, who lived in an age of culture and hence of unbelief, could not refrain in his *Fasti* (which only his antiquarian enthusiasm led him to write) from expressing his surprise at the belief of his pious ancestors that all offenses, even the terrible crime of murder, could be washed away by river water. But contradictory as are faith and love, religion and ethics, ethics is not only linked to religion as I showed above, but is actually based on it, though not at all for the reason ordinarily alleged. Religion is all-powerful; it controls heaven and earth, the course of the sun, which it can even cause to stand still, thunder and lightning, rain and sunshine, in short, everything that man loves and fears, fortune and misfortune, life and death; and so it makes the commandments of love or ethics into *objects of human self-love, of the striving for happiness,* by rewarding obedience to them with all manner of desirable goods and punishing disobedience with all manner of terrible evils.

But it will come to pass, if thou wilt not hearken unto the voice of the Lord thy God, to observe and to do all his commandments and his statutes which I command thee this day, that all these curses shall come upon thee, and overtake thee. Cursed shalt thou be in the city, and cursed shalt thou be in the field. . . . [etc.] The Lord shall send upon thee cursing, vexation, and rebuke in all that thou settest thine hand unto for to do, until thou be destroyed. . . . The Lord shall smite thee with a consumption, and with a fever, and with an inflammation, and with an extreme burning, and with the sword, and with blasting, and with mildew; and they shall pursue thee until thou perish. . . . The Lord will smite thee with the botch of Egypt, and with the emerods, and with the scab, and with the itch, whereof thou canst not be healed. The Lord will smite thee with madness, and blindness, and astonishment of heart; and thou shalt grope at noonday, as the blind gropeth in darkness, and thou shalt not prosper in thy ways. . . . [etc.] See, I have set before thee this day life and good, and death and evil; in that I command thee this day to love the Lord thy God, to walk in his ways, and to keep his commandments and his statutes and his judgments, that thou mayest live and multiply; and the Lord thy God shall bless thee in the land whither thou goest to possess it.

This classical passage shows how religion makes the love of virtue into the love of a long and happy life and the fear of infringing on the precepts of morality* into the fear of the botch of Egypt, of emerods, the scab, and the itch, in short, of all possible calamity and misfortune, and that to say that morality is based, or must be based, on religion is merely to say that morality must be based on egoism, self-love, and the striving for happiness, that otherwise it has no foundation. The only difference between Judaism and Christianity is that in Judaism morality is based on the love of temporal, earthly life, and in Chrisianity on the love of eternal, heavenly life. If it is not generally recognized that egoism alone is the secret of faith as distinct from love, the secret of religion as distinct from ethics, it is only because religious egoism does not have the *appearance* of egoism; in religion man affirms his self in the form of self-abnegation, he does not assert his ego in the first person or his will in the form of a command, but asserts them in the form of supplication, not actively but passively; he does not love himself but humbly lets himself be loved. Thus the content of the Lutheran faith, in contrast to love or ethics, is simply self-love in the *passive* form: God loves me, or I am beloved of God; but because God loves me—and this is the connection between faith and ethics—I love men; because my egoism is satisfied in religion, I have no need to satisfy it in ethics; what I give away and lose in ethics, I recover, or possess a hundredfold, in faith, in my certainty of being loved by the all-powerful being who disposes of all treasures and goods.

But back to our Old Testament passage! What is the part of re-

* This passage contains religious as well as ethical commandments, but since we are dealing here with the distinction between morality and religion, we stress only the latter.

ligion and what of ethics, what is the part of God and what of man? Man's part is the prohibitions—do not murder, commit adultery, steal, bear false witness, covet your neighbor's wife, house, field, etc., for even though the prohibition of theft seems inhuman to the thief and radically opposes his egoism, it is in perfect harmony with the egoism of the property owner. Ethics and law in general are based on the very simple principle: "Don't do to others what you don't want them to do to you." And no man wants his life, his wife, his field, his good name to be taken away from him. It is perfectly natural that this will, which is the will of every man—for even a thief doesn't want to be robbed of what he has stolen and even a murderer doesn't want to be deprived of his own life—should be explicitly translated into a universal law and that the offender against it should be punished. What then is the part of God or of religion? On the one hand, the botch of Egypt, the emerods, the scab, the itch and other evils which He visits upon the wicked, on the other hand, long life, fertility of body, land, and flocks, which He promises to the good, for neither these benefits nor these evils are in man's power.* But both are objects of the striving for happiness, the benefits in a positive way as objects of love and desire, the evils in a negative way as objects of fear and revulsion.

What then is *specific and proper to religion? Solely the striving for happiness, egoism,* and in particular *that* egoism whose satisfaction is not in the hands of man. For myself, my wife, my field, my flocks I wish all possible blessings; but I curse the man who lays hands on my wife, my flocks, my life, and wish him every possible evil, especially if, as is often the case, he is not in my power; but the omnipotence of God or of faith does or can grant both these

* The gods, it is true, are moral powers insofar as they punish wrongdoing or sin and reward righteousness or virtue. Nevertheless, their characteristic, essential feature is not morality, but only the *power* to punish and reward. "God demands of you not only Christian faith; He also demands that you be kind, charitable, and loving to your fellow man." Wrong; *all God demands of you is faith, it is man who demands that you be kind, charitable, and loving,* for *God is interested only in faith, but man is interested in morality*. What you believe is all the same to me, but not what you are, what you do. To the "I," faith is closer than morality; but to the "Thou," morality is closer than faith, for my faith is of no concern to my fellow man, but my morality is.

wishes, both the blessings and the curses. Thus, because religion rules over life and death, heaven and hell, because it transforms laws into the commandments of an all-powerful being—the essence of all human wishes and fears—religion gains control of, or is favored by, human egoism and so exerts a terrible power over man, especially uncivilized man, a power beside which the power of ethics, especially of abstract, philosophical ethics, pales to nothingness, and which for this reason seems indispensable.

But no one can fail to see that religion exerts this power through the imagination alone, that its power resides solely in the imagination; for if the power of religion were anything more than imaginary, if religion were really the positive foundation and support of justice and ethics, the promises and punishments of religion would have sufficed for the founding and preservation of states, men would never have devised all the many exquisitely cruel punishments they employ for the prevention of crime. Or if you will, we acknowledge that religion is the foundation of states, but with this limitation: only in the imagination, in belief, in opinion, for in reality states, even Christian states, are built not on the power of religion, though they have used it too (i. e., credulity, man's weak point) as a means to their ends, but on the power of bayonets and other instruments of torture. In reality men act out of entirely different motives than their religious imagination leads them to *suppose*. In his chronicle of Louis XI, the pious Philippe de Commines writes: "All evils or transgressions come from lack of faith; if men firmly believed what God and the Church tell us about the eternal and terrible torments of hell, they could not do what they do."

But whence comes this weakness of faith? From the fact that the power of belief is nothing other than the power of imagination, and that reality is an infinitely greater power, directly opposed to the imagination. Like the imagination, faith is hyperbolic; it moves only in extremes, in exaggerations; it knows only of heaven and hell, angels and devils; it tries to make more of man than he should be, and consequently makes less of him than he could be; it tries to make him into an angel and consequently, given the opportunity, makes him into a true devil. Faced with the resistance of prosaic reality, the hyperbolic fantasies of faith shift into their direct opposite! Human life would be in a bad way if law and ethics had no other basis than religious faith, which so easily turns into its opposite, because, as even the greatest heroes of faith have confessed, it flies in the face of sensory evidence, natural feeling, and man's innate tendency to disbelief. How, indeed, can anything built on constraint, on the forcible repression of a sound inclination, anything exposed at every moment to the mind's doubts and the contradictions of experience, provide a firm and secure foundation? To believe that the state—I mean of course the state as such, not our artificial, supranaturalistic political edifices—cannot exist without religious faith is to believe that our natural legs are not sufficient for man to stand or walk on, that he can only stand and walk on stilts. And these natural legs, the support of ethics and law, are love of life, self-interest, egoism.

Accordingly, nothing is more groundless than the fear that the distinction between right and wrong, good and evil, must vanish with the gods. The distinction exists and will continue to exist as long as there is a difference between me and thee, for this is the source of ethics and law. My egoism may permit me to steal, but my fellow man's egoism will sternly forbid me; left to myself I may know nothing of unselfishness, but the selfishness of others will teach me the virtue of unselfishness. My masculine egoism may be inclined to polygamy, but feminine egoism will oppose my inclination and champion monogamy: I may be unaware of the beam in my own eye, but the merest mote in it will be a thorn in the critical eye of others. In short, though it may be of no concern to me whether I am good or bad, it will always be a matter of concern to the egoism of others.

Who has always been the ruler of states? God? Good heavens, no! The gods rule only in the heavens of the imagination, not on the profane ground of reality. Who then? Egoism and egoism alone, though not simple egoism, but the dualistic egoism of those who have devised heaven for themselves and hell for others, materialism for themselves and idealism for others, freedom for themselves but servitude for others, enjoyment for themselves but resignation for others—the egoism of those who as rulers punish their subjects for the crimes they themselves have committed, who as fathers visit their own crimes on their children, who as husbands punish their wives for their own weaknesses, who in general forgive themselves all offenses and assert their egos in all directions, but expect others to have no egos, to live on air, to be as perfect and immaterial as angels. Not the limited egoism to which the term is ordinarily confined but which is only one variety, though the most common; but the egoism which comprises as many varieties as there are aspects of human nature, for there is not only a singular or individual egoism, but also a social egoism, a family egoism, a corporate egoism, a community egoism, a patriotic egoism. True, egoism is the source of evil, but it is also the source of good, for what else but egoism gave rise to agriculture, commerce, the arts and the sciences? True, it is the source of all vices, but also the source of all virtues, for what gave rise to the virtue of honesty? Egoism, through the prohibition of theft! What molded the virtue of chastity? The egoism of those who did not wish to share their beloved with others, through the prohibition of adultery. What produced the virtue of truthfulness? The egoism of those who do not wish to be deceived and cheated, through the prohibition of lying.

Egoism was the first lawgiver and promoter of the virtues, though only out of hostility to vice, only out of egoism, only because what opposes my egoism strikes me as a vice—just as conversely, what to me is a blow against my egoism is to others an affirmation of theirs, and what to me is a *virtue* is to them a *benefit*. Moreover, vices are just as necessary, if not more so, for the preservation of states, at least of our despicable, unnatural and inhuman states, as are virtues. To cite an example that is close to me because I am writing on Bavarian soil, though not in a Bavarian spirit (or in a Prussian or Austrian spirit either, for that matter): if Christianity in our country were anything more than a clerical phrase, if the spirit of Christian asceticism and subjugation of the senses should take hold of the Bavarian people, leading them to abstain from beer drinking, or only from immoderate beer drinking, what would become of our Bavarian state? And despite its "substantial faith," the Russian state finds its chief source of revenue in poison—in vodka. Without beer, then, there would be no Bavaria, and without distilled liquor no Russia or even Bo-Russia.*

Yet, despite these and countless other equally well-known facts,

* The Latin form of "Prussia."—Tr.

certain people have the gall to tell us that religion is the cement of states—states which in fact are held together solely by prison chains, by crimes against human nature. But enough of the horrors of politics. Morality, it is said, must be built on religion, on God and not on man, for otherwise it loses all firmness and authority. What is more relative, more changeable, more unreliable than human nature? How can the moral law be built on such a foundation? But isn't it jumping from the frying pan into the fire, to exchange human nature for divinity? For all its infinite variety, is there not something unchanging and reliable, is there not even a concrete certainty in the basic human impulses? "*All* men want the same thing" says the proverb, "namely well-being."

And is there anything more uncertain, more dubious, more contradictory, vacillating, indefinite, and relative than the divine nature? Is it not at least as changing and varied as times and men? If at a given moment God hands down these particular laws and not others, these revelations and not others, is it not because these laws and revelations, and no others, are suited to human nature as it is at this particular time? But when a legislator gives me a law consonant with my nature—and only such a law is a true and valid law—isn't my *nature* the law and foundation of the law? What then is the difference between the human and the divine as a foundation for morality? The difference between the simple truth and the religious illusion or fantasy which personifies man's *alter ego,* his essence in contradistinction to his will and knowledge. "God cannot command what is evil," says an eighteenth-century orthodox polyhistor (Gundling), "because He is supremely good and wise; consequently He commands the good. The good precedes *in signo rationis,* the commandment follows; therefore He *commands* man to do *what is good for him* and *forbids him to do what is harmful to him. Finis Dei noster quoque finis sit oportet,* God's purpose must also be our purpose."

Of course; for our purpose is *God's purpose;* what we do not want, what conflicts with our nature, what is evil and harmful, is also unwelcome to God. God and His law presuppose and are grounded in human nature, but the religious imagination reverses this relationship. On this occasion, the same theist observes that though an atheist can "understand the ethical truths that have a connection with human nature," only religion supplies the means of "putting them into practice, because to practice them is contrary to our concupiscence and passions." "Where the opposite view is held," says the same author in agreement with all theists, "nothing remains but *utilitas* to deter me from stealing, from murdering or from offending my fellow man. But now suppose," he continues, "that you met your mortal enemy in a lonely spot, as Saul met David in the cave, with no reason to fear that you would be discovered and punished if you were to satisfy your lust for vengeance. You do not fear God. . . . You are an atheist. What then is to deter you from massacring your enemy?"

The same thing that deters you, vainglorious theist! For in such casuistic situations the decisive element is what you *are,* not what you *think* or *believe*. If you are a malignant, vengeful man, you will commit murder in spite of your faith, in spite of your fear of God, for passion and opportunity will carry you away; but if you are the contrary, if your nature is not crude but noble, if you are really a man and not a beast, you will find sufficient reason within yourself, without fear of God or man, to deter you from such a shameful act. First of all, your sense of honor, your unwillingess to do in secret what you are ashamed to do in the presence of others—a sentiment which unfortunately Christianity has utterly neglected in favor of its belief in God—the feeling that restrains you from deceiving others, that makes you want to *be* what you seem in the eyes of others; and in the present case, the feeling that enables a man to triumph over his passion at the very moment when its object, the triumphant feeling of holding the highest power, the power over life and death, is within reach, but for that very reason makes him disdain to act as an executioner.

As in physics, so also in morality, men have resorted to theology out of ignorance alone, and in so doing have neglected to develop the impulses and elements of virtue within man himself, so condemning the multitude down to our own day to the deepest moral barbarism. As to the above-cited proposition that in atheism morality depends only on considerations of utility or harmfulness —a doctrine which even today theology and its camp followers, the speculative lackeys of theology, continue to mouth, though in other words and phrases, it should be remarked that even from the standpoint of religion it involves a spurious opposition. Believers and atheists are agreed in seeking the useful and in shunning the harmful. The difference between them is the difference between uncertain benefit or harm on the one hand and certain benefit or harm on the other. To the atheist the harm is uncertain, while to the believer harm, the object of his fear, God's anger and punishment, is certain; but conversely the atheist's benefit is also uncertain, while the believer's benefit, God's love and reward, is certain. In other words: the true difference between religion and atheism is the difference between *infinite* egoism and *finite* egoism. In the fear of God, to be sure, egoism vanishes, for fear is the trembling of the ego before a power that destroys or can destroy it; but in God's certain and infinite reward, infinite egoism reappears all the more clearly. Thus the atheist is at a moral disadvantage over against the believer, insofar as he has no fear of God, but he also has the moral advantage of having no divine reward in view.

At this point I wish to dissociate myself from the limited, superficial atheism of the early days, in particular of the French. French atheism is as far from true atheism as the French republic from the true republic. As I have shown elsewhere, the belief in divine punitive justice is based on the belief in nemesis, in the defeat of evil, in the triumph of the good, a belief which is the foundation of all historical actions. But this belief is independent of religion, for the good lies in human nature and even in human egoism; the good is merely what falls in with the egoism of all men, and evil is simply what falls in with the egoism of certain classes of men at the expense of others, but the egoism of all, or at least of the majority, is always more powerful than that of the minority. One glance at history is sufficient. When does a new historical epoch set in? Always when a repressed mass or majority asserts its justified egoism in opposition to the exclusive egoism of a nation or caste, when classes of men or whole nations triumph over the arrogance and presumption of a patrician minority and so emerge from the darkness of the despised proletarian mass to the light of historical fame. In the same way, the egoism of the now oppressed majority of mankind must and will come into its own, ushering in a new historical epoch. I am not for eliminating the cultural aristocracy. Far from it; I reject a state of affairs in which some men are aristocrats and all the rest plebeians, and am looking forward to the day when all men at least enjoy the advantages of education. I am not for abolishing property. Far from it, I am opposed to the ownership of the few while others have nothing, and look forward to the day when all men have property.

The original object of religion is something which is differentiated from man and independent of him, but on which he is nevertheless dependent. And that is *nature*. The classics are most illuminating on this point. A few examples: "May the gods only give you years [i. e., long life]," says Ovid to Germanicus in his epistles from Pontus, "and you will achieve the rest by yourself." Young Caeso Quinctius, says Livy, was of noble birth and large, powerful stature. To these *gifts of the gods* he himself added brilliant feats of bravery in battle and of eloquence in the Forum. Indeed, Livy goes on, he was endowed with all the gifts or benefits of *nature* and *good fortune*. And again according to Livy: "What I fear most," says Scipio to the Roman soldiers after Hannibal's crossing of the Alps, "is that it may appear as though not you but the Alps had defeated Hannibal, although it is perfectly natural that the *gods themselves,* without human aid, should combat and defeat a perjured general." "The gods," writes Tacitus in his *Annals,* "also visited storms and plagues upon a year desecrated by so many [human] horrors." In Plutarch's Lives, Lucullus drives Mithridates from the seas with the *help of the gods,* for a storm destroys his fleet, while in Florus it is the waves and storms, in alliance as it were with Lucullus, that cause the defeat of Mithridates.

But whether we speak of "nature" or "the gods," the meaning is the same, for the gods are merely poetic embodiments of nature. "All men," says Cotta in Cicero's *De Natura Deorum,* "hold that they derive from the gods the outward good things of life, vineyards, fields, olive groves, the fruits of field and orchard, in short, all the prerequisites of a happy, pleasant life. Has anyone ever thanked the gods for making him virtuous? No! We thank them only for health, wealth and honor.* In short, it is the opinion of all men that we must pray to the gods for good fortune, but must find

* Sadi, the Persian poet, says: "We do not attain *wealth* and *power* by our cleverness, but by the divine omnipotence alone."

wisdom in ourselves." "May Jupiter," says Horace in his *Epistles,* "give me only life and possessions; I myself will achieve peace of mind." And in Aulus Gellius, the censor Metellus Numidicus says: "The gods must reward virtue, but not give it." "Who can doubt," says Seneca in his Letters, "that life is a gift of the immortal gods, but to live *well* [that is, virtuously] is the gift of philosophy." All these passages show with exemplary clarity that divinity, or the gods, means nothing other than nature. What is beyond the power of man, what is not the result of human activity, life, for example, is the work of God, that is, of nature.

Nature is man's God; but nature is in perpetual movement and change, and the changes or events of nature frustrate or favor, hinder or abet human desires and purposes; consequently, it is they more than anything else that arouse religious feeling, that make nature an object of religion. A favorable wind springs up and carries me to the land I have been yearning for: I have sailed "with God"; a windstorm blows dust in my enemies' faces. God has blinded them; after long drought a shower suddenly refreshes me: the gods have sent rain; a pestilence breaks out among men or beasts: the "hand" or power of God is at work. In most cases it is purely a matter of chance whether such natural happenings favor or oppose man's desires, whether they are fortunate or unfortunate for man. Chance—especially favorable chance—is therefore the principal object of religion. It seems contradictory that, as Pliny the Elder puts it, the very thing which makes man doubt the existence of a God, should itself be taken as a god. But chance has this essential and original characteristic of divinity: it is something unintended and unwilled, independent of human knowledge and will, and yet man's fate depends on it. What the pagans attributed to Fortuna or Fatum, fate, the Christians attribute to God, but though they do not regard chance as a special deity, they deify it as much as the pagans did.

The universal concept *God* is a sack, a catchall; but I do not change the nature of a thing by putting it into a sack; I merely cease to *see* it, it loses its *visible* attributes. The content remains the same whether I say God willed it, or chance willed it; God disposes, or you never can tell; God gave a plentiful harvest, or the harvest turned out well. It is all one whether I say "If God wills, a broomstick will flower," or "With luck, your ox will calve"; "God smiles on fools," or "Luck smiles on fools"; "The Lord giveth, the Lord taketh away," or "Fortune is fickle"; "Things are going as God wills," or "Things are doing the best they can"; "Whom God makes wet, He makes dry again," or "Your luck will change"; "God sends rain," or "*It* has chosen to rain." God is the impersonal "it," transformed into the personal "He." He is more comforting, more edifying than the "it" for fortune or misfortune, but that is the only difference. The injury remains the same whether the droppings of a swallow or a deliberate punch in the eye robs me of my eyesight, whether an accidental *It* falls off the roof, or a capricious He, my most serene and gracious sovereign, for example, shoots at me from the roof for his amusement.

Thus it is not to be wondered at that the Greek word *Theos,* god, carried the meaning of *tyche,* fortune, chance,* and that (as I pointed out in *The Essence of Christianity* to the consternation of modern Christians) our Christian forefathers in their pious simplicity guessed that natural chance and divine chance were identical. The naïvely pious Aventinus wrote, for example: "Our forces were already confident of victory, but *God and nature and fortune* had decided otherwise." And on another occasion, when "the Hungarians were put to flight by wind and storm," he says: "And then by God's grace, or perhaps by chance, the sun was blotted out," etc.

The object of religion is nature, which operates independently of man and which he distinguishes from himself. But this nature is more than the phenomena of the outside world; it also includes man's inner nature, which operates independently of his knowledge and his will. This statement brings us to our most crucial point, the true seat and source of religion. The ultimate secret of religion is the *relationship* between the *conscious* and *unconscious,* the *volun-*

* Instead of our "In the name of God," the Greeks began their official documents and decrees with the words "With good fortune." The Romans too sometimes said god instead of fortune or chance, and sometimes chance instead of god. "*Nisi qui deus vel casus aliquis subvenerit,*" writes Cicero, for example, in a letter to Tiro. Fortuna had in Rome no less than twenty-six temples. Just as with us "it" and God are equivalent, the Romans said interchangeably: *bene vertat Deus!* or *Quae mihi atque vobis vertat bene!*

tary and *involuntary in one and the same individual.* Man wills, but often he does so unwillingly—how often he envies the beings who have no will; he is conscious, yet he achieves consciousness unconsciously—how often he deprives himself of consiousness, and how gladly he relapses into unconsciousness at the end of his day's work! He lives, and yet he is without power over the beginning and end of his life; he is the outcome of a process of development, yet once he exists, it seems to him as though he had come into being through a unique act of creation, as though he had shot up overnight like a mushroom; he has a body, in every experience of pleasure of pain he feels it to be his own, and yet he is a stranger in his own house; pleasure is an unearned reward, every pain is an undeserved punishment; in happy moments he feels that life is a gift he has not asked for, in unhappy moments a burden inflicted upon him against his will; he feels the torment of his needs, yet satisfies them without knowing whether the impulsion to do so comes from within or without, whether he is satisfying himself or some outside being.

Man with his ego or consciousness stands at the brink of a bottomless abyss; that abyss is his own unconscious being, which seems alien to him and inspires him with a feeling which expresses itself in words of wonderment such as: What am I? Where have I come from? To what end? And this feeling that I am nothing without a *not-I* which is distinct from me yet intimately related to me, something *other,* which is at the same time my *own* being, is the religious feeling. But what part of me is I and what part is not-I? Hunger as such, or its cause, is not-I; but the painful sensation or awareness of hunger which drives me to direct all my motor faculties toward an object that will appease this pain, is I. The elements, then, of the I or man, of the real man, are consciousness, feeling, voluntary movement—voluntary movement, I say, because involuntary movement is outside the sphere of the I, in the realm of the divine not-I—and that is why certain disorders, such as epilepsy, why states of ecstasy or madness have been looked upon as divine revelations or manifestations.

What we have just said about hunger applies also to the higher, spiritual impulses. I feel a desire to write poetry, I can satisfy it only by voluntary activity, but the underlying impulse is not-I; although I and not-I are so closely intertwined that one can be substituted for the other—for there is no such thing as a not-I without an I or vice-versa—this fusion of I and not-I is the secret, the essence, of *individuality*. The one determines the other. Where, for example, the appetite is the dominant element in the not-I, the I or individuality is characterized by a pronounced development of the teeth and jaws. Every not-I has its corresponding I. If it were otherwise, if the not-I were not itself individualized, the phenomenon or existence of the I would be just as inexplicable, miraculous, and monstrous as the incarnation of God or the union of man and God in theology.

And the foundation of individuality is also the foundation of religion; namely, the relationship between, or the fusion of, I and not-I. If man were a mere I, he would have no religion, for he himself would be God; but he would also have no religion if he were a not-I, or an I undifferentiated from his not-I, for then he would be a plant or an animal. What distinguishes man is not that his not-I is just as much an object of his consciousness, of his sense of wonderment, of his feeling of dependency—just as much an object of religion—as is external nature. What am I without senses, without imagination, without reason? Wherein is an outward stroke of chance better than a happy inspiration that saves me in a difficult situation? Of what use to me is the sun in the sky unless my eyes watch over my steps? And what is the sun's light beside the magic light of the imagination? What, in general, are the outward miracles of nature compared to the miracle of our inner nature, of the mind? But is the eye a product of my hands, is the imagination a product of my will, is reason my invention? Or have I "given" to myself all these magnificent powers and talents, which are the foundation of my being and on which my existence depends? Is it my *achievement,* my *work* that I am a man?

No! I humbly recognize—and to this extent I am entirely in agreement with religion—that I have made neither my eye nor any of my organs or talents. But that is as far as I can go along with religion. Shall I say, with religion, that someone gave me all my human capacities? No, I say that they grew from the womb of nature along with my I. Religion transforms everything that is *not a product of the human will* into a product of the *divine will,* everything that is not a human achievement, a work of man, into the achievement, the gift, the work of God. Religion knows no other productive activity than the voluntary activity of the human hand, it knows indeed *no other being than man* (in his subjectivity); to religion, man is the *absolute,* the *only* being, preceding all the gods; and nevertheless, to its great surprise, the religious mind encounters a not-I in man, whereupon it transforms the not-human part of man into a human being, transforms the not-I into an I who, just like man, has hands (and all the instruments or powers of voluntary activity), the only difference being that the divine hands make what human hands can *not* make. Thus we observe two things in religion. One is the humility with which man recognizes that he did *not* obtain *from himself* what he is and has, that he does not possess his life and being but merely holds a lease on them and can therefore be deprived of them at any moment—who can guarantee that I will not lose my reason?—and that he consequently has no ground for self-conceit, pride, and arrogance."*

"Though his body be ever so powerful," says Sophocles in *Ajax,* "man must always be mindful and fear that the most trifling accident may be his downfall." "We men," he says elsewhere in the same play, "are nothing other than light, unsubstantial shadows. If you bear that in mind, you will never utter a presumptuous word against the gods, or puff yourself up with pride because you are stronger or richer than others, for a single day can take away everything you have." When Ajax left home, his father said to him: "Son, try to be victorious in battle, but to be victorious only with God." But Ajax gave the foolish and overweening answer: "Father, even a nobody can triumph with the gods; I hope to gain warlike fame

* The concept of the I, of what man attributes to *himself,* is extremely indefinite and relative, and accordingly as man broadens or narrows its scope, his conception of divine activity is narrowed or amplified. Indeed—often out of sheer religious gallantry and desire to flatter the gods—a man can go so far as to disclaim all credit; for ultimately my feeling, my consciousness, my very being result from premises which are situated outside the I, which are the work of nature or of God. Indeed, the deeper man looks within, the more the distinction between nature and man or I vanishes, the plainer it becomes to him that he is only *consciously unconscious,* a *not-I that is an I.* That is why man is the deepest and most complex of all beings. But man cannot understand or endure his own depth, and for that reason he splits his being into an I without a not-I, which he calls God and a not-I without an I, which he calls nature.

without them." These words were not only irreligious but also thoughtless, for the bravest and strongest of men can be incapacitated before he knows it by a mere attack of rheumatism or some other unfortunate accident. Even if Ajax wanted no truck with the gods, he should at least have tempered his declaration with a little "if"; he should have said: if no misfortune strikes me, I will triumph. Religiosity, then, is nothing more than the virtue of modesty, of moderation in the sense of the Greek *sophrosyne*—God loves the *sophrones,* says Sophocles—the virtue which deters a man from overstepping the limits of his nature, from striving for what is beyond the capacity of man, from laying claim to the proud title of an author; it is the virtue which forbids him to look upon his achievements as his own, for he derives the predisposition, the principles underlying even such skills as metalworking and weaving, not from himself but from nature. To be religious means: remember what you are, a man, a mortal.

The first source of religion (in its enduring positive sense) was not so-called God-consciousness, but consciousness of the nature of man, the consciousness or feeling that I am a man but not the cause of man's being, that I live but am not the cause of life, that I see but am not the cause of sight. Any attempt to do away with this aspect of religion is as absurd as the attempt of a talentless individual to become an artist by mere determination and industry. To undertake a task without talent and therefore without vocation is to undertake it without God; to perform a task with talent is to perform it successfully, with God. "*In us there dwells a god,*" says Ovid in his *Fasti*. "We burn when he enflames us." But what is this god the poet speaks of? He is the personified art of poetry, he is poetic talent objectified as a divine being. "All attempts," says Goethe most aptly, "to introduce a foreign innovation unless the need for it is rooted in the heart of our own nation, are absurd, and all calculated revolutions of this kind are doomed to failure, for they are without God, who draws back from such bungling efforts. But if a nation feels a real need for a great reform, God is with that nation and the reform succeeds." In other words: what is done without necessity and consequently without law—for the first and fundamental law is the law of necessity—is done without God. Where there is no need for a revolution, the true impulse, the talent, the brain for a revolution are also lacking, and it must inevitably fail. A godless, or what amounts to the same thing, an unsuccessful undertaking is a brainless, indiscreet undertaking.

The other feature of religion that I wished to remark on, though we have already discussed it, is the self-centered arrogance that leads man to see everything in human terms and to transform the not-I in man into a personal being, who then becomes an object of prayers, thanksgiving, and honors. By turning the involuntary into something voluntary and the forces and products of nature into gifts and benefits which obligate man to gratitude and reverence toward their bestowers, the gods, religion takes on a *semblance* of profound humanity and culture, while the contrary attitude, according to which the good things of life are involuntary products of nature, seems barbarous and unfeeling. "You say that all these good things come from nature," write Seneca in *De beneficiis*. "But are you not aware that in saying this you are merely employing another name for God? For what is nature but God? Thus you are saying nothing, most ungrateful of mortals, when you say that you owe nothing to God but are indebted only to nature, for there is no nature without God or God without nature; they are one and the same." But we must not let the religious aura blind us to the fact that this human tendency—to trace all the workings of nature back to a personal cause, to derive its good effects from a good will or being and its bad effects from an evil one—is grounded in the crudest egoism, and that this tendency is alone responsible for the human sacrifices ordained by religion and for countless other horrors of human history; for the same tendency that requires a personal being to thank and love for the good that man enjoys, also requires a personal being—Jew or heretic, sorcerer or witch—to hate and strangle for the evil that befalls him. It was *one and the same fire which flamed heavenward in thanks for nature's benefits and which consumed heretics, sorcerers, and witches to punish them for the evils of nature.* If it is a sign of culture and humanity to thank God for a beneficial rainfall, it is equally a sign of culture and humanity to blame the Devil and his crew for a destructive hailstorm.

Where *all good things* come from *divine goodness, all evil* must necessarily stem from *diabolical malice.* The two notions are inseparable. But to blame an evil will for the natural phenomena that are opposed to my egoism is an obvious sign of barbarism. To convince ourselves that this is so, there is no need to go back to Xerxes, who, according to Herodotus, punished the Hellespont with three hundred lashes in his rage at the disobedience of the sea; there is no need of a trip to Madagascar, where babies who give their mothers trouble and pain during pregnancy and childbirth are strangled, since they must obviously be evil. Right before our eyes we can see how our barbarous and ignorant governments put the blame for every historical necessity and human development that is not to their liking on the ill will of individuals; we see ignorant boors mistreat their cattle, their children, their sick, simply because they take the failings or peculiarities of nature for willful obstinacy, and everywhere we see the rabble gleefully attributing a man's natural failings, which he cannot possibly help, to his ill will. Accordingly, it is also a sign of men's ignorance, barbarism, egoism, and their inability to look beyond themselves, when they attribute the benefits of nature to a good or divine will.

Differentiation—I am not you, you are not I—this is the basic condition and principle of all culture and humanity. But the man who attributes the workings of nature to someone's will fails to differentiate between himself and nature, and consequently his attitude toward nature is not what it should be. The proper attitude toward an object is an attitude consonant with its nature and its dissimilarity to myself; such an attitude is not a *religious* one, but neither is it *irreligious* as is supposed by the vulgarians, learned or common, who are able only to distinguish between belief and unbelief, religion and irreligion, but are unaware of a third and higher principle above them both. Kindly give me a good harvest, dear earth, says the religious man; "whether the earth wants to or not, it must yield me fruit," says the irreligious man, Polyphemus. But the true man, who is neither religious nor irreligious, says: The earth will give me fruit if I give it what is appropriate to its nature; it does not *will* to give, nor *must* it give—"must" implies reluctance and coercion—no, it will give only if I for my part have fulfilled all the conditions under which it can give, or rather produce; for nature gives me nothing, I myself must take everything, at least everything that is not already a part of me—and moreover I must take it by extreme violence. With intelligent egoism we forbid murder and theft among ourselves, but toward other beings, toward nature, we are all murderers and thieves.

Who gives me the right to catch a rabbit? The fox and the vulture are just as hungry as I, just as much entitled to exist. Who gives me the right to pick a pear? It belongs just as much to the ants, the caterpillars, the birds, the four-footed animals. To whom then does it really belong? To the one who takes it. Is it not sufficient that I live by murder and theft—should I in addition thank the gods? How foolish! I have reason to thank the gods if they can show me that I really owe them my life, and this they will not have done until pigeons fly ready roasted into my mouth. Did I say roasted? No, that is not enough; I should say chewed and digested, for the tedious and unaesthetic operations of mastication and digestion are unbefitting the gods and their gifts. Why should a God who at one stroke makes the world out of nothing in a twinkling need so much time to provide me with a bit of chyme? Here again it becomes evident that the Godhead consists as it were of two components, one originating in man's imagination, the other in nature. "You must pray," says the one component, the god differentiated from nature. "You must work," says the other, the god who is not differentiated from nature and merely expresses the essence of nature. For nature is a worker bee, while the gods are drones. How can I derive the image and law of industry from drones? To derive nature or world from God, to maintain that hunger comes from satiety, need from abundance, gravity from levity, work from sloth—is attempting to bake common bread from ambrosia and to brew beer from the nectar of the gods.

Nature is the first God, the first object of religion; but religion does not look upon it as nature; religion views it as a human being, characterized by emotion, imagination, and thought. The secret of religion is "the *identity of the subjective and objective*," that is, the unity of man and nature, but this unity is arrived at in disregard of their true character. Man has many ways of humanizing nature and, conversely (for man and nature are inseparable), of objectifying and externalizing his own being. Here, however, we shall confine ourselves to two of these ways, to the metaphysical form and the practical-poetic form of monotheism. The latter is characteristic of the Old Testament and the Koran. The God of the Koran as of the Old Testament is nature or the world, its real, living being as opposed to artificial, dead, man-made idols.* He is not any part of the world or fragment of nature, such as the stone which the Arabs before Mohammed worshiped, but all nature, immense and undivided. In the tenth Sura of the Koran, for example, we read: "Say: 'Who provides food for you from the earth and the sky? Who has endowed you with sight and hearing? Who brings forth the living from the dead, and the dead from the living? Who ordains all things?' They will reply: 'Allah.' Say: 'Will you not take heed then?' " Or the sixth Sura: "Allah splits the seed and the fruit-stone. . . . He kindles the light of dawn. He has ordained the night for rest and the sun and the moon to measure time. Such is the ordinance of Allah, the Mighty One, the All-Knowing. . . . He sends down water from the sky and with it we bring forth the buds of every plant, green foliage and close-growing grain, palm trees laden with clusters of dates, vineyards and olive groves and all manner of pomegranates. Behold their fruits when they ripen. Surely in these there are signs enough for true believers." And the thirteenth Sura: "It was Allah who raised the heavens without resting them on visible pillars. . . . It was He who spread out the earth and placed upon it rivers and unchangeable mountains. He gave all plants their male and female parts and drew the veil of night over the day. . . . It is He who makes the lightning flash upon you, inspiring you with fear and hope, and makes the clouds heavy with rain. The thunder sounds His praises and the angels too for awe. He hurls His thunderbolts and crushes whom He pleases. Yet the unbelievers wrangle about Allah. Stern is His punishment."

Thus the signs or effects of the true God—the original God as opposed to His copies the idols—are the workings of nature. An idol cannot bring forth living things, tasty fruits, fruitful rain, or terrible storms. This can be done only by the God who is not fashioned by man but is God by nature, and who therefore not only

* Jalal-ud-din relates that Mohammed sent a zealous Mohammedan to convert an unbeliever to Islam. "What manner of being is your God?" the unbeliever asked him. "Is He of gold, silver, or copper?" Lightning struck the godless man and he was dead. This is a crude but convincing lesson on the difference between the *living* God and the man-made god.

appears to be but is a real living being. But a God whose signs and works are the works of nature is nothing more than nature. Yet, as we have said, He is not a part of nature which is in one place and not another, which is here today and gone tomorrow and which for that very reason man makes eternally present in an image; He is the whole of nature. "When night drew its shadow over him [Abraham]," we read in the sixth Sura, "he saw a star. 'That,' he said, 'is my God.' But when the star faded into the morning light, he said: 'I will not worship gods that fade.' When he beheld the rising moon, he said: 'That surely is my God.' But when it, too, set, he said: 'If Allah does not guide me, I shall surely go astray.' Then, when he beheld the sun shining, he said: 'That must be my God: it is larger than the other two.' But when it, too, set, he said to his people: 'I am done with your idols. I will turn my face to Him who has created the heavens and the earth.' "

Thus eternal omnipresence is a hallmark of the true God; but nature, too, is everywhere. Where there is no nature, I am not, and where I am there is also nature. "Whither shall I go" from thee, O Nature? "And where shall I flee" from thy being? "If I fly heavenward, Nature is there. If I bed myself in hell, Nature is there too." Where there is life there is nature, and where there is no life, there too is nature; everything is full of nature. How, then, would you escape from nature? But the God of the Koran, as of the Old Testament, is nature and at the same time *not* nature, for He is also a *subjective,* i. e., personal being, knowing and thinking, willing and acting like man. As an object of religion, the works of nature are at the same time *works* of *human ignorance and imagination,* the being or cause behind them is a product of *human ignorance and imagination*. Man is divided from nature by a gulf of ignorance; he does not know how the grass grows, how a child forms in the womb, what causes rain, thunder and lightning. "Hast thou perceived the breadth of the earth?" we read in Job. "Declare if thou knowest it all. . . . Hast thou seen the treasures of the hail? . . . . Hath the rain a father? . . . . Knowest thou the ordinances of heaven?"

Because man does *not* know what the works of nature are made of, where they come from and under what conditions, he regards them as the works of an absolutely unconditioned and unlimited power, to which nothing is impossible, which even brought forth the world out of nothing, just as it continues to bring forth the works of nature from nothing, the nothing of human ignorance. Human ignorance is bottomless, and the human imagination knows no bounds; deprived of its foundations by ignorance and of its limits by the imagination, the power of nature becomes divine omnipotence. Once the works of nature are attributed to the divine omnipotence, they cease to be distinguished from supernatural events, from miracles, the products of faith; *one and the same* power produces natural death and the supernatural resurrection from the dead which is purely a product of faith, *one and the same* power engenders man in a natural way and brings him forth from stones or from nothing if it so chooses. "We have sent down blessed water," says the fiftieth Sura, for example, "thereby giving new life to some dead land. Such shall be the Resurrection. . . . Were We worn out by the first creation? [Or according to Savary's French translation: Did the creation of the universe cost us the slightest effort?] Yet they are in doubt about a new creation," i. e., the resurrection.

"After winter," says Luther in his Short Explanation of the 147th Psalm, "He brings summer; if He did not, if winter were everlasting, we should die of the cold. But *how* or *by what means* does He bring summer?" "He speaks and the ice melts." "Through the *word* He creates all things. He needs no more than one word; the Word is a Lord." In other words: the divine omnipotence is the power of nature identified and merged with the power of the human imagination, the power of nature differentiated and detached from sensuous reality until it signifies little or nothing more than the *power of the human imagination.* But insofar as nature creates, destroys, and impresses man with its might, he personifies it as an all-powerful individual; insofar as it confers innumerable benefits and seems to embody all the good things of life, he personifies it as a supremely *good* individual; and insofar as it inspires the human mind with extreme wonderment, he personifies it as a supremely *wise* and *omniscient* being. In short, an *object* considered as *subject,* the essence of nature *differentiated from nature* and seen as a *human being,* the essence of man *differentiated from man* and seen as a *not-human being*—this is the essence of divinity and religion, the secret of mysticism and speculation, this is the great *thauma,* the wonder of all wonders, which fills men with the profoundest amazement and rapture.*

Like man, God has will, but what is the will of man beside the will of God, beside the will which calls forth the great works of nature, which makes the earth quake, piles up mountains, moves the sun, commands the raging sea: Thus far and no further. Is anything impossible to this will? "God creates what He will," we read in the Koran and in the Psalms. God has speech like man, but what is man's word beside the word of God? "Does He will something to be?" says the Koran. "He says: Be, and it is." "When He wills to give existence to beings, He says: Be, and they are." God has reason like man, but what is man's knowledge beside God's knowledge? It embraces all things, it embraces the infinite cosmos. "He knows," says the Koran, "what is on earth and at the bottom of the sea. Not a leaf falls without His knowledge. There is not a grain in the earth but is recorded in the book of evidence." God is man, but a man who is nature and whose imagination embraces the cosmos; the same being and yet a very different one, as far removed from us as the sun from the eye, the sky from the earth, as different from us as nature is, an entirely different being and yet the same—hence the profound mystical impression made by this being and hence the sublimity of the Koran and the Psalms.

The only difference between Mohammedan and Jewish monotheism on the one hand and Christian monotheism on the other is that in the former the religious imagination or fantasy looks outward with open eyes and builds directly on the perception of nature, while in Christianity it closes its eyes, separates the personified essence of nature entirely from sense perception, and so transforms what was originally body, or mind and body, into an abstract, metaphysical being. The God of the Koran and the Old Testament is still filled with the sap of nature, still wet and cold from the cosmic ocean whence He sprang, whereas the God of Christian monotheism is a withered, dried-out God in whom all traces of His origin in nature is effaced; there He stands like a creation out of

* It goes without saying that this fusion of man and nature into a single being, who is termed the supreme being precisely because he is the summit of the imagination, is involuntary. And "the instinct for religion or divinity" owes its name and existence to the involuntary character of this fusion.

nothing; on pain of the rod He even forbids the inevitable question: "What did God do before He created the world?" or more correctly: What was He before nature? In other words, He makes a secret of His physical origin, hiding it behind a metaphysical abstraction. Whereas the first God sprang from the union of the feminine power of thought and imagination with the masculine faculty of material perception, the metaphysical God sprang from the mere union of thought or abstraction with imagination.

In his thinking, man separates adjective from substantive, attribute from essence, or, as the ancients put it, form from matter; for he cannot grasp the subject itself, the matter, the essence, and sets it aside. The metaphysical God is nothing other than a compendium of the most universal attributes abstracted from nature, which compendium however—and precisely in its dissociation from the sensuous reality or matter of nature—man transforms by his imagination into an independent subject or being. But the most universal attribute of all things is being, the fact that each thing *is* and is *something*. Being as such, being as differentiated from existing things, differentiated from nature and personified as a being—that is the first and second element of the divine metaphysic or essence. But apart from being and the characteristics which he shares with the other things and beings of nature, man has characteristics that belong to him alone: he has reason, mind. Consequently the divine metaphysic has a third element in addition to the first two, namely, logic; the element abstracted from nature is combined in man's mind with the element abstracted specifically from man. God, therefore, has as much existence or reality as has Being, Essence, or Spirit as such—in other words, He has subjective, logical, metaphysical existence; but can anything be more absurd than the attempt to transform metaphysical into physical, subjective into objective, logical or abstract existence into an alogical, real existence?

And yet how convenient, how comforting it is to take the abstracted being—the figment of thought which we carry around in our heads and can deal with as we please—for a real being, and then look down with contempt upon recalcitrant, inaccessible reality! True, "what we think, *exists*," but only as thought; thought is one thing, reality is another; no sleight-of-hand can make them the same. "Is there then an eternal cleavage and opposition between being and thought?" Yes, in the mind; but in reality the contradiction has long been resolved. The cleavage has been bridged over by no less than five senses, perhaps not in accordance with dogmatic concepts, but in a manner quite consonant with reality.

3. A bird flits by; I follow it and come to a marvelous spring; consequently, the bird is a harbinger of good fortune. A cat crosses my path as I am starting on a journey; my journey is unsuccessful; consequently, the cat is a prophet of disaster. The area of religious superstition is absolutely limitless, for its only causal nexus is chance. Thus an animal or other natural being can become an object of religious faith or superstition for no objective reason.* This lack of objective justification does not invalidate my explanation of the animal cult, for what a thing has not or is not in reality, it has or is in faith. Is the spider poisonous? No, but faith has made it so. Is *Euphrasia officinalis* good for the eyes? No, but faith has made it into "eyebright." Does the swallow bring good fortune? No, but faith lays its cuckoo's eggs even in swallow's nests. To reject what I have said to be the principle of animal worship on the ground that men have worshiped animals which are neither useful nor harmful, is tantamount to denying that men have ever attributed magic power to such words as *abracadabra,* on the ground that these words are meaningless and therefore not true words. The suprasensory, that is, nonsensical, and suprarational, that is, the irrational, are precisely the essense of religious faith or superstition.

Moreover, the other factors of religion we have mentioned also

* Usually, to be sure, superstition attaches to a conspicuous attribute or peculiarity of its object, but the significance it reads into this attribute is purely arbitrary or subjective. Speaking of animal cults in his *Recherches philosophiques sur les Egyptiens et les Chinois* (1774), Pauw remarks that some years ago French peasants, thinking they discerned clear signs of divinity in the pupae of the caterpillars who make their home on the stinging nettle, made them the object of a kind of religious cult. These signs of divinity were obviously nothing other than the shiny golden dots on their surface. Pauw prefaces his story with the apt observation: "*L'esprit du petit peuple peut être fortement frappé par de petites choses.*" But this "*petit peuple*" in man is the so-called religious feeling, the state of mind that allows itself to be bewitched and mystified, or in plain language hoodwinked, even by the golden dots on a pupa.

occur in animal cults. We have seen how a religious fondness for animals sacrifices man even to bedbugs, fleas, and lice. In his *History of the United States of America* Bancroft says very aptly of the Indians' nature and animal cults: "The bird, that mysteriously cleaves the air, into which he [man] *cannot soar*; the fish, that hides itself in the depths of the clear, cool lakes, which he *cannot fathom*; the beasts of the forest, whose unerring instincts, more sure than his own intelligence, seem like revelations;—these enshrine the deity whom he adores." But Bancroft's preceding remark—"His gods are not the offspring of terror. . . . The Indian venerates what excites his amazement or interests his imagination"—calls for comment. Mere amazement and imagination do not give rise to *prayers* or *sacrifices*. Bancroft himself goes on to say: "The piety of the savage was not merely a sentiment of passive resignation—he sought to propitiate the unknown, to avert their wrath, to secure their favor. . . . Every where among the red men . . . . they had some kind of sacrifice and of prayer. If the harvest was abundant, if the chase was successful, they saw in their success the influence of a manitou; and they would ascribe even an ordinary accident to the wrath of the god. 'O manitou!' exclaimed an Indian at daybreak, with his family about him, lamenting the loss of a child, 'thou art angry with me; turn thine anger from me, and spare the rest of my children.' "

Here he has hit on the core of religion. Man is a practical, not a theoretical being, he is motivated not by ethereal imagination but by hungry, painful reality. Hence it is no wonder that, as Loskiel reports, the Indians hold a sacrificial festival in honor even of a certain *gluttonous goblin* whose hunger in their opinion can never be appeased. Why, even the "greatest mind of the pagan North," Eywind Skalldaspillir, immortalized in song "a fortunate catch of herring, which freed him from his distress." The height of absurdity, by the way, is for the theists to put the suave distinctions of theology into the mouths of savages, to quote them as saying that what they really worship is not the animals themselves, but "the God within them." What can be worshiped in an animal but the nature and being of an animal? Speaking of the Egyptian animal cult in *De Iside et Osiride,* Plutarch writes:

If the foremost philosophers perceived images of divinity even in lifeless things, how much more are they to be sought in living and feeling beings. But only those are deserving of praise who worship not these beings and things themselves but through or by means of them [*dia toutōn*] worship the divine. It is easy to see that no lifeless thing is better than a being that has life, that no unfeeling thing is more excellent than a being endowed with feeling; the divine nature does not reside in colors or figures or smooth surfaces, for the most lifeless is the most inferior. What lives, sees, moves, and distinguishes the useful from the harmful, has in it a share of the Providence which, as Heraclitus says, rules the universe.

Must the ground for animal worship not therefore be sought in the animals themselves? If divine nature is essentially different from animal nature, I cannot honor it in or through animals, for then I find in them no images of divinity, no resemblance to God; but if the opposite is true, such a distinction is meaningless. Those who conceive of and depict the gods in animal form unconsciously worship the animals themselves, even if their consciousness and reason deny it.

4. Another fine example is Pliny's panegyric to the sun in his Natural History.

In the midst of the so-called comets courses the sun, immense in size and power, ruler not only of times and countries, but even of the stars and the heavens themselves. When we consider its effects on the soul, we are bound to look upon it as the spirit of the whole world, as the preeminent ruler and god of nature. It provides the light of the world and dispels the darkness; it blots out the other heavenly bodies, it orders the changes of the seasons and the ever regenerating year to nature's profit, brightens the dark sky and banishes the clouds of the human soul. It lends its light to the other luminaries, outshining and standing out from them all, and, as Homer says, it sees and hears all things.

Here we have all the elements of religion in a nutshell.

5. The statement that the Greeks regarded only Greek gods as gods, that paganism, as I formerly held, is patriotism while Christianity is cosmopolitanism requires comment, for it seems in direct contradiction to the generally accepted view that polytheism went hand in hand with tolerance and open-mindedness. In his book *Die altteutsche Religion oder Hertha* (2d edition) the learned Barth

goes so far as to say: "Although every religion takes on something of a national coloration and every nation is in some degree colored by its religion, religions are not separated like nations or political leagues; we cannot speak today of a Spanish, Swedish, or Russian religion but only of one Christian religion and its sects, nor was there any such division in antiquity." But if the unity of religion in antiquity is to be deduced from the fact that all modern nations are or call themselves Christian, the unity of ancient religion is in a bad way, for although we do not *speak* of a German or Russian religion, there is in fact just as great a difference between German and Russian religion as between the German and Russian peoples. To ask whether religions are one or diversified is to ask whether mankind as a whole is one or diversified. And the answers will differ as long as men themselves differ from one another and think differently, some stressing the common, identical factors and others the diverse and individual factors.

But as far as our specific question is concerned, politics and religion were so intimately joined among the Romans and Greeks that if their gods are separated out of this union, only so much or so little remains of them as if I were to remove the Romanness from a Roman and the Greekness from a Greek, and leave nothing but the human being as such. "Jupiter, who by his universal character was a god for every situation, represented every variety of kinship and civic relationship; thus we may say, with Creuzer, that the concept of Jupiter was developed into an ideal *corpus juris*. He is Polieus (protector of the city), Metoikios, Phratrios (protector of phratries), Herkeois," etc. (E. Platner, *Beiträge zur Kenntniss des attischen Rechts*.) But what is left of Jupiter if I take away this *corpus juris,* these political epithets or titles? Nothing, or no more than if I as an Athenian were deprived of all the rights grounded in these predicates or than if I were shortened by a head. Just as spiritual Athens was bound up with geographical Athens and spiritual Rome with geographical Rome—with the immovable *Fortuna loci,* as Livy's Camillus puts it in his speech admonishing the Romans not to leave Rome—just so the Roman and Greek gods were by necessity territorial or local gods.

Jupiter Capitoline, to be sure, lives in the mind of every Roman even outside Rome, but his real existence, his "seat," is on the Capitol in Rome and nowhere else. Every corner of this city, says Camillus in his speech, is full of gods and religious usages (that is, religious ties). And you mean to leave all these gods? *Here* is the Capitol where once a human head was found and where the oracle gave answer that the head of world dominion would be in this place. *Here* is the place where, when the site of the Capitol was cleared and several earlier altars were removed, the Youth and the Boundary gods, to the utmost joy of our fathers, refused to budge. *Here* are the vestal fires, *here* the shields fallen from heaven, *here* are all the gods, devoted to you if you stay. When, as Tacitus tells us in his *Historiae,* Vitellius' soldiers set fire to the Capitol, there spread among the Gauls and Germans the belief, perfectly consonant with Roman conceptions and pagan conceptions in general, that the end of the Roman Empire was at hand. Once, to be sure, the city had been captured by the Gauls, but it had retained its dominant position because the seat of Jupiter had not been harmed. The present fire, it was held however, was a sign of divine wrath and announced to the peoples beyond the Alps that they would rule the world. We know that when the Romans wished to capture a city, they first summoned its tutelary gods by magic and incantations, for which reason, as Macrobius tells us in his *Saturnalia,* they kept secret the identity of Rome's tutelary deity and even its Latin name. They believed, then, that the protective power of the gods was confined to their dwelling place, that it was effective only where the gods were physically present. Thus it is no wonder that when a polytheistic people can get no help from its native gods, it welcomes foreign gods into its midst to test their saving, protective power. Even Cicero, in *De Legibus,* praises the Greeks and Romans because they did not, like the Persians, assign the whole world to their gods as a temple and dwelling place, but believed that they lived *in the same cities as themselves* and wanted them to go on living there.

6. Herodotus, it is true, says only that a he-goat publicly mated with a woman; his account does not make it clear whether the woman was a voluntary or involuntary victim of bestial lust. But if we consider that this happened in Mendes where goats and especially

he-goats are worshiped, where the god Pan was depicted with the face and hoofs of a goat and even bore the name Mendes, i.e., "he-goat"; if we further bear in mind that this mating of he-goat and woman was taken as a favorable omen—so at least certain authors have translated Herodotus' unclear *es epideixin anthrōpōn*—there can be no doubt that the woman was driven solely by religious enthusiasm, that is, suprahumanism and supranaturalism, to overcome the egoist and exclusive tendency of the human female to mate only with a human male, that she sacrificed her human nature and dignity to the sacred he-goat for the same motive as leads a Christian to sacrifice his human reason to the *divine unreason* of faith—*credo quia absurdum est.*

7. Moreover, as everyone knows, the Christian Church has offered up plenty of human sacrifices to its faith or, what amounts to the same thing, to its God. If the "Christian state," and hence also the Christian penal code, are mere creatures of the Christian faith, Christians to this very day offer up bloody human sacrifices to their faith or to what, as we have said, amounts to the same thing, their God, every time they haul a poor devil to the scaffold. Why, if the newspapers are to be believed, it was purely for religious reasons that His "Christian" Majesty the King of Prussia refused to abolish the death sentence!

8. In 356 B.C., as Livy relates in the fifth book of his history, the first *lectisternium,* or banquet for the gods, was held on the occasion of an epidemic that had broken out in Rome. For eight days running the Romans feasted the gods in the hope of propitiating them, and the liberality of the citizens extended also to their fellow men. Doors were left open throughout the city, the people put all their possessions at the disposal of the community, invited strangers as well as friends to dine with them, abstained from lawsuits and quarrels, and spoke amiably even to their enemies; prisoners were unshackled. And in 359, when news reached Rome that after a ten-year siege Veii had finally been taken, the rejoicing, as Livy relates in the same book, was so great that Roman mothers thronged to the temples to offer up thanks to the gods; the Senate decreed that the people should pray and give thanks to the gods

for four whole days—longer than in connection with any previous war.

9. Though the learned scholar E. Röth arrived at his conclusions by different means, his views on the subject are similar to my own. In his above-cited work on the Egyptian and Zoroastrian religion, he writes: "In all ancient religions the names of the gods were at first simple common nouns which merely designated things—water, wind, fire, and the like—and carried no personal connotation. This notion of a personal being developed only very gradually from the attributes that were imputed to divinity; thus a god's name sprang from one of the many epithets that were originally used to designate the various attributes of divinity. Consequently, the closer a god-concept is to its beginning, the more indeterminate it becomes, so that the divine names ultimately go back to *mere common nouns* or *adjectives.*"

10. The passage here cited is taken from the notes of Dionysius Vossius on the *De Idolatria* of Maimonides. I own that the meaning I have found in it is not explicitly stated in the text, but if this passage is collated with others, such as those from Eisenmenger's *Entdecktes Judenthum* quoted in *The Essence of Christianity,* in which it is said expressly that the world exists only for the sake of the Jews, it becomes evident that the passage from Vossius carries the meaning I have indicated.

11. No more than the multiplicity and diversity of nature in general can be derived from the monotheistic God, a being fundamentably differentiated from nature, no more can the multiplicity and diversity of human nature and its corollary, the justification of the diverse religions, be derived from Him. All that can be deduced from the unity of the monotheistic abstraction is the *unity* and *identity* of men, hence also the *unity* of faith. The diversity and multiplicity of human nature, which are the foundation of religious tolerance and indifference, stem solely from the *polytheistic principle* of *sensory intuition.* Only my senses, only nature tell me that I am not the only man, that there are other men beside me; but the inner light of the Quakers, the God differentiated from nature, dis-

embodied reason, tells me only that *I am the one and only man,* and consequently, if someone else should turn up, demands that he should think and believe *as I do,* for confronted with the reality of monotheistic unity, the reality of difference, the reality of the other, vanishes and becomes a mere sensory illusion: *Tout ce qui n'est pas Dieu n'est rien,* or in other words, *tout ce qui n'est pas Moi n'est rien.*

Thus if faith in the One God is accompanied by tolerance toward those of different belief, this One God must be grounded on nature with its diversity and tolerance. "Naturalism," says C. F. Bahrdt in his *Würdigung der natürlichen Religion* (1791), "leads by its very nature to tolerance and freedom. It is nothing other than a belief in subjective truth." "But the positivist regards *only his own* faith as true, because he believes it to be ordained by God; he can accept no *diversity* of any kind with indifference, because diversity is a deviation from the one belief which God, as he supposes, has ordained." "Can I still love a man whom my God hates and whom my God has given over to the Devil for all eternity?" But what or who is the God of nature religion? He is the 'God of Love,' who finds beatitude in doing good and in making his creatures happy." "If God is love. . . . the man who loves his fellow men must be the image and likeness of God."

But to love a man is to recognize his individuality. A lover of flowers loves all flowers, takes pleasure in their infinite variety, and gives to each one what its individual nature demands. But what is the principle or source of these infinite varieties and individualities that the senses disclose to us? It is nature, whose very essence is diversity and individuality, because it is not, like God, a spiritual, that is, abstract, metaphysical being. God too, of course, has been described as an "infinite number of diversities," but even this conception is merely abstracted from nature and the perception of nature. What then is the God of nature religion? Nature and nothing else, but nature represented as a personal, feeling, well-disposed being, hence an anthropomorphism. In this connection I must observe that not only the pagans or pantheists but the Christians as well are always *connecting* and even *identifying nature with God,* that is, using the two terms interchangeably. A few examples: In his *Icon Animorum,* J. Barclaius writes:

"In the customs of these people we encounter the richness of nature, which behind similarity in outward appearance has brought forth so many different usages and intentions." Even Melanchthon, in his *Psychology,* says of the gall bladder: "Creative nature wisely hid it." And speaking of the lungs: "The reason why nature placed the lungs around the heart is evident from their function." And in his collection of proverbs Erasmus explains the phrase "to fight the gods" as follows: To fight the gods after the manner of Titans means simply to oppose nature.

12. This becomes most evident in the idea of death, that greatest of evils in the eyes of primitive man. Originally man did not know what death was, and still less what caused it. Man is an absolute egoist; he cannot conceive of a refusal of his desires, hence of an end to his life, for he desires to live. He knew nothing of nature, nothing of an entity differentiated from man and his will; how then could he have looked upon death as something natural, let alone necessary? Consequently, death had for him a human, personal, voluntary cause; but death is an evil, therefore its cause was the *envy* of the gods who begrudged man all joy and happiness ("Hades, thou art envious," says an epigram of Erinna), or the *anger* of the gods over some offense. According to W. Mariner in *Nachrichten über die freundschaftlichen oder die Tongainseln,* the inhabitants of the Friendly Islands believe that all calamities are inflicted on men by the gods for neglect of some religious duty—or the *sheer malice* of the spirits and of those men who are in league with them, that is, the magicians.*

The Khonds of Gondwana attribute death "to the magical powers of certain persons and gods. They hold that death is not the necessary lot of man, but that man is by nature immortal (just as with the Christians) and death strikes him only if he has

* According to Charlevoix (*Histoire du Paraguay,* Vol. I) the Lulles of the Chaco attributed all diseases, with the exception of chicken pox, to the malice of an invisible animal which is not distinguished from a "spirit," while the Chiquitos believed (Vol. II) that *women were the cause of all diseases.* The Kaffirs believe that if the magician in command of the elements fails to make rain, some man must be responsible for the drought. This individual is then pointed out by the magician and murdered (*Ausland,* May 1849).

offended a god or if malignant persons endowed with supernatural powers bring it upon him. All deaths, those brought about by tigers for example, are attributed to such persons, for in the belief of the Khonds (and also of Christians, or at least of the orthodox among them) the tiger was made for man's benefit, but is employed by angry gods or magicians for their own purposes" (*Ausland,* January 1849). These conceptions of the cause and nature of death and other evils are also the source of the human sacrifices* and other monstrosities which men in religion inflict on themselves or others. Either from envy or from desire for vengeance or for some other personal reason, God takes pleasure in the death of men, and therefore men must be killed in His honor. It is the war-god who takes the most evident delight in human blood, for victory, the war-god's gift, hinges exclusively on the enemy's death; no wonder, then, that this god should have been the foremost beneficiary of human sacrifices. For one reason or another the gods in general take pleasure in the sufferings and torments of man; to please them, to gain their favor, we must therefore anticipate involuntary with voluntary sacrifices and torments.

13. Literally, in August Schlegel's translation: "I am eternal time (*le temps infaillable,* according to Wilkins' French translation of 1787), I am all-seeing and all-destroying death, I am the source of the future."

14. Then you espouse the absurd view of the nominalists who recognize no other universality than concepts and names?—Yes, but I believe I am espousing a very reasonable opinion; for, good Lord, I ask you, you who assume the existence of universals, what do you perceive in the world that is not individual? Most individual of all is God (*singularissimus est Deus*),† individual are all his beings, this angel, this sun, this stone; in short, there is nothing that is not individual. You say, for example, that there is a universal human nature. But where can this universal nature be seen? I, for my part, see Plato's human nature, Socrates' human nature, and so on, but all these natures are

* Though not the only source, for the belief in immortality has alone destroyed countless numbers of men by fire and sword.

† This thought is also to be found elsewhere, in Scaliger, for example.

individual. If you are more keen-sighted than I, tell me where you see the other, universal nature. Since there are so many individual natures, you say, there is in all of them a universal nature. Indeed? But how can you prove it? I, for my part, am content to have an individual nature, and to you too, say what you like, *one* individual nature suffices; for my part, I see no nature that is common to us, identical in you and in me. You have your body, your soul, your own organs and talents, and I have mine. What then is this nature that is supposed to be identical in you and in me? . . . . You say, and you have been much applauded for it: even when no one thinks of it, is not human nature in many? and if it is in many, is it not universal? I admit that human nature is in many, even when no one thinks of it, but I add that it is diverse. You wished to say that it is one in order to assert its universality, but I say it is manifold in order to assert the existence of individual natures. . . . Tell me, if you please, when it is said that Plato is a man, is the man in this statement Plato *himself* or *someone else*? None but himself, of course; similarly, when it is said that Socrates is a man, the man is no other than (or no different from) Socrates himself; and because human nature is the possession of both these men, it is not simple but twofold. Then, you will argue, the statement that Plato is a man is an empty tautology, for it merely states that he is identical to himself. I reply that every statement, to be true, must be a tautology, because nothing can be said of a thing that is not that thing itself or in it.

So Gassendi in his *Exercitationes paradoxicae adversus Aristoteleos*. Of course the universal exists, but when it exists, not merely in thought, it is not universal but individual, so that we can just as well say with the realist that it exists, as with the nominalists that it does not exist. Mankind exists in men, each man is a man; but each man is an individual, differentiated from other men. And it is only in thought, but not in reality, that you can separate that which distinguishes me from others from that wherein I resemble them without reducing me to nothing. Reality is an absolute, undifferentiable one; there is in me no point, no atom that is not individual.* What the theologians say of God—that in Him subject

* Leibniz is therefore quite right in saying in his scholastic dissertation *De principio individui* that every individual's principle of individuation is his whole being.

and predicate, being and essence, are identical, that no statement can be made as to what He himself is—actually applies to individuality, to *reality*. But thought separates that wherein I resemble others from that whereby I differ from them and am an individual; it separates predicate from subject, adjective from substantive, and makes the adjective itself into a substantive for the simple reason that the adjective is the primary factor by reason both of its nature—for the individual, the subject, cannot encompass it—and of its function. For abstract thinking, consequently, God is the essential, the principal being, although, as I have shown in these lectures and elsewhere, He is nothing other than a *Thesaurus Eruditionis Scholasticae,* a *Lexicon philosophicum,* a *Catholicon seu lexicon ex diversis rebus contractum,* in other words, a collection of names, of epithets, of adjectives without essence, matter, or substance, which is nevertheless made into a substance and, what is more, the supreme substance.

From the standpoint of abstract thinking, already replete with universal propositions, the derivation of the universal from the particular seems irrational and absurd; for in thought the universal appears to be essential and necessary, while the particular appears to be contingent, exceptional, and indifferent. Thought, for example, subsumes infinitely many neighboring grains of sand under the common or collective concept: pile of sand. In forming this concept, I gather the grains of sand with *one* glance into a pile without distinguishing them, and considering this pile as an entity with an independent existence of its own, I look upon the grains of sand which I in thought or with my hands one after another remove from it, as individual, contingent, and nonessential in contrast to the pile, because the pile remains a pile even if they are removed. But are the remaining grains not equally individual? What is there in the pile but a multiplicity of individuals? Does it not cease to exist if I set no limit to the number of individual grains I remove? But where is this limit?

It is where the thinker becomes bored with giving his attention to individuals. With one arbitrary leap, he jumps from grains of sand to sand pile, that is, from the individual to the universal. Universality is the infinite, the absolute of thought, individuality is the infinite, the absolute of sensuous reality, for it is not only this individual, it is *all* individuals; but "all individuals" are beyond our grasp, for the totality exists only in the infinitude of time and space. This place is limited, but there are innumerable other places that annul its limitation; this time is limited, but the limit loses itself in the stream of past and future times. How then does thought, abstract thought at least, transcend these limits? By a qualitative transformation of concepts; to the limitation of this place it opposes omnipresence, i. e., spaceless being; to the limitation of this time it opposes eternity, i. e., timeless being. Thus thought leaps straight from the particular to the universal and makes it into an essentially different, independent entity. "Men pass away, but mankind endures." Indeed? But what becomes of mankind if there are no men? Who are the "men who pass away"? The dead and those who are now living. And what is the mankind which remains? The men who are to come.

But as this example shows, man, in his thinking, always takes *some part* selected at random for the *totality, a few* individuals for *all* individuals, and so substitutes the genus, mankind, for the future individuals whom his thought has swept away and eliminated. The brain is the parliament of the universe, in which the generic concept represents the infinitely many individuals for whom the brain has not room enough. But precisely because the generic concept is the representative of individuals, and because when we hear the word "individuals," we think only of specific individuals, it strikes us as perfectly natural and reasonable—especially if our minds are full of generic concepts and we have become estranged from the perception of reality—to derive the particular from the universal, that is, the real from the abstract, existing things from thought, and nature from God. But such a derivation suggests the medieval political fiction to the effect that the head of the state is its foundation and that the emperor—for in the political realm emperor is the generic concept, in Rome the emperor alone was looked upon as a public person while all others were regarded as private persons—is the source and foundation of all law, all power, and all nobility, though in reality, in accordance with the actual course of development, the exact opposite was the case, since the "rule of the masses, or of free men, as the ancients put it," preceded the monarchic principle.

15. In thought and speech (where the succession of ideas in itself causes us to dismember all totalities and to consider the parts as independent entities, to tear the stomach out of the body, the heart out of the breast, the brain out of the head, and so to arrive at the *idée fixe* of an isolated individuality, i. e., a mere specter, a scholastic fiction), the opposite also occurs, that is, the individual also presupposes the universal concept; for what would an individual be without content, without the properties, talents, or powers which make man a man, but which in thought we differentiate from the individual, lending them independent existence as generic concepts? He would be comparable to a knife from which the blade has been abstracted. True, the idea or cause for which I live does not die with me, reason does not cease to be if I cease to think, but this is so only because other individuals take it up, because other individuals think in my place. "Interests endure, individuals change," but only because others have the same interest as I, because they too wish to be free, happy, educated men.

16. Concerning the political views stated in these lectures, only this brief observation. Aristotle has already said in his *Politics*—which treats of almost all our present-day problems, though of course in the spirit of antiquity—that it is necessary not only to know the best form of government, but also to know what form is suited to what men, for even the best form of government is not suited to all men. Thus I wholly agree with those who from an historical point of view, that is, a point of view taking account of space and time, regard constitutional monarchy—*true* constitutional monarchy, that is—as the only form of government that is practicable, suitable for us, and therefore reasonable. But when it is maintained that monarchy is the one and only absolutely rational form of government, regardless of space and time, that is, of this particular time (even a millennium is a particular time) and this particular place (even Europe is only one place, one point in the world), then I protest and maintain that the republic, the democratic republic is the form of government which reason must recognize to be consonant with human nature and therefore best, that constitutional monarchy is the Ptolemaic system of politics while the republic is its Copernican system, and that in the future

of mankind Copernicus will therefore triumph over Ptolemy in politics just as he has already triumphed in astronomy, even though the Ptolemaic system was formerly represented by philosophers and scholars as unshakable *"scientific truth."*

17. The same, incidentally, applies not only to the pagans but also to the ancient Israelites. When the children of Dan had taken Micah's idol, he cried out to them: "Ye have taken away *my* gods [or in other translations, my God] *which I made.*" And not only the maker of plastic images, but also and above all the maker of spiritual images, the poet, is a maker of gods. We need think only of Homer and Hesiod. Ovid says expressly in the fourth book of his epistles from Pontus: "Gods too are made in [or through] poems" (or by poets). *Di quoque carminibus (si fas est dicere) fiunt.*

It is maintained that a religious man does not worship the image or statue itself as God, but only worships God in the image. But such a distinction is justified only insofar as the god also exists outside the statue or image, namely, in the head, in the religious man's mind, hence only insofar as there is a difference between a real sensuous being and the mental representation of that being. Moreover, such a distinction is meaningless. The thing *in which* man worships God is his *real* and true God, the God existing above and outside of this one is a mere figment of the mind. Thus, for example, Protestantism—true, positive Protestantism at least—finds and worships God in the Bible, that is to say, it worships the Bible *as God.* The Protestant, to be sure, does not worship the book as a book after the manner of the king of the African Ashantis, who worships the Koran though he understands not a letter of it; he worships its content, the word of God, the word in which He expressed His essence, but this word exists, or at least exists undistorted, only in the Bible.*

It is all-important [says Luther in an Easter Monday sermon delivered in Coburg] that we should know the value of Scripture, namely, that it is a *testimony* to all articles concerning Christ, and moreover, the *highest*

* The word of God is also God's thought, God's will, God's mind, hence His essence, the content of the Holy Scriptures is therefore the content and essence of God.

testimony, *far exceeding all miraculous signs,* as Christ explained to the rich man in Luke 16: 29-31: "If they hear not Moses and the prophets, neither will they be persuaded, though one rose from the dead." The dead can deceive us, Scripture cannot. That is what impels us to hold Scripture in such high esteem, and in this passage He holds it to be the best testimony. As though He wished to say: You read the prophets and yet you do not believe? True, it is paper and ink, and yet it is the most eminent sign. Thus even Christ stresses it *more than his manifestations. . . .* [etc.]

Who then can be surprised that in the Protestant Church "the power of the divine word" or "the divine power of Holy Scripture" should have become a central theme of theological controversy, that Protestants should have quarreled over the "ethical, natural, supernatural, physical, quasi-physical, objective, subjective power of the divine word," and expressly asserted the *divinity of Scripture* in statements such as the following: "The divine and supernatural power by which man is enlightened and converted is not *with* Holy Scripture but *in* it *(non adesse scripturae, sed inesse),* man is converted not by the *coexisting* but by the *inexisting* power of Scripture" (J. R. Schlegel, *Kirchengeschichte des achtzehenden Jahrhunderts*). In the first half of the nineteenth century G. Nitsche, general superintendent and Pastor Primarius, wrote: *On the Question of Whether Holy Scripture Is God Himself* and *The Question Rescued.*

18. As has been amply shown, a god is indeed an image of nature or its imaginary essence—nature is indeed the first, original, object of religion, its enduring background—but from the standpoint of religion man imagines and represents nature in terms of himself, so that the imagination of nature is merely a projection of man.

19. Combustion of course also requires a degree of temperature that varies with the fuel, and poetry requires a degree of temperature—the inner and outward warmth needed to create enthusiasm—which varies with the individual. When we become spiritually inflamed, a physical fire is also kindled; we grow warm even while sitting still in a cold room. And conversely, physical heat also pro-

vokes poetic heat within us. When the blood freezes, the poetic pulse beat also ceases.

20. The capricious visions in a feverish sleep [writes G. Bancroft in his *History of the United States of America*] are obeyed by the village or the tribe; the whole nation would contribute its harvest, its costly furs, its belts of beads, the produce of its chase, rather than fail in their fulfillment; the dream must be obeyed, even if it required the surrender of women to a public embrace. The faith in the spiritual world, as revealed by dreams [more properly, in dreams which men took for spirits, gods, or supernatural beings], was universal. On Lake Superior, the nephew of a Chippewa squaw having dreamed that he saw a French dog, the woman traveled four hundred leagues over ice and through snow to obtain it.

What heroism! And all for the sake of a dream.

21. Among the Guaranis, as we read in the above-cited *History of Paraguay,* death was often induced by the *mere fear* of magic. The Brazilians, too, "feared evil spirits so much that some of them died from the *mere sight of an imaginary apparition*" (Bastholm, *Historische Nachrichten zur Kenntnis des Menschen in Seinem wilden und rohen Zustand,* Part 4).

22. God fulfills man's desires, and man's desires determine His nature; the only difference between God and desire is that in Him the mere potentiality of desire becomes reality; He is fulfilled desire, or a desire that is certain to be fulfilled;* in other words, He is objectified and realized desire. "They [the gods]," says a Greek poet (Pindar) in Plutarch, "are without sickness, they do not age, they know no hardships, they are exempt from the hollow-echoing passage across Acheron." Could it be stated more plainly that the gods are men's desires? "There is nothing which men can

* In his *Intellectual System* Cudworth asks: "If there is no God, how does it come about that all men want to have a God?" The question should be turned around: If there is a God, we should ask, why and to what end must men want Him? Realities need not be desired, the desire that there should be a God demonstrates precisely that there is none.

desire of the gods," says Velleius Paterculus, "nothing which the gods can grant men. . . . that Augustus. . . . has not given the Roman state." "What is to be learned, I learn," says Sophocles (Plutarch, *de Fortuna*); "what is to be found, I seek; what is to be desired [or the desired, or the desirable, ta d'eukta] *I beseech of the gods.*"

Hannah was childless. "The Lord had shut up her womb." So she "rose up. . . . and prayed to the Lord: if thou wilt indeed look on the affliction of thy handmaid. . . . and not forget me, but wilt give unto thine handmaid a man child, then I will give him unto the Lord all the days of his life. . . . And the Lord remembered her. . . . And the Lord hath given me my petition which I asked of him. . . . Wherefore it came to pass. . . . that she bare a son and called his name Samuel [Besought-of-God, or Theaiteton, as Josephus translates the name] saying, Because I have asked him of the Lord." Concerning this passage, Clericus comments that the words "the Lord shut up her womb" do not imply a miracle (that is, a special act of God's omnipotence) and that the opening of her womb was therefore no miracle either. But what is God, what is prayer, if they have no other power and function than to mature the preformed germs of nature? Faith does not concern itself with anatomico-physiological questions and investigations. For faith, God or the divine power of prayer, of pious desire was the *cause* of Hannah's conception. A God who cannot create, who can only hatch out the eggs laid by naturalism, is no God. A God is just as much *above* nature, just as free, just as independent of anatomico-physiological conditions as are man's desire and imagination.

To cite a few more examples and proofs of the connection between God and desire, Odysseus says to Eumaeus: "For your kind hospitality to me, may Zeus and the other immortal gods grant you *what you most desire.*" And in the twenty-first book of the Odyssey, the chief cowherd says to Odysseus: "Father Zeus, oh, if only you would *grant this wish,* that the hero may return home and that an immortal may lead him." And in Ovid's *Fasti* Jupiter says to Hyrieus, the Boeotian peasant who had received him hospitably along with his brother Neptune and with Mercury: "If you desire something, state your wish: You will obtain it, everything will be granted you." The old man replied: I had a beloved wife, but now the earth covers her. I swore in your name to touch no other woman beside her. I have kept my word, but my heart is torn, I would gladly be a father, yet I do not wish to be a husband. The gods granted his entire wish; they pissed into an oxhide and at the end of ten months a little boy rose from the divine urine. If we disregard the watery admixture in this fable, it means exactly the same as the words of the Old Testament, uttered in a similar situation: "Is any thing too hard for the Lord?"—that is, is anything impossible for the imaginative power of the human heart, of human desire?

23. Because of its simplicity and fervor I cannot refrain from including the following Indian hymn to water from the *Rigveda* (Colebrooke, *Treatise on the Sacred Writings of the Indians,* with fragments of the oldest religious poetry of the Indians):

I invoke the waters, the goddesses that give our cows to drink; we must offer sacrifices to the rivers. In water is immortality [nectar], in water is the power to heal, ye priests, be untiring in the praise of water. Soma has revealed to me that all remedies are in water, that Agnis [fire] rejoices all and that water heals all. Ye waters, fill my body with balms that destroy sickness, that I may long behold the light of the sun. Ye waters, take away from me everything that is evil in me, all the violent deeds I have done and every curse or lie I have uttered. Today I have worshiped water, I have united myself with the spirit of the waters [by bathing]; come, Agnis endowed with water, surround me with radiance.

24. Insofar as parents are private beings, while the gods are public beings who concern and encompass the entire state and all its citizens, parents are inferior to the gods, for, as Valerius Maximus says, the state lives on despite the downfall of any particular house or family, but the destruction of the city or state necessarily brings with it the destruction of all the *penates.* In his scale of duties, Cicero therefore assigns first place to duties toward the gods, second place to duties toward one's country, and third place to duties toward one's parents. But differences in degree or rank are not differences of essence. Moreover, first in the order of thought is not first in the order of nature. The source of my country's sanctity is

the sanctity of my own hearth;* penates, ancestors, and the source of the gods' sanctity is the sanctity of my country, because my main reason for worshiping them is that they are the gods of my country, the *Di Romani,* and before there was a Rome there were no *Roman* gods.

25. Since the ancient pagans, especially the Greeks, regarded not only all material, but also all spiritual goods and powers as gods or gifts of the gods, and were aware that without virtue and intelligence or wisdom there can be no happiness—"Injustice is disastrous to poor mortals," says Hesiod, for example, and Solon: "I wish indeed to acquire wealth, but not unjustly"—therefore not only material goods, but spiritual goods as well were the objects of their desires and prayers. The poets, indeed, always began their songs with prayers to the gods! However, they knew of no virtue independent of outward goods—hence the poets' lamentations over the misfortune of poverty, which corrupted men and drove them to base thoughts and actions—"O Plutos [Wealth]! You most beautiful and lovable of all the gods," says Theognis, for example, "even if I am bad, with thee I will become a good man"—nor is there any happiness without bodily health. "Without thee no one is happy," we read, for example, in a Greek scolion, a prayer to Hygeia, goddess of health. Even so late a writer as Aristotle held that there can be no virtue or happiness without outward, "temporal goods."

26. The pagans, to be sure, also deified poverty, misfortune, sickness. The only difference is that good is what is desired, bad or evil is what is wished away, or cursed. Theognis, for example, sings: "O wretched Poverty! Why won't you go to another man, why do you love me against my will? Can't you leave me alone?"

* "What is more inviolable," says Cicero or the author of *Oratio pro domo,* "what is more hedged around in every religion than the house of each citizen? . . . This place of refuge is so inviolable that no one is permitted to seize a man out of it." What a contrast between the pagan state's respect for the home and the brutality and insolence with which the Christian state, even on the most meager suspicion, breaks into a man's house like a thief in the night and drags the owner off to prison!

27. Because in *The Essence of Christianity* and my other works I have not moralized, nor raised an uproar about sin, nor even devoted a special, expressly titled chapter to it, my critics have accused me of not understanding Christianity. But here, as in other cardinal points—this, I own, is only an unproved contention, but I have no time or desire for such proofs or for empty, meaningless criticisms*—here then as in other cardinal points, my astute critics have reproached me precisely for my soundness of instinct and judgment. No more than virtue or morality is itself the aim or object of Christian love, no more is vice or sin in itself the object of Christian hatred. God is the Christian's goal; but God is not, or at least not exclusively, an ethical being; a purely ethical being is a mere abstraction, a mere concept, and a concept has no existence. But for faith, God is a real, existing being. He is, of course, holy, good, without sin; He encompasses ethical goodness or perfection, but only because He is the sum of all goods; for He is nothing other than the personified and objective imagination, adorned with all the treasures, goods, and perfections of nature and mankind.

God's ethical perfection or virtue is not the Kantian virtue, opposed to inclination, to the striving for happiness; God as the sum of all goods is happiness; thus, though a man whose goal is God aims at freedom from sin, at ethical perfection, he strives all the while, immediately and inseparably, for happiness. In seeking thee, my God, says Augustine in the tenth book of his *Confessions,* I seek eternal life. Christians call God the highest good, but they also say that *Vita aeterna,* a life of everlasting bliss, is the highest good. A Christian does not condemn sin alone or in itself, he also condemns its conditions, its causes, its accomplices, the entire context in which sin is a necessary component: the world, nature, flesh. Is marriage a sin? No; but marriages are not made in heaven, the goal of Christian desires. Are eating and drinking sins? No; but they are ungodlike and therefore excluded from the ideal of Christianity. The essence of Christianity, as I correctly define it in the work so titled, is subjectivity in both the good and the bad sense of the word—subjectivity is man's soul or personality freed from the limits imposed upon it by nature, hence from the lusts

* A note to this note, grown to inordinate length in spite of me, will be found at the end, after Note 28.

but also from the burdens of the flesh; or rather, it is the deified, unrestricted, supernatural striving for happiness.

28. In a Christian hymnbook we read, for example: "Wilt Thou lay me on my sick bed? I will. . . . Shall I be in need? I will. . . . . And wilt Thou give me death? I will. . . . Thy will be done, O God! Wilt Thou have me in heaven? Lord, that is the height of my desires. Shall I then go to hell? I know, Lord, *that is not Thy will.* The death of Thy son willed that Thy will should not be thus." And in another hymn, by Christian Titius, we read: "Help held in wait is not denied. Though He may not help on every occasion, He helps when it is necessary." And in another: "As God wills, so be it. The birds will provide. If happiness does not come to me today, it will come tomorrow. Be undismayed. Though it be long in coming, thank God with all your heart. What should be will be; He will surely bring about my happiness." In a hymn by N. Hermann: "Trust in God, the Lord. He does what he wills. He *wills nothing but what is beneficial to us,* He wishes us all well." Another, by P. Gerhard: "The torments of Christians are meant for the best: Those who have wept in this temporal world will not lament forever; they will find perfect joy in Christ's garden, which alone they await, sure to attain it in the end."

* * *

(To note 27:) Rebuttals of criticism are pointless, senseless, useless, boring, and repulsive, because the critics, in their eagerness not to understand the author but to confute him, take appearance for content, uncritically twist terminology into substance, the local into the universal, the particular into the characteristic, the temporal into the enduring, the relative into the absolute; they connect factors that are unrelated, and separate factors that necessarily go together; in short, they arbitrarily confuse all the issues, so that the rebutter is left not with a philosophical task, but with the philological chore of unscrambling quotations. Or rather, he is obliged first to teach the critics *how to read,* and in particular how to read books that are written with spirit; for one characteristic of spirited writing is that it presupposes intelligence in the reader, that it does not dot all the i's but leaves it up to the reader to bear in mind all the relationships, conditions, and limitations which he presupposes in making his statements, and which must be borne in mind if the statements are to be valid. If the reader, whether out of stupidity or cantankerousness, fails to fill in these omissions, these ellipses, if he does not by his own effort complement the author, if he has no understanding for him but only *against* him, it is not to be wondered at that a book, which cannot after all stand up to defend itself, should be torn to shreds by such arbitrary criticism.

A few examples will show what I mean. Professor von Schaden,* for example, takes an article written by me in 1838, reflecting a mere stage in my development, as the *main, definitive* foundation of his criticism of my "concept of thought"; to this early work he arbitrarily and uncritically juxtaposes contrary statements from my later works. What, for example, is his point, in p. 47, in citing Par. 24 of the *Grundsätze,* which opens with the words: "It is admitted, to be sure, that the soul feels identity with itself." My own work provides organic links between the ideas of 1838 and the later "amplifications, which are in every respect odd, and more or less at variance with the earlier statements." These are: first the direct and indirect critique of my earlier work and opinions contained in my article "Against Dualism," in which I trace the psychological development of men's belief in the suprasensory, immaterial nature of the soul, and explain how it came about that man is unable to identify thought with the action of the brain; secondly, my demonstration, supported by innumerable examples, that suprasensory ideas are mere fictions derived by thought or imagination from the world of the senses; and lastly, the theme of all my later works, namely, that man is the *subject* of thought, whereas I formerly regarded thought itself as the subject.

But the uncritical critic leaps over all these intermediate links, abstracts an opposition between mind and matter from a few sentences shuffled together at random, and on this foundation builds the dream castle of his critique of my "concept of thought." Equally arbitrary and uncritical is his critique of my "concept of

* Of Erlangen University, b. 1814, d. 1852. The book in question appeared in 1848 under the title: *Ueber den Gegensatz des theistischen und pantheistischen Standpunktes, ein Sendschreiben an Dr. L. Feuerbach.*

being." He writes, for example: being "becomes [in F.] a shadow . . . . degraded into a part of the thinking subject, the ego. He harps incessantly on the proposition that one cannot renounce matter without renouncing reason or recognize it without recognizing reason." What on earth has this proposition to do with the case? It is simply an historical fact stated in general terms. And how can anyone infer from such a statement that I reduce being to thought? "True," our critic continues, "he says: 'to be is to be an object,' but he immediately adds: 'and so presupposes consciousness. Only as an object of consciousness is a something a real something. . . . hence consciousness is the measure of all existence.' " How can this "conscientious" critic fail to see that this statement merely reflects the spirit of Fichtean idealism, a discussion of which forms part of my development, since in the very next sentence I write: "And so theology finds its fulfillment in *idealism*."

Moreover, the utter irrelevance of his criticism can be seen from the fact that he reduces the content of my works to the abstract concepts being and thought, when in reality I hold that all philosophy which deals with thought independently of the thinking subject, with being independently of the existent which only the senses disclose, in short, all philosophy which does not seize upon things *in flagranti*, is idle and fruitless speculation; when I explicitly replace being with nature and thought with man, and for this very reason deal not with abstract but with *dramatic* psychology, that is to say, I treat of psychology only as related to the objects in which the whole human psyche manifests itself, hence only in its objective manifestations. Herr von Schaden surely thinks he has confuted or at least criticized me; but I contend that he has only dreamed of me, and extremely wild dreams at that.

And now a few words about the "critique" of Herr Professor Schaller.* Here again, if I wished to let myself in for true counter-criticism, I should have to reply with a philological analysis of my own works; for its author is so far from having cast a remotely pertinent glance even at the formal aspect of my work that all his judgments and developments are the exact opposite of the

* Born in 1810, became professor at Halle in 1838, died in 1868. The work in question, *Darstellung und Kritik der Philosophie Ludwig Feuerbachs,* was published in Leipzig in 1847.

truth. He goes so far in his petty critical malice as to contradict or at least to criticize my clearest and most self-evident statements, in which I merely record historical facts or formulate universally recognized truths, the statement for example that nature religion is the first or original religion. Setting aside all his detailed criticisms, all the contradictions and absurdities which my critic either finds in my ideas or deduces from them, I shall stress only *one* point; but it is the cardinal point on which everything hinges. That is the concept of the *individual.* The essential difference between my standpoint and that represented by my critic is this; he distinguishes the genus or the universal from the individual and opposes the genus as "self-positing," that is, as an independent, objective reality, to the individual, which he regards as negative, finite, relative, and contingent, so that emphasis on the individual is for him a choice in favor of "arbitrariness, immorality, and sophistry"; I, on the other hand, identify the genus with the individual and individualize the universal but for this very reason generalize the individual; in other words, I broaden the concept of the individual, which thus becomes for me the true, absolute being.

Thus, according to Herr Schaller, man or the individual has in him "a *self*-positing, inherently necessary universality," through which the individual can practically and theoretically transcend himself, a "fundamental universality of the I," which is the foundation of language, an "essential universality, whereby the individual is placed above his *individual inclinations,*" "overcomes his *individual will,*" as in morality, whereby, as for example "in artistic enthusiasm he is impelled by the idea and not by his own *individual representations,*" whereby, as in knowledge, my thoughts "are not only my own, but express essence, and are in themselves energy and communication." Here, then, we have two beings in man: a universal and an individual; whereas in my view individuality embraces the whole man and the human essence is one, the universal being itself individual.

True, man is differentiated—he is obviously composed of different and even opposing organs and forces—but what he differentiates from himself is just as much a part of his individuality as that from which he differentiates it. If I combat an inclination, the force by which I combat it is just as much a part of my individuality as the inclination itself; it is merely a force of a different kind.* The head, seat of man's intelligence, is something very different from the belly, seat of his material drives and needs. But does my being stop at my navel? Doesn't it extend to my head? Is my entire individuality contained in my belly? Is my head no longer I? Or is it not, rather, in my head that I truly become myself? Is thinking not an individual activity, an "*individual state*"?

Why then do I find it so strenuous? Is the head of a thinker, i. e., of a man who makes the individual activity of thinking his main and characteristic task, not different from the head that does not think. Do you really believe, Herr Professor, that Fichte philosophized against his individual inclination, that Goethe wrote against his individual inclination, that Raphael painted against his individual inclination? What makes the artist an artist if not precisely that his individual inclinations, representations, and intuitions are artistic? And what is the idea by which the artist is inspired, if not "a more or less indeterminate image of another individual," in this case of a work of art, "or of an individual state" of art, different from its present state?

And what are "individual inclinations and ideas"? They are ideas and inclinations which are not circumscribed by my profession, by my position in life, or by the task in hand, but which are just as important, just as positive as the others. For example, I am engaged in writing a sublime poem; meanwhile, all sorts of comic scenes, toward which I have a special inclination, occur to me, and interrupt me in my flight; these are "individual" ideas that I must dismiss if I wish to carry out my project; but they cease to be such if I put them in their proper place and make them the subject of a separate work. This man is a painter; his art is the whole basis of his material and spiritual or moral existence; chosen from inclination, it is his officially recognized wife, but he has other passions; he is also a lover of music, horseback riding, hunting, etc.;

* The phrase, "to overcome oneself," "to transcend oneself," finds its explanation in other idioms, such as "to outdo oneself." Can an individual really outdo himself? Isn't that which enables me to outdo myself simply my own individual energy and predisposition, which has been released and developed on this particular occasion? But most people mistake phrases for reality.

for their sake, he neglects his art, so bringing ruin on himself and his family.

These passions, it is true, are "individual inclinations"; but are they reprehensible in themselves? Have they not a recognized, objective existence in other individuals? Are not some men horsemen, musicians, or hunters both by inclination and profession? A servant girl chances to find her mistress's jewel box open; her eyes light on some costly rings; she glances at her bare fingers and the wish is born: oh, if I could only wear these splendid things! The seduction of opportunity turns wish into deed—the poor thing steals and is sent to the workhouse. Is such an inclination toward jewelry in itself "individual" and therefore, as our speculative philosophers would say, a sinful, punishable inclination that should be overcome? No; for in the owner of the jewels, this same inclination is held to be legitimate, since its object is recognized to be her inalienable property. In fact, the poor servant girl's inclination to glitter and finery becomes "universal power" when it shines forth from the gold and jewels that grace the sovereign's crown.

Every man has countless desires, inclinations, passions which he cannot indulge because they conflict with his official situation, his profession, his mode of life, his condition—desires and inclinations which therefore have only an ephemeral, microscopic, spermatozoic existence, because he lacks the *space, time,* or other means of gratifying them, but which in other individuals play leading roles for good or evil. But to deduce a "self-positing universality," an intellectual spook without inclination, without desires, without individuality, from this negation of wishes and inclinations, is merely to revive, disguised in logical forms and phrases, the old dualistic leap or inference from the world to an unworldly being, from matter to an immaterial being, from the body to a bodiless being; for the striving to which I sacrifice these inclinations and desires is itself nothing other than an individual predisposition or inclination, or rather the most individual of all, which I have favored before others and raised to mastery by diligent practice, so gaining recognition for it.

The difference between "individual" and universal is indeed relative and evanescent, for what in me is only a private person is in others a public, universal person. You yourself, Herr Professor, were you not formerly a *Privatdozent*? And what is a *Privatdozent*? An individual whose desire to lecture is repressed as an unjustified "individual inclination" by the "universal powers" of the university in their learned arrogance. But now, glory be, you are a professor and your former private inclination has actually become your official duty, your "moral necessity." But what a difference between then and now! No more than a professor wishes to be reminded that he was once an instructor, no more does duty, once it has disengaged itself from life and mounted the lecture platform of abstract morality, wish to admit that it, too, originated in an "individual inclination." But where does the law, and consequently the duty, not to kill come from? From the "categorical imperative." Yes, but what does this categorical imperative say? It says: *I don't want to die, I want to live,* and what *I want, you should do*; that is, you should let me live. Where does the law and hence the duty not to steal come from? From self-established, self-seated universality? Why not from the self-seated behind? To possess something is to sit on it, and you can't sit without a behind. "Thou shalt not steal" means simply: thou shalt not pull the seat of my individual inclination and will—be it a couch or a straw tick, a royal throne, or a papal chamberpot—out from under my behind, which is the final argument and foundation of property rights.

Why did hunting play so important a part in the laws of the Germans; why was the theft or killing of a stag trained for the hunt punished more severely than the murder of a slave? Because of the Germans' "individual inclination" toward hunting. But what was unjust and barbarous about their game laws? The inclination toward hunting? Not at all. The laws were unjust because the great lords asserted the legitimacy of only *their* inclination and, anticipating our philosophers, condemned the same inclination in everybody else as merely individual. "The princes and nobles," says Sebastian Münster in Wirth's *Deutsche Geschichte,* "are all given to hunting and believe that *they alone* are entitled by long custom and God-given right to engage in it; they forbid all others to catch stags, roes, rabbits, and game birds on pain of losing their eyes and, in some localities, their heads."

And where does "speculative philosophy" with its polemics against *individual* caprice, *individual* inclinations, and *individual* representations or ideas come from? It comes directly from the army barracks or the Jesuit schools—which is roughly the same thing, for what is a barracks but a secularized version of a medieval monastery? The barracks man, whether military or clerical, Catholic or Protestant, is not allowed to eat, drink, walk, sleep, act, feel, think as he would like and as his individuality demands; no, all individual caprice, all thought, feeling, and will, is suppressed; for if someone deprives me of my *own individual* will, he leaves me *no will at all,* and if someone denies me the right to my own thoughts, to my own individual reason, he denies me the right to all thought and reason, for there is no more a universal reason than there is a universal stomach, although every man has a stomach just as he has an organ or faculty of thought.

We need only listen to the Jesuits themselves to be convinced that the Jesuit order is the unconscious model and ideal of our speculative philosophers, just as it is the deliberate model and ideal of our desperate conservative statesmen. A Jesuit, we read in the Rule of the Society of Jesus, resists the *natural inclination,* innate in all men, to have and follow their *own* judgment (Letter of St. Ignatius Loyola on the virtue of obedience); he must with blind obedience renounce all opinion and conviction of his own; he must be as a cudgel, which is a will-less instrument in our hand, or as a *corpse* with which one can do what one pleases (*Summarium Constit.,* Nos. 35, 36). Exactly. To suppress the "individual will," and hence also voluntary movement, is to suppress life. Like the Jesuit, like the monarchist, the speculative philosopher is the mortal enemy of life, for what he loves above all else is "peace and order," lest he be disturbed in his ideas; but life is essentially restless, disorderly, anarchic; it can no more be understood by the narrow concepts of the philosopher than it can be contained by the narrow laws of the monarch.

But what is the universal to which the Jesuit sacrifices his individual inclination, will, and reason; what is the same, the identical—according to the Jesuit Rule, we should all know and say the same thing—in all Jesuit individuals? This identical universal is nothing other than the will, the "individual caprice," of the superior, who to the Jesuit is the vicar of God, i.e., God himself, just as the monarch is to the monarchist. A Jesuit, says St.

Ignatius, must not only will, but also feel *the same* as his superior, to whose judgment he must subordinate his own. Do you see now, Herr Professor, that the negation of one individuality is simply the affirmation of another, in short that the universal is also the individual, but an individual who has the power to dominate other individuals either by forcibly repressing their individuality or by appealing to their individual inclination, for even Jesuitry presupposes a special predisposition?

For Christians, to cite another example, the Bible is *the* book. "The spirit," writes Luther, commenting on the words "in the . . . . book it is written of me" (Psalm 40), "speaks as if it knew of no other book (though the world is full of them), but only of this book, the Holy Scriptures." But are the Holy Scriptures to which the Christian sacrifices his subjective and "individual" reason, not themselves an individual book? Are the ideas of the Bible those of the Koran, of the Vedas, of the Zend Avesta? Is what is universal to the Christian not individual to a Mohammedan or Hindu? Was what our pious forefathers regarded as the "Word of God" not long ago recognized to be the word of man? How relative, here again, is the distinction between universal and individual! What in this time and place passes as "individual caprice" is taken in another time and place for universal law. And what here and now is a subjective, heretical opinion becomes tomorrow or elsewhere a sacred article of faith. In our country today, republic is held to be identical with anarchy, monarchy with law; but among the Romans "monarchic" was a predicate of lawlessness, arbitrariness, immorality, and overwhelming pride—monarchy, the Romans said, is a crime.

And has this statement not been confirmed by history, including German history? In Germany, it is true, monarchy responded to the desires of the masses opposed to the evils of aristocratic polyarchy; but did it not, here too, spring from *individual striving for power, individual greed,* and *individual blood lust*? Is it not true that in our country the *death penalty,* at least in its application to solvent free men, originated with the *monarchy*? (Wirth, *Deutsche Geschichte.*) And in monarchy, at least in genuine, absolute monarchy, is the *individual caprice* of the monarch not universal law, is his individual inclination not universal custom? Is the rule in absolute monarchy not *l'État, c'est moi,* or *qualis rex, talix grex*?*

There is indeed a difference, and a very real one, between universal and individual, but it does not argue in favor of our political and speculative absolutists. Individual—as language defines the word—is that which only this or several individuals, to the exclusion of other individuals, have or want; universal is what every individual, though singly, each in his individual way, has and wants; every man, for example, has a head, but it is his own individual head, every man has will, but it is his own individual will.† We distinguish the state—I am not referring to the modern state, which has its existence solely in individuals bearing the state uniform, but to the state as such—from individuals. But what is the state, what is the nation if I take away the individuals who constitute it? The state is nothing other than what all (or at least the majority) wish, the nation nothing other than what all (or at least the majority) are; for the majority alone decides; consciously or unconsciously, the majority, though an indeterminate and very relative conception, is taken as the measure of universality.

No law, Livy quotes Cato as saying in his oration in behalf of the *Lex Oppia,* is entirely to the liking of *all*; the question is therefore: is it beneficial to the majority and totality? What crime, says Cicero or whoever may have been the author of *Ad Herennium,* can be compared to the crime of treason against state or country? In all other crimes the injury is limited to *individuals* or to *a few,* while this crime brings the most dire misfortune upon *all* citizens, destroys the happiness of all. The early Germans knew no crime of *lèse-majesté,* but only "a crime against the nation" (Eichhorn, *Deutsche Staats- und Rechtsgeschichte*). "Concerning lesser matters the notables or princes deliberate, concerning the more im-

* In Book 5, Livy speaks of the "multitude which almost always resembles its ruler."

† Consequently, the universal is also individual, but because every individual has it, thought abstracts it from the individuals and sets it up as a thing in itself, though a thing common to all—a conception from which result all the tedious scholastic and idealistic difficulties and questions concerning the relation between the universal and the particular. In short: thought takes the discreteness of reality for a continuum, the infinitely many events of life as one identical event. Knowledge of the essential, ineffaceable difference between thought and life (or reality) is the beginning of wisdom in thought and life. Here differentiation is the only true connective.

portant matters all decide" (Tacitus). "In certain questions every single free man had not only the right to join in deliberations but also an absolute veto" (Wirth, *loc. cit.*). "I shall not shrink," Brutus wrote to Cicero, "from leading *our state* out of slavery. If my undertaking is successful, we shall all be glad, if not, I at least shall be glad, for in what actions or thoughts should I spend my life, if not in actions and thoughts whose purpose is the liberation of my fellow citizens?" Thus a man who lives and dies for the idea of freedom thinks only of *free men, free individuals,* even if he does not think precisely of this or that individual.

But do you believe, my dear Herr Professor, that when I stress the particular over against the universal of philosophy, the individual over against the class, I have in mind only *this* particular to the exclusion of other particulars, this individual to the exclusion of other individuals, that I am speaking in favor of the *aristocratic* principle which has hitherto asserted itself as the universal and dominated the world? How can you think me capable of such an absurdity? My principle embraces all individuals, past, present and future: *the principle of individuality is the principle of infinity and universality,* the "bad" kind of infinity and universality from the standpoint of the presumptuous and envious concept, but the very best kind from the standpoint of life, for this is the only creative and fruitful kind of infinity and universality.*

In conclusion, just a word about the genus in the light of biology. "In the mating season, animals demonstrate *ad oculos* the universality of the genus." Not at all. The heat of animals, the violence of the sexual drive even in man, demonstrate nothing more than what is demonstrated by every violent drive. Anger, the frustrated instinct of self-preservation, unsatisfied hunger, all have the same effects as the unsatisfied sexual drive, namely, that they provoke fury and madness in animals and men. Long ago Homer said of hunger: "For nothing is more terrible and furious than hunger, which at all times impresses itself forcibly on the mind of man, even of the afflicted, whose soul is weighed down with grief. My soul too is

* Practically speaking, individualism is socialism, but not the French variety of socialism which negates individuality or, what amounts to the same thing, freedom (freedom being merely a more abstract expression of individuality).

weighed down with grief; yet the tyrant hunger still demands food and drink; and I forget all my sorrow until my hunger is sated."

Thus if the sexual drive demonstrates the reality of generic universality, the pangs of hunger also demonstrate the generic universality of my stomach; my rage over some injury or offense demonstrates the generic universality of my ego. Far from being a friend of philosophy, and especially of speculative philosophy, far from the arguing the reality of universal concepts, the sexual drive expresses the reality of individuality in its most extreme form, for it is in the sexual drive that individuality is first consummated, that it first becomes flesh. The difference between the sexes is the flower, the culmination, of individuality, the most sensitive point, the *point d'honneur* of individuality; the sexual drive is the most ambitious, the proudest of drives, it is the impulse to be a creator, an author. Spiritually as well as physically, man achieves the highest sense of self at the moment when he becomes an author, for then alone does he manifest what distinguishes him from others, then alone does he produce something new; in other activities he is a spiritless, selfless, mechanical repeater.

The higher a man stands in the scale, the more individual he is. The less spirit men have, the lower they stand in the scale, the less they differ among themselves, the less individual they are. The sexual drive has as its object a being who corresponds exactly to my individual drive, need, and being, and in this it resembles other drives. In general, nature is apprehended and assimilated only by itself, that is, by what is similar and related to it: the air by the lungs, the airiest organ as it were, the light by the eye, organ of light, sound by the elastic, vibrant ear, solid matter by the rough, materialistic sense of touch, the edible and nutritious by the alimentary organs. Respiration is therefore the mating of the lungs with the air, vision is the mating of the eye or optic nerve with the light. And this mating of the lungs with the air, of the eye with the light, and of the other drives or organs with their objects, is just as productive as mating proper, except that each drive engenders a product in keeping with itself and its object.

For productivity is the essence of nature, the essence of life. The lungs as receivers of air engender fire, the eye as the organ of light engenders visual images, and the sexual drive, as a male and female drive, engenders only male and female young. But is the individual productive? Is it not God or the genus that makes or creates children? But why then do so many individuals perish in mating or childbearing? Whence the well-known dejection after the sexual act if my own essence does not participate in it? Whence the individual resemblance of children to their parents if the genus, "self-established universality" and not individuality, is the principle of reproduction? True, I cannot beget children if I lack some known or unknown organic condition or faculty; but neither can I see, hear, walk, eat, or piss if I lack the necessary organic conditions and predispositions; indeed, I cannot do anything, I am a mere name, if the other part of me, the not-I, nature, is removed from me.

I have spoken of all this before, Still, it goes without saying, I wish to deny no one the freedom to restrict the concept of the individual as he sees fit, to remove its entrails from its body and then to stuff the empty carcass with a God, a nameless substance, or some other monster of the speculative fantasy. Nor do I wish by these remarks to deprive my adversaries and their public of the pleasure of believing that their picture of me is my true self, their caricature of me my portrait.

Bibliography

of works cited in the text. Standard works available in recent editions are not included.

AGRIPPA, HENRICUS CORNELIUS. *De Incertitudine et Vanitate Scientiarum & Artium Liber*. Strasburg, 1622. (Many later editions and translations.)

AL SENUSI (YUSUF, ABU ABD ALLAH). *El Senusi's Begriffsentwicklung des Muhammedanischen Glaubensbekenntnisses.* Leipzig, 1838.

Ausland (a periodical). Stuttgart, 1828–93.

BAHRDT, CARL FRIEDRICH. *Würdigung der natürlichen Religion.* Halle, 1791.

BARTH, CHRISTIAN CARL. *Die altteutsche Religion.* Leipzig, 1835, 1836.

BASTHOLM, CHRISTIAN. *Historische Nachrichten zur Kenntnis des Menschen in seinem wilden und rohen Zustande.* Altoona, 1818–21.

BAUMGARTEN, SIEGMUND JAKOB (ed.). *Algemeine Welthistorie.* 72 parts. Halle, 1744–1810.

BERNIER, FRANÇOIS. *Voyages de François Bernier.* 2 vols. Amsterdam, 1699.

BODIN, JEAN. *De la demonomanie des sorciers.* Paris, 1580.

BOHLEN, PETER VON. *Das Alte Indien, mit besonderer Rücksicht auf Aegypten.* Königsberg, 1930.

BRETSCHNEIDER, CARL GOTTLIEB. *Die religiöse Glaubenslehre nach der Vernunft und der Offenbarung.* 3d ed. Halle, 1844.

CHARLEVOIX, PIERRE FRANÇOIS XAVIER DE. *Histoire du Paraguay.* 3 vols. Paris, 1756.

COLEBROOKE, HENRY THOMAS. *Essays on the Religion and Philosophy of the Hindus.* London and Edinburgh, 1858.

CONSTANT DE REBECQUE, HENRI BENJAMIN. *De la religion.* 5 vols. Paris, 1824–31.

CUDWORTH, RALPH. *The True Intellectual System of the Universe. . . . To which are added the notes and dissertations of Dr. J. L. Mosheim, translated by John Harrison.* London, 1845.

DUMAS, JEAN BAPTISTE ANDRÉ and BOUSSINGAULT, J. B. *Essai de statique chimique des êtres organisés.* 3d ed., Paris, 1844.

ECKERMANN, CARL. *Lehrbuch der Religionsgeschichte und Mythologie der vorzüglichsten Völker des Altertums.* Halle, 1845–46.

EISENMENGER, JOHANNES ANDREAS. *Entdecktes Judenthum.* 2 vols. Königsberg, 1711.

ERSCH, JOHANN SAMUEL and GRUBER, JOHANN GOTTFRIED. *Allgemeine Encyclopädie der Wissenschaften und Künste.* Leipzig, 1818–89.

GRIMM, JACOB LUDWIG CARL. *Deutsche Mythologie.* 2 vols. Göttingen, 1835.

HECKEWELDER, (The Rev.) JOHN GOTTLIEB ERNEST. *An Account of the History, Manners, and Customs of the Indian Nations.* Philadelphia, 1818.

HUELLMANN, CARL DIETRICH. *Theogonie.* Berlin, 1804.

KLEUKNER, JOHANN FRIEDRICH (trans.) *Zend-Avesta, Zoroaster's lebendiges Wort.* Riga, 1776–77.

KOLB, GEORG FRIEDRICH. *Geschichte der Menschheit und der Kultur.* Pforzheim, 1843.

KRASHENINNIKOV, STEPAN PETROVICH. *La Description de Kamtschatka.* 2 vols. Lyon, 1767.

LICHTENSTAEDT, JEREMIAS RUDOLF. *Über die Ursachen der grossen Sterblichkeit der Kinder des ersten Lebensjahres und über die diesem Übel entgegenzustellenden Massregeln.* St. Petersburg and Leipzig, 1837.

MANU. *Hindu Gesetzbuch oder Menu's Verordnungen nach Cullucas Erläuterung. Aus der Sanscrit-Sprache ins Englische übersetzt von Sir W. Jones und verteutschet . . . von J. C. Hüttner.* Weimar, 1797.

MARINER, WILLIAM. *An account of the natives of the Tonga Islands.* 2 vols. London, 1817.

MARSDEN, WILLIAM. *Natürliche und bürgerliche Beschreibung der Insel Sumatra* (tr. from the English). Leipzig, 1785.

MARTIUS, CARL FRIEDRICH PHILLIPP VON. *Von dem Rechtszustande unter den Ureinwohnern Brasiliens.* Munich, 1832.

MEINERS, CHRISTOPH. *Allgemeine kritische Geschichte der Religionen.* 2 vols. Hannover, 1806–1807.

MEISTER, JACQUES HENRI. *De l'Origine des principes religieux.* Paris, 1768.

MUELLER, WILHELM. *Geschichte und System der altdeutschen Religion.* Göttingen, 1844.

MULDER, GERRIT JAN. *Versuch einer allgemeinen physiologischen Chemie.* Braunschweig, 1844–51.

NEMESIUS, Bishop of Emesa. *De Natura Hominis.* (Numerous editions and translations.)

PAUW, CORNELIUS DE. *Recherches philosophiques sur les Egyptiens et les Chinois.* [?] 1773.

PAULINUS, a Sancto Bartholomaeo (JOANNES PHILLIPUS WERDIN, or WESDIN). *Das Brahmanische Religionssystem.* Calcuttta, 1795.

PENNANT, THOMAS. *Artic Zoology.* 2 vols. London, 1784–87.

PLATNER, EDUARD. *Beitraege zur Kenntniss des Attischen Rechts.* Marburg, 1820.

RHODE, JOHANN GOTTLIEB. *Die heilige Sage und das gesammte Religionssystem der alten Baktrer, Meder und Perser.* Frankfurt, 1820.

RITTER, AUGUST HEINRICH. *Ueber unsere Kenntniss der Arabischen Philosophie.* Göttingen, 1844.

ROETH, EDUARD MAXIMILIAN. *Die ägyptische und die zoroastrische Glaubenslehre.* (*Geschichte unserer Philosophie,* Vol. I.) Mannheim, 1846–58.

SCHADEN, EMIL AUGUST VON. *Über den Gegensatz des theistischen und pantheistischen Standpunktes.* Erlangen, 1848.

SCHALLER, JULIUS. *Darstellung und Kritik der Philosophie L. Feuerbachs.* Leipzig, 1847.

SCHEUCHZER, JOHANN JACOB. *Kupfer-Bibel, in welcher die Physica Sacra, oder geheiligte Natur-Wissenschaft derer in Heil. Schrifft vorkommenden natuerlichen Sachen, deutlich erklaert und bewaehrt.* [?], 1731.

SCHLEGEL, JOHANN RUDOLPH. *Kirchengeschichte des achtzehenden Jahrhunderts.* (J. L. Mosheims vollständige Kirchengeschichte, Vols. 5–7.) Heilbronn, 1770–96.

SONNERAT, PIERRE. *Voyage aux Indes Orienales et à la Chine.* 2 vols. Paris, 1782.

STUHR, FRIEDRICH. *Die Religionssysteme der heidnischen Völker des Orients.* Berlin, 1838.

VOSSIUS, GERARDUS JOANNES. *De theologia gentili, et physiologia christiana; sive De origine ac progressv idolatriae.* Amsterdam, 1668.

ZIMMERMANN, EBERHARDT AUGUST WILHELM VON. *Taschenbuch der Reisen.* 17 vols. Leipzig, 1802–1817.

Format by Sidney Feinberg
Set in Linotype Times Roman
Composed, printed and bound by The Haddon Craftsmen, Inc.
HARPER & ROW, PUBLISHERS, INCORPORATED